3 4-60

The Inter-War Years

AND OTHER PAPERS

The Inter-War Years

AND OTHER PAPERS

A SELECTION FROM THE WRITINGS OF

HUBERT DOUGLAS HENDERSON

━━━━━

EDITED BY HENRY CLAY

OXFORD
AT THE CLARENDON PRESS
1955

Oxford University Press, Amen House, London E.C.4

GLASGOW NEW YORK TORONTO MELBOURNE WELLINGTON
BOMBAY CALCUTTA MADRAS KARACHI CAPE TOWN IBADAN

Geoffrey Cumberlege, Publisher to the University

———

PRINTED IN GREAT BRITAIN

PREFACE

HUBERT HENDERSON's printed lectures and contributions to journals were numerous enough to fill a substantial volume. By themselves, however, these would not have shown the development of his ideas and the change in his approach to economic problems with widening experience of affairs. I have made a selection of them, and I wish to acknowledge the kindness of the original publishers in giving permission to reprint them. A selection of Leaders written while he was editor of *The Nation* illustrate one important phase of his work. But much of his most important work was neither published nor written for publication, being done when he was in the office of the Economic Advisory Council or the Treasury in the course of his two long terms of Government service. Permission to include in this volume a number of typical memoranda on general economic problems from documents written by Henderson while in Government service has been given on behalf of H.M. Government by the Secretary of the Treasury and the Secretary of the Cabinet.

Lady Henderson and Sir Piers Debenham will not allow me to associate their names with mine on the title-page as editors. The least I can do is to explain that that would be the proper place. I wish to acknowledge also my indebtedness to the editors of, and contributors to, the Supplement to *Oxford Economic Papers*, 1953, devoted to Henderson and his work, on which I have drawn freely in the Introduction.

HENRY CLAY

Acknowledgement is made to the following publishers for permission to reproduce articles:

The American Economic Association for 'A Criticism of the Havana Charter', from *American Economic Review*, June 1949; the Stamp Memorial Trustees and the Athlone Press of the University of London for *The International Economic Problem* (Stamp Memorial Lecture, 1946); the Royal Economic Society for 'The Price System', from *Economic Journal*, vol. lviiii, no. 232, December 1948; the Coventry Engineering Society for 'Controls and the Price System' (Herbert Lecture, 1950) from *The Coventry Engineering Society Journal*, June 1950; the District Bank Limited for 'The Economics of International Tension', from *District Bank Review*, September 1950; the Cambridge University Press for *The Uses and Abuses of Economic Planning* (Rede Lecture, 1947); Lloyds Bank Limited for 'The Problem of Retrenchment', from *Lloyds Bank Review*, January 1950; the Clarendon Press and the editors for 'The Function of Exchange Rates', from *Oxford Economic Papers*, January 1949.

HENRY CLAY died, as the result of a road accident in Holland, on the 31st of July 1954, when the final proofs of this book were available. We, who shared his conviction that it should be prepared, and collaborated with him in some degree for its publication, wish to record our great debt of gratitude to the Editor, and our feeling of personal loss at his death.

FAITH HENDERSON
PIERS DEBENHAM

CONTENTS

INTRODUCTION   xiii

PART I

Leading Articles from *The Nation*, 1923–30

1. Editorial Foreword. 5 May 1923   1
2. Monetary Policy. 14 July 1923   5
3. The McKenna Duties. 17 May 1924   9
4. Will Unemployment Increase? 4 April 1925   13
5. Diagnosis and Remedy. 9 May 1925   18
6. The Economic Trend. 6 November 1926   23
7. The New Industrial Revolution. 27 November 1926   28
8. The Limits of Insular Socialism. 30 November 1929 33
9. The McKenna Duties again. 4 January 1930   39
10. Our Heresy. 18 January 1930   43

PART II

Memoranda written when Secretary of the Economic Advisory Council, 1930–4

1. The Falling Price-Level and its Implications. 24 April
   1930   49
2. The Present Unemployment. 10 July 1930   56
3. The Development of New Industries. 21 August 1930 61
4. The Background of the Problem. 18 September 1930   66
5. The Economy Report. 7 August 1931   71
6. The State of Economics. 14 October 1931   78
7. Internal Credit Policy—and International. 27 October
   1931   81

8. Sterling and the Balance of Trade. 28 January 1932   87

9. German Reparations and British Industry. 24 February 1932   91

10. A Monetary Proposal for Lausanne. 17 May 1932   103

11. Some Notes on the Exchange Question. 23 June 1933   107

12. International Monetary Problems: Note for Discussion. 13 September 1933   110

13. Increasing Productivity and the Demand for Labour. 12 December 1933   126

PART III

All Souls College, 1934–9

1. Do we want Public Works? 11 May 1935   151

2. Mr. Keynes's Theories. 2 May 1936   161

3. The Significance of the Rate of Interest. January 1938   178

PART IV

Memoranda written while at the Treasury during the War, 1940–5

1. The Principles of the Beveridge Plan. 4 August 1942   191

2. Great Britain's Post-war Commercial Policy. 6 January 1943   209

3. Notes on the Problem of Maintaining Employment. 20 May 1943   220

4. International Economic History of the Inter-war Period. 3 December 1943   236

5. Notes on Planning and on the Land Values Problem. 26 January 1944   296

6. Lord Keynes and Employment Policy. 1 March 1944   316

Contents

PART V

Post-War, 1945–51

1. The Uses and Abuses of Economic Planning   327
2. The Price System   342
3. The Function of Exchange Rates   357
4. The International Economic Problem   377
5. The Havana Charter   388
6. The Problem of Retrenchment   402
7. Controls and the Price System   413
8. The Economics of International Tension   425

LIST OF PUBLICATIONS   435

INDEX   438

Portraits of H.D.H. appear as plates facing pages 5 and 336

INTRODUCTION

HUBERT DOUGLAS HENDERSON was born at Beckenham, Kent, on 20 October 1890. He was the son of a Scotch banker, the joint manager at the time of the London office of the Clydesdale Bank. When Hubert was eight his father was appointed manager of the North of Scotland Bank in Aberdeen; later he moved to Glasgow as general manager of the Clydesdale Bank. His mother was a Thomson, an Edinburgh ship-owning family. The family had a large Victorian house in Kelvinside and kept a carriage and pair. Hubert was the youngest, by five years, of six children. His two elder brothers became respectively a solicitor and a stockbroker in Glasgow. He was educated at the Grammar School, Aberdeen— where he said he had the best school-teaching he ever received— and then at Rugby. He did not enjoy the change to an English public school, at any rate not until he reached the sixth form and discovered the pleasures of the school library. At the same time he left the classical side to specialize in mathematics. He was elected to a mathematical exhibition at Emmanuel College, Cambridge, and went up in October 1909.

His father, recognizing his son's promise and proud of him, destined him for the Bar. Henderson took the first part of the Mathematical Tripos; but his interest was not kindled, his energies were absorbed elsewhere, and he was placed in the Third Class. What had happened was that he had awakened for the first time to the interest of the world of politics. At home the atmosphere had been, so far as it was political at all, conventionally Conservative. School had not excited an interest. In Cambridge he found himself in the stream of an enthusiastic and exciting intellectual movement, in which he found he could immerse himself and could play an active and positive part. The advent of a Liberal government in 1906, defending Free Trade against a revival of Protection, formulating a novel social policy for relieving the chief causes of poverty, and financing its reforms by attacking the inequality of personal incomes, stimulated a fresh interest in economic studies, and provided undergraduate politicians with a new world to conquer. Henderson had been attracted by the opportunities of debate offered by his college debating society; encouraged by another freshman of his college, an older man, Norman Birkett, he began to take part in the debates of the Union. His aptitude for debate, and enjoyment of it, ensured success, and he was in due course elected, first Secretary and then President. This political interest also turned his mind to economics; he read for the second part of the Economics Tripos and was placed in the First Class in 1912. His own disposition and the Liberal tradition of Cambridge economics ensured that his party associations (though he was never much of a party politician) would be with the Liberals, and not with the Socialist group which was another product of the political revival of the time. The reforms with which the name of Lloyd George was associated alarmed his elders as revolutionary; as such he himself welcomed them, but it was their practical character that made sure of his support.

After graduating he proceeded to read for the Bar. But he did not wish to leave Cambridge, nor to be dependent any longer on his father for support; and he was able to support himself by teaching. He took pupils for his college, which also gave him a small bursary, and for a time he took a W.E.A. class. At this time he came into touch with Norman Angell, whose book *The Great Illusion* impressed him as it did many of his generation. War took him by surprise, and for a time he was associated with the Union of Democratic Control; but he had no doubts about the necessity of supporting the country's policy. He did not think he would have made a good soldier; nevertheless he volunteered for service and was rejected on physical grounds, being graded C3—probably his eyesight disqualified him, for his general health then was good.

He was employed in the war first in the statistical section organized by Walter Layton in the Board of Trade, and lived at Toynbee Hall. In 1917 he was sent to Manchester to serve as Secretary of the Cotton Control Board, set up to deal with the problems with which the industry was confronted by the curtailment of American raw cotton supplies. He contributed a history of the experiment to the Carnegie Economic History of the War. The work was very heavy, the more so that he was now married and living in London and had the strain of much travelling. But the experience was valuable; it gave him an insight into the effect of shortages and redundancies in the daily conduct of an industry and the way in which industrialists and trade union officials face such problems. He had already the advantage of growing up in a family of business men: his Lancashire experience widened and deepened his knowledge of the kind of people who actually run the trades and industries of the country.

In 1915 he had married Faith Bagenal; the arguments that the older generation in his social class urged—that he was young, had no regular job, and that he had still to establish himself at the Bar —did not weigh with him. He had a small legacy from his mother, as well as his Civil Service salary, and settled down at 45 Downshire Hill, Hampstead, for the next four years. When the war ended he had still to choose a career. The Board of Trade invited him to stay with them as an established civil servant. His father was still anxious that he should make the law his profession, and offered to relieve him of the responsibility for his family's support until he was established in it; and Clare College invited him back to Cambridge as a teaching Fellow. The last offered him the most attractive life; he ascertained that he would be given a university lectureship with it, and accepted. It was two years before he was able to move his family to Cambridge; till then he lived in college in term, and at home in the vacations. He found it a full and a hard life—lecturing, tutoring, examining, and taking his part in college business. He enjoyed it and had no wish to change it. In the long vacation of 1922 he wrote his volume *Supply and Demand* in the series of Cambridge Economic Handbooks which he edited. It illustrated already his capacity for making an argument watertight and lucid, and explained his success as a teacher. He remained a teacher for the rest of his life, but in less well-organized classes.

Even when he had moved his household to Cambridge, Henderson maintained his contacts with London. Throughout his life he found unending interest and enjoyment in the informal discussion of current economic and political questions in societies, dining clubs, and similar occasions. His gift for such discussion was early recognized, and his friends would not have allowed it to rest unused, if he himself had not been always eager to use it. It was in mixed gatherings of financiers, economists, civil servants, and business men that he found the most congenial opportunity; and his friends in the City, Whitehall, the business world, and the world of journalism and politics were never willing to let the acquaintance slip, once they had enjoyed it. Among the overlapping circles in which he moved in the beginning of the twenties was a group drawn together by the hope of reviving the Liberal Party. They were philosophical Liberals rather than party politicians; but they felt themselves left homeless by the break-up of the historic Liberal Party, without finding any attraction in either the doctrinaire Socialism of the Labour Party or the refusal to face the country's need of drastic change of the dominant Conservatives. A Manchester circle, which included Ramsay Muir, Ernest Simon, and E. T. Scott, joined with a group of Cambridge men, of whom Keynes and Layton were the centre, to organize a summer school in the Lake District in 1922. The school was repeated every year, and out of the association the possibilities of a new party, Liberal in its philosophy and practical in its approach to the problems facing the country after war, emerged.

Henderson was in the centre of this group, drawn to it by personal friendship and his own political ideals. The group needed an organ through which to put its criticism and proposals before the public. They had the chance of acquiring *The Nation and the Athenæum*; Keynes was chairman of the company formed for the purpose, and on behalf of the group approached Henderson in 1923 to act as editor. Lady Henderson[1] has described the interview, and its outcome:

I have a vivid picture in my mind of Maynard standing in front of our drawing-room fire with his hands in his pockets, warming his posterior, and plunging into the subject with all his accustomed enthusiasm and tenacity. He propounded the scheme. He himself was to be the chairman of the paper. Would Hubert become editor? Hubert raised the obvious objections. He had never edited anything; he had done very little journalism. Maynard, like a prancing steed, overrode all his objections. He wanted him as editor, and Hubert must not and could not refuse.

For the next seven years Hubert worked in the closest collaboration with Keynes. No chairman could have given his editor more scope, more encouragement, more support. Hubert had a completely free hand to write what he liked. Maynard wrote constantly in the paper himself, but always under his own name. He never encroached on the editor's ground. He was in and out of the office every week discussing what line the paper should take on whatever issue was foremost at the moment. Then, when the paper was all ready for bed on Wednesday evening, and everyone else had left the office, Hubert would settle down to write his leader. Hour after hour he would scribble and smoke, scratch out and tear up. Never did anyone write with such blood and sweat. Sometimes he would catch the last train back to Hampstead, sometimes the first tube train on Thursday morning. However long the leader took to write, it had to

[1] *Oxford Economic Papers*, Supplement, 1953, p. 8.

come up to the standard he set himself. However difficult the argument, however closely reasoned, it had to be clear and comprehensible to the ordinary reader. That was his criterion.

In the first part of this collection are ten of Henderson's leaders. The writing of leaders was only one part of the editor's duty; but it was the most important part, and the medium through which for seven years he influenced political thinking in a circle wider than his own rather ill-defined party. The choice of subjects was dictated by the economic issues facing governments at the time—monetary policy, unemployment, coal, the Socialist challenge, protection. His treatment, while always effective and pointed as a contribution to immediate policy, carried the discussion far wider than the immediate issue; always he would contrive unobtrusively to relate the immediate question to be decided to the broad principles on which long-term policy should be based. They afford also an admirable illustration of his approach to a subject; to quote Lady Henderson[1] again:

His method of writing was the method of debate, in which he played the parts of both proposer and opposer of the motion, and of the chairman who sums up at the end. He liked to take a subject for discussion, give the arguments on both sides, and then decide at the end which side should win. His arguments were closely reasoned, the conclusions clear and definite. The whole made up a pattern from which it is difficult to quote, unless at undue length, without losing much of the urgency of the argument, except for the places where he let himself go, as he sometimes did, in rhetoric which had all the more force by contrast with the sweet reasonableness which preceded it.

A little later the same group organized an inquiry into the state and the needs of the country's industry. The results were embodied in *Britain's Industrial Future*, published in 1928. Henderson's part in conducting the inquiry and drafting the report was considerable, though it cannot be disentangled from a large co-operative work. It marked a shift of interest from the analytical and monetary approach to the country's problems (which was included but not stressed) to an examination of the structural elements, which he had always recognized, and the institutional reforms called for. It led also to his only incursion into party politics in the narrow sense. In March 1929 Lloyd George, in anticipation of the General

---

[1] Op. cit., p. 9.

Election, gave certain pledges on the subject of unemployment, and supported them by the issue of a pamphlet, *We can conquer unemployment*. The Government published a reply in the form of a White Paper, *Memoranda on Certain Proposals relating to Unemployment*; whereupon Keynes and Henderson came to Lloyd George's support with a pamphlet, *Can Lloyd George Do It?*, aimed at a wide circulation, which it secured. But the electorate did not give Lloyd George the chance. There was a clash of personalities in the Liberal Party as well as a difference of views; the two-party basis of British Parliamentary Government (which Henderson defended brilliantly in *The Nation*) limits the opportunities of any third party; and the subsequent development of Henderson's own views was to throw doubt on the accuracy and adequacy of the Liberal diagnosis of the country's needs. He himself was about to move into a position in which party politics was prohibited, and it may be doubted whether he would ever have made a good party man.

One of the innovations for which the Liberal Industrial Report had argued was what Beveridge had earlier called an Economic General Staff, and the Report described as 'a thinking department within the administration, at the elbow of the inner ring of the Cabinet, which shall warn Ministers of what is ahead, and advise them on all broad questions of economic policy'. The new Prime Minister, Ramsay MacDonald, faced with an economic situation much more threatening than had faced him in 1923, and feeling the need of advice, set up in January 1930 an Economic Advisory Council with the same purpose as the Liberal proposal, though differently constituted. Its membership consisted of the Ministers primarily concerned with economic policy, supplemented by a number of independent members, under the chairmanship of the Prime Minister. Thomas Jones, the Assistant Secretary of the Cabinet, was its first secretary, and Henderson was invited to join him as assistant-secretary; he accepted, and, when Thomas Jones retired, became joint secretary with a civil servant colleague. The Council did not prove an appropriate device for its work. It ceased to meet after the middle of 1931, and functioned thereafter only through committees, which reported to the Prime Minister. The change, if it lessened the influence of the Council, increased that of Henderson. He was the only professional economist giving his whole time to its inquiries, and among economists he was the one most likely, both by lucidity of exposition and willingness to examine any argument or plea, to help overworked Ministers and civil servants with whom he was now associated.

The memoranda included in Part II of this collection were written by him during the four years he was working in Whitehall Gardens. They are chosen to illustrate his method of approach to the problems with which the Government was faced rather than the full range of subjects he dealt with. While the subjects were mainly given by events, he took a broad view of his responsibility. His approach was academic in the good sense of the word, relating policy to principles as he had sought to do in *The Nation*, but with a more mature consideration and ampler space than was possible in a weekly paper. He could not write for publication, but some of these memoranda are among the most characteristic of his writings; and certainly it was in these four years that he formed the general outlook on economics which he was to elaborate in his published writing later. He paid his official readers the compliment of offering them serious argument, fully worked out and backed by theory when it was applicable, and realistic research. It should be remembered that what he wrote was supplemented by what he said in committee and personal discussion: he was available and always willing to discuss his own memoranda or anyone else's ideas. From this intercourse he gained as well as gave. Compared with most economic reformers, he had always been more disposed to recognize the administrative and political difficulties which the ministers, civil servants, or business men might have to meet in carrying out a proposal or policy attractive on theoretical grounds. Now he had always to be aware of the conditions under which governments act; their actions must be defensible in debate, they must command the public support which makes administration in a democracy possible, they must not overload the central organs of government nor require a degree of discrimination at the periphery with which the subordinate officials in contact with the public cannot fairly be charged. Occasionally he put forward a project of his own; but mainly he was engaged in explanation and criticism.

Two of the committees with which he associated may be referred to. In July 1930 the Prime Minister invited a committee of economists, of which Keynes was chairman and Henderson the only 'official' member, 'to review the present economic condition of Great Britain, to examine the causes which are responsible for it, and to indicate the conditions of recovery'. The committee was not unanimous and their reports were not published; but the systematic review of the country's position which it undertook in the three months of its existence was an appropriate overture to the next nine years of Henderson's work. The other was a standing committee, of which Stamp was chairman, to report on the current economic situation. This survived until the outbreak of the second war, and it was the occasion of a regular monthly report which Henderson made orally to the Prime Minister.

The four years of study and comment on current economic problems, though he was no longer diverted by the exigencies of periodical journalism or academic teaching from the large issues that interested him, left him unsatisfied. In 1934 he was given the opportunity of working exclusively on inquiries of his own choice by an invitation to a research fellowship in All Souls. He was now able to concentrate on the study of the fundamental changes in economic conditions and economic policy, which were to be discerned before 1914 but which war had accelerated and enormously extended. The essay printed here on _The International Economic History of the Inter-war Period_ is probably the most significant indication of the questions on which his mind was longest engaged. Though not written until later, during the war, and embodying conclusions he did not perhaps reach until then, it reflects a trend in his ideas already apparent before war broke out, and followed after war ended, when it was used as a basis for his main course of lectures when he returned to Oxford as professor. But it was not in his nature to withdraw into academic seclusion and allow nothing to distract him from the writing of a book. He retained his contacts in London and elsewhere with the societies and friends, which provided an outlet for his love of discussion, and found new opportunities in Oxford. Now that he was free to publish he took some part in the public discussion of current events, as the list of his published work shows. He was conscripted for two inquiries, contemporary and practical, which bore on his central interest and contributed to its study but delayed his carrying out of it. One was an inquiry into the position of British agriculture, for which Seebohm Rowntree and Lord Astor were responsible, the results of which were published in a volume entitled _The Agricultural Dilemma_; to both compilation and writing of this Henderson made perhaps the principal contribution. And there was a Royal Commission of Enquiry into the economic problems of the West Indies, on which he served in 1938 and 1939 under the chairmanship of Lord Moyne. This took him to the West Indies from October 1938 to April 1939, and he was occupied in drafting the report in the summer before war broke out. This stimulated him by offering the spectacle of a community widely different from that of Britain, population problems also very different, and a condition of poverty which could not be explained by the monetary and cyclical fluctuation theories which then dominated English economics.

It will be convenient to refer here to the other important commission of inquiry on which Henderson worked—the Royal Commission on Population, appointed in March 1944. His old interest in the effect of population changes on employment, intensified by his visit to the West Indies, made the subject interesting to him, and the divergence of views and aims represented on the Commission gave ample scope for his gift of clarification and conciliation. He became chairman when Lord Simon retired, and was very largely responsible for the form, and actual drafting, of the Report.

He was, again, inevitably drawn out of the course of his historical studies by the revolutionary impact on economic thinking of Keynes's *General Theory*. He reviewed the book in the *Spectator* and examined it at greater length in the paper included in this volume. He was inclined to defend the approach of the classical economists to the problems of production and distribution as valid on a longer view than Keynes's novel approach took, and to treat Keynes's thesis as only one contribution to an understanding of economic processes. His criticisms are evidence of a change going on in his attitude to economic studies—a growing reliance on an historical approach (which Keynes shared, though his intense concentration on the subject in hand and his analytical brilliance led him to give an analytical treatment to the problems he took up); and a growing preoccupation with the international element in British economic difficulties, which may have made him unsympathetic to a sustained argument on the hypothesis of a closed economy.

To these years belongs the essay on *The Significance of the Rate of Interest*. Apart from its importance as a late re-statement of his views on a branch of theory which had long interested him, it illustrates the part he had begun to play in the organized study of economics in Oxford. His younger colleagues were seeking opportunities of supplementing the theoretical analysis in which they were trained by a realistic examination of some of their questions. They formed a group, of which Henderson acted as chairman, to approach business men and cross-examine them on their practice and reasons for it. Henderson was their mainstay, not only because he could draw on a wide circle of acquaintances in business, but also because the patience, clarity, and even temper with which he would always pursue an argument made him an ideal chairman: the same qualities made him invaluable on the West Indies Commission. The effect on business behaviour of changes in interest rates was one subject investigated; the other was the methods by which business men arrived at their prices, the results of which were published by other members of the Group. Simultaneously, Oxford was remedying a deficiency in its equipment, the lack of any teaching or systematic facilities for the study of statistics, by establishing an Institute of Statistics. In this Henderson saw a possibility of remedying the deficiencies he thought he saw in current economic studies, when in 1931 he wrote the paper on *The State of Economics* included in this collection. He took an active part in the organization and administration of the Institute before war broke out, and, when he returned to Oxford after the war, succeeded Lord Lindsay as chairman of its committee and its chief friend and adviser in the University.

In July 1939 Lord Stamp was asked by the Government to survey the departmental plans made for the war that threatened, so far as they concerned the domestic economic life of the country; munitions production and the manning of the armed forces were excluded. Stamp asked for certain colleagues, Henderson and Henry Clay, and began his survey, with Henderson's former joint secretary, A. F. Hemming, and assistant, Piers Debenham, on the Economic Advisory Council. When war broke out the Survey was continued, and associated with two committees, one of official heads of Departments, the other of Ministers concerned with economic affairs. Out of the staff which it collected as its work expanded, both the Central Statistical Office and the Economic Section of the Cabinet Secretariat, under heads originally recruited by the Survey, were to grow; something like the 'thinking department' he had suggested in peace was realized in war. This development took place only after the Survey was discontinued after Stamp's death, and Henderson had moved into the Treasury for the duration of the war. In its initial work, however, the wide range of his

knowledge, his skill in examining witnesses, and his gift of clear
and rapid drafting made possible an amount of review and report-
ing which, considering the improvized character of the agency, was
remarkable.

Henderson's work in the Treasury has been described by a colleague, Sir David Waley,[1] and its character is indicated by the
selection of his memoranda given in Part IV. These, as it happens,
all belong to a phase which Sir David Waley refers to as 'a curiosity
of history' that 'during a total war in which unexampled efforts and
sacrifices had to be made to avert defeat . . . a large proportion of
the time and energy of the Treasury was devoted to the elaboration
of post-war Utopias'. At first, it would seem, Henderson's advice
was wanted as a complement and perhaps corrective of the advice
of other experts and officials which was primarily financial. In effect
he resumed the kind of work he had done for Ministers from 1930
to 1934. It was, however, impossible, with his background, that he
should not have been continuously looking for the shifts and dis-
locations, which an economically greater war than the first would
produce, both during hostilities and when they ceased. Equally it
was certain that his attitude to Utopias would be critical. Without
any change in ultimate social aims and the kind of society he wished
to realize, he had grown more and more sceptical of the possibility,
by abstract reasoning, either of understanding the economic
processes of society or of constructing policies for modifying and
controlling them. More and more had he turned to a realistic, quantitative, historical examination of the actual situation with which
governments find themselves faced; more and more did he rely
on the adaptation and use of tried administrative and legislative
devices to secure ends he had in view.

From the first he insisted that the fundamental problem the
country would have to face after the war was its international
economic situation. Any early return to unrestricted imports, uncontrolled exchanges, and freedom of trade would be out of the
question; such a *laissez-faire* policy belonged to a world which had
passed away. The measures forced on governments by the difficulties not only of war but of the thirties, were necessary and legitimate instruments of economic policy; we should only increase our
difficulties if, under American pressure, we discarded them, and
associated 'the idea of international economic co-operation with

[1] *Oxford Economic Papers*, Supplement, 1953, p. 47.

the subordination of human welfare to the arbitrary sway of market prices under the influence of doctrinaire abstractions, misplaced idealism and nostalgia for the past'. Taking his stand on this general position, he found himself in opposition to much of the war-time planning for post-war needs, and the details of the plans were often equally unsatisfactory to his mind. He criticized the proposals for an international monetary clearing agency on the ground that it proposed to give large credits without any reasonable security, which was contrary to all good banking practice; he objected to commodity buffer stocks, that they would react on excessive production too slowly, and were dangerous if they were not supported by the regulation of production; he protested against renouncing quantitative import restrictions, which were far more effective than tariffs in stabilizing domestic production and reducing the impact of world market fluctuations. In the discussions on full employment which led to the White Paper of 1945, he criticized 'the chief defects of the momentarily fashionable approach to the problem' which, he said, was 'to combine an eventual return to economic *laissez-faire* (after a transition period during which it is recognised that many controls will be necessary, but which, it is hoped, will be brief) with throwing financial orthodoxy to the winds'. As a recipe for full employment he thought both parts of the prescription were mistaken, and would, under present conditions of external weakness, lead to currency collapse.

These criticisms were provoked by the projects against which they were directed. They did not mean that he expected or desired an authoritarian economy in which government agencies planned and co-ordinated everything. When he returned to academic life and was free to speak and publish, he enjoyed himself in criticizing both the extremes of current thought. He had moved a long way from the confident Lloyd George Liberalism of the twenties. The dogmatic adhesion to Free Trade he had dropped early—with Keynes. The insistence on the return to gold standard as the chief cause of the country's difficulties was gradually modified; in 1933 he was already arguing that the notion that there was some definite point of exchange equilibrium capable of precise determination was an illusion, and after the experience of the second war's effects he argued that 'the true function of exchange rates is to provide a constant factor round which the more variable elements may move, and by reference to which they can be adjusted; in other words, to provide a focus of stability in an orderly price system', and advocated a modernized version of the Cunliffe Committee's scheme of automatic contraction to support the fixed exchange. Similarly his view of the scope for public works programmes in dealing with unemployment steadily contracted, and their use as a trade cycle tap 'which you turn on when trade is bad and turn off when it is comparatively good' he demolished by pointing out that the tap was too stiff. His scepticism of the policy of controlling the whole economy by State planning he justified in his Rede Lecture; long before the second war he had realized the incompatibility of the current popular aims, 'internationalism' and 'planning', so long as the controlling or planning body was bound to be the national state.

Penetrating and entertaining as these criticisms were, they were more than the immediate reaction of an administrator or journalist to an unacceptable proposal. They sprang from a consistant theoretical position, to which he sought to relate policy. The changes in his attitude to particular projects or policies were the fruit of experience. The scepticism of the popular *nostrum* or current fashion of thought sprang from a wide observation of government in action. He looked back to the economists of the nineteenth century, not only because he thought their theories were entitled to more respect than under the influence of Keynes's *General Theory* they received, but because they took as their field the broad complex of social relations implied in political economy, not the narrower specialism of economics. Of the more extreme policies of planning he was sceptical for a more fundamental reason; his innate modesty combined with his observation of others to make it impossible for him to believe that man's foresight and comprehensiveness of vision would ever be equal to the requirements of the planner's policies. In his general outlook—in his belief in personal liberty, freedom of intercourse and expression, equality of opportunity and in his distrust of an overweening State—he ended as Liberal as he began.

His pleasure in discussion has been mentioned. It led him to take an active part in the clubs and societies formed for this purpose— the Political Economy Club and Tuesday Club in London, the Oxford Political Economy Club, Chatham House, and the National Institute of Economic and Social Research, and other less regular occasions—which eagerly enlisted his help. The college of which he was a member in Oxford, All Souls, was the most congenial environment that could have been provided. It had no undergraduate members to make the chief claim on the Fellows' attention; its resident Fellows represented a wide range of research and teaching in the field of social study in its widest definition; and it provided a link with the world of affairs he had left in its quondam Fellows, engaged in finance and business, public administration, the practice of law, and university work elsewhere, who kept a regular contact with the college. It was a college of talkers, and he fitted easily into it. A colleague has described his conversation, and the description explains much more than the affection and admiration which he inspired in his college:[1]

He liked conversation; he was interested in many topics and was glad to speak about them with anyone who responded to his own detached, disinterested, and essentially middle-road notions; he did not particularly expect or take pleasure in agreement. He was a man of deep convictions, which he held with clarity and a kind of tranquil passion; in argument he was eloquent, lucid, and tenacious; and since he was free from solemnity and priggishness, and liked to discuss whatever interested him, he took equal pleasure in analysing personalities and in dissecting abstract topics or political issues, and treated them always in the same scrupulous, and sometimes animated, fashion. He talked well, and with a courtesy of manner which never abandoned him even in moments of acute provocation; nor were either his juniors or his seniors ever made to feel that he put them into any category or box, or was conscious of being in one himself. This made the experience of talking with him, whether *à deux* or in company, particularly delightful and profitable. . . . He had a genuinely independent personality, and held sharp ideas and opinions both about persons and about issues, and spoke about them without rancour, without self-consciousness, moderate in judgment, intellectually intense, and naturally civil. . . . He liked to talk an issue through and he liked argument; he wished to make his own views entirely clear to others and grasp theirs as fairly and accurately as he could; and since he had an intellect of exceptional acuteness and integrity, and a genuine desire to establish the truth, and sincerely believed that this could sometimes be done by means of rational discussion, he used to argue on and on, with tenacity and absorption, and infectious spontaneity. His face would assume a puzzled, sometimes bewildered or incredulous expression, when, as occasionally happened, his opponent seemed to him to advance opinions which no sane or well-informed person could conceivably hold. He would ruffle his hair, his voice would rise in pitch, he would make gestures of despair, but, whatever the hour, he would go on. He would never willingly let go. He would never grow angry, nor

[1] Isaiah Berlin, in *Oxford Economic Papers,* Supplement, 1953, p. 55.

rude, nor waspish, no matter how maddening his opponent seemed to him to be. The hour would grow late, it would be past midnight, and the ash-tray beside him would become filled and over-filled with stumps of du Maurier cigarettes. If, as sometimes happened, the argument broke down under a hail of mere counter-assertions, he would simply grow silent and avert his thoughts; if the tone grew too sharp he would look at a newspaper or quietly leave the room.

When he left Cambridge to return to London in 1923, Henderson had bought a house in Upper Park Road, N.W. 3. This was his home, until (more than two years after leaving the Economic Advisory Council) he moved to 5 South Parks Road, Oxford, in April 1937. He lived quietly, but enjoyed entertaining a few friends, and was an admirable host. In 1926 he bought a cottage at Inkpen, under the Berkshire Downs, where his family spent the school holidays, and he would come down when he could. He seldom gave much time or thought to holidays for himself. During the war he first shared a flat with D. H. Robertson, and then ensconced himself in the Reform Club, getting down to Oxford for the week-end when he could; he had to find other accommodation when a bomb fell next door to the Reform Club, but he returned as soon as he could get a room in the basement, and stayed till the end of 1944. He took no account of the strain of the life until August 1942, when he had a coronary thrombosis attack in his room at the Treasury, and was taken to the Westminster Hospital. He made a quick recovery and was back at work by the end of the year. He returned to Oxford, to the Drummond Chair of Political Economy, at the end of 1944.

The Chair carried with it a Professorial Fellowship in All Souls, so that he was able to resume the social relations the war had interrupted. He had another coronary thrombosis attack in 1947. Again he made a rapid recovery, so rapid that he allowed himself to be persuaded to take over the chairmanship of the Royal Commission on Population. The only concession he made to his illness was the purchase of a small car and the engagement—for the first time—of a part-time secretary. His life in Oxford, quite apart from the Commission and his public lectures, was a full one. He was Chairman of the Committee of the Institute of Statistics, a member and for some time Chairman of the Board of the Faculty of Social Studies, one of the Delegates of the University Press—a duty he much enjoyed —and active in the affairs of his college, especially the administration of its financial affairs and estates. At the same time his colleagues, both in administration and in the world of economic studies, sought to honour him and to claim his services; he was knighted in 1942, elected President of the Economic Section of the British Association in 1948, elected a Fellow of the British Academy the same year, and President of the Royal Economic Society in 1950. In 1951 his college elected him to the Wardenship. It was an ideal position in which to complete his active life, with as much administrative work as he would enjoy, in a community into which he had grown, with relief from compulsory lectures and yet an academic position in which he could continue to exercise the wide influence he had both on economic studies and the shaping of economic policy. Though he was not able to travel to Lambeth to be confirmed in his office by the Visitor, he took up his duties in May and carried them out with intense enjoyment, in spite of the interruption of illness, until the following January. But he had a third coronary thrombosis attack during Encaenia, and although to his friends who visited him, frail as he was, his mind seemed as active and interesting as ever, his doctors decided that he was unequal to the duties of Warden. On their advice he resigned the Wardenship in January. He died on 22 February 1952.

PART I

Leading Articles from *The Nation*

1923–30

1

EDITORIAL FOREWORD[1]

THE present issue marks a change in the editorship and control of
THE NATION AND THE ATHENÆUM. Mr. Massingham has edited THE
NATION since its foundation in 1907. It is he who has made the paper
and has won for it its reputation for distinction and integrity. Few
men have done more to keep the true spirit of Liberalism alive and
its essential principles clear, in days of adversity and amid the
temptations of electoral success. He never forgot that Liberalism
was, in his own phrase, 'a larger and more fruitful thing' than the
formularies of a political party; and no concession to mere ex-
pediency or to personalities has ever been countenanced by THE
NATION. We deeply regret the termination of his long connexion
with the paper. We shall do our best to continue his honourable
traditions and to maintain and extend the influence of the paper in
the political and intellectual life of the country.

We write our first Leading Article at a moment of extraordinary
confusion of ideas and aims in the political world. Many of the old
party programmes are either obsolete or accomplished. The new
banners are not yet unfurled, or the lines of demarcation clearly
drawn.

The problem of 'Reunion', or, as it would be better described,
of 'Segregation', is not at all peculiar to the Liberal Party. It is, in
many respects, more acute in the Conservative Party. And in the
Labour Party the question as to exactly who, in a tight place, really
and truly at the bottom of his heart belongs to it, is just as difficult

---

[1] 5 May 1923.

to answer. Nor is it quite so much a matter of personalities as many people make out—though personalities come in, too. It is mainly a question of where the party lines of the future are going to be drawn.

Now, as always, the political opinions of individuals stretch in a continuous series, each man separated from his neighbour in the row by a scarcely distinguishable difference, all the way from Right to Left—from Lord Carson to Lord Salisbury, to Lord Derby, to Lord Curzon, to Mr. Bonar Law, to Mr. Baldwin, to Mr. Austen Chamberlain, to Sir Robert Horne, to Lord Birkenhead, to Mr. Churchill, to Mr. Lloyd George, to Sir Alfred Mond, to Lord Grey, to Sir John Simon, to Mr. Asquith, to Lord Buckmaster, to Lord Haldane, to Mr. Clynes, to Mr. Webb, to Mr. Ramsay MacDonald, to Mr. Snowden, to Mr. Lansbury, to Mr. Newbold; graded on a scale of belief in the existing structure and objects of society, like Gibbon's Theological Barometer, 'of which the Cardinal Baronius and Dr. Middleton should constitute the opposite and remote extremities, as the former sunk to the lowest degree of credulity, which was compatible with learning, and the latter rose to the highest pitch of scepticism in any wise consistent with Religion'.

The present confusion of politics exists because no one yet knows where the new party fissures are going to break through. It shows, for example, no special lack of principle in Mr. Lloyd George that he should flirt with the 'Centre Party' on one day and with the Liberals on the next. He is unluckily placed—somewhere very near the spot where, when the world divides into continents, the waters will break through. He cannot yet tell on which side of him, when the day comes, he will find dry land and a friend.

Our own sympathies are for a Liberal Party which has its centre well to the Left, a Party definitely of Change and Progress, discontented with the world, striving after many things; but with bolder, freer, more disinterested minds than Labour has, and quit of their out-of-date dogmas. We should like to play a part in forming and expressing the new thoughts of the world which grows up since the war, and in building something to which enthusiasm is appropriate, and which is based on firm foundations of reason and good sense.

All through the nineteenth century questions of government and of religious opinion played a very big part in politics—the Suffrage, Home Rule, the powers of the House of Lords, Catholic Emancipa-

tion, Church Establishment, Religious Education, Licensing. Of
these great questions only the House of Lords—and that in a form
which interests the country very little—lingers on alive. What sort
of issues are going to take their place? Proportional Representation,
Divorce Reform, Prohibition, Eugenics, freedom of opinion and of
propaganda on sex and birth-control problems? Perhaps. Some of
these may be burning questions within ten years. But these are not
the controversies at present which are tending to divide the country
into solid groups of opinion. They cut across party divisions, and
have not reached the crucial point at which people are prepared to
sink their differences on other things to promote their agreement on
these.

The great dividing questions of the near future seem to us to
belong to other categories. They fall into two great groups: Peace
and Disarmament; and the Economic Structure. The political
aspect of both these problems is utterly different from what it was
ten years ago. Before the war the range of controversy upon British
Foreign Policy was narrow. Groupings of Great Powers, with expanding ambitions and expanding armaments, faced one another;
and the only basis of accommodation was an anomalous but long-
established *status quo*. In such an atmosphere a British Minister,
intent on peace, must needs walk in the pathways of tradition. But
today the old European order is dissolved, and the new forms are
not yet shaped. The hopes of peace are staked upon the attainment
of that ideal of a new international polity which has given birth to
the League of Nations. In this work Britain may have a decisive
part to play, for which a new type of foreign policy will be required,
certain to lead to profound differences of opinion.

With the other problem the change is hardly less marked. From
1906 to 1914 a common economic policy united, for most practical
purposes, the parties of the Left—the development of social services
involving public expenditure, and the raising of the money by stiffer
taxes upon wealth. As an instrument of radical social change, this
policy has been shattered by the weight of the War Debt; and
economic discontent is now focused on the vague issues of industrial control. Here the ideas of all of us are so confused and
incomplete that the real points of controversy have scarcely begun
to emerge. It is a mistake to suppose that 'Socialism', whatever that
may mean, is going to be the issue. It is merely a word, only useful
so long as it cloaks decently the nakedness of Labour policy. The

thing it once stood for is fifty years antiquated, the product of a different atmosphere, and is largely irrelevant to the real problems of today.

We have no programme to offer ready-made. But we have our views of the lines along which sound policy must proceed. And we aspire to offer a lively spot where, out of controversy and conversation, a comprehensive policy may gradually take shape.

H. D. H. 1917

2

MONETARY POLICY[1]

WE dwelt last week on the immediate issue involved in the increase of Bank Rate to 4 per cent.; and we expressed the hope that this event would provoke a lively public controversy. In this, it seems, we were unduly optimistic. The action of the Bank of England (which is of importance, not only in itself, but as a revelation of a general policy, of which it is by no means the first step) has aroused small attention, and next to no criticism. It has been the subject, of course, of general comment in the City columns of the newspapers; where, for the most part, it has been treated, as regards its causes, as though it were some inexorable natural phenomenon, and, as regards its effects, as though these were confined to the money market and the Stock Exchange. Even where a city editor has had sufficient perception to realize that trade and employment may be prejudiced, this perception has not penetrated beyond his own columns. Leader-writers, Ministers, and Sir Eric Geddes have joined in asserting that the set-back to trade is due solely to the Ruhr position; and the public is left completely unaware that any other influence tending in the same direction is at work. The 'dear money' policy now being pursued is certainly such an influence; and it ought to be avoided all the more because of the existence of other obstacles. The worst time to put on the brake is when the cart is labouring uphill. The suggestion that restricted credit cannot injure trade much just now, because bad trade is inevitable owing to the Ruhr, is like saying that the brake cannot make much difference, because the slope must in any case retard the progress of the cart. As is argued in our Finance and Investment columns, unless it succeeds in depressing trade, and so reducing prices, the policy will do little to achieve its purpose of maintaining the New York exchange.

We seek to concentrate attention on the matter, not only because it is important in itself, but because behind it there lies a larger and even more important issue. The last few years have seen not, indeed, the birth, but the first serious public discussion of an idea

[1] 14 July 1923.

which contains potentialities of far-reaching improvement in social conditions—which may, indeed, hold the key to any real social advance in our generation. We refer to the idea of attempting to diminish, perhaps even to eliminate, general trade fluctuations by means of a monetary policy designed to keep the price level stable. Shortly stated, the idea runs as follows. Hitherto a state of active trade has been allowed to pass into a stage in which the demand for commodities in general exceeds their supply; prices rise, speculative purchases accentuating this tendency, until finally the process is brought to a halt by the inability of the banks to supply the additional purchasing power required to sustain the increased price level. Credit is then restricted; and a converse sequence of falling prices and withholding of orders is set in motion, which continues until credit conditions have become so easy as to stimulate enterprise once more. Such, it is argued, is the main explanation of the trade cycle, and the suggestion is made: let credit be curtailed somewhat whenever the demand for commodities shows signs of outrunning supply; let the upward movement of prices be thus nipped in the bud; conversely, when prices are falling, or there are other signs of incipient depression, let credit be supplied more readily, and on easier terms. A policy of this kind would certainly do something to diminish trade fluctuations; in the opinion of many competent authorities it might go a long way towards solving the problem.

It is worth letting our imaginations play on the possibilities which a real mastery over the trade cycle would open out. The general trade depression is the crux of the unemployment problem, and if the former could be got rid of, the latter would be reduced to easily manageable proportions. The saving of the waste arising from the periodical idleness of much of our machinery and labour power would do more to increase the national income than can be expected from technical invention in a generation. The effect on distribution might prove even more important. It is because Capital undertakes the risks of industry and commerce, and because these risks are so great under present conditions, that it is able to command so high a reward. But the trade cycle accounts for a considerable part of these business risks; and, if this element could be removed, the play of ordinary economic forces would do much to reduce Capital's share in the product of industry, more, certainly, than trade-union action or nationalization is ever likely to achieve.

Moreover, the smaller share of Capital would be steadier; there would be fewer failures on the one hand, fewer easily won fortunes on the other; and, with a diminution thus effected in the flow of 'profiteers', it might then be possible to attempt—what is hardly worth doing otherwise—an attack on another big cause of inequality, the perpetuation by inheritance of accumulated inequalities over distant generations. The problem of the relations between management and labour might prove to be a much simpler problem than now appears. The real difficulty at present in meeting Labour's aspiration for a more responsible status is the feeling that it would use any influence accorded to it to thwart the management in its aim of making profits. This hostility to profits is always greatest in times when huge fortunes are being made, and might largely disappear if profits became both lower and less fluctuating. To take a less remote and more definite matter, wage disputes, together with the strikes and bad feeling they entail, would be greatly diminished by a stable price level. When prices move far in either direction, even though the movement may be a gradual one, wage questions are bound to come up, and are likely to engender friction, which otherwise might never have been raised at all. The present dockers' strike shows that there is no royal road out of this difficulty by agreements for automatic adjustment by a cost-of-living index number.

With such issues at stake we ought not lightly to reject any policy which offers a real prospect of diminishing the severity of trade fluctuations. But here a curious fact emerges. In the regions of social and industrial policy there is a general readiness to consider new suggestions, to experiment with untried devices, even when the advantages which they promise are not very great, and when serious practical difficulties stand in the way. On monetary questions, on the other hand, the minds of most men are not open. Old maxims, born of bygone circumstances, are allowed undisputed sway; and it is enough for a proposal to involve some departure from tradition for it to be deemed 'unsound', and dismissed with the peculiar kind of disapprobation attaching to religious heresy. Even those who suspect that much good might be done by a new policy are apt to be cowed by the prevailing atmosphere.

Such an attitude is, perhaps, natural, in view of the intellectual difficulty of monetary problems, and the mischief which has been done in the past when plausible quacks have been allowed to experiment with the currency. But it is not an attitude in which today we can afford to acquiesce. Least of all can Liberals afford to do so. For Liberals are dissatisfied with the existing social order, have little faith in the nostrums by which Labour hopes to effect a transformation, and are eagerly searching for a policy adequate to the evils which they recognize. It is not for them to dismiss a project, containing vast possibilities of social improvement, by a mere appeal to tradition and ancient saws.

What are the corollaries which the pursuit of such a policy would involve? Under pre-war conditions it would have been inconsistent with the maintenance of an ordinary gold standard, since prices in a gold-standard country must move along with gold prices elsewhere. It is not certain that this incompatibility will continue in future. A new situation has been created by the Federal Reserve Board system in the United States, and by the large surplus stores of gold now under their control. It is suggested that it may be within their power to keep gold prices stable, and that, when we ourselves return to a gold basis, we—and later on, other countries —may co-operate with them in this endeavour. It may be that such a scheme will prove feasible; and we should certainly not exclude the possibility of its realization. But it is uncertain yet what course monetary events will take in the United States; and the kind of international co-operation suggested raises difficulties.

In these circumstances it is far better, in our judgement, that, instead of hastening, at the expense of trade activity, the day when we can revert to the gold standard, we should employ the considerable period of inconvertible paper, which must in any case intervene, in finding out what we can ourselves achieve by a stable price level policy. If it should prove possible just now, despite the Ruhr, to secure by cheap credit a considerable measure of trade activity without an inflation of the price level, it would be a strong testimony to the feasibility of mastering the trade cycle under more normal conditions. We cannot tell whether this is possible unless we try.

3

THE McKENNA DUTIES[1]

SOME faint idea of the atmosphere in which politics would be conducted in this country if we embarked upon a protectionist policy may be gleaned from the clamour over the repeal of the McKenna Duties. So little that is intelligible can be heard amid the din, that it may be well to explain the character and origin of these duties. In 1915, in order to restrain the importation of luxuries and thus to save tonnage for more urgent uses, Mr. McKenna imposed an *ad valorem* duty of 33⅓ per cent. upon light motor-cars, cinema films, clocks, musical instruments, and a few additional trifles. By that time the manufacture of light cars had practically ceased in this country, as the factories were devoted to the making of munitions. At the end of the war, therefore, there was a strong case for maintaining the duty, in order to give the industry a chance of recovering its position before exposing it to the full competition of foreign products. The manufacture of cars in this country was virtually an 'infant industry' in 1920 to 1922. It was on this ground that a Committee of the Ministry of Reconstruction recommended in 1918 that 'the British motor industry should be assisted by the imposition of an import duty on foreign motor vehicles and parts for a period of at least three years after peace'; and it was on this ground that a succession of Chancellors of the Exchequer with protectionist leanings were permitted by their free-trade colleagues to retain the McKenna Duties after their original purpose had disappeared.

In repealing these duties now, Mr. Snowden is accused of pedantry. We fully agree that a belief that Free Trade is the best fiscal system for this country does not necessarily make it wise to sweep away immediately every duty that can be shown to have a protective effect. Every change in the fiscal system is liable to have disturbing effects; and it is certainly right therefore to consider each case carefully on its merits, provided it is borne in mind that the advantage that one industry obtains from protection is always at

[1] 17 May 1924.

the expense of others. What, then, is the case for retaining these duties, when we consider them on their merits?

There is nothing to be said for singling out the motor-car industry as a special case for *permanent* protection in a free-trade country. It is in no sense a key industry. We are not subject to any peculiar handicap in its development. It is indeed an industry which may legitimately expect to carry on a considerable export trade, and not by any means one which should be confined to a sheltered home market. No claim to permanent protection has, so far as we are aware, been put forward, and none, we are certain, can be established. The question at issue, therefore, narrows down to whether it is better to repeal the McKenna Duties now or to retain them for a time.

The advocates of the duties ask, in the first place, whether it is wise to choose a time when British trade is admittedly in difficulties, when there are still a large number of workers unemployed, and when we are laboriously struggling out of an unexampled depression, to take a step which, whatever its ultimate effects may be, will inevitably cause immediate dislocation in a comparatively flourishing industry and swell the volume of unemployment. They ignore the fact that any loss of employment which may occur in the motor-car industry will be offset, at least to a considerable extent, by a corresponding expansion of other occupations. If foreign motor-cars are imported in greater numbers under free-trade conditions, they must be paid for in goods and services, and our shipping and export industries, which are the greatest sufferers from the depression, will derive a proportionate advantage. The main question, however, is whether it is true that any considerable number of workers will be deprived of employment by the repeal of the McKenna Duties. If we believed that they would, we should be in favour of delay.

Fortunately there is no danger whatever that employment in the motor-car trade will diminish. Financially, the industry is admittedly in an unsound condition. Some firms are certain to go into liquidation before long, duties or no duties, owing mainly to the severe competition of other British firms. Perhaps the number of these failures will be increased by repeal, but it is perfectly safe to predict that there will be as many workers employed in the industry next year as there are today. For the market is a rising one. The practice of owning a small car is rapidly spreading among people of moderate means in this country. In 1922 about 35,000 British made and 37,000 imported cars were retained in Great Britain. In 1923 the number of British-made cars sold in this country rose to 59,000, while the number of foreign cars imported and retained was about the same as in the preceding year. And still the demand increases. It may be that the industry will afford less employment if the duties are repealed than it would if they were retained, but an actual decrease in employment, once the matter is finally settled, is out of the question. For is it conceivable that of the large number of cars demanded so great a proportion will be supplied from abroad as to leave British manufacturers with a smaller market than they have at present? The duty is a very minor factor in the competition of American cars, such as the Ford, which is so cheap that it can undercut every other make after paying the duty in full. But it does not pay in full. The parts are either manufactured here or come from Canada, which receives preferential treatment, and they are assembled in this country. It is said that a Ford car sold in England today only pays about £3 in tax. But a Ford is not everybody's car. It supplies essentially a different market from the more expensive British and French-made cars. It is indeed from France that the most formidable competition comes. The Citroen car fulfils the conditions demanded by the most numerous class of motorists in this country, and competes directly with the products of Mr. Morris, who has taken so prominent a part in this controversy. Until quite recently, moreover, French production for the British market has received a bonus through the depreciation in the exchange value of the franc. For many months the internal value of French currency was higher than its external value, and the export trade reaped an advantage. With the recent recovery of the franc that advantage disappeared, and it is stated that a rise in the British price of French cars was only averted by the announcement that the import duty would be removed. If, therefore, the import duty is ever to go, the present moment is by no means an unfavourable one.

The spectacle of an infant industry growing so powerful under protection that it is able to exert the political pressure necessary for the maintenance of its protection is a familiar one in tariff countries. That process constitutes indeed the most important practical objection to the fostering of industries by the device of import duties. We are told that the Tory Party has now abandoned the advocacy of a general tariff for this country, but still seeks to benefit particular industries by protectionist means. Do Mr. Baldwin and his friends realize how damaging to their cause is an agitation such as that in which they are now participating? The fantastic forecasts of unemployment quoted by Mr. Snowden in the House of Commons last Tuesday, the absurd mental processes displayed by protectionist correspondents of the newspapers, the attempt to exploit the natural apprehensions of workers in the trade concerned and the threats of employers to discharge their operatives must all react injuriously upon the chances of such defensible measures as the McKenna Duties being adopted in the future. If there is any temporary dislocation in the motor-car trade, it will be mainly due to the political activities of those who sought to retain the duties. Mr. Snowden is to be congratulated upon his firmness, and the motor-car industry may in time recognize the advantage of having been put upon a permanent footing before it had become too dependent upon the crutch of protection.

4

WILL UNEMPLOYMENT INCREASE?[1]

AN unusual realism marked the debate on unemployment, which took place in the House of Commons on Thursday of last week. Hitherto the House has had two styles for the theme. Sometimes, responding eagerly to some such challenge as 'Socialism is the only remedy', it has plunged into one of those interminable discussions of a vague abstraction which are the delight and the stand-by of an undergraduate debating society. At other times it has pre-occupied itself with the technical details of administration— canvassing the exact sums of public money spent by successive governments on relief works, or, as happened only three weeks ago, disputing hotly the policy and the parentage of Circular 8213. In either case the note of party faction has been supreme; damaging points, triumphant retorts, smashing speeches have been made; the doctrinaires and the swashbucklers in all parties have thoroughly enjoyed themselves; and chill despair has crept over those who realize how vital and how difficult the problem of unemployment is, and how severe an intellectual effort is needed, if we are to master it.

But last week the whole atmosphere was different. Members, on all sides, were obviously trying to get to grips with the problem. Party gibes were indulged in very sparingly, and even then with an apologetic note. Panaceas were at a discount. In their place was a readiness to face facts, to tackle new and difficult ideas—a real effort to talk sense. Not everything that was proposed was wise. We trust, for instance, that Sir Alfred Mond will not convert any of his colleagues to his idea of using the unemployment insurance funds to subsidize employers who engage additional work-people. But behind his proposal there was a serious attempt to think the matter out; and most of the speeches conveyed a similar impression that the member's mind had really been at work. The results were not, indeed, strikingly illuminating; but at least we had a discussion not markedly inferior to, say, a week-end conference at an Oxford or Cambridge college of persons interested in industrial problems.

[1] 4 April 1925.

For this gratifying change credit is largely due to Sir John Simon, who initiated the debate on behalf of the Liberal Party in exactly the right key. It was helped by the chastened mood of the Labour Party, who cannot, after last year's experience, repeat their old speeches with any satisfaction to themselves. Perhaps, also, the House was still under the influence of Mr. Baldwin's appeal for 'sweetness and light'. But another factor helped to account for the serious mood. There is a growing uneasiness about the industrial outlook. At a season of the year when the volume of trade normally expands, it is not expanding. The metallurgical group of industries —coal, iron and steel, engineering, shipbuilding—which are the centre of industrial *malaise*, are encountering growing difficulties, and have almost lost the hope of better days ahead. The most optimistic, indeed, can no longer convince themselves that a steady expansion of trade upon normal lines is about to take place, which will reduce unemployment to pre-war dimensions. On the other hand, though we may hope that the pessimists may prove wrong, the possibility cannot be ruled out that trade may shortly suffer a definite set-back and unemployment grow formidably worse. Over the whole outlook, moreover, there hangs the menace of grave labour disputes, which it will take all the industrial statesmanship which Mr. Baldwin calls for to avert.

Let us take stock of the situation. As Sir John Simon pointed out, unemployment today is practically the same as it was two years ago —a figure of over 1,200,000 persons, including well over 900,000 men. That figure of two years ago represented a considerable recovery from the depths of a trade depression, a recovery which was still in progress, and which, in fact, continued fairly steadily, allowing for seasonal movements, until May 1924, when little more than a million persons were unemployed. Since then employment has fallen away again; and we are back where we were in 1923. What are the morals to be drawn? In the first place it is fairly clear, not only from the unemployment figures but from other signs, that by the spring of last year the ordinary process of recovery from an ordinary trade depression was virtually exhausted. Trade as a whole could not properly be termed depressed last spring. So far as the ordinary trade cycle is concerned, that roundabout of the phases of normal trade activity, boom, crisis, slump, depression, slow recovery, normal trade again, which accounted for the major part of any serious pre-war unemployment, we had reached the phase of normal activity—with over a million persons unemployed. That was the problem which presented itself last spring.

We ourselves felt so convinced that unemployment was not going to be solved by a mere continuance of ordinary trade recovery that we initiated last April in THE NATION a searching discussion of the trade outlook, opening with a letter from Mr. Lloyd George, whose claim last week that he has always sought to make people face the seriousness of the position is abundantly justified. The conclusions which we drew then we venture to summarize today. The main and obvious explanation of the co-existence of large unemployment with normal conditions as regards the trade cycle is the decline in foreign trade. This is a factor which it is not within our power to correct. It is not our *share* of world trade, but world trade as a whole, which is down. Nor is it a matter which is likely to right itself very soon. Nor, again, is it necessarily an unmitigated evil. If we are selling less abroad, we are selling that less on better terms. We are not in the smallest danger of finding ourselves in difficulties about purchasing our essential supplies of foodstuffs and raw materials, which are the ultimate purpose and *raison d'être* of our export trade. It ought not to be impossible to secure such a diversion of our labour power to new industrial purposes as would get rid of abnormal unemployment and increase our national income. It is in this direction that we should turn our minds. What prevents our using, where there is need for them, the labour power and resources lying idle in the export trades?

To this question we give two answers. The appropriate remedy for unemployment in the metallurgical industries, arising from diminished exports, is the undertaking of schemes of capital development at home, which call for the services of just this type of industry. Unfortunately, such development is handicapped at present by various obstacles, and it should be one of the primary tasks of statesmanship to see how these obstacles can be overcome. Secondly, the situation calls for the greatest possible *mobility* of labour—between different occupations, between different districts in the same occupation: and for many reasons the mobility of labour is much less today than it has ever been. Admittedly, these are difficult problems; but it is no use pretending that they are not the real problems, because they are difficult to deal with. In the case of the coal-mines, for example, the only possible means of raising the standard of the miners is to press on rapidly with the development

of new and profitable pits in place of those which will never again
be economic. Capital development and greater mobility are the
two essential conditions of a reduction of unemployment substantially below the figure of a million; and Mr. Lloyd George is, we
believe, entirely right in the persistence with which he stresses both
these points.

But, at the moment, another aspect of the problem is even more
important. General trade conditions could not, we say, be rightly
called depressed twelve months ago. Nor are they really depressed
today. But unfavourable symptoms abound, and the possibility that
trade may take a turn for the worse in the near future must be
seriously reckoned with. In this connexion, the decisions that will
shortly be taken with regard to our monetary policy are of critical
importance. The Government is under strong pressure from the
pundits of financial orthodoxy to promise a definite return to the
gold standard by the end of the present year. The Act which imposes an embargo on gold exports lapses at that date; it must be
specially renewed unless we are ready to take the plunge back to
gold, and it is certainly desirable that we should know well before-
hand whether it is to be renewed or not. It is, therefore, entirely
right that the question should be raised at this juncture. Nor is it
surprising, in view of the fact that sterling is not very far below par,
that the stalwart advocates of gold should argue that the present
opportunity is much too good a one to miss.

We make bold to say that a return to gold this year cannot be
achieved without terrible risk of renewed trade depression and a
serious aggravation of unemployment. A boom in the United States
and a big rise in American prices would, it is true, bring us back to
gold without these sacrifices. A few months ago it seemed quite
likely that this was about to happen, and it remains a probable
development of the next few years. But at the moment activity is
tending to slacken in America. We cannot count on a boom there
this year sufficient to put sterling firmly at par without deflation on
our part. In these circumstances, to announce that we shall return
to gold this year is to announce that a curtailment of credit, further
increases in Bank Rate, a deflation drastic enough to force prices
down by a considerable percentage, which it can only do through
the medium of depressing trade, will in all probability be called
for. Surely business confidence is not so strong that such threats
can be lightly thrown over it.

It is not as though we could feel confident that the present high exchange rate of sterling was justified on the basis of our present price level. On the contrary, as Mr. Keynes points out this week in our Financial Section, there are good reasons for believing that sterling is considerably overvalued by the exchanges. It has been buoyed up by that most untrustworthy of all supports—the anticipation that it would shortly return to par. In our judgement this overvaluation of sterling has been a factor in the recent set-back to our export trades. Everyone recognizes that our export trades are hit by an undue depreciation of the mark or the franc or the lira; but there is a curious failure to grasp that an undue appreciation of sterling has precisely the same effect, is really only the other side of the same shield. Indeed, it is not too much to say that we have been already suffering from an anticipated deflation, working through unduly high exchange rates, the whole brunt of which has fallen on the 'unsheltered' trades.

There were many references to monetary policy in the House of Commons debate, not all of them reassuring. Mr. Snowden, after stressing the 'intimate connexion between our monetary policy, currency and credit, and unemployment', and denouncing the 'rapid deflation' of post-war years, urged the need for caution in general terms. He then expressed the hope that 'the Government will take an early opportunity of announcing that, if they do not propose to go back to the gold standard before the end of the year, they do not intend to renew the Act when it automatically expires at the end of this year'. It is disconcerting to find that Mr. Snowden evidently thinks this a moderate and cautious programme. Mr. Lloyd George brushed monetary questions aside as unimportant details. Sir Arthur Steel-Maitland thought it enough to say that Germany has a Bank Rate of 9 per cent. It is difficult to resist the impression that most of our public men try to minimize the importance of monetary influences, because they find the subject an intricate and difficult one. We venture to say that while the public has reconciled itself to the failure of successive parliaments to solve the unemployment problem, it will not show itself complacent if it should prove that unemployment has been aggravated, gratuitously and on a substantial scale, in the interests of a return to gold. Nor will it avail members then that the course they supported was eminently respectable.

5

DIAGNOSIS AND REMEDY[1]

THE more Mr. Churchill's Budget policy is studied, the more incredible does the folly of it seem. When its various aspects have been fully digested, certainly when its consequences have become apparent, it will surely rank, both from the financial and political standpoints, as an ineptitude without parallel in our recent history. Already it has provoked a storm of opposition as vehement in Conservative as in other circles. The most faithful of the Government's supporters advise that certain features should be dropped, and display their uneasiness by reminding us of Mr. Churchill's difficulties. 'Was he not', asks Mr. Garvin in the *Observer*, 'given the hardest task of its kind that was ever set to man?' He certainly was not. Other Chancellors have had deficits to face. Mr. Churchill, on his own showing, started off with a surplus of £26 millions. When Mr. Snowden last year produced a popular Budget there was a natural tendency to minimize his achievement. 'Any fool', said the chagrined Conservatives, 'could make a popular Budget with a surplus of £40 millions; and the surplus is really ours.' Mr. Churchill commenced, on his own showing, with at least £26 millions to distribute. Confident in his prowess, he had encouraged industry to look to him for benefits, and the Conservative Party to look to him for votes. But he has so framed his policy that it is a nice question whether it will prove more embarrassing to the Government which he serves, or to the industry which he professes to relieve.

The Budget exposes so large a surface to criticism that it is difficult to know what points to take. It contains items of great and, in some cases, of disastrous importance which call for searching examination in themselves. Some of these are dealt with in later articles. But more extraordinary than any of the items (if indeed anything could be more extraordinary than the silk duties) is the tenor of the Budget as a whole. British industry is labouring under great and growing difficulties. In comparison the salaried and rentier classes of the community are reasonably prosperous. Mr. Churchill pays rhetorical recognition to this contrast, and he has

[1] 9 May 1925.

£26,000,000 to play with. Yet he adds materially to the difficulties of industry and concentrates his favours upon the rentier and salaried man. The point has been made by many critics, but we doubt if its full force has yet been generally recognized.

Consider how the cotton industry of Lancashire fares at Mr. Churchill's hands.

1. It is gravely prejudiced by the duty on artificial silk yarn, which means a tax of not far short of 50 per cent. on a raw material which is already important to it, and the growing use of which represents perhaps one of its best chances of renewed prosperity.

2. It is subject like other trades to a substantial increase in the already heavy tax upon employment, represented by insurance contributions.

3. The return to gold rivets upon it an unduly high exchange which serves to diminish the sterling prices which its foreign customers can offer for its products. There is, indeed, partial compensation in a proportionate reduction of the sterling prices of raw cotton. But this compensation is partial only. Moreover, by virtue of the same policy the cotton trade will suffer, and probably very soon, from a higher Bank Rate and diminished credit.

Thus Mr. Churchill presents the cotton trade with a crushing tax upon a new and promising variety of trade, with higher labour costs, and with the prospect of dearer credit and diminished prices for its products. As against this, there is only the reduction of 6*d.* in the standard rate of income-tax, a reduction which is of benefit only to those firms (and they will not be many when Mr. Churchill has done with them) who succeed in making profits.

Compare this result with the position of the salaried man. No new burdens are imposed upon him. He will be relieved not only by the reduction of the standard rate, but by the increased allowance for earned income, and perhaps by the reduction in supertax as well. A man with a wife and three children who has an earned income of £1,000 has his income-tax reduced by almost exactly a quarter. If his income is £3,000, he saves in income-tax and supertax together nearly £120, or about one-fifth of what he now pays. In addition, the purchasing power of his income is likely to be increased by the deflation consequential on the return to gold. What sort of justification can be offered for this sharply contrasted treatment in present circumstances? It is true that the salaried man is heavily taxed; he would be entitled to consideration if trade were

active and employment good, but he has no urgent claim for relief.
Industry, on the other hand, has, and Mr. Churchill admits it, yet
he contrives to produce the result set out above. Was there ever so
glaring a contrast between diagnosis and remedy?

What has led Mr. Churchill to produce a scheme so utterly at
variance with the real needs of the situation? Most of the items are
easy enough to explain if they are taken by themselves and regarded
in watertight compartments. We can only suppose that it is in
watertight compartments that Mr. Churchill has dealt with them,
and that he has not stopped to consider their cumulative effects.
Indeed, it is obvious that the Budget proper had been framed
before any decision upon the crucial question of the gold standard
had been taken, and without any regard to the consequences of
the decision which has actually been taken. Mr. Churchill ought to
have recognized that the question of gold must govern everything
else. The spirit of those who have pressed for the return to gold is
an austere Spartan spirit, ready for the sake of ultimate benefits
(doubtful on balance as we think them) to face 'difficulties', 'painful
readjustments', indeed they are not afraid to say 'sacrifices', in the
immediate future. This is a spirit which consorts ill with the benevo-
lent expansive spirit of new insurance schemes. The postponement
by the Government of its ambition to show itself in earnest in the
field of social reform is indeed just one of the sacrifices which the
Moloch of gold demands. You cannot combine the roles of Cromwell and the brothers Cheeryble.

In short, it was Mr. Churchill's duty, if he decided to take the
plunge back to gold, to insist that expensive social measures must
be ruled out meantime. Nor is that all. Relief to the income-tax
payer should no less have been ruled out. The sacrifices of the
return to gold fall entirely upon business and do not touch the
salaried man. Mr. Churchill should accordingly have used his
Budget surplus, 'fortified' as it might still have been by the increase
in the death duties, exclusively to help industry through the transition. This he could best have done in our opinion by spending most
of it in reducing the existing taxes on employment. At the present
time industry has to pay, through insurance contributions, not only
for the benefits which are rightly on a contributory basis, but also
for uncovenanted unemployment benefit. Uncovenanted benefit is
not insurance at all. It really is (as the other benefits are not) a 'dole',
and there is no justification, even in principle, for throwing this

charge mainly upon industry. In our present economic circumstances it is really preposterous to do so, for unquestionably these insurance contributions (this is the grain of sense in the proposals of Sir Alfred Mond) tend in the direction of aggravating unemployment. Largely on account of uncovenanted benefit, the contributions both of employers and employed are 4d. a week higher than the rates prescribed by Parliament as the proper rates when the 'deficiency' period expires. Mr. Churchill offers industry the hope of ending the 'deficiency' period by a strenuous weeding out of bogus claims. This hope is utterly futile in view of the return to gold. But Mr. Churchill had ample resources with which to relieve industry forthwith of these abnormal charges. If he had done this, if he had postponed the new insurance scheme and abstained from the folly of the silk duties, he would at least have done something to help industry to adapt itself to the return to gold.

This is not the policy that we should have chosen. We should have preferred to launch the insurance scheme and to put off the return to gold. But, even so, we should have coupled the new insurance policy with the assumption by the State of the liability for the abnormal unemployment of the 'deficiency' period. In this way the contributions of employers and workers would not on balance have been increased, and the new scheme would have had an easy passage. This would have meant postponing substantial relief for the salaried man, and coupling his chances of future relief with the chances of improving trade. But surely, in all the circumstances, he would have had no reason to complain of this.

The present situation is not devoid of irony. Industrialists have largely themselves to thank for the way they have been treated. They have joined in the general cry against high taxes, and have displayed an utter absence of discrimination. They never seem to have grasped that, as the Chancellor of the Exchequer must obtain his revenue somehow, the vital question is which taxes he shall choose, and that the true criterion of a bad tax is the damage it does to industry in comparison with the revenue it yields. On the contrary, their one criterion of a specially objectionable tax has been the magnitude of the sums they have had to pay; and as income-tax brings in the largest revenue, it has seemed to them accordingly the most objectionable. In the matter of insurance contributions, on the other hand, they have been very reticent, because these contributions are expressly linked with social policies which it would seem 'hard-faced' to attack. They have thus helped to make it possible for an undiscerning Chancellor to assume that he is helping industry by reducing the income-tax at the expense of an equivalent sum raised by weekly contributions from employers and employed. But this is no defence for Mr. Churchill. He ought not to have been so undiscerning. He ought not to have accepted current clichés so readily at their face value.

We are driven to the conclusion that Mr. Churchill's great but peculiar abilities are not well suited to the realms of finance. He has filled a large variety of public offices with (in the main) conspicuous success. His general reputation deserves, indeed, to rank far higher than it does, for his administration of the Admiralty has been most ungenerously judged. It is with regret that we are disposed to write him down as one of the worst Chancellors of the Exchequer of modern times.

6

THE ECONOMIC TREND[1]

A VAGUE apprehensiveness is widespread in the business world today. A well-founded suspicion is spreading that the comparative immunity from obviously disastrous consequences with which we have sustained six months of national coal stoppage may have been purchased at the expense of piling up heavier troubles for the future. A long time-lag separates economic cause and consequence; and many of the consequences of the coal stoppage are only beginning to come home. Clearly we must be substantially on the wrong side of equilibrium in the balance of external trade. Shall we succeed in getting through the winter without a drain of gold heavy enough to entail restricted credit and general trade depression? What sort of Budget will Mr. Churchill produce next year? These are questions which might well cause uneasiness even if the coal-mines were to resume normal work tomorrow. And behind them the suspicion is deepening that the stoppage is not likely to end either soon or clean.

It is becoming urgent that we should take stock of the situation. We shall not, however, see it in its true perspective, if we regard it merely as a case of a temporary emergency, as a trying time to be passed through with the aid of whatever rough-and-ready expedients we can improvise. The coal stoppage will leave enduring marks upon our economic structure. It will serve, we believe, to give a lasting impetus to certain profoundly important tendencies, which had already acquired a strong momentum before it began. These tendencies are not only profoundly important, they are profoundly disagreeable to conventional minds, because they disturb the whole code of saws and maxims which, carelessly accepted without much scrutiny, have done duty for generations past as an analysis of the sources of our national well-being. And because they have seemed so disagreeable, there has been an obstinate reluctance to face them squarely. Most of our leaders of opinion, in the industrial, financial, and political worlds, have tried to shut out of mind as far as possible, and, in so far as it has not been

[1] 6 November 1926.

possible, to treat as a passing abnormality, tendencies which were manifestly growing stronger year by year. They would not adjust their minds to them and shape their policies thereby; and it is largely for this reason that we have blundered as badly as we have in our handling of the coal dispute. It is imperative that we should adjust our minds to the situation now.

For years past we have all been accustomed to deplore the depression which has lain on our staple export industries. For years past we have talked of the sharp contrast of fortune between the 'sheltered' and the 'unsheltered' trades—which leads to the most highly skilled workmen, such as the British engineer, whose equal, we boast, is not to be found in the outside world, receiving less wages than many other workers performing functions which call for no special skill, or any high degree of general competence or intelligence or character. We have recognized, though perhaps not vividly enough, for it is not a matter which mass statistics force upon our notice, the profoundly unsatisfactory consequences of that contrast; its subtle but powerful influence in promoting social unrest, the low estimation of the value of training which it breeds; the loss by emigration of the most skilled and desirable sections of our population. But, though this state of things has steadily persisted, and indeed has tended to get steadily worse, we have hugged ourselves in the complacent assumption that it was all just a passing difficulty, which would soon right itself. We had become so proud of a Britain whose development was based on an exuberant expansion of export and metallurgy, that we could not bear to think of a Britain developing along other lines. And so we consoled ourselves with any consolations which statistics could suggest. We might be exporting much less; but we were still doing our old *share* of the world's trade; and the settlement of Reparations, or Locarno, or whatever was going forward, would soon set matters right. Our staple export trades had always emerged triumphantly from their difficulties; they always would; it was un-British to doubt it. There was no need even to take any special care to avoid making matters worse. And so, quite complacently, we made matters materially and perhaps permanently worse, by restoring the gold standard, in satisfaction of another ingredient in our pre-war pride, namely, that whatever might be the case in other lands, London was always a free gold market, and the British sovereign worth precisely 123·274 grains of gold, eleven-twelfths fine.

It is, we believe, an indispensable condition of dealing wisely with the economic difficulties that lie ahead, that we should grasp the real significance of what is taking place. A combination of causes, technical (like the growing industrial efficiency of competing countries and the growing economic nationalism in the East), and monetary (like the return to the gold standard coupled with a high level of wages in the sheltered trades, which has clearly come to stay) are gradually but increasingly transforming our economic life. The transformation has many aspects. It effects our equilibrium as a nation accustomed to export on a steadily and rapidly expanding scale, and to leave abroad as investments a large portion of the proceeds. It has an occupational aspect; the staple industries, coal, iron and steel, shipbuilding, cotton, whose expansion was the chief pride of industrial Britain in the nineteenth century, tending rather to decline, and yielding pride of place in the process of development to industries of a new type. And it has a very important geographical aspect; most of the new industrial development—and industrial development has been proceeding on a very considerable scale during the last few years—taking place in districts remote from the old centres of industrial population.

It is surprising that this last aspect of our economic transformation has not received more public attention; for it is not merely a matter of some places expanding while others are declining in a featureless sort of way all over the country. A large regional change is in process. The old 'industrial North' is losing ground to the Midlands and the South. This tendency is, of course, largely the result of the comparative decline of the type of industry which was localized in the old centres. But it goes far beyond that. For example, while the coal industry as a whole is losing ground, its centre of gravity is shifting south and east—away from South Wales, the Tyne, and Scotland—to the newer and richer coalfields in South Yorkshire, the Midlands, and in Kent. This is an accident of Nature and discovery. In other instances the tendency to avoid the old regions, when setting up new enterprises, is perhaps less fortuitous. There is a tendency for highly skilled labour to become less important, and, accordingly, for the advantages offered by the old centres to diminish; on the other hand, their disadvantages, in such shapes as high local rates, and militant trade unionism, are tending to increase. Whatever the causes, the trend is unmistakable. We find the factory inspector writing in his annual Report of 'the areas surrounding London which continue to develop industrially in a remarkable manner', and of 'the astonishing prosperity of Coventry and district'. In its October issue the MINISTRY OF LABOUR GAZETTE publishes for the first time a table giving the percentages of unemployment among insured work-people separately for each employment exchange division. This yields the following results:

	Percentage unemployed at 20 September 1926	Increase (+) or Decrease (−) in percentages as compared with a year ago
London	6·7	−0·2
South-eastern . . .	4·8	−0·1
South-western . .	7·7	−0·5
Midlands . .	13·2	+3·4
North-eastern . .	19·6	+3·1
North-western . .	17·3	+4·4
Scotland . . .	17·3	+1·8
Wales	20·6	−0·1
Northern Ireland . .	22·1	−2·4
Great Britain and Ireland . . .	13·9	+1·9

The contrast between the three southern divisions and the rest of the country, revealed in the first column, is noteworthy; hardly less noteworthy, we would suggest, is the divergent trend during the past year under the influence of the coal stoppage. If, in place of figures of *un*employment, we could obtain figures showing the changes that have taken place in the volume of employment during the past five or six years, it is safe to say that a much more striking contrast would be exhibited.

The picture disclosed by these various tendencies is not, we would emphasize, by any means wholly a discouraging one. If there is depression and decline in some industries, there is expansion and development in others. If an appallingly large part of the productive powers represented by our work-people and our machinery have been standing idle for years past, and, unless we bestir ourselves about the matter, seem likely to stand idle for years to come, we have none the less been producing enough to maintain the general standards of life. If the volume of our exports, instead of increasing steadily as it used to do, is deplorably below the pre-war level, we have none the less been exporting enough, year in and year out, to purchase our necessary imports and leave a margin over for foreign investment which is quite substantial. In short, the tendencies which are at work, if only we can adapt ourselves to them, and make clear-sightedly any readjustments that may be necessary, point to a new sort of equilibrium which is perfectly consistent with increasing national well-being.

But if we refuse to recognize what is happening, if we invest all our hopes for the future on a restoration of the pre-war equilibrium, we are likely to plunge deeper into trouble. At the root of the mishandling of the coal problem, at the root certainly of the encouragement which industrialists and financiers have prevailingly extended to the coal-owners in their disastrously uncompromising attitude, there lies a complex of false notions linked together by the assumptions that it is possible to get back to the sort of equilibrium that we had before the war, and that our national prosperity is staked upon our doing so. It is not by looking in this direction that we shall shake off our industrial *malaise*.

7

THE NEW INDUSTRIAL REVOLUTION[1]

WE may now reasonably hope that we are within sight of some sort of end of the coal stoppage, though it is still doubtful whether the end will be a really clean one, and we have still to reckon with many of the more formidable consequences which it will leave behind. What lessons are we going to draw as a people from this lamentable experience? Will the coal stoppage serve, as observers in Soviet Russia delightedly prophesy, to give a decisive impulse to the forces making for class-warfare, to propel us more rapidly along the road of industrial conflict and confusion to the final downfall of our industrial greatness? Or will it rather prove the darkest hour that precedes the dawn, the last fling of the forces of folly and unreason, before the phase of disturbance which is the usual sequel to a great war gives place to a phase of genuine reconstruction?

The issue is uncertain. It depends upon many factors; but, above all, we believe, on whether we understand the nature of the problems that confront us. It is greatly to be hoped that within the Labour movement the influence of those will grow who recognize the essentially suicidal nature of industrial warfare and the narrow limits to Labour's power, and that the cult of militancy, which so many silly-clever intellectuals have set themselves in recent years to glorify and idealize, will wane. But it is not only Labour that has lessons to learn; and Labour is unlikely to learn its lessons unless others learn theirs. Unhappily there is little sign that the Conservative middle-class opinion now dominant is disposed to draw wise conclusions. On the contrary there are many signs of the growth of a really alarming attitude. For example, industrial disputes are attributed to the excessive legal privileges of the trade unions. To clip their powers is therefore the way to industrial peace; and the Government will get into trouble unless it satisfies this sentiment. Again, unemployment is attributed to 'the dole', which prevents men seeking work; accordingly an attack is developing, which considerations of economy are likely to reinforce, upon unemployment benefits and indeed upon the whole system of national insurance.

[1] 27 November 1926.

Now, it may be desirable to overhaul and revise both trade-union law and our system of unemployment relief. But it is certain that both these tasks need to be approached in a very different spirit from that which is now prevalent. And the first condition of approaching them and the other tasks that await us in the right spirit is to understand the nature of the causes which underlie both the unemployment and the industrial strife.

We have repeatedly called attention to the transformation that is coming over our economic life, amounting almost, as Mr. Baldwin put it at the Guildhall, to a new Industrial Revolution. A fortnight ago we dwelt upon the regional aspect of this process, pointing out that 'the old industrial North is yielding place to the Midlands and the South'. We may perhaps convey our meaning more exactly and more vividly as follows. Draw a line across the map of England, starting from the mouth of the Severn, and proceeding straight to Stafford, from there to the High Peak, and from there to Scarborough. This line divides Great Britain into two parts of almost equal economic importance, but presenting an extraordinary contrast of fortune. The numbers of insured work-people on either side of the line are approximately the same; but to the left of it (i.e. to the north and west) unemployment is almost exactly double what it is on the right (i.e. to the south and east); or rather it was double just before the coal stoppage began; the contrast must be much sharper at the present moment. To the left of the line lie all the 'black spots', the regions of the Tyne, the Clyde and South Wales, the Potteries, the textile districts of Lancashire and Yorkshire. Almost every area of present development or future promise, for example, Doncaster, Coventry, Kent, lies to the right.

Now it is of considerable interest to observe that the voting of the miners last week, which preceded the decision to negotiate district settlements, corresponded almost exactly with this line of demarcation. To the right of our line, the vote was for peace; to the left for a continuation of the struggle. The reason is not, of course, far to seek. To the right, in the Doncaster area and the Midlands, the terms offered to the miners are better than elsewhere because the coal-mines there are comparatively prosperous. It was largely for this reason that the breakaways developed first and have gone furthest in the Midlands. This contrast may have important consequences in the near future. For one thing, it seems by no means unlikely that the dispute may drag on in other areas for a consider-

able time after Yorkshire and the Midlands have come to terms.
Whether this happens or not, the way in which the miners react to
their defeat is likely to be very different in the two parts of the
country. The newspapers are making much just now of various
symptoms of disillusionment with the militant policy of the Miners'
Federation. We learn, for example, that a new union is being
formed in Notts., which is to eschew politics and cultivate friendly
relations with the owners. But this is a Midlands phenomenon. In
South Wales, in Northumberland and Durham, and in Scotland,
the prevailing reaction will almost certainly be an increased bitter-
ness of feeling, manifesting itself in the growth of Communist
opinions. It will not be surprising, in short, if, as the result of the
struggle, the mining population is divided, by the line we have indicated, into two sections, sharply contrasted in temper and policy
and economic prosperity.

Let us now turn to the occupational changes which are taking
place. The November issue of the MINISTRY OF LABOUR GAZETTE
contains some very important tables, to which we referred briefly
last week, which throw fresh light upon the matter. They show,
industry by industry, the changes over the last three years in the
numbers of work-people insured. In one of the tables, industries are
arranged in two groups; according as their personnel has increased
or diminished. We give below the figures for the latter group, simplifying the classification a little:

Industry	Numbers of insured work-people				Decrease over the three years
	July 1923	*July* 1924	*July* 1925	*July* 1926	
Coal mining . .	1,256,000	1,260,350	1,240,450	1,227,870	28,130
Woollen and worsted .	271,000	260,890	257,700	254,750	16,250
Bread-, biscuit-, cake-, &c., making . .	157,700	144,540	141,790	145,830	11,870
General engineering .	669,000	627,380	627,280	615,920	53,080
Marine engineering .	66,300	66,110	61,720	58,370	7,930
Shipbuilding . .	270,200	255,090	241,700	224,120	46,080
Iron and steel . .	242,000	237,460	225,910	218,340	23,660
Railway service (non-permanent workers) .	191,100	173,210	168,610	160,650	30,450
National government .	179,600	160,970	156,490	151,470	23,130
Vehicle building . .	27,700	24,550	24,630	21,700	6,000
Total of above industries	3,330,600	3,210,550	3,146,280	3,079,020	251,580

There are many features of this table which deserve attention. In the first place, it should be observed that the figures cover all insured persons attached to the industry, whether in or out of work; so that to obtain the decline in the volume of employment, we need to add the figures of the last column to any increase which there may have been in unemployment. All our basic metallurgical industries appear in this list. It is hardly less noteworthy that, while the woollen industry also appears, the cotton industry, which has fared materially worse, does not. The cotton industry has actually increased its personnel by about 8,000, an interesting sidelight on the working of the short-time system. The table of industries which have increased their personnel is too long for us to reproduce in full. The distributive trades alone show an increase of 260,000, or more than the aggregate decrease in the declining industries. Building and public works have increased by 128,000; the motor-car industry and road transport by 75,000; furniture, brick-making, printing, silk, the electrical trades, all show important increases.

Now figures such as these convey a very inadequate impression of the real magnitude of the changes that are taking place. The changes are partly occupational, and partly regional; and figures relating only to one or to the other tendency do not do justice to the combined effects of the two. Engineering, for example, as a whole, presents an unsatisfactory picture; but engineering is a large category comprising many essentially different trades, with very diverse fortunes and localized to a large extent in different centres. General figures for engineering thus tend to cloak the plight of engineering on the Tyne, say, or in South Wales, as can be seen from the following figures from the same issue of the LABOUR GAZETTE:

Engineering

Percentages Unemployed at 25 October 1926

London	.	.	.	6·9	North-eastern	.	.	26·9
South-eastern	.	.	.	6·1	North-western	.	.	19·0
South-western	.	.	.	6·3	Scotland	.	.	23·6
Midlands	.	.	.	13·2	Wales	.	.	33·6
					Northern Ireland	.	.	29·0

Such are the diversities concealed beneath the average unemployment percentage for engineering of 16·4.

Let us recapitulate the general contention, in support of which we adduce the above figures as merely such straws of evidence as are available. Our economic life is shifting, we believe, from one sort of equilibrium to another. Our unemployment and our labour troubles represent essentially the difficulties and the pains of that transition. Those difficulties and pains are being aggravated unnecessarily in a great variety of ways by a general and obstinate failure to recognize that transition and to adapt ourselves to it. To organize and to direct that transition is today the central task of economic statesmanship. These are general phrases; and we shall not attempt this week to translate them into concrete terms. We are concerned now to emphasize the facts. But assuredly there is no lack of practical morals to be drawn. It is, indeed, not easy to exaggerate the difference it will make in the sort of policy we shall pursue, and the sort of results we may expect, according as we envisage the problem in its true perspective, or treat it as the natural outcome of twenty years of indulgence of trade unions and extravagance in social reform.

8

THE LIMITS OF INSULAR SOCIALISM[1]

We argued last week that Mr. Snowden, in framing his Budget next year, will be faced with the necessity of finding additional revenue to the tune of at least £40 millions, and very likely substantially more. We observed further that, in our judgement, this about exhausts the limits of the additional money which can safely be raised during the present Parliament, at any rate by the method of direct taxation. And we concluded that it was a very serious state of affairs that the financial resources, prudently open to the present Parliament, should already have been mortgaged for purposes which are entirely unconstructive and unproductive in their character.

Now, in writing thus, we are, we believe, writing very moderately. So far from seeking to lay the dark colours on thick, we are conscious rather, at every point of our diagnosis, of exercising considerable restraint; and we are convinced that the misgivings we have expressed are shared to the full by the Chancellor of the Exchequer, and by every man of sense in the present Government who is in touch with the realities of the financial position. But, of course, very few, even among intelligent and well-informed people, have given their minds seriously to the practical problem of next year's Budget; and most members of the Labour Party, even those of moderate opinions, seem to us to be living in a Fool's Paradise. Holding a general belief (which we share) in the twofold policy of the graduated taxation of wealth on the one hand and the provision of social services on the other, they have no inkling of the very real dangers of pushing that policy much further at the present time; and they still think it sufficient to say with a facile plausibility: 'Can we afford it? Of course we can. We are a rich country, with plenty of rich people to tax. We can afford anything which we really want to do.' Such a mood must lead sooner or later to disillusionment; and the earlier the process of disillusionment begins the better for everyone.

The yield of supertax last year was £56 millions. (It will probably be a good deal less in the current year.) Let us set that figure against the £40 millions, or more, which Mr. Snowden will have to

---

[1] 30 November 1929.

find next April. If Mr. Snowden were to attempt to meet his coming
deficit entirely by means of supertax he would have practically to
double the rates of tax. No one, we imagine, will suggest that this
would be feasible. The supertax is already stiff and steeply graduated, beginning at the income-limit of £2,000 a year, and ranging
from a rate of 9*d.* to one of 6*s.* in the £, payable, of course, on top
of income-tax. The notion of doubling such a tax is clearly utterly
chimerical. But another fact must be borne in mind, which makes
it very dangerous to raise the supertax at all. The yield of supertax
has been declining steadily, substantially and ominously in recent
years. The significance of this decline is clear. The practice of evad-
ing or avoiding supertax is becoming increasingly widespread.
There are all sorts of entirely legitimate ways by which supertax
can be avoided, if the motive for doing so is strong enough; and it
is idle to suppose that it is possible to stop them up effectively by
ad hoc legislation. There is an obvious danger that even a mild
increase in the rates of supertax would give a powerful stimulus to
the practice of evasion. It is a wise financial maxim that you should
beware of increasing the rate of tax on any source of revenue which
is showing a declining yield.

In our judgement, therefore, Mr. Snowden will be well advised
not to touch supertax at all. In any case, it is clear that he can hope
for very little from this source, and that, if he has to find £40 millions in his next Budget, and limits himself mainly to direct taxation, his main reliance must be upon the ordinary income-tax. Now
it would require an addition of at least 8*d.* to the standard rate of
income-tax to bring in £40 millions in a full year of operation; and,
of course, Mr. Snowden will only get the benefit in his next Budget
of a half-year's yield of any increase he imposes. If he were to increase the income-tax by as much as 1*s.* in the £, this would only
bring him next year about £30 millions, and he would still have to
raise a considerable sum in other ways to make ends meet. If he
were content with 6*d.*, he would have to lean heavily next year on
indirect taxes, a course which would be repugnant to his principles
and extremely distasteful to the Labour Party. We suggest, therefore, that we have to reckon very seriously with the possibility of
1*s.* on the income-tax in the next Budget, not standing alone, but
supplemented by, say, some addition to the death duties and some
new miscellaneous imposts. It is true that this would give Mr.
Snowden a substantial margin in subsequent years with which to

meet the rising tide of social expenditure, and this consideration
has some reassuring value in connexion with the argument that
follows.

We do not suggest that there is anything necessarily or inherently
disastrous in the difference between a 4s. and a 5s. income-tax.
Most of the arguments which stress the damage done by high direct
taxation to industry and enterprise are, we believe, essentially fallacious. If no one was in the least apprehensive that taxation would
be increased any further, the burden of a 5s. income-tax is one
which, we believe, could easily be borne without any serious repercussions detrimental to the national well-being—though not, of
course, without considerable soreness on the part of those who
would have to bear it for the sake of nothing better than a miscel-
lany of such uninspiring trivialities as the raising of unemployment
pay and the granting of pensions to widows who *ex hypothesi* are
of working age and have no children to support. But the question
assumes an altogether different aspect if taxpayers are fearful that
the end has not been reached, but that there may be something
more on next year, and more again the year after; if they are persuaded, in short, that increased taxation has become the order of
the day, and may go to almost any lengths. In that case, the repercussions of the next Budget may be very serious indeed, and, what
is more, very speedy in their operation. The man who makes light
of them is either ignorant and irresponsible, or is burying his head
in the sand.

We must return at this point to the phenomenon of tax evasion
or avoidance. At present its commonest form is the creation of
trusts, by which a rich man parts with the legal ownership of a
portion of his capital in favour of his children or relations. In this
case, the Inland Revenue loses in supertax, but that is all; no loss
of national income is involved. But there is a form of tax avoidance
which, if it were to develop on a big scale, would be immeasurably
more formidable, namely, residence abroad. The number of British
persons who, stimulated mainly or largely by the taxation motive,
are domiciled beyond the reach of the Chancellor of the Exchequer,
is already by no means negligible. The practice, it should be observed, is not confined to wealthy persons of the supertax-paying
class. It extends to comparatively small rentiers who are thinking
only of the income-tax. Now, when a man goes abroad to avoid
taxation, the State loses all the revenue it at present gets from him

—income-tax as well as supertax, the duties on his tobacco, his wine, and his motor-car. But that is not all. The national income is reduced thereby. He may own overseas investments, the income from which has hitherto helped us in the balance of international payments, tending to support the sterling exchange, and contributing to the means by which, as a people, we pay for our food and raw materials. In future, his income will tell the other way.

The practice of moving abroad to escape taxation has not gone very far as yet; nor do we think it likely to go very far, so long as nothing is done to give the rentier classes an acute feeling of insecurity. But who feels confident that it would not acquire a greatly increased momentum if apprehensions were to be widely and seriously entertained that taxation in Great Britain was going up and up, more or less indefinitely? We put the question in that form: Who feels confident that it would not? because it is not necessary that such a movement should actually develop. If such a movement appears probable or even likely, trouble begins to arise at once.

Before a man moves abroad to escape taxation, before he definitely makes up his mind to do so, before he has got much further than a vague feeling that, if things go on like this, he may do so one day, he is apt to do something else. He is apt to put his money, or a large part of it, abroad, by way of preparation or precaution. And if a sufficient number of people are doing this, others are apt to follow suit, merely as a matter of prudent investment, because the situation threatens a steady decline in the value of British securities. The result, in other words, is apt to be a 'flight from the pound', serious in proportion to the seriousness of the apprehensions about high taxation. At the present time, with the foreign-exchange position precarious for quite other reasons, such as the repatriation of French balances, we can ill sustain even the mildest flight from the pound. Quite a mild flight would entail a series of reactions, higher Bank Rate, slackened trade, increased unemployment, which would serve to defeat the purpose of the increased taxation and to make the Budget deficit larger than before. There is always the danger that the movement might gain a gathering momentum and develop into a real *dégringolade*.

These are dangers which we believe to be latent in the Budget situation which confronts Mr. Snowden. To avert them it is essential, in our judgement, that he should be able to convince the public that the increased taxation he imposes does not represent the first instalment of an indefinite series of increases, but rather a temporary reversion, under the pressure of unfortunate circumstances, to an abnormally high level of taxation, from which some relief can be expected fairly confidently in the future. We do not doubt that Mr. Snowden will endeavour to represent matters in this light, and in some respects he is strongly placed for doing so. It is quite true that he finds himself this year in a position of exceptional difficulty. A large part of the deficit which faces him is attributable, as we pointed out last week, not to the commitments of the present Government, but to Mr. Churchill's improvidence. Moreover, whatever taxes Mr. Snowden decides to impose, it is almost certain that they will be such as will yield a larger revenue in the following year, so that he will have a sufficient margin in prospect to finance the binding commitments of the Government to further expenditure under such heads as the raising of the school age.

But such facts, together with all the personal assurances which it is in Mr. Snowden's power to give, will not carry conviction, unless the Labour Party as a whole modify the ideas about future social expenditure which at present they so clamorously proclaim. It is the reverse of helpful to Mr. Snowden when Mr. Shaw, in defending the Unemployment Insurance Bill, asserts heatedly that the increase in the scale of benefits represents only a very modest instalment of what the Government want to do, mean to do, and indeed would do at this moment if only they had a majority in the House of Commons. Almost every Minister, in introducing almost every Bill, speaks after this fashion. It is done, of course, to placate the rank and file. But the Labour rank and file, and, we dare say, some of the Ministers too, need today not so much to be placated as to be educated.

We have laid stress in the foregoing analysis on the danger of a flight from the pound, because that, we believe, is the way in which the consequences of imprudent taxation would most immediately make themselves felt. But behind that there is, of course, a more fundamental factor. We live in an age of international tendency, of highly developed international communications, of international travel, of international trusts, of a projected International Bank, of international groupings and *camaraderies* of every sort and description. The power of all organizations resting on a purely national basis, including national governments, is necessarily limited by this tendency; and in most connexions no one is quicker than the Socialist to point this out. No one, for example, argues more insistently that the coal problem is an international problem and can only be solved satisfactorily by international agreement. No one lays more stress—as we are disposed to think, undue stress —on the importance of the work of the International Labour Office. In most connexions, in short, no one recognizes more clearly the need for some degree of conformity between the practice of different nations. Now this need for some degree of international conformity does not disappear when we come to taxation. Just as with hours and wages, it is difficult to move very far in advance of the prevailing practice of other countries in the taxation of wealth.

We have already, of course, gone a long way in advance of other countries in this matter, as in others. Is it surprising that it should be really difficult and dangerous to go much further? The *a priori* justice or injustice of redistributing wealth by taxing the rich for the benefit of the poor is beside the point. The point is the power of the national State. In the modern world the national State is not omnipotent, and there are limits to its power to remould the structure of its domestic society without reference to what is happening in the world outside. The large majority of rentiers are willing to pay a large 'ransom', to use Mr. Joseph Chamberlain's old phrase, rather than take themselves off to a strange land. But the hold over them possessed by the national State is not absolute, and it is dangerous to speak and reason as though it were.

There is, we believe, no escape from the conclusion that we should eschew for the time being measures which are primarily redistributive in character, and concentrate our energies for the next few years on the attempt to restore and improve our national productivity. This is a conclusion which is necessarily extremely unpalatable to the Labour Party. Yet perhaps they are not quite so far from accepting it as appearances suggest.

9

THE McKENNA DUTIES AGAIN[1]

On Monday of Christmas week Mr. Snowden made a statement designed to relieve the uncertainty of traders and manufacturers as to the position in which they might find themselves if he should decide to repeal the McKenna duties or certain other indirect taxes in the next Budget. The assurances contained in the statement were not extensive. They were limited to an undertaking that, if the silk and sugar duties were repealed, some scheme of rebates on duty-paid stocks would be introduced, and that, if the McKenna duties were repealed, there would be, as in 1924, the usual drawback on exports. On the question of whether any of these duties were likely to be repealed, Mr. Snowden refused to throw any light whatever, taking his stand on 'the invariable rule that Budget decisions cannot be anticipated'. He even appeared doubtful whether it was really quite proper to give the foregoing assurances; for he was at pains to emphasize that 'it is only in consideration of the exceptional circumstances of the present time and of their bearing on the pressing problem of employment that I have agreed to make this statement', and that it must not be assumed that 'the same course would be followed in different circumstances or in future years'.

For our part, we entertain only a limited veneration for such rules and traditions as that by which Mr. Snowden professes to be bound. They are useful servants but bad masters. If Mr. Snowden seriously thinks that the repeal or the reduction of the McKenna duties or the silk duties or the sugar duties is a possible feature of his coming Budget, he is perfectly right not to commit himself in any way. But, if it is already clear to him that he must put such thoughts aside for the time being, he might well say so, as it seems to us, without any sort of disadvantage, immediate or ultimate, belonging to the domain of reality, and with considerable advantage, as indeed he recognizes, to business confidence and to employment in the meantime.

The propriety of making such a statement is, however, a very secondary matter. The question of real importance is whether it

[1] 4 January 1930.

would be wise or defensible policy to repeal or reduce any of these duties in the coming Budget. In our judgement it would be the height of folly, and utterly indefensible to touch a single one of them. We think it desirable to state our opinion plainly and emphatically; since it might be most unfortunate if the impression were to get abroad that Free Trade opinion would be solidly behind a course which, under present economic conditions, must do wanton mischief to trade and employment, and would, incidentally, we believe, do irreparable damage to the Free Trade cause.

In the first place, Mr. Snowden, in his coming Budget, will be in no position to throw away any part of his existing revenue. In recent articles we have attempted to call attention to the gravity of the financial outlook, and the revenue returns which have just been published make it clear, as we thought probable at the time, that our analysis erred on the side of understatement. Formidable increases in direct taxation, such as another shilling on the income-tax, or some variant of the surtax proposal which will have much the same significance and psychological effect, are already inevitable; and the man who supposes that such taxation will not react prejudicially on business activity and economic welfare is—a rude word is the most appropriate—an ass. The situation is indeed so difficult that on merits there is much to be said for not leaning entirely on direct taxation, but for increasing indirect taxes as well in order to make ends meet. This would, of course, be so distasteful to Mr. Snowden and the Labour Party that it is not very likely to be done. But for Mr. Snowden to go out of his way to enlarge the gap which he will have to meet by repealing or reducing existing indirect taxes which bring in a modest but useful revenue would, in all the circumstances, be a most irresponsible proceeding. It would only be justified if it could be shown that the taxes which it was proposed to repeal were not merely obnoxious on grounds of general principle, but were doing serious practical mischief, mischief exceeding any which might be caused by a still further increase of the income-tax. With regard to none of the duties referred to by Mr. Snowden, not even with regard to the McKenna duties which represent the heart of the controversy, can such a contention possibly be sustained.

On the contrary, even if we had not to face a condition of exceptional financial stringency, it would be very difficult, on industrial grounds, to justify the choice of the present year for the repeal of

the McKenna duties. We have to reckon this year with the repercussions of the Wall Street slump as the dominating factor in the
world economic situation. Many of those repercussions should
prove very helpful to us, notably cheap money throughout the
world. But one repercussion which it is idle to ignore is that many
of our industries will have to face keener American competition in
our domestic and in export markets. In no industry is this factor
likely to be more important than in the production of motor-cars.
For the automobile industry stands out pre-eminent among the
'luxury' industries of the United States, which are already finding
it difficult to sell their products at home owing to the sense of impoverishment resulting from the collapse of stock values.

This constitutes an extraordinarily unfavourable environment for
withdrawing the protection which the British motor-car industry
has hitherto enjoyed. The removal of protective duties, on which
an industry has been built up, is, of course, always liable to cause
immediate dislocation; so that the present year, with unemployment very high and showing ominous signs, when all seasonal
influences have been allowed for, of moving upwards, with the assurance of business confidence perhaps our most pressing economic
need, would in any case be a bad time for repealing the McKenna
duties. But the force of this consideration is increased tenfold, so
far as the motor industry is concerned, when we remember that we
may have to face something fairly deserving the name of dumping
from the United States. The repeal of the McKenna duties, under
those conditions, would undoubtedly entail a large addition to the
numbers of the unemployed; and it is idle to suppose that there
would be compensation in other directions on anything approaching a commensurate scale.

In our judgement, either this industrial argument or the previous
financial argument would, by itself, be sufficient to forbid the repeal
just now of the McKenna duties. Together they form a case of overwhelming strength, so overwhelming, indeed, that the possibility of
repeal could safely be ruled out, if it were not for the high authority
which Mr. Snowden is believed to attach to the claims of Free Trade
principle.

Now, it is surely to misconceive altogether the place of principle
in economic affairs to suppose that you ought to do things in deference to it which are likely to be mischievous in their results. It is
absurd to claim for economic principles the dignity of categorical

imperatives. Their whole purpose is, or should be, to indicate generally what you should do in order to obtain good results; and it is the sheerest pedantry to suppose that it is in some way virtuous to follow them when you recognize that they will produce bad results. There is, indeed, one principle, above all others, which is at present unduly neglected in our economic statesmanship, namely, the principle that policy should be related to circumstances. It would be at least as ill-judged to repeal the McKenna duties in 1930 in deference to Free Trade principles as it was to restore the gold standard in 1925 in deference to sound money principles.

It is not as though it were in the least likely that the repeal of the McKenna duties by Mr. Snowden would serve to fortify Free Trade, and scotch the possibility that Protection may gradually spread itself throughout our fiscal system. On the contrary, it would inevitably stimulate Protectionist agitation, and, if the immediate effects of repeal proved as patently injurious as we believe they would, it might lead, by way of reaction, to the establishment of a considerably more extended tariff system than we possess at present.

This leads us to our final point. In approaching tariff questions today, it is vital that we should consider the bearing of our actions on the project of the World Economic Conference, the endeavour, by international agreement, to reverse the tendency towards rising tariffs throughout the world. Would the repeal of the McKenna duties help or hinder that endeavour? We are convinced, for our part, that it would hinder it; and we believe that our opinion is shared by those who are closely in touch with the actual work of Geneva. We cannot attempt now to elaborate our reasons for taking this view; we must be content with a summary indication of their nature. If we are to pursue the method of international agreement, it will be important that the British governments should be able to give undertakings relating to tariffs which succeeding governments will not repudiate. If anything comes of Mr. Graham's proposal for a tariff truce it will involve such an undertaking; he is proposing in effect to tie the hands of succeeding governments. But if we are to proceed upon these lines, we must cultivate some degree of continuity of policy in regard to tariffs; and we must modify our national tradition of treating them as the favourite Aunt Sally of our domestic politics.

10

OUR HERESY[1]

A CURIOUS fate has attended the article which we wrote a fortnight ago on the subject of the McKenna duties. It has caused, it
seems, so at least we are assured on all sides in the Press, a minor
political sensation. The MANCHESTER GUARDIAN describes it as a
'sensational Protectionist article' which has 'created doubt and
dismay' in the Liberal ranks, brackets us with Lord Beaverbrook
and Lord Rothermere, and adds reassuringly that the Liberal Party
is in no way associated with our 'backsliding'. Conservative papers,
while congratulating us on our dawning sense of the error of Cob-
denite opinions, are no less astonished, and some of them display
considerable ingenuity in their search for an adequate explanation
of so remarkable a phenomenon. 'Its meaning', says a paragraph
writer in the YORKSHIRE POST, in a reference to our article, 'is a
matter of general speculation. There is a suggestion that it is kite-
flying, and those who would discover the politician who is indulg-
ing in this pastime go back some six years. In 1923, when he went
to America, Mr. Lloyd George was credited with plans which
implied a wide departure from the historical fiscal policy of the
Liberal Party. . . .' The same suggestion appears in other papers.

We are as much staggered by this reception of our article as any
of our critics can have been by the article itself. It has never been
our practice in this journal to fly kites for political leaders, and we
are at a loss to understand why such an explanation should be
thought necessary in the present case. The view which we advanced
—that it would be a grave mistake to repeal the McKenna duties
in this particular year—is not, among Free Traders, a bizarre, or
indeed at all an uncommon view. On the contrary, we believe that
it is easily preponderant among those Free Traders who approach
the question primarily from the standpoint of economic policy
rather than from that of the political platform.

It is fairly clear, indeed, that no one would have regarded our
article as in any way sensational if it were not for the quasi-
theological atmosphere which surrounds the fiscal issue. There is

[1] 18 January 1930.

a widespread impression—whether it is well founded we shall not presume to say—that on any matter where a theological atmosphere prevails, no one ever says exactly what he means. We think it highly probable that many of our Free Trade critics really agree with us —for, after all, many of them are men of sense—that it would be a mistake to abolish the McKenna duties in the present year; but they are none the less genuinely shocked that we should say so, for they cannot conceive that we should say this in public unless what we really meant was that we are in favour of imposing a tariff on wool and steel. Nor do we suppose that anything which we can say now will have the effect of removing such suspicions. We have some knowledge of Scottish theological controversy, and, when we read the phrases of rebuke that have been addressed to us: 'backsliding', 'cowardly advice', 'weakening in the fight', 'the effect of such an article must be to put the quality of their Free Trade opinions under grave suspicion', we despair of rehabilitating, in the eyes of such guardians of the faith, our Free Trade reputation.

Nor, shocking as it may be, are we particularly anxious to do so. We have never regarded Free Trade opinions as an ingredient of moral virtue; and, if we thought that a system of Protection would represent the best economic policy for Great Britain, we should advocate it without any sense of sin. It so happens that the case for Free Trade seems to us, on prosaic utilitarian grounds, a very strong one, so strong that we have never felt the need for theological buttresses. A horrid doubt suggests itself that perhaps our Free Trade theologians are not equally convinced of the strength of the economic case. Mr. Brunker, for instance, who flings 'coward' at us this week in the name of the Free Trade Union—what exactly is his state of mind? He seems to us to imply—we cannot make sense of him otherwise—that we may be right in maintaining that the consequences of repealing the McKenna duties would be bad, but that courage requires us to damn the consequences. Apparently, a really brave and noble Free Trader is one who believes in it entirely independently of its practical results.

Possibly, therefore, it may come as a welcome surprise to Free Traders of this type to learn that, when you have thrown quasi-theological prepossessions overboard, and have put yourself into the frame of mind which is ready to accept facts and make reasonable admissions, the case for Free Trade remains, as we have said, extremely strong, and when we say the case for Free Trade, we do not mean merely as an abstract academic theory, but as the fiscal policy for Great Britain at the present time and in existing circumstances. The case, in a nutshell, is that our economic welfare is dependent on our continuing to do a large export trade, and we can only retain a large export trade on the basis of world prices. The effect of Protection is necessarily to cut our industries adrift from world prices, and accordingly to turn them away from world markets. It enables this or that protected industry to maintain a prosperous home trade on the basis of prices raised above the international price level; it enables it to maintain wages and costs of production which would be impossible but for the shelter of protection; and, since the finished product of one industry is the raw material of another, all this increases the difficulties of exporting industries in world markets. Protection, in short, means the aggravation of that contrast between sheltered and unsheltered industries, which is admittedly at the root of our present economic troubles.

We do not suggest that our existing Protectionist duties have contributed appreciably to our exporting difficulties. They are too trivial for that. It is monetary, rather than fiscal policy, that is mainly responsible for the present contrast between sheltered and unsheltered trades. But to go out of our way to aggravate that contrast, when our exports have already fallen to a level that is disconcertingly low, to make every industry think in terms of abandoning the laborious export game for the easier task of doing a sheltered trade at home, or (for that matter) within the Empire, would be, in our judgement, as perilous a policy as we could well adopt. We by no means underrate the danger that some such policy may, amid the confusion of political issues, win the electoral day. On the contrary, we regard it very seriously; we are anxious to avert it; and it is largely for this reason that we urge Free Traders to recognize the sheer folly of repealing the McKenna duties in the present year.

We gave our reasons at length in our previous article; and our critics, while eloquent on the moral issue of our backsliding, have not made any very serious attempt to answer them. We think it desirable, however, to deal with one point which the controversy has brought out. Some of our critics evidently labour under the belief that an increase of imports must be balanced immediately by a commensurate increase of exports. We do not know whether they imagine that exports are increased the next day, the next week, or the next month; nor do we know by what chain of causation they suppose this happens. In any case, this idea is a complete delusion. The only immediate effect produced by an increase of imports is an alteration in the balance of short-period international indebtedness; and it is only through a rather disagreeable series of reactions, embracing weak foreign exchanges, dear money, trade depression, wage reductions, that the change, if on a sufficiently big scale, filters ultimately through to exports. The 'imports pay for exports' proposition provides, therefore, no sort of answer to our objection that the repeal of the McKenna duties must have the immediate effect of increasing unemployment.

Indeed, it is not really possible for anyone who has a glimmering of an understanding of the way in which international trade works to deny that the repeal of the McKenna duties would cause immediate dislocation. Opinions may legitimately differ as to how serious the dislocation would be. We pointed to the reactions of the Wall Street slump as our reason for fearing that it might be very serious in the present year. But, leaving the question of degree aside, the contention that there would be an immediate increase of unemployment is really not open to dispute; and we are surprised that Free Traders should be anxious to dispute it. That tariffs, once imposed, cannot usually be removed without causing unemployment, is a weighty reason against imposing them.

Now this immediate dislocation is a factor which Liberals must, in our judgement, weigh very seriously. They fought the last election on the proposition that large-scale unemployment constituted so urgent an evil as to call for remedy by avowedly emergency measures. We cannot, for our part, understand how Liberals who used this language at the last election can now turn round and say in effect: 'The McKenna duties must go, and we do not care two hoots whether this will increase unemployment or not. Principle does not permit us to take such considerations into account.' Let them, at all events, not blind themselves to the dangers of such an attitude. When people sacrifice realities to abstractions, the abstractions soon fall out of favour. The unemployment figures are as bad as they were last year; under the shadow of the Budget they may well become worse. If they should be palpably increased by serious unemployment in the motor industry the Protectionists will be supplied with an object-lesson which will carry a weight far exceeding its deserts.

In our previous article we pleaded that we should have some regard to the bearing of our actions on the project of the World Economic Conference. Nothing in the attitude of our Free Trade critics surprises us more than their apparently complete indifference to this plea. Some of them, indeed, find the main offence of our article in the passage in which we urged that, if we are to seek international agreements regarding tariffs, 'we must modify our national tradition of treating them as the favourite Aunt Sally of our domestic politics'. Possibly they have failed to grasp our meaning. In 1924 Mr. Snowden repealed the McKenna duties. In 1925 Mr. Churchill reimposed them. Our critics urge Mr. Snowden to repeal them once more in 1930. If he does the next Conservative Government will certainly reimpose them, possibly in 1931. We say that such oscillations of policy, which are damaging enough from a domestic standpoint, are incompatible with the effective prosecution of the World Economic Conference idea.

At this moment Mr. Graham, in the name of Great Britain, is proposing to the world a tariff truce. The proposal is to be considered next month by an *ad hoc* Conference at Geneva. Mr. Graham has indicated 'two or three years' as the period he proposes for his truce; but obviously an agreement even on this limited basis might, in not unlikely circumstances, fall to be honoured by a Conservative Government. It is not, we hope, unreasonable to expect a Conservative Government to honour it, if the tariff issue is not forced meanwhile into the forefront of acrimonious party controversy. But, if Mr. Snowden is to repeal the McKenna duties—well, frankly, we do not see how the present Government can decently conclude such an agreement. Perhaps some of our Free Trade critics, when they have exhausted their virtuous indignation, will tell us how they answer this point. We should really like to know.

PART II

Memoranda written when Secretary of the Economic Advisory Council

1930–4

1

THE FALLING PRICE LEVEL AND ITS IMPLICATIONS[1]

1. THE falling tendency of prices throughout the world is the governing economic fact of the present time. It exercises a profound and far-reaching influence on the whole economic situation; and its repercussions spread out into the political and psychological spheres. If, for example, we ask why it is that the attempt to secure an international tariff truce has met with such a meagre measure of success, the answer is that it has been frustrated by the falling tendency of world prices. If we ask why the position of the national finances has become increasingly tight and difficult in recent years, again the essential answer lies in the falling price level. It is highly important, if policy is to be wisely directed, that the implications of this tendency should be clearly appreciated and steadily kept in mind. Maxims and precepts which may be eminently sound under conditions of stationary or rising prices may lose all their virtue if applied to a condition of falling prices such as now obtains. The trend of the price level constitutes, indeed, the most important element of that background of economic circumstance to which economic statesmanship must pay regard.

2. In the first place, it is important to appreciate that the falling price level may prove to represent a long-period, continuing tendency which has by no means run its course. Everyone is aware of

---

[1] 24 April 1930.

the heavy fall in wholesale prices during the past year; but this is commonly referred to as though it were an episode peculiar to the last twelve months, attributable to a transient condition of the over-production of primary commodities, and having no relation to any general trend. This is a possible interpretation; and some evidence can be advanced in its support. Certainly it was not until the beginning of 1929 that the downward movement of prices throughout the world became clearly marked. But a long-period trend of falling prices never takes the form of a steady fall year by year at a more or less constant rate. The normal course is that every now and then there occurs a sharp fall of prices, of just such a character as we have recently experienced, then follow a few years in which prices are stationary or perhaps even recover slightly, then comes another break, then another stationary period and so forth. This was the experience of the period from the late seventies to the middle nineties, during which the wholesale price level fell by 30 per cent.

3. In the present case, there are various indications which suggest that the break in prices which occurred last year was attributable to forces which had been pressing in the direction of lower prices for some time previously. Money rates had ruled high throughout the world for a considerable period, for reasons unconnected with the needs of the commercial or industrial situation, without, that is to say, there being anything in the nature of an inflationary tendency to call for high money rates. An eventual general trade depression is the natural and normal result of such a monetary condition; but it always takes time for this to come about, and on the present occasion there were special factors which made for delay. The *modus operandi* by which dear money reduces prices is the creation of conditions under which the demand for most commodities falls short of the supply. There were many signs of such a condition in the primary commodity markets considerably further back than a year ago; but the sequel of falling prices was delayed by resistances set up by the many experiments in organized marketing which have come into existence throughout the world. Selling pools accumulated stocks and held them off the market, in the hope that the apparent condition of over-supply would prove transient. The essential significance of the break in prices during the past few months is that the forces making for lower prices have at last broken these resistances down.

4. The important question, however, is whether the forces which

have led to the recent fall in prices are likely to continue to operate in future. This is not a question which admits of a clear-cut answer. The future course of prices will depend in large measure on the policies pursued by the principal central banks; and any change in those policies, such as might result, for example, from the progress of the idea of concerted action by the central banks with the object of keeping trade and prices steady, would alter the whole outlook. None the less, it would be useful to form some idea of what we may expect to happen, if there are no such developments and the policies of central banks remain essentially unchanged. This is a question upon which different opinions are entertained by competent authorities. On the one hand, we have to reckon with the fact that the present annual production of gold serves to increase the total stocks of gold held by central banks at a rate which is considerably less than the rate of growth of world commerce; and this suggests the probability of a prevailing deflationary trend, in the absence of banking changes which will make a given amount of gold go further. On the other hand, there are some grounds for holding that the existing stocks of gold are fully adequate to sustain an expanding volume of trade for some time to come, without any change in central-banking policies, and that the stringent monetary conditions of recent years have been due to abnormal circumstances, in France and the United States particularly, which are not likely to recur. This is a question on which it seems wisest to suspend judgement. But, while there can be no certainty about the matter, it would be imprudent to ignore the possibility that, after a brief period of comparative stability, showing some recovery from the recent slump, the downward trend of prices may reassert itself. In any case, we have still to reckon with the consequences of the recent slump.

THE REACTIONS OF FALLING PRICES

5. The most obvious of the reactions of a period of falling prices is that it must be a period of prevailingly bad trade. Indeed, as has been observed above, it is only through the medium of trade depression that the forces making for lower prices can produce their effect. Broadly speaking, prices only fall when sellers find it difficult to sell what they have to sell, in other words when supply exceeds demand, and a state of things in which this is true of all or most commodities is precisely what we are accustomed to call a trade

depression. Falling prices and depressed trade are inseparable bed-fellows.

6. Next, falling prices give rise to various maladjustments and disequilibria in the economic system. The pressure of the forces making for lower prices does not fall on every trade with equal severity. Industries engaged in international competition feel it more acutely than industries working for a sheltered market. Industry, as a whole, feels it more acutely than the distributive trades. Thus anomalous and inequitable contrasts are set up between the fortunes of both employers and work-people in different occupations. The current complaints in Great Britain of the high level of distribution charges are in large measure the outcome of the movement of prices. Falling prices play into the distributor's hand.

THE EFFECT ON TARIFFS

7. A period of falling world prices is a period of rising world tariffs. When trade is depressed and unemployment widespread, protectionist arguments gain greatly in their appeal. The pressure of foreign competition in the home market is more acutely felt, and the mere fact that prices are falling lends colour to complaints of dumping and unfair competition. Public sympathy is aroused for the work-people who have lost their employment, and the feeling grows that it is unwise national economy to allow imported goods to enter which might be made at home. In a period of rising prices, on the other hand, Protection becomes relatively unpopular. Public attention is then preoccupied, not with unemployment, but with the high cost of living: and agitations for lower tariffs accordingly make headway.

8. The course of history affords striking confirmation of this view. From the Repeal of the Corn Laws in 1846 to the Franco-German war, Free Trade or low-tariff ideas were in the ascendant not only in Great Britain but throughout the world; and this was a period when prices were rising, under the influence of the Californian and Australian gold discoveries. It was during this period that Cobden was able to negotiate his famous commercial treaty with France. From the middle seventies to the middle nineties, when prices were falling, there was a general recrudescence of Protectionism, culminating in the McKinley tariff in the United States. When prices moved upwards again, as the result of the gold

production of the Transvaal, this tendency made no further head-way, despite the fact that the political atmosphere was becoming increasingly one of preparation for war. In countries which were unaffected by this atmosphere, indications were accumulating be-fore the war, e.g. the Wilson tariff in the United States, that a new phase of lower tariffs had begun.

9. Thus general considerations and experience combine to sug-gest that the present downward tendency of prices constitutes an extremely unfavourable environment for any project directed to securing a reduction of tariffs. This applies, it should be observed, not merely to attempts at Geneva to get tariffs down throughout the world, but in hardly less degree to attempts to secure lower tariffs within the Empire. Under present conditions, the Dominions are far more disinclined to consider reducing the protection which their local industries enjoy against British competition than they would be if prices were moving upwards. They may be ready enough, as part of a programme of increased protection, to grant larger Imperial preferences. But, even if Great Britain were willing to make sub-stantial reciprocal concessions, it would be extremely difficult just now to secure any arrangement with the Dominions which would entail an actual reduction of tariffs on British goods. Mr. Joseph Chamberlain's chief difficulty was to convert the British public, because prices were rising when he commenced his agitation. Lord Beaverbrook has launched his campaign under conditions in which the British public may be more likely but the Dominions are less likely to make a favourable response.

10. The sharp fall in prices of recent months has already pro-duced a marked upward movement in tariffs. Since last summer proposals for tariff increases have either been adopted or put forward by the governments in the United States, Australia, South Africa, India, Italy, Turkey, Portugal, Egypt, Greece, Finland, Estonia, Peru, and Mexico, while special temporary increases in the duties on particular agricultural commodities have also been imposed in France, Germany, Poland, Czechoslovakia, and Japan. This ten-dency means that the development of our export trade is likely to encounter growing obstacles. The notion that our problem of large-scale unemployment will be eventually solved by the recovery of our lost export markets is, therefore, when viewed against the back-ground of the trend of tariffs and prices, an extremely optimistic one.

11. The reactions of the falling price level on the national finances are of the first importance. The level of money incomes tends to decline with the fall in prices and the normal buoyancy of the revenue is accordingly checked. On the other hand, with a large part of the expenditure of the State fixed in terms of money, there is not a commensurate relief on the expenditure side. The more, accordingly, that prices fall, the greater become the difficulties of the Chancellor of the Exchequer. In view of the heavy burden of the British national debt, and the high level which direct taxation has already reached, a further substantial fall in the price level would cause an almost intolerable strain, and something would have to give way beneath it.

12. The financial situation which emerges from the Budget of 1930 is worth examining closely.[1]

.   .   .   .   .

19. These considerations suggest that it is likely to prove impossible during the next few years, within the limits of the assurance against further increases of taxation, to finance any net increase in the aggregate national expenditure, and that measures involving fresh expenditure can only be financed by economies in other directions. Moreover, apart from new measures, expenditure under certain heads, e.g. unemployment relief, may have to be increased, if trade continues bad.

20. This difficult situation alters the perspective of various issues of financial policy; and it seems desirable that certain traditional precepts should be reconsidered in the light of the tendencies which are now at work. In the first place, these tendencies have an important bearing on the merits of indirect taxation. When prices are falling, the customary objections to indirect taxes lose much of their force; for under such conditions the effect of indirect taxes is not to increase the cost of living, but to avert a reduction of it, and this is not necessarily a decisive objection, if revenue is required for useful purposes. Moreover, it must be borne in mind that when prices are falling there is apt to be a long time-lag before the fall works through to the consumer. For a considerable time the benefit is apt to be intercepted by the distributive trades. In such circumstances

---

[1] This examination is not reproduced.

increased indirect taxation may serve to some extent to deprive distributors of this windfall advantage, and thus fall for a period on them rather than on the consumers.

21. The fixed debt charge of £355 millions is another matter that may deserve reconsideration in the light of present conditions. The one compensating advantage that has resulted from the trade set-back of the last few months is cheap money. This serves to reduce the interest charge for the floating debt, and may, if it continues, make possible advantageous conversion operations. There is a possibility, therefore, of a substantial decline in the interest burden of the debt; and, on this assumption, the retention of the present fixed charge in the Budget would be equivalent to a substantial increase of the sinking-fund. It may be doubted whether a time of depressed trade and financial stringency is an appropriate time for such an increase. It must be borne in mind in this connexion that there are grounds for believing that a high sinking-fund acts in practice as a deflationary influence, and may serve therefore to aggravate the tendency which lies at the root of our troubles.

22. In conclusion, I may emphasize the profoundly important part played by the falling tendency of prices in the difficulties of the Budget situation. The present Budget involves the paradox that while on the one hand it marks a very formidable development in the progressive taxation of wealth, it holds out little prospect of meeting the demands of any extensive programme of social expenditure. At the root of this paradox lies the falling tendency of prices; and much misunderstanding may be attributed to the general failure to appreciate the extreme importance of this factor. If prices should continue to fall in future, the problem of producing a Budget reconcilable both with democratic aspirations and with the honouring of the financial obligations of the State might become well-nigh insoluble. There is no objective which is more vital both to our financial solvency and to our commercial prosperity than to put an end to the present world deflationary trend.

2

THE PRESENT UNEMPLOYMENT[1]

[A FRAGMENT]

THE present volume of unemployment as measured by the weekly Live Register figures falls into three broad categories, which, though they may shade into one another, represent essentially distinct problems. These are:

1. the unemployment figure which would exist even if industry were in a healthy and prosperous condition;

2. the unemployment arising from the post-war difficulties specially affecting particular British industries;

3. the unemployment attributable to the present world-wide trade depression.

MINIMUM UNEMPLOYMENT

In pre-war days the unemployment percentages derived from trade-union returns did not fall below about 2 per cent. even in years of good trade. These trade-union figures related for the most part to skilled workers and did not cover occupations where a large degree of casual employment exists. For industry as a whole, accordingly, the minimum unemployment in times of good trade must even before the war have been considerably higher than 2 per cent. This minimum unemployment is attributable to various causes, of which the following are among the most important:

(a) Even when trade is good there are bound to be a large number of workers who at any one time are in process of changing from one job to another and take a little time to find other employment. The concern which previously employed them may have lost business to its competitors and so been compelled to reduce its number of employees, or it may have introduced labour-saving machinery or reorganized its methods; or the workers themselves may desire to change their occupation. The labour 'turn-over' due to such causes and quite apart from bad trade is considerable.

[1] 10 July 1930.

(*b*) In many trades activity varies regularly in accordance with the season, building, for example, being relatively slack in winter and coal relatively slack in summer. In the best of years, therefore, there is always a certain amount of unemployment of a seasonal character.

(*c*) The nature of some trades exposes them to fluctuations in activity from week to week or even from day to day, e.g. the docks.

(*d*) Interruptions in the continuity of work may occur for innumerable miscellaneous reasons, e.g. the breakdown of machinery, the failure of materials to arrive in time, and these interruptions give rise to temporary stoppages of work.

(*e*) There are always a certain number of workmen of poor industrial quality whom it does not pay an employer to engage at the prevailing wage rates except possibly in times when trade is so abnormally profitable that the conditions are those of boom rather than healthy activity. This group includes people of various sorts and ages, e.g. young persons who have been demoralized in blind-alley occupations, oldish people whose quality has declined, &c.

Developments since the war have tended to increase the number recorded as unemployed at the employment exchanges under most of the above headings. First there are the effects of the system of unemployment insurance. This tends to increase unemployment under (*e*) by making employers less reluctant to discharge workpeople who have been in their employment for some time but who are not really worth their pay. Similarly it increases unemployment under (*b*), (*c*), and (*d*) by weakening the desire of employers to keep their men together and to make shift to find some sort of occupation for them when work is interrupted or slack. In this connexion, moreover, it is to be noted that temporary stoppages which would not have been reckoned as unemployment at all before the war are now so arranged as to enable the work-people affected to qualify for unemployment pay, thus swelling the unemployment figures; while in some cases workers stopped for perhaps only a day or two will register as a precautionary measure. Furthermore, the unemployment insurance system serves to some extent to introduce a new element into the unemployment figures by its effect in inducing certain classes of persons (for example a number of married women) who have to all intents and purposes withdrawn from the employment market, to register and draw benefit as unemployed.

Apart from the effects of unemployment insurance the general tendency of modern industry is in the direction of discharging men more ruthlessly when it is no longer strictly profitable to the employer to keep them on. In the United States it is notorious that the labour turn-over is far higher than here and it is part of the insistence on efficiency as compared with easy-going and paternal methods that British employers should move to some extent in the direction of the American practice. The higher rates of wages now prevailing and the more widespread standardization of wages are factors which tend in the same direction.

Finally it must be remembered that the mere fact that unemployment has continued for many years on a large scale must have served to increase the number of work-people whose industrial quality is too poor to permit of their employment at current wage rates.

For these various reasons it is probable that a high aggregate unemployment figure would remain, under the present unemployment-insurance arrangements, even if industry were in an active and healthy condition. It is difficult to compute this figure with any precision; but it is worth noting that, although the London and South-eastern divisions have in recent years been expanding industrial areas, drawing in labour from other parts of the country, the unemployment percentages in these divisions have never fallen appreciably below 5 per cent. even during the more favourable seasons of the year. These figures would no doubt have been lower if the general economic condition of the country had been one of healthy activity; for some of the occupations in the London and South-eastern divisions were affected by the depression existing in other areas. On the other hand, we have now to reckon with the effects on the Live Register figure of the recent alterations in the conditions of benefit. On the whole, therefore, we doubt whether the minimum Live Register figure for the country in years of good trade, can be placed lower, under existing conditions as regards unemployment benefit, than about 5 per cent., or 600,000 persons.

The problems presented by the unemployment figures which fall under this first broad heading are, for the most part, problems of statistics and finance rather than of remedial policy directed to increasing employment. We discuss later the practical questions that arise in this connexion; but we would emphasize here that, as regards about 600,000 of those included in the weekly unemployment figures, there is no real *unemployment* problem.

THE WORLD DEPRESSION

As regards (3), the unemployment attributable to the present world trade depression amounts today to a very substantial figure. The total Live Register figure is today about three-quarters of a million higher than that of a year ago and though a small part of this increase is attributable to the easier conditions of benefit under the Act of last year, the figure of a year ago was already swollen to a slight extent by the beginnings of the world set-back to trade, so it is, perhaps, fair to take about 750,000 as representing the unemployment arising under this heading. This world depression is quite certainly a purely temporary phenomenon. While different opinions may be entertained as to its precise causes and as to its probable duration, all economists are agreed that it is, in type and character, a cyclical depression of the familiar pre-war type, and that recovery, though it may be delayed for many months, will certainly come sooner or later.

If, however, this country is to be in a position to take its full share in the recovery in world trade when it comes, it is important that nothing should be done in the meantime which would be likely to check business enterprise or to disturb confidence. There is a danger both in Great Britain and elsewhere that Budget deficits and consequential increased taxation may enter into the vicious circle of reactions which every trade depression sets up and which tend to prolong its course; and in the case of Great Britain the danger is increased by a growing nervousness as to the soundness of our financial situation which it might not take very much to convert into real alarm. It is important, therefore, in the interests of employment, to avoid, as far as possible, measures likely to aggravate a necessarily difficult Budget situation.

The possibilities of action that arise under this heading are those of broad policy, e.g. whether anything can be done to hasten a recovery of world trade, which raises the question of co-operation among the central banks to economize the use of gold; or whether anything can be done to insulate Great Britain from the effects of the depression, which raises the question of Protection, Imperial Preference, &c. But unemployment under this heading does not lend itself to a detailed attack industry by industry or age-group by age-group, designed to provide for the workers unemployed in some other way than re-employment in their former occupations.

Unemployment representing a temporary general set-back to trade is precisely the sort of unemployment which the insurance system is designed to relieve. The problem is essentially one of tiding over a bad period.

THE BRITISH POST-WAR DIFFICULTIES

There remains (2), the unemployment attributable to the special post-war difficulties of British industry. Putting the minimum unemployment at 600,000 and the effects of the world depression at 750,000 we are left with about 500,000 persons unemployed as the measure of the real, obstinate, post-war unemployment problem. The heart of this problem is the long-continued depression of some of our leading exporting industries, many of them of a highly localized character whose depression involves the stagnation of the whole economic life of the localities in which they are situated. There attaches accordingly to industries like coal and cotton a large surplus of labour which we have not as yet succeeded in absorbing in other occupations. Apart from these specially depressed industries, a large variety of occupations have failed to show for several years past a satisfactory rate of progress and expansion.

3

THE DEVELOPMENT OF NEW INDUSTRIES[1]

1. From the long-range standpoint, perhaps the most disquieting fact in British economic life is our comparative failure to keep in the van of new industrial and commercial developments. Our staple exporting industries have experienced in the post-war decade an exceptional combination of adverse circumstances, and their plight is necessarily one of our most formidable problems. In some degree, however, it was inevitable and in the nature of things that our old-established industries should lose ground. The law of life for an industrial country which seeks to maintain a materially higher standard of living than its neighbours is that it should be constantly adaptable, constantly turning over from activities which fresh competitors are taking up, to new developments. It is therefore profoundly unsatisfactory that Great Britain should have been comparatively laggard in the new economic activities which have come into prominence in recent years.

2. The recent Report of Lord d'Abernon's Economic Mission to South America contains passages which are highly pertinent in this connexion. After noting that the share of Argentina's total imports derived from the United Kingdom has fallen from 31 per cent. of the total in 1913 to 19·4 per cent. in 1927, while the United States share had increased from 14·7 to 25·4, the Report proceeds:

The decrease in the British percentage and increase in the American has been caused not so much by the displacement of old trades as by the development of new trades in which we have taken an insignificant share.

Demand for New Commodities.—We now come to the most striking feature of the changed trend of Argentine trade, and an explanation, serious in its implications, of our having lost ground. It probably applies in other of our great overseas markets. The large Argentine demand is for the new commodities of commerce and we do not supply them. Either we do not make them or we do not market them; at least not on the scale worthy of our position as an industrial and exporting nation. Yet this demand absorbs the fresh purchasing power and diverts a large

[1] 21 August 1930.

portion of the old. The average Argentine household thinks more now in terms of motor-cars, gramophones and radio sets than of Irish linen, Sheffield cutlery and English china and glass. The expenditure on new luxuries has diverted money which would otherwise have gone to the staple trades. The rapid increase in United States trade in the Argentine market is particularly marked in the new industries—motor-cars and accessories, films and cinematograph goods, electrical appliances, radio apparatus, typewriters, cash registers and office appliances, sewing machines, domestic refrigerators, gramophones, new types of agricultural and road-making machinery, oil-well plant and supplies. The trade which the United States had during the war and post-war period in textile piece-goods, coal, iron and steel, and chemicals has, to a large extent, been lost to European competitors. Great Britain holds the position she has on account of her staple exports—principally textile goods, coal and railway material. But for the large orders for plant placed in England during recent years by British railway and other companies in Argentina for their programmes of extension and development, which fortunately coincided with the worst period of depression in British industry, the falling off in the proportion of British trade would have been far more pronounced.

3. Some of the causes which have contributed to our relative backwardness in new developments are obvious enough. The war and the needs of war absorbed the whole economic attention of Great Britain in a way in which they did not absorb the whole economic attention of the United States, and the United States thus emerged from the war with the advantage of a good start in some of the characteristic developments of the day comparable in kind with the advantage of the first start as a manufacturing people which we acquired in the nineteenth century. Furthermore, the possession of a large home market composed of consumers with some money to spare above what is necessary to purchase the necessaries of life, and predisposed to novelties and experiments in consumption, gives the United States a special advantage for developing such specialties as those which are indicated in the above extract from the d'Abernon Report. But when every allowance has been made for such considerations, cause for dissatisfaction remains with the small headway which Britain has made in new lines of trade.

4. Nothing is more essential to the future of Great Britain as an industrial country than to keep well abreast with new economic developments. Yet much less attention is paid to our efficiency in

this respect than to our efficiency for retaining the old-established lines of trade. Take, for example, the question of our comparative failure to secure an important export trade in motor-cars. It has always been recognized that the horse-power basis of motor-vehicle taxation militates against the production of a type of motor-car likely to secure a wide sale in overseas markets; it has accordingly been urged that an entirely different system of motor-taxation should be introduced; and, as a broad proposition, this proposal has commanded general support. None the less the horse-power basis of taxation still remains. For a long time doubts were cast on the practicability of the suggested alternative of a petrol duty; and eventually a petrol duty was imposed, not as a substitute for the horse-power tax, but to supplement the general revenue. At every stage there were, of course, good arguments for the course adopted, but it is difficult to believe that the question would have been treated in the same way if it had been a matter of succouring a declining trade, instead of promoting the expansion of a growing one. Indeed, since the petrol duty was associated with the derating scheme which was designed primarily to relieve the depressed industries, the story illustrates very clearly the tendency to subordinate the needs of expanding industries to those of industries which are in difficulties.

5. This tendency is, of course, entirely natural. An industry which is losing trade presents a tangible problem of unemployed workpeople and idle plant, which cannot be ignored, and the urgency of which is palpable. There is nothing so arresting to the attention in the possibility that a new industry may not be developing in Great Britain on the scale of which economic opportunities permit. Yet, in reality, the latter phenomenon may be the more serious of the two.

6. The question arises, therefore, whether the time has not come to review more systematically than hitherto the progress that is being made in new or developing lines of business, to consider whether there are any opportunities indicated by the economic trend of the present day which we, as a nation, are neglecting, whether there are any defects in our administrative arrangements responsible for such neglect, and generally whether any steps can usefully be taken to keep the nation in the forefront of new economic activity.

7. The scope that an inquiry along these lines might assume

might be very wide. It would be undesirable, for instance, to confine it to the narrowly industrial sphere. One of the most obvious
examples of the economic opportunities which we are largely
neglecting at present is provided by the average small English hotel
or inn. With the advent of the cheap motor-car, hotel services are
clearly marked out as an industry with great possibilities of development. Travel has become a pastime for a largely increased number
of persons of very moderate means; and this provides the managers
of hotels and inns with a great opportunity, of which in most other
countries they are making full use. For rich persons Great Britain
provides many of the best-equipped and most expensive hotels in
the world. But in comparison with the Continent, the standard of
efficiency and the amenities provided by the average small English
hotel are notoriously low. In a very large number of cases, even the
essential business mentality of considering and attempting to meet
the wishes of customers is almost wholly absent. No industry, in
short, provides a more glaring case of the need for drastic change
and modernization of methods.

8. It would be a mistake to despise such a possibility as hotel and
inn development merely because it lies outside the main industrial
world. It may prove that the commercial opportunities of the future
will lie very largely in the direction of the development of services,
as contrasted with the mass production of commodities. Moreover,
hotel and inn services, associated as they are with travel, enter as
an important element into the balance of foreign trade. One of the
principal imports of the United States is represented by the vast
sums which her citizens expend annually on European travel; and
if a larger portion of this tourist traffic could be diverted to Great
Britain, or visitors from other parts of the world attracted here, or
a greater number of British people induced by better amenities to
spend their holidays at home, the results would be as beneficial,
from the standpoint of employment and the foreign exchanges
alike, as that of a commensurate increase in our exports of manufactured goods.

9. It is difficult to believe that the modernization of our hotel
system would not do something in this direction. Accordingly the
question whether something might not be done to promote the
modernization of our hotel system deserves to be treated as a
serious part of our economic problem.

10. Within the more strictly industrial sphere, questions of a

different character present themselves; for example, Does a lack of technical and scientific knowledge on the part of British boards of directors lead to undue reluctance or lack of discrimination in the adoption of new processes? Are the rather haphazard arrangements by which capital is obtained for new and speculative ventures satisfactory? Are our provisions for industrial research adequate? Are there any new developments of great potential importance which the State might advantageously promote and control? But before it can be determined whether it would be really fruitful to examine such large questions in any detail it would seem desirable to review systematically our comparative progress in the newer lines of industry.

4

THE BACKGROUND OF THE PROBLEM

[A memorandum circulated to a Committee of Economists][1]

I⊤ is, or, I submit, ought to be one of the main virtues of a committee composed exclusively of economists for the task set out in our terms of reference that such a body should be able to analyse and appraise the situation with a wider sweep and in a truer perspective than a committee chosen with a view to its knowledge of practical affairs. As against the advantage which the business man possesses of a more intimate knowledge of the detailed facts of the industries and markets with which he is concerned, the economist is in a position to supply qualities which should include more than familiarity with certain technical methods of theoretical analysis, and the habit of systematic study of current economic statistics. He ought, for instance, to bring to the task a more ordered knowledge of economic history, and a greater power accordingly of interpreting the essential significance of the present drift of tendency. He may be expected to measure the present world depression against a fairly clear background of previous world depressions, and equally to measure the post-war tendency for Great Britain to lose ground to other countries against a background of what has happened in the past to other countries when they have begun similarly to lose ground. He may be expected to recognize, more clearly than the practical man, the sort of tendencies that are likely to prove ephemeral, and the sort that are likely to prove cumulative. He may be expected, in short, to bring to the task of a diagnosis a surer general perspective.

I preface my observations with these platitudes because I seem to have detected a complaint that the sort of approach to our problem which I am about to suggest is an inappropriate one for economists. I maintain, on the contrary, that there is no function which we can more usefully and appropriately perform than to appraise in the broadest way the significance and the implications of the complex depression from which we are at present suffering.

[1] 18 September 1930.

For my part, I believe that the period through which we are now passing is an exceptionally critical period, and that there are immense dangers latent in the situation which economists ought to be the first to appreciate and to emphasize. I suspect that the present slump will be known in history as the Great Slump, that it will prove more prolonged and more severe than even the most pessimistic of us like to admit as probable, and that it will put to a most searching test everything that is unstable, makeshift, and unsound in the economic arrangements which obtain in Great Britain and throughout the world. I predict that the international historian will regard the Great Slump as forming an essential part of the story of the Great War and its Aftermath, and that there is nothing that will strike him as more curious than the way in which informed contemporary observers, who in the years immediately succeeding the armistice had a most vivid sense of the precarious and explosive nature of the foundations on which the economic structure of the post-war world was built, were deluded, like the people who live on the slopes of Mount Vesuvius, by a few years of comparative tranquillity, into assuming tacitly a quasi-permanence for arrangements the inherent instability of which they had previously emphasized.

I refer here particularly to the vast system of inter-governmental indebtedness arising out of Reparations and inter-Allied debts, which, after all the revisions and abatements that have been made in recent years, remains a prodigious phenomenon without a parallel in the history of the world. Few intelligent persons, I imagine, feel much confidence that Germany will in practice continue over two generations to make payments to other countries of the order of magnitude of £100 millions annually as the penalty of defeat in the late war. But, particularly in the light of the recent German elections, I regard it as very doubtful whether the Young Plan will survive the present slump. For just as here, so in Germany, the slump throws a severe strain on the public finances; and Germany is faced like us with a formidable budget problem. If Reparations go into the melting-pot, so assuredly will inter-Allied debts; and a most ugly international situation may easily ensue, which might entail unexpected repercussions in other parts of the world, and which would certainly destroy all hopes of successful international cooperation for such purposes as concerted reductions of tariffs, and economy in the use of gold. Moreover, even if no such developments actually materialize for some time to come, the possibility that they *may* will serve increasingly to impair confidence in the stability of Government loans. If it really be a prior condition of a substantial improvement of trade that the rates of interest at which governments can borrow should fall to a decidedly lower level than now obtains, I suggest, in view of the clouds that are already on the horizon, that the prospects of a substantial recovery of trade are very remote indeed.

Regarded as an ordinary economic phenomenon, the present world depression has all the marks of an exceptionally severe depression. It has set moving all sorts of vicious circles which will take time to work themselves out, and has established many gross and palpable maladjustments which will take time to correct. Disregarding, therefore, such complications as I have mentioned above, we should have to expect a long time to elapse before recovery really begins. When we take account of such complications, we must, I submit, reckon very seriously with the possibility that the present depression may break all records in point of both duration and severity.

It is against this uncertain and menacing background that we have to consider the special position and the special problems of Great Britain. The outstanding fact that confronts us here is the unsatisfactory rate of our economic progress in recent years as compared with that of other countries. We may have continued to go forward absolutely, but relatively we have certainly been losing ground; while in the light of the present depression a doubt suggests itself as to whether the small degree of absolute progress we have made is not attributable to the fact that we have been during these years in the better phase of the trade cycle. We must also bear in mind that we carry a much heavier burden of public debt in relation to our resources than any other country, that our level of direct taxation is extremely high and that our Budgetary position has been decidedly dubious for some time past. Moreover, several of the factors which have adversely affected our relative economic position, e.g. a diminished world demand for the goods on which we largely specialize and the intensification of difficulties in the way of international trade, particularly in India and the East, show signs of continuing to operate with cumulative force. Altogether, therefore, our relative economic position seems to me of very doubtful soundness quite apart from the present world depression. It is certainly unsatisfactory but it may be sound in the sense that the worst before us is a very slow rate of progress. On the other hand, it may not be sound at all and the present may merely be the opening phase of what would necessarily be a prolonged process, viz. the decline and fall of Great Britain as a prosperous industrial country.

I indicate summarily a few broad morals which are connected in my mind with the foregoing analysis:

(i) It is utterly wrong under present circumstances to embark on anything in the nature of a gamble, i.e. to pursue policies which one hopes will be beneficial immediately, but will certainly aggravate the situation later on, on the strength of an optimistic assumption that the situation will be much better in a few years' time. We have no warrant to take for granted that the situation will be better in a few years' time. Moreover, in view of the present condition of business confidence I am very doubtful whether anything which is clearly calculated to make things worse a little later on would yield any immediate advantages on balance.

(ii) I apply this general consideration in particular to any proposal to raid the Sinking Fund on a large scale. With the Unemployment Fund piling up debt at a rate of about £30 millions a year, and with the addition year by year of various fresh liabilities to the Budget in respect of housing subsidies, &c., the existing Sinking Fund is mainly illusory and though I agree that the present is certainly not a time for extreme financial austerities, I regard it as essential that we remain clearly on the right side of the line.

(iii) I am of opinion that the situation calls for the adoption of a system of Protective tariffs, the main considerations in my mind being:

(a) the need for an extended revenue without increasing direct taxation further;

(b) the need for a more satisfactory balance of international payments in a world in which it may be increasingly difficult for us to export;

(c) the importance of maintaining certain basic industries such as steel against progressive decline.

But there seem to me fairly narrow limits to what can possibly be accomplished by any system of tariffs, and it would be quite idle to suppose that we could by this means effectively insulate ourselves from the consequences of what is happening in the world outside.

I am unsympathetic to the approach of starting by assuming that we are 'a closed system' and then introducing qualifications later on. One is so apt to omit half the qualifications in the process and it is clearly impossible for us in Great Britain even remotely to resemble 'a closed system'.

(iv) I don't therefore regard tariffs as necessarily an alternative to lower money wages except in the sense that they may serve to make the reduction of wages less than would otherwise be necessary, but if world prices continue to move downwards I think it likely that both tariffs and lower money wages may be necessary.

(v) I am strongly of opinion that the broad question of the present system of unemployment pay is one which we ought not to neglect. It is not properly to be regarded as a mere detail. It represents a phenomenon essentially new, possessing the most subtle and far-reaching reactions affecting profoundly the mobility of labour and serving directly to account for the added difficulty of this year's Budget situation, thus creating a new vicious circle in the story of the trade cycle.

5

THE ECONOMY REPORT[1]

1. The *Report of the Committee on National Expenditure* cannot be adequately considered without reference to the peculiar circumstances in which it has been published. The *Report* could hardly have appeared at a more unfortunate moment. It appears at a time when confidence in the stability of British credit has been shaken for reasons which have little or nothing to do with Budgetary difficulties, and when withdrawals of foreign balances from London are taking place on a scale which raises misgivings in even the most responsible quarters as to the possibility of maintaining the parity of sterling. In these circumstances the main immediate effect of the extremely sombre picture of the Budgetary position contained in the May *Report* is of a kind which its authors can hardly have envisaged. They evidently regarded it as their main duty to call domestic opinion sharply to its senses, to arouse the country, and political parties in particular, from a Fool's Paradise. With this object in view they laid on the dark colours very thick indeed; and the effect was further heightened by the tenor of most of the commentaries in the Press. Unfortunately, the impression produced by the *Report* has not been confined to domestic opinion, but has extended to that of the foreign financial world, an opinion which was far from harbouring any optimistic illusions about the financial situation of Great Britain. There appears to be no doubt that the May *Report* has been a material factor in the renewed disquieting weakness of sterling in the present week; and the change of tone, resulting from an appreciation of this fact, in the British financial press is noteworthy. There is a striking contrast, for example, between two leading articles in the *Financial News* dealing with the May *Report*, the first, dated Saturday, 1 August, and headed 'The Rake's Progress', the second, dated Thursday, 6 August, and headed 'Unreasoning Fears'.

2. Without adopting an alarmist view, the position of London *vis-à-vis* other financial centres seems likely to remain weak and precarious for a considerable time. In these circumstances, perhaps

[1] 7 August 1931.

the dominating aspect of the question of the policy which should be adopted towards the May *Report* is the effect of what is done or not done on the confidence felt in British credit both at home and abroad.

3. The picture of the Budgetary position portrayed in the *Report* is, as has been said, an extremely sombre one. The Committee estimate that to produce a 'properly balanced Budget' in 1932, a deficiency of approximately £120 millions must be made good by fresh taxation or by economy. This formidable estimate, moreover, is put forward with an air of understatement, since no account is taken in the calculations of the effect of the Hoover plan or of further expenditure under pending legislation. The Committee then make proposals for economy, which, though extremely drastic in character, so drastic that no one can entertain any expectation that they will be carried out in their integrity, yield none the less a total of only £96½ millions for the first year of their full operation. There thus remains a gap of from £20–30 millions, which the Committee imply must be met by additional taxation, unless some scheme should be adopted for an all-round reduction of incomes which might justify a further saving on the Budget by cutting the pay of public servants and pensioners.

4. If the Committee's criterion of a properly balanced Budget be accepted, their calculations do not, in my judgement, overstate but rather understate the magnitude of the prospective deficiency. There is no prospect now of any early recovery in trade or decline in unemployment. On the contrary, the probability is that revenue next year will fall off even more than the Committee assume, and that the cost of unemployment benefit will increase further by what may easily prove a very formidable figure. Nor, in view of the precarious position of sterling, does there now seem a reasonable chance of any important offsetting advantage from debt conversion.

5. On the other hand, the Committee's criterion of a properly balanced Budget seems to me unreasonably austere. The prospective deficiency of £120 millions is reached by adding in the whole of the expected borrowing for the Unemployment Fund and the Road Fund, while maintaining the Sinking Fund at £52 millions. Thus the Committee in effect lay it down as essential to a sound budgetary position that every penny spent on unemployment benefit and road construction during the very worst phase of an unprecedently severe depression should be met out of current

revenue while debt repayment is maintained on the customary scale. This is to go far beyond what would have been regarded as the requirements of prudence in the hey-day of orthodox finance. It was, after all, an integral part of the idea of an Unemployment Insurance Fund that the Fund would spend more than its income in bad years, accumulating commensurable surpluses in good years, and though, as the latter has never been done, it is undeniable that the financial basis of the Fund is at present thoroughly unsound, the notion that unemployment benefit should be defrayed wholly from revenue at a time like this is unreasonable.

6. No other important country, moreover, would pass just now the Committee's test of a properly balanced Budget. The United States has ended the past financial year, not with a small margin on the right side (as was the case in Great Britain even after allowing for borrowing for unemployment), but with a deficit substantially exceeding the provision for debt repayment. Moreover, the deficiency in the American budget is likely to grow in the near future, since all the indications are that, with another bad winter ahead, money will have to be voted on a substantial scale for the relief of unemployment and distress, while the revenue is likely to languish further, there as here. In France, also, the equilibrium of the Budget is deranged; and neither in France nor in the United States is the principle acted on of meeting development expenditure out of current revenue. On the whole, indeed, the British budgetary system has so far stood the test of depression decidedly better than those of most other countries; and the suggestion conveyed by the May Committee that our position is exceptionally unsound and will remain so, unless a gap of £120 millions is bridged next year, is thus, from the standpoint of international comparison, misleading in the extreme.

7. It is true that in many respects the financial position of Great Britain is weaker than that of either France or the United States. Our burden of debt is heavier, our level of taxation is higher and cannot therefore so easily be increased, and our national income has ceased to grow at so rapid a rate. We entered, in short, into the depression with smaller reserves of financial strength; and, for this reason, we cannot afford to view so lightly a prospective deficit in our Budget, even though this is, in itself, no larger and perhaps decidedly smaller than the corresponding deficits which face other countries. In the light of our recent experience, it is clear that we

have been increasing expenditure over the last half-decade on the tacit assumption of a normal buoyancy of the revenue far greater than we had any right to assume, and there can be no disputing the May Committee's moral that political parties must approach reforms entailing expenditure in a very different spirit from that of recent years 'if democracy is not to suffer shipwreck on the hard rock of finance'.

8. At the same time, the Committee's diagnosis of the causes which have led to our present difficulties is far too simple. The major factor in these difficulties is the prodigious fall of the commodity price level in recent years. The *relative* weakness of the British financial position is largely attributable, as the Minority rightly pointed out (1) to the exceptionally heavy debt burden which we still carry (a consequence of past financial strength and virtue) and (2) to our special industrial difficulties during the post-war period.

9. If wholesale prices fail to recover appreciably from their present level, the financial position is certainly at least as desperate as the May Committee represent it to be. For in that event, we must expect a continuous sagging of the revenue, and the indefinite continuance of even heavier unemployment than we have today. Nor, unfortunately, is it possible to rule out the contingency that wholesale prices may fail to recover, until irreparable damage has been done. But for the financial situation which would result on this hypothesis, I do not believe that the policy of the May *Report* would provide an effective remedy. Apart from repercussions on confidence, the immediate effect of increased taxation and drastic cuts in Government expenditure must be to aggravate the trade depression further, to reduce the public revenue still further, to plunge us still deeper into the vicious circle of deflationary consequences from which it is so difficult to break through. On the assumption of no recovery in world prices, we might make all the cuts recommended by the May Committee and find as large a deficiency as ever still remaining at the end. If, therefore, the question of confidence could be disregarded, there would be little to be said, in my judgement, for aiming at a time like this at a budget properly balanced by the criterion of the May *Report*.

10. The question of confidence is, however, vital. An important treasury committee has proclaimed in effect to the world: 'The British Budget is hopelessly unbalanced. It has got into a thoroughly

unsound position as the result of the inherently profligate tendencies of our competitive party politics. If our politicians have the courage to make drastic and unpopular retrenchments, it is not too late to put our house in order. But if they lack this courage, it is all up with us.' This picture may be fair or unfair. In my opinion, as I have indicated, it is largely unfair. But if after this has been said so authoritatively, and with so much publicity, nothing, or nothing substantial, is done along the lines indicated by the Committee, the conclusion will be widely drawn that sterling is doomed, and, having regard to the weakness of the position of London, it would prove impossible in my judgement to maintain sterling at parity throughout the ensuing year. The ill consequences of an abandonment of the gold standard can no doubt be exaggerated; but they would be formidable and enduring; and I cannot think that the time has yet been reached when we should reconcile ourselves to so serious a step. But I feel convinced that an indispensable condition of maintaining the gold standard is that we should go, not necessarily the whole way, but at least the greater part of the way, towards bridging the gap in the Budget indicated by the May Committee.

11. To bridge the gap, there are two broad alternative means (*a*) retrenchment, (*b*) increased taxation. The view of the Majority Report is that the gap must be bridged mainly, if not wholly, by the former. The view implied by the Minority is that it must be bridged mainly by the latter. A wise national policy must in my judgement employ both methods. If no economies are effected, or no more than the trifling economies that might be secured by winding up a few not very prominent departments—if, in other words, no substantial *unpopular* economies are effected—an increase in taxation, particularly in direct taxation, would probably be as disastrous to British credit as leaving the deficiency unmet. For this would confirm the belief that Britain was going rapidly down the slope to the abyss. To an increase of taxation, on the other hand, which was coupled with substantial and unpopular economies, the psychological reaction would, I should judge, be quite different. There would then be a feeling that the situation was being faced responsibly and courageously, and the sense of the necessity for all-round sacrifices to meet a national emergency would be enlisted.

12. Unless, therefore, we are ready to abandon forthwith the

attempt to maintain sterling at parity, I conclude that the situation calls imperatively for retrenchments amounting to a substantial proportion of the savings indicated by the May Committee. I am not qualified to review their proposals in detail. But it is noteworthy that, though their recommendations are numerous, very few offer a substantial yield. By far their largest item is Unemployment Insurance, accounting for £66½ millions; teachers' salaries come next, at £13½ millions; next the curtailment of roads at nearly £8 millions; the remaining recommendations are comparatively trifles. In these circumstances, a substantial policy of economy must, as it seems to me, involve cutting unemployment benefit. As regards teachers' salaries, it is to be noted that the Minority, while protesting that the Majority's recommendations are too drastic, give tentative support to 'an adjustment of teachers' salaries in the region of 12½ per cent.' As regards roads, the proposal to abolish the Road Fund seems to me retrograde and definitely bad; and I have little sympathy with the suggestion that the Government should now go out of its way to slow down work which it has been endeavouring in the past two years to stimulate, though it would doubtless be wise to abandon the policy of stimulation.

13. In addition, however, to these detailed proposals for retrenchment, there is the question of the fresh expenditure which is likely to arise from pending legislation. Any serious policy of retrenchment, designed to reassure opinion effectively, must, as it seems to me, entail an announcement that, save for the most exceptional and indispensable purposes, no such legislation will be proceeded with.

14. To sum up: the conclusions which in my judgement emerge clearly with regard to the situation created by the Economy Report are as follows:

1. the picture of the British financial position which the *Report* presents is in many ways unfair, and coming at the present juncture, most unfortunate;
2. none the less, distrust of British credit is so widely spread that unless the attempt to maintain sterling at parity is to be abandoned, it is essential to go the greater part of the way towards bridging the gap of £120 millions;
3. it would be useless to rely mainly upon increased taxation for this purpose; substantial and unpopular economies are essential to restore confidence in British credit, though some in-

crease in taxation will not be disastrous if such economies are made;

4. these economies must at least include (*a*) considerable cuts in unemployment benefit and (*b*) the postponement of pending legislation entailing substantial expenditure.

6

THE STATE OF ECONOMICS[1]

THE most conspicuous defect of the present state of economics is
the lack of adequate contact between the work of theoretical analysis on the one hand and realistic study on the other. In both compartments there has been a very rapid development in recent years
of the work that is being done, and much of the work is character-
ized by a high degree of thoroughness and intellectual integrity.
But the compartments are essentially watertight compartments.
The theoretical economist is concerned with the elaboration of a
highly complex and abstract logical system. The foundations on
which he rears his analysis are not for the most part generalizations
of fact, but distinctions between alternative logical possibilities. He
will point out, for example, that a given change will have different
consequences according as the elasticity of the demand for a commodity is greater than, equal to, or less than unity, or according as
its supply obeys the law of increasing constant, or decreasing costs.
His professional conscience is preoccupied with the logical validity
of the reasoning based on such distinctions, not with their fertility
as guides for the interpretation of concrete phenomena. On the
other hand, the professional statistician or research institute worker
is concerned, properly enough, with the accurate collection, assembly, and presentation of economic facts, and not with their
explanation.

Clearly, however, the application of the scientific method to
economic phenomena must involve something else. It must involve
first the attempt to extract tentative generalizations from a patient
study of the available facts, secondly a thoroughgoing and scrupulous testing of those tentative generalizations by reference to a
wider range of facts, and thirdly the precise formulation of the
revised generalizations that emerge from the process. That is the
essence of what we mean by the scientific method in all other
branches of knowledge; study, hypothesis, verification. In economics, unfortunately, partly, I think, on account of the philosophical
and logical origins of economic analysis, and partly on account of

[1] 14 October 1931.

the inevitable association between practical economics and politics, this essential work is very imperfectly done.

Whereas, as has been said, high standards of intellectual thoroughness and integrity prevail in each of the strict spheres of theoretical analysis and realistic study, a very different tradition prevails when attempts are made to extract generalizations from the body of economic facts. The prevalent mood is either essentially that of a political partisan or that of a journalist endeavouring to be brilliant, seldom that of a genuinely scientific inquirer. One economist will hold fast to an old-established doctrine, being influenced in so doing by the feeling that loyalty and reverence for the great names of the past oblige him to do so. Another will make war on the old doctrine in the spirit of a rebel against authority. Both will be swayed by polemical emotions which are destructive of the disinterested patience which is the soul of scientific inquiry. Thus an essential amateurishness mars most of the work of economic generalization at the present time.

It is possible, I think, that a great advance might be secured by the establishment of some authoritative institute, organization, or group, the primary purpose of which was to apply severe critical standards to the principal economic generalizations which are currently advanced. Take, for example, a generalization which has lately been the subject of a vast amount of discussion both in Great Britain (Keynes) and the United States (Foster and Catchings), that a tendency towards an excess of savings over investment is the essential underlying feature of trade depressions. At present the discussion is too predominantly polemical and propagandist. It is a doctrine which has advocates and opponents; and both are more anxious to make out their case than to establish the truth. The issues accordingly are confused, the terms are loosely defined, the question of whether the fundamental proposition is true is mixed up with the question of whether a remedy, hastily suggested as a corollary, is wise and sound. I can imagine that much good might be done if an influential group of men, able to enlist the co-operation of others, were to make it their business to disentangle the various issues, define them clearly, and submit them to a searching scrutiny in the light of the available facts, were to draw up, in other words, a *plan* of investigation, in which they would then invite others to co-operate. I am aware that organizations at present exist (e.g. the Industrial Institute) which at first sight may appear to attempt to discharge this sort of function. But, as I see the problem, the most important part of the task is the preliminary sorting out and definition of the issues which would call for much time, trouble, and intellectual effort on the part of those who would undertake it; and in most types of collective economic investigation, this work is apt to be done in too perfunctory and mechanical a way.

7

INTERNAL CREDIT POLICY—
AND INTERNATIONAL[1]

1. I AM a little apprehensive as to the possible consequences of one part of what seems to be the accepted view as to the monetary policy to be pursued in the situation created by the suspension of gold payments. The point of view to which I refer runs something as follows: Now that the pound is divorced from gold it is above all things essential to maintain its internal purchasing power. Everything possible must be done to avert the danger of the development of a spiral process of rising prices, wages, and costs of production, which if unchecked might lead to an indefinite depreciation. As a safeguard against this danger it is essential to prevent anything that might make for an internal inflation, to maintain a high Bank Rate and high money rates generally, to watch jealously the movements of the note issue and the volume of bank credit, to prevent any expansion in either, and if possible to secure a contraction.

2. I am far from disagreeing with this view in its entirety. I agree that it is vital to prevent the development of a vicious circle of rising prices, rising wage costs, and a continually falling exchange. For this reason among others, in the controversy as to whether we should wish to see the exchange settle at something like a 15 to 20 per cent. depreciation on the one hand or at a 30 per cent. depreciation on the other, I am on the side of the higher level of exchange. Undoubtedly dear money and a restricted volume of credit are factors tending to some extent to strengthen the exchange. In so far, therefore, as the exchange can only be prevented from falling to a dangerously low level by employing these instruments, I do not wish to question the wisdom of employing them.

3. This consideration, indeed, clearly suffices to my mind to rule out anything like a cheery, hearty policy of cheap money. If our official attitude were to be 'Now that we have got rid of the incubus of the gold standard, let us disregard all exchange considerations and throw ourselves with a single mind into an attempt to secure the utmost possible expansion of trade activity from what has

---

[1] 27 October 1931.

happened', there would be, in my judgement, a serious danger of a renewal of foreign distrust of sterling, and of a consequent fall of the exchanges to a point which would threaten the commencement of the spiral process. We cannot afford to run such a risk, and for this reason it is essential, for the time being at least, to maintain money rates at a higher level than those prevailing in, say, New York and Paris.

4. There is not, however, any practical danger of the pursuit of such a policy as that indicated in the preceding paragraph. Or rather, the only practical danger of such a policy is that it may come by way of reaction from an excessive application of the opposite policy. The practical danger at the moment seems to me to be that we shall carry a dear money and restrictive credit policy beyond the limits which exchange considerations really justify.

5. It is only exchange considerations that supply, in my opinion, any valid ground for anything in the nature of dear money just now. The danger of the development of the spiral process depends entirely upon the possibility of a heavy increase in the prices of imported commodities, and of consequential reactions on the cost of living and on profits in industries exposed to foreign competition. It is a mistake, I suggest, to suppose that we ought to be very careful to prevent industries and occupations which do not benefit directly from a low exchange from receiving any direct stimulus whatsoever. On the contrary it seems to me that it should rather be our objective that the potential stimulus which the fall of the pound offers to our trade should be diffused as widely as possible, making itself felt in a greater degree of activity in every sort of trade and occupation instead of being concentrated in a substantial windfall gain to the industries which compete with foreigners. We don't want, of course, to see sheltered prices rise to any greater degree than may be appropriate as the result of the higher prices of imported materials which they buy, but it is possible that the prospect of a slight upward movement of sheltered prices arising from this cause might help to increase the volume of business activity, and it should not be our policy, as I see the problem, to regard this increased activity as a dangerous thing and to seek to check it.

6. There is the less need for adopting a jealous restrictive attitude towards internal trade activity in that there are other forces at work making for a decline of this activity. The impoverishment resulting from the prolonged depression is beginning to curtail the consump-

tion of the British public. Well-to-do persons are deciding that it is
essential for them to retrench; others are affected by the cuts and
economies of recent months. A general disposition towards retrenchment is abroad, and in these circumstances the activity of
trades which cater for the home public, which kept up so well
during the earlier phases of the depression, is likely to be seriously
prejudiced. Domestic employment may be expected to feel next
spring the effects of the curtailment of road programmes and housing schemes. These being the underlying conditions the danger of
any undue inflation of sheltered prices seems to me so slight as to
be negligible. On the other hand, it seems to me that there is a real
danger that internal trade activity may be quite unnecessarily discouraged by restrictive credit tendencies.

7. Indeed, so far as internal trade is concerned, the prevailing
conditions are such as to indicate the desirability of the encouragement of cheap money rather than the discouragement of dear
money. It would be unwise, in view of the precarious exchange
position, to pursue a really cheap-money policy. But it would be
equally unwise, in my judgement, to push a dear-money policy any
further than exchange considerations really require. Approaching
the question from this standpoint, the maintenance of Bank Rate
at 6 per cent. does not seem to me justified. I am aware that the re-
discount rate in New York has lately been increased in two stages
from $1\frac{1}{2}$ per cent. to $3\frac{1}{2}$ per cent. This, however, represents doubts
as to the stability of the dollar which, while they exist, are a factor
tending to strengthen sterling and to make relatively high money
rates here less necessary. In any case, the existing disparity between
our money rates and those abroad seems to me excessive. A 6 per
cent. Bank Rate serves to strengthen the exchanges only, in so far
as it attracts money here which would not stay if Bank Rate were
5 per cent. or 4 per cent. The amount of money in question cannot
surely be very large. Moreover, such money must be a factor making
for future weakness in the exchanges, just as the large-scale foreign
balances accumulated in London in recent years have proved a
source of weakness. It seems to me improbable, therefore, that the
exchanges would fall very much if Bank Rate were gradually reduced towards 4 per cent. The resultant exchange position would
be sounder and healthier, and internal trade activity would have
a better chance of making some headway.

8. The foregoing considerations are linked up in my mind with

some reflections on the development of the world economic situation as a whole, which it may perhaps be useful to set out.

9. Great Britain's example in suspending gold payments has already been followed by a number of other countries, most of them, paradoxically enough, countries in a comparatively strong economic position, like the Scandinavian group. Most countries in Central Europe, influenced by memories of the unlimited inflations of the post-war period, are making strenuous efforts to maintain some sort of gold parity, and for this purpose are resorting to a complex network of restrictions which are seriously prejudicial to world trade, and the ultimate efficacy of which is very doubtful. It is only in very few countries that the gold standard can be said to be functioning at all normally at the present time. Everyone recognizes that the movement away from the gold standard is very likely to extend in the fairly near future, and that conceivably it may become virtually world-wide. What will be the effect of this movement on world trade? Will it produce a better or a worse world economic situation than existed last summer?

10. Before answering this question it is convenient to consider first a hypothetical one. Supposing on the 1st of June last all the countries of the world had agreed to reduce by 20 per cent. the gold equivalent of their currencies, how would the world economic situation have been affected? The foreign exchanges would have been unaltered. No country would have gained any competitive advantage in world trade over another. But the gold reserves of every central bank would have been increased (in terms of money) by 20 per cent. The positions of all central banks would thus have been strengthened. The Reichsbank and the Bank of England could each have met more easily an external drain, and this being so, an external drain might have been less likely to arise. Possibly, therefore, such an agreement might have sufficed to avert the financial crises which have supervened. But would the strengthening of all central bank reserves have served to break through the vicious circle of falling prices and start a trade recovery in motion? It would have helped in this direction, but we cannot be certain that it would have been sufficient. An all-round reduction of the gold value of currencies would have no *direct* effect on the price level: it would only tend to raise it in so far as the stronger position of central banks succeeded in stimulating trade.

11. Suppose now that the process of departure from gold stan-

dards were to end in the foregoing result, i.e. that all currencies were devalued by 20 per cent. in terms of gold. Would the fact that this had come about by successive departures first by one country, then by another, then by a large group, instead of by a simultaneous process, alter the resultant situation, and if so, in what way? The present drift of events makes clear one important difference. The long-drawn-out process entails financial strains and embarrassments which (i) seriously aggravate the pre-existing maldistribution of gold between different countries, and (ii) stimulate in many countries, including some of the financially strongest, a disposition on the part of the public to hoard currency. Thus, if the process of exchange depreciation were to become general and were to be finally completed by a 20 per cent. devaluation of the French franc, the world would emerge with the reserves of many central banks possibly in a far weaker position than they were last June. It is doubtful, in other words, if we should retain anything of the advantage which would have been secured by an agreed all-round devaluation before the crisis began.

12. There are, however, other possible differences between the two cases. Each country, as it departs from gold, acquires an advantage in world markets over its competitors; but these relative advantages and disadvantages disappear when the process is completed. What does not necessarily disappear is, on the one hand, the *momentum* which may have been supplied to internal trade activity in the countries first undergoing depreciation, and, on the other hand, the *retardation* of internal trade activity which the process may have entailed in the countries which clung to gold longest. The ultimate state of world trade activity would largely turn on whether the momentum in the former countries outweighed the retardation in the latter. It is conceivable, if first we in Great Britain and then other countries get much busier in our domestic trade activity as the result of the depreciation of our exchanges, while internal trade in the countries remaining on gold is not appreciably affected, that the working out of the process might supply a stimulus which would result in a general improvement of world trade. But the actual tendencies at work suggest that it is more likely in practice that the depression of internal trade in the countries remaining on gold will be considerably greater than the stimulus to internal trade in the countries which depart from gold. In this event the final consummation of the process would probably

leave world trade decidedly worse than it was before the process began.

13. We are not, of course, likely to see a development of the monetary situation on precisely the lines of the foregoing hypothesis. But we are likely to see a considerable approximation towards it, i.e. a state of affairs in which departures from gold parity, though not universal, are very widespread, in which accordingly the competitive advantage which our industries have derived from the fall of the pound will count for less than it does at the moment, and our economic welfare will depend largely on what has happened in the meantime to world trade as a whole. In the light of the probability of a development along these lines, I view with misgiving the policies which are being pursued both in the countries which have departed from gold and in those which are desperately clinging to it. A 6 per cent. Bank Rate in London and the extreme restrictions on exchange dealings which are now common in central Europe, must make for a deterioration in the world economic situation. Any country which has either undergone an exchange depreciation or is afraid of one in the near future, is naturally preoccupied with the question of maintaining confidence in its relative position. But if each country acts independently under the influence of this preoccupation in a way that is prejudicial to world trade, the outcome is likely to be a general disaster.

14. The economic fate of every country is vitally dependent on an improvement in the world economic situation. No local restorations of confidence or local improvements in the trade balance which are achieved at the expense of a deterioration in the general world position can possibly prove an adequate solution for the difficulties of any country.

15. I suggest that these general considerations are relevant to our own internal credit problem, to our tariff problem, and also, though I have no immediate concrete moral to propose, to the idea of international co-operation in regard to gold and credit.

8

STERLING AND THE BALANCE OF TRADE[1]

1. IT is commonly assumed or implied that there is a far closer and simpler relation between the British balance of trade and the strength of sterling in the exchange markets than is really the case. Inasmuch as the prospect of restoring the balance of trade to an even keel in the near future is not very good, there is a danger that an unduly unfavourable impression may thus be given to the world of the position of sterling. It is important, therefore, that the following considerations should be borne in mind.

2. If Great Britain were to import an increased quantity of goods from India, Australia, or New Zealand, the British adverse balance of trade would be correspondingly increased; and on the basis of the assumptions that are current, the position of sterling would be correspondingly weaker. In reality, however, this would not be so. The increased imports would cast no strain whatever on the sterling exchanges. All that would happen would be that the London balances of the central banks of India and Australia would be strengthened, with the result that the governments of India and Australia would find it easier to meet their sterling obligations without recourse to fresh borrowing. So far from weakening sterling, this would actually tend to strengthen it, by diminishing fears of eventual financial default by these countries, which form an intimate part of the British financial system.

3. Conversely, and for the same reasons, it would do nothing to strengthen sterling but something to weaken it, if we were to reduce our imports from India or Australia, whether by consuming less or by replacing these imports by home production.

4. For the same reasons again, increased exports from India and Australia to the outside world, particularly to gold-absorbing countries like France and the United States, would strengthen sterling just as much as would increased exports from Great Britain. This has been shown very clearly by the effect of the large exports of gold from the private hoards of India in recent months.

5. In short, any change in the balance of trade of countries like

[1] 28 January 1932.

India, Australia, and New Zealand has fully as much bearing on the strength of sterling as a commensurate change in the balance of trade of Great Britain. Apart altogether from capital movements, the income position which is relevant to the exchange-value of sterling is the balance of payments not of Great Britain alone, but of a group of countries.

6. What then are the countries which constitute this group? India, Australia, and New Zealand clearly belong to it, but they are not the only ones. The criterion is not that of a currency which moves with sterling. South Africa remains on gold: none the less everything that has been said above with reference to India and Australia applied with almost equal force to South Africa, and for the present purpose South Africa must therefore be included in the sterling group. Nor is political sovereignty the criterion. In a very important degree Argentina is associated with the British financial system; in a lesser, but still important degree so are Brazil, Norway, Sweden, and Denmark. On the other hand, Canada should probably be ranked with the American system.

7. The main criterion is whether the country in question may be said to bank with London, in the sense that any increased payments accruing to it on international account will be reflected in increased London balances, and vice versa. The extent to which the country normally raises its long-term capital in London is also relevant.

8. The answer to the question as to whether a given country belongs in this sense to the British system is necessarily in many cases doubtful. It is a matter of degree. It is, therefore, not possible to define the range of countries which may be called sterling countries for the purpose of the present argument with precision.

9. It is worth noting, however, that the marked deterioration in the British balance of payments in the past year has been accompanied by a marked improvement in the balance of trade of countries like Australia and Argentina, which are closely linked with London. It is probable, therefore, that an adverse balance of payments on income account has not been so important a source of weakness to sterling as the estimates of the British balance of payments appear to suggest. Moreover, so far as 1932 is concerned, there would appear to be a good prospect of a further improvement in the balance of trade position of sterling countries other than Great Britain.

10. The above argument can indeed be pushed further. What we

are really concerned with in regard to the exchanges is the strength
of sterling relatively to the franc and the dollar. It is the possibility
that the rest of the world may have to make large payments,
whether on income or capital account, to France, the United States,
and countries associated with them, that constitutes the real menace
to the pound. It is as much therefore to the purpose to consider the
balance of trade of what may be termed the Franco-American system, as it is to consider the balance of the sterling system.

11. Now the balance of trade of the Franco-American system has
deteriorated steadily in recent years, and is continuing to deteriorate
very rapidly indeed. If we add together the figures for France and
her colonies, Belgium, Czechoslovakia, Poland, Romania, Yugoslavia, the United States, Central America and those parts of South
America within the orbit of American finance, we get the following
results for the merchandise balance of trade.

Franco-American System

Excess of exports

	£ millions
1928	198
1929	99
1930	47
1931 (first nine months)	−33

These figures relate to the merchandise balance of trade only, ex-
cluding gold movements. To compute the complete balance of payments on income account for these countries, it would be necessary
to make adjustments, for the contraband imports of the United
States, for shipping services and payments, and for all the many
invisible items in international transactions. None the less, the
change of the visible balance for the Franco-American group from
a large export surplus to a rapidly growing import surplus is a
highly significant phenomenon. Moreover, this visible import surplus is likely to be largely increased by the departure of Great
Britain and other countries from the gold standard.

12. In the light of these considerations it may be doubted
whether the position of sterling is really as weak as current discussions of the balance of trade position are apt to suggest, apart from
the possibility of adverse capital movements on a large scale.

13. The foregoing observations should not be taken as implying
that the British balance of trade is of no particular consequence
and that we could view the indefinite continuance of an adverse

balance with equanimity. In the long run it is vital that our British balance of payments should be on the right side. As a nation, we are living on our capital until it is. But in the long run there are good grounds for expecting not only an improvement in our commodity balance of trade, but also a recovery in our income from overseas investments. The point is that while it is desirable in the meantime to take all reasonable measures to strengthen the balance of trade position, there does not attach to the elimination of the current deficit the vital and almost desperate urgency from the standpoint of the stability of sterling that is often implied.

9

GERMAN REPARATIONS AND BRITISH INDUSTRY[1]

I. THE BASIC FACTS

THE payment of Reparations by Germany is liable to be of special detriment to the economic life of Great Britain, because Germany and Great Britain are largely specialized in similar forms of productive activity. The principal categories of German export trade are as follows:

	German exports in 1928	Percentage of total German exports
	£ millions	
Coal and iron products . .	118	20·1
Textiles	89	15·0
Chemicals . . .	63	10·8
Machinery and vehicles . .	53	9·1
	323	55·0

But these are also the principal exporting industries of Great Britain, the corresponding figures being as follows:

	British exports in 1928	Percentage of total British exports
	£ millions	
Coal and iron products . .	110	15·1
Textiles	244	33·8
Chemicals . . .	25	3·5
Machinery and vehicles . .	96	13·3
	475	65·7

Thus these four groups of industry account for well over one-half of the recorded export trade of Germany, and for nearly two-thirds of that of Great Britain. A more detailed comparison of the export trade of the two countries is given in the table appended,[2] and

[1] 24 February 1932. [2] Not reproduced.

confirms this impression of a broad similarity of industrial development in the two countries.

It is important to add that these export figures take no account of the shipping services which represent a most important item in the 'invisible exports', by which Great Britain adjusts her trade balance. Great Britain is the leading shipbuilding and shipping country, about half the tonnage launched in the world being British built. Both in shipbuilding and shipping, Germany is one of the most important of our competitors.

This similarity of economic structure between the two countries is of fundamental importance, because in the long run Germany can only pay Reparations by means of a so-called 'export surplus'. An export surplus can be built up (1) by checking imports, (2) by stimulating exports; and the obligation to pay reparations exerts a pressure on German economy in both these directions. Great Britain stands to suffer to some extent from the former tendency, because Germany is normally an important consumer of British goods. Of the total volume of British exports, 8 per cent. went to Germany in 1928. But she stands to suffer still more seriously from the latter tendency, because an artificial stimulus to German exports is necessarily to the detriment of a country whose industrial life is developed along such similar lines. The considerable, though short-lived, improvement which the British heavy industries enjoyed in 1923–4, during the occupation of the Ruhr, despite the unfavourable influence which that event exerted on general business confidence, was a testimony to the importance of the influence of German competition on British industrial activity.

The potential damage to British industry, it should be observed, arises because Germany has to pay reparations, not because Great Britain receives them. On the contrary, granted that Germany has to pay a given sum in reparations, our industries would suffer no more, while our taxpayers would benefit, if we received a larger share of them. The detriment to British interests is, therefore, in no way mitigated by the fact that our receipts from war debts and reparations are roughly equal to the payments we make to the United States. The position may be likened to that of a self-contained village community, in which there are two cobblers in keen competition with one another. If a heavy annual fine were imposed on one of the cobblers, which he could only pay by cutting his prices and working overtime, the result would be bad for the other cobbler, and would not be any the less bad if he had to pass on his share of the receipts from the fine to the lord of the manor.

II. THE PHASE OF GERMAN BORROWING

During the period 1924–9, i.e. the period of the operation of the Dawes Plan until the onset of the world depression, the menace of the consequences indicated in the foregoing section remained for the most part latent. During this period Germany as a people was borrowing from abroad on a large scale, which substantially exceeded the reparation payments which she had to make. It was estimated by the Bankers' Committee in August 1931 that the influx of foreign capital into Germany between 1924 and 1929 amounted to Rm. 18 milliards (at par £900 millions) as against reparation payments of Rm. 10·3 milliards (i.e. just over £500 millions). In these circumstances the accumulation of foreign exchange for the transfer of reparations presented no difficulties, and the general pressure on German economy towards the creation of an export surplus was consequently postponed. It is true that during this period British industries lost ground in world markets relatively to German industries; British exports declined from 12·2 per cent. in 1925 to 10·8 per cent. in 1929 of the total trade of the world, while German exports increased from 6·8 per cent. in 1925 to 9·7 per cent. in 1929. The increase in German exports in this period represents, however, a recovery to normal from the abnormally low level of the phase of currency disorganization and the Ruhr occupation, and it seems improbable that it was swollen in general in any considerable degree by the pressure of reparations. Even during this period, however, certain leading British industries, notably the coal industry, suffered materially from the artificial German competition arising from the system of deliveries in kind. The damage done to the British coal industry by deliveries in kind serves to indicate the extent of the damage to which British industries would be exposed if German exports in general were artificially stimulated by the pressure of large reparation payments unrelieved by commensurate foreign borrowing.

III. DELIVERIES IN KIND

Of deliveries in kind the most important have taken the form of coal and coke. The following table illustrates the extent to which

TABLE I

Exports of British and German Coal, Coke, and Manufactured Fuel (in terms of coal) to France and Italy, 1913 and 1927–31

(in millions of metric tons)

| Year | To France | | | | To Italy | | | |
| | From Great Britain | From Germany | | | From Great Britain | From Germany | | |
		Total	of which Free	Reparations		Total	of which Free	Reparations
1913	13·23	6·74	..	..	10·15	1·26	..	..
1927	9·67	10·60	1·28	9·34[1]	7·20	4·55	1·49	3·06
1928	9·31	10·09	0·26	10·25[1]	7·06	4·91	0·35	4·57
1929	13·45	10·63	2·75	8·16[1]	7·65	5·69	0·17	5·52
1930	13·41	9·70	7·37	2·31	7·61	3·80	0·89	2·90
Jan. to June 1931	5·67	4·14	2·59	1·55	3·06	1·76	0·45	1·80

[1] Including Reparation deliveries to Algeria, Tunis, and French Morocco.

German coal has been substituted for British in the French and Italian markets.

The figures for Italy are very significant. Before the war Italy, a country with practically no fuel resources of her own, was predominantly a British market. When after the war the creditor Powers had to absorb a large proportion of their reparation credits in deliveries in kind, Italy took the bulk of these deliveries in coal, on the ground that this was the form in which they would be least noxious to Italian industry. The result has been that whereas in 1913 Great Britain supplied 86·7 per cent. as against Germany's 8·9 per cent. of Italy's coal requirements, these proportions became under the reparation régime, approximately 50 per cent. from Great Britain and 35 per cent. from Germany. Moreover, the reduction in the quantity of coal imported into France and Italy in 1930 as deliveries in kind, as the result of the coming into force of the Young Plan, did not bring about a corresponding reduction in the total imports of coal from Germany in that year.

The figures for 1929 and 1930 direct attention to two points. First, so long as Germany is under an obligation to achieve an enormous export surplus, a reduction of deliveries in kind will have little effect in lessening the competition of German goods in our export markets. Secondly, the injury suffered by British industry through the diversion of trade into German hands is not confined to the direct loss of profit and employment involved, but must include the injury to our established trade connexions. The system of deliveries in kind has given rise to the employment in France, at any rate, of a number of German technicians, who naturally give preference to German products.

IV. REVERSAL OF THE TIDE OF BORROWING

Towards the end of 1928 the rate of influx of foreign capital into Germany began to slacken off, and Germany's reparations obligations gradually came to exceed the amount of the foreign exchange resources put at her disposal by foreign borrowing. In these circumstances the latent pressure of reparations payments on German economy towards the creation of an export surplus began to make itself felt, and was all the more powerful because of the necessity of paying interest on the sums which had been previously borrowed. It has been estimated by the Young Plan Advisory Committee that the sums due by Germany in respect of interest and normal amortization on her foreign liabilities amounted for 1931 to Rm. 1·5 milliards (or, at par, £75 millions). Except in so far as Germany is able to borrow additional sums from abroad, she is thus under the necessity of creating an export surplus big enough to cover this amount in addition to her reparations obligations.

The resultant pressure on the German economic system reached an acute stage in 1930, when a movement towards wage reductions was initiated by the Government, which reduced the salaries of State employees and appealed to private employers to do likewise towards their employees. A substantial reduction in the costs of production of German industries was thus effected, and their competitive power in world markets was increased, to the detriment of that of other competitors, of whom, as has been pointed out, Great Britain is chief. By this and similar means, Germany succeeded in building up a growing export surplus which, as the following figures show, had reached impressive dimensions up to the time of the departure of Great Britain from the gold standard.

TABLE II
German Imports and Exports
(*in millions of Rm.*)

	Imports	Exports	Surplus of	
			Imports	Exports
Monthly average, 1925–9 .	1,051	959	92	..
Monthly average, 1930 . .	866	1,003	..	137
Monthly average, Jan.–June 1931	634	794	..	160
1931: July	562	827	..	265
August. . . .	454	803	..	349
September . . .	448	835	..	387
October . . .	483	879	..	396
November . . .	482	749	..	267

It will be observed that the growth of the export surplus took the form of a heavy reduction of imports rather than an increase of exports, but two points must be borne in mind in this connexion: (1) the big fall in the level of prices, and (2) the decline under conditions of depression of the aggregate volume of world trade. The German export figures in the above table represent a rapidly increasing share of the total world trade. It has already been pointed out that between 1925 and 1929 British exports declined from 12·2 per cent. to 10·8 per cent. of the total trade of the world, while German exports increased from 6·8 per cent. to 9·7 per cent. Since 1929 these tendencies have been accentuated, and for the twelve months ended 30 September 1931 British exports were only 10·1 per cent., while German exports had risen to 11·8 per cent. of the total world trade. For the first time, that is to say, German exports had come to exceed British exports by a substantial margin.

V. THE WORLD SLUMP

The occurrence of the severe world depression of trade has served, as the preceding section suggests, to obscure somewhat the part played by reparation payments in the decline of British export trade, since the aggregate value of German exports has not in fact been increasing during the period of depression, although intensified German competition has none the less exerted serious effects upon British industries. It is important to note, however, that the sequence of events connected with reparations described in the preceding sections has played an important part, in the opinion of some a major part, in causing the world depression. So long as capital continued to flow into Germany on a large scale, a reasonable equilibrium in the balance of international payments was maintained, and no great strain was cast upon the world economic and financial system. It was impossible, however, in the nature of the case, that so large a flow of capital into Germany could continue indefinitely, and when the flow ceased, as it was bound to cease sooner or later, the inevitable first consequence was to release the tendency towards a maldistribution of gold which had all the time been latent in the situation. Gold began to flow on a formidable scale from Germany and other countries which were in a weak position as regards the balance of international payments, towards countries in a strong position, of which the two outstanding cases were France and the United States. The countries which began to lose gold were forced to raise money rates and restrict the volume of credit in order to protect their gold reserves, with a consequent tendency towards the restriction of the volume of business. On the other hand, in France and the United States the accumulated gold was rendered virtually sterile from the economic standpoint. Thus a prevailing tendency towards a trade depression in certain countries, unaccompanied by an adequate countervailing tendency in

H

other countries, was set in motion and contributed materially to the general trade depression that ensued.

The part which reparations coupled with the changes in the tide of German borrowing have played in causing the maldistribution of gold is well brought out in the following table in a memorandum by Sir Henry Strakosch in *The Economist* of 9 January 1932. It will

TABLE III

Reparations and War Debts
(*Millions of dollars*)

	Receipts on account of Reparations and War Debts	Change in Gold Reserves
1 Jan. 1925 to 31 Dec. 1928:		
FRANCE	557	+544
UNITED STATES . . .	807	−344
	1,364	200
1 Jan. 1929 to 30 June 1931:		
FRANCE	343	+958
UNITED STATES . . .	555	+847
	898	+1,805

be observed that, taking the two periods together, the increase in the gold reserves of France and the United States between 1 January 1925 and 30 June 1931 was just over $2,000 millions, while the receipts of these two countries in respect of reparations and war debts was about $2,250 millions. The correspondence between these two figures suggests that the system of reparations and war debts has been the dominant factor in leading to the maldistribution of gold. In so far, therefore, as it is correct to attribute the world depression to the maldistribution of gold, the ulterior responsibility must be laid at the door of the reparations and war debts system.

VI. THE FINANCIAL CRISIS

The system of reparations has an even clearer responsibility for the aggravation of the world depression by the financial crisis which began in the summer of 1931. The occurrence of the depression found Germany faced with the obligation to pay abroad not only large sums in respect of reparations, but also, as has been pointed out above, large sums in respect of interest on loans which she had previously borrowed. It was inevitable that in these circumstances distrust should have arisen as to the ability of Germany to discharge her obligations, and that the influx of capital into Germany should have been followed by a reverse movement of foreigners attempting to get their money out of Germany. A very large part of the German borrowing had been of a short-term kind, and a process of withdrawing short balances from Germany accordingly commenced. It is of the essence of such a movement that once it has started it grows rapidly and assumes formidable dimensions. For the very withdrawal of capital serves to give grounds for the distrust which had first given rise to it. It soon became evident, however, that Germany was incapable of repaying all the sums which her creditors were demanding from her, despite the big export surplus which she was beginning to achieve, and to prevent an actual catastrophe it was necessary to negotiate the Standstill Agreement in August 1931, by which the various banking interests which had short-term money in Germany undertook to leave the greater part of it there. The difficulty of withdrawing money from Germany aroused in its turn distrust of the position of those financial institutions which were known to be important short-term creditors of Germany, and there thus came into existence something in the nature of a world financial crisis and a tendency to withdraw money from other centres, notably from London, which culminated in the suspension of the gold standard in Great Britain.

VII. TRADE RESTRICTIONS

The course of the present depression has been marked by an unprecedented development of restrictions placed in the way of trade which greatly increase the difficulties of securing a recovery, and again a definite connexion can be traced between these restrictions and German reparations. The extent to which the world is suffering from regulations affecting foreign trade and foreign exchange transactions may be seen from the following brief summary of exchange restrictions, import restrictions, and new tariff regulations which have been brought into force during the present phase of the world depression.

(i) *Exchange restrictions*

Exchange restrictions are of two kinds, those designed to prevent the flight of capital from the country in question, and secondly those also designed to limit directly the volume of imports. In most cases the control of exchange is effected by the centralization of exchange dealings in the hands of the national bank.

The European countries in the first or less severely restricted group are: Bulgaria, Czechoslovakia, Germany, Italy (where, though powers have been taken, no control is actually exercised), and Yugoslavia.

In the second group are: Austria, Denmark, Estonia, Greece, Hungary, Latvia, Norway, Spain, and Turkey.

Sweden and Finland, in which foreign dealings were at one time restricted, have now abolished control.

Restriction, in the countries enumerated above, operates with a varying degree of effectiveness. In some instances, e.g. Austria and Hungary, a 'black bourse' has sprung up where the exporter can dispose of his foreign currency on more advantageous terms than are offered him by the central institution.

Restrictions are also numerous in South America.

(ii) *Import restrictions*

Import restrictions in some form have been adopted by Czechoslovakia, Estonia, France, Hungary, Italy, Latvia, the Netherlands, Persia, Poland, Spain, Switzerland, and Turkey. Quotas in some cases are applied to a wide range of goods, e.g. in Czechoslovakia and in Estonia, with a view to correcting an adverse balance of trade. In other cases they are retaliatory measures aimed at countries which have adopted restrictions inimical to the interest of the country in question. For example, the quotas in Poland are said to be directed against Germany, and those in Spain against France. Finally, they have been adopted by countries whose exchange position is exceptionally strong, e.g. France and Switzerland, as a protective measure of immediate effectiveness against the dumping which has inevitably followed the damming up of customary channels of trade. The Swiss restrictions are of interest as being specially directed against the importation of goods from Germany. They have, therefore, an immediate connexion with the problem of reparations.

(iii) *Tariff increases*

There have been in addition a number of tariff increases during the year, including the imposition of surtaxes in France on goods coming from countries with depreciated currencies, a general 15 per cent. *ad valorem* duty in Italy, and an increase in the level of duties imposed in the Netherlands. Nor has this country remained inactive in this respect.

In general, it may be said that countries have been influenced by one of two motives towards the adoption of the various restrictive practices set out above. Either they have found themselves in a weak exchange position and have been under the necessity of correcting their balance of payments as best they might; or, on the other hand, being in a comparatively strong exchange position themselves, they have seen their own industries suffer from the forced competition of their weaker neighbours, and have resorted to restriction as an alleviation of their domestic distress. As each country can operate more expeditiously on the volume of its imports than on that of its exports, a general determination to improve the balance of trade on the part of one group of countries, combined with a determination on the part of the remainder that no existing industry shall suffer through foreign competition, inevitably leads to a reduction in the total volume of trade. In this way the existence of a debt, the payment of which demands of the receiving countries a greater elasticity in their industrial structure than psychological and physical facts permit, leads to the gradual extinction of the trade, not only of themselves, and their debtors, but also of those outsiders who have the misfortune to be dependent on the trade of both. That the struggle on the part of Germany to achieve a favourable balance of payments is one of the main factors in the present disturbed state of the world can no more be doubted than that the necessity for the payment of reparations is the ultimate, though perhaps not the immediate, cause forcing her to take this course.

VIII. THE TERMS OF TRADE

The principal ways in which German reparations have caused damage so far to world trade in general and British industry in particular have been summarized in the foregoing sections. It is important to add, however, that we have not as yet had much experience of one of the ways in which British interests would be likely to suffer from German reparations in normal circumstances. As has been pointed out above, British industry did not really feel the pressure of the reparations system between 1925 and 1929, apart from the special case of deliveries in kind. Since 1929 reparations have served chiefly to cause or to aggravate the world difficulties of depression and financial crisis, and the special injury which we are apt to suffer has been obscured by the general world confusion. If, however, the world were to settle down to anything like normal trade conditions, with Germany under the obligation to pay reparations on a large scale, but without commensurate German borrowing from other countries, the consequences indicated in Section I would for the first time come into play without being obscured by the operation of other factors. Great Britain would then tend to suffer not only by a diminished volume of export trade but by selling her exports on less favourable terms for the products of other countries. It is important in this connexion to realize to what extent the position of Great Britain has been strengthened during the past decade by the improvement in the terms upon which it exchanges its products abroad. A reversal of this tendency, in view of the declining demand for British goods, might have disastrous consequences for this country.

10

A MONETARY PROPOSAL FOR LAUSANNE[1]

A. THE PROPOSAL

1. A SPECIAL currency, to be called, say, International Certificates, shall be issued by the Bank for International Settlements. An international certificate shall be declared to be the equivalent of so many grains of gold, but shall be without backing or cover of any kind.

2. On the basis of this issue, the Bank for International Settlements shall place to the credit of every government which complies with the conditions set out below, a sum payable in international certificates as an interest-free advance. The amounts thus advanced to the different governments shall be determined in accordance with some criterion of economic importance. For example, the value of a country's export trade might be adopted; and the amount advanced to each government might be 50 per cent. of the gold value of its exports in 1928.

3. These advances shall only be made to governments which

(a) pass legislation recognizing international certificates as the equivalent of gold for all purposes, including the gold reserve requirements of central banks, the obligation of Mints or central banks to supply domestic currency in exchange for gold or gold in exchange for domestic currency, and the discharge of international debts fixed in terms of gold;

(b) where the currency is not at present on an effective gold basis, fix the value of the currency in terms of gold, undertake to maintain effective convertibility in gold or international certificates at the value so fixed, and abandon any restrictions on exchange dealings;

(c) undertake to repay the advances when called upon to do so in accordance with (6) below.

4. The governments receiving the advances shall be free to put them to any use they choose, e.g. to pay external debts, to improve the reserve position of their central banks, to lighten their burden of taxation, or to expend on measures of reliefs or public works.

[1] 17 May 1932.

5. The volume of international certificates to be issued under
(1) shall be limited to the extent of the advances actually made
under (2) plus a certain percentage, say 5 per cent., designed to
strengthen the position of the Bank for International Settlements,
and to enable it to make additional advances on an ordinary
interest-bearing basis in special cases.

6. If and when the gold prices of commodities rise more than
half-way towards the level of 1928, the Board of the Bank for
International Settlements shall call upon each government to repay
a percentage of the interest-free advance made to it, and shall be
obliged to contract proportionately the issue of international certificates. If commodity prices continue to rise thereafter, the amounts
recalled shall be increased continuously; but the extent of the repayment to be demanded at any time shall be at the discretion of
the Board of the Bank for International Settlements, subject to the
condition that if commodity prices return to the 1928 level or above,
the advances shall be entirely recalled. If any government is unable
to make immediate repayment of any sum, it shall be required to
pay interest on the sum in question at the rate of 5 per cent. per
annum. The Board of the Bank for International Settlements shall
select the index-number which they consider appropriate for the
purpose of measuring the extent of the rise in prices.

B. THE ARGUMENT

1. It is generally agreed that a recovery of the world's economic
system requires some recovery in the gold prices of commodities.

2. In the United States the Federal Reserve authorities are now
endeavouring to turn the tide of prices by employing a monetary
means often recommended, namely the large-scale purchase of
securities with the object of increasing the cash reserves of the
member banks. The Bank of England is also keeping credit fairly
abundant and may conceivably enlarge the basis of credit further
in the near future. It would be premature as yet to pass judgement
on the efficacy of these experiments; but it is clearly possible that
they may prove futile in face of the rapid deterioration of the world
position.

3. The fundamental difficulty is that the only orthodox means
of increasing the effective supply of purchasing power is through
increased loans. This method may fail when things have reached

such a pass that solvent people are reluctant to borrow and those anxious to borrow are insolvent.

4. This difficulty has two aspects, international and internal:

(a) It is essential to increase the international purchasing power of certain countries such as those of Central and south-eastern Europe and Central and South America. It is difficult, however, to do this by means of loans when these countries are unable to meet their existing obligations.

(b) It is also essential to increase the volume of internal purchasing power in creditor countries like the United States, France, and Great Britain. All that open-market policy can do, however, is to increase the readiness of the banks to lend. With large surplus stocks of almost every commodity and with the demand of the consuming public so restricted by the impoverishment of the depression as to fall short in most cases of existing production, manufacturers and traders have little inducement to enlarge their business operations, however ready the banks may be to lend them money.

5. Logically, therefore, the first requirements of the situation are to secure an increase, as a matter of right and not of borrowing, in:

(a) the international purchasing power of embarrassed debtor peoples, and

(b) the domestic purchasing power of the consuming publics in the creditor countries.

6. To secure the latter of these objects, schemes of public works and doles (such as soldiers' bonus schemes) are sometimes advocated. Such schemes, however, run up against the difficulty of governmental finance. The governments must either tax or borrow to defray the cost. If they tax there is no net gain to consumers' income: if they borrow the growth of deficits disturbs confidence, keeps up the rate of interest, and may stimulate a tendency to hoard or a flight from the currency, even a strong currency like the dollar. Today, indeed, governments represent one of the most impecunious elements in society; and it is difficult, therefore, to use them, unless their resources are first strengthened, to increase internal purchasing power.

7. The danger of a flight from the currency, which may make it difficult to carry very far, even in the United States, the orthodox policy of increasing the supply of credit by open-market purchases, suggests the need for concerted international action.

8. But the needs of different countries are so different that a policy which might be appropriate in some cases would be utterly inappropriate in others. It would be impossible, for example, for all countries to agree to enlarge the supply of bank credit together, much less to indulge in expansionist policies of governmental expenditure. For a country which has now to restrict exchange dealings cannot afford to inflate, while retrenchment is clearly an imperative duty for all governments which cannot meet their obligations.

9. The scheme outlined in this Memorandum represents an attempt to overcome these various difficulties. It provides a common international policy. It contemplates that this policy will be applied in different ways in different countries according to the needs of the local situation. It is based on the principle of increasing the financial resources of governments.

10. If all governments agreed to participate in the scheme, its effects would be substantially the same as if in every country there were discovered on the same day a vast hidden treasure of gold, becoming Government property. It can hardly be doubted that such a discovery would be of immense advantage. The governments are asked in effect, under the scheme proposed, to agree to act on the assumption that such a discovery has been made, until such time, at least, as prices have risen sufficiently to permit normal conditions of trade.

11. The scheme could not, of course, be worked unless most countries agreed to participate. The abstention of a single strong country would not, however, be fatal to it. If we suppose that all countries agreed to participate except, say, France and Belgium, the latter countries would have to face the prospect of a possible appreciation of the franc which might jeopardize their trade, while the rest of the world was trading normally with mutually stable exchanges. Indeed, it may be claimed for the scheme that it provides a possible framework for a managed international currency system extending over a wide area.

11

SOME NOTES ON THE EXCHANGE QUESTION[1]

1. THE American refusal to contemplate immediate stabilization raises an obvious possibility that the deterioration of the dollar may now acquire a gathering momentum. The international speculator has become for the time being the effective civil service of the United States Government, endeavouring faithfully to anticipate and to execute his masters' wishes. The speculator will presumably interpret the pronouncement against stabilization as indicating with sufficient distinctness that his masters have made up their minds in favour of a further and substantial depreciation.

2. The problem of British exchange policy in this situation is one of extreme difficulty. A big exchange depreciation of the dollar, however much it may be accompanied or followed by a rise in American wholesale prices, would almost certainly be highly prejudicial to our industrial competitive position, since it would be unlikely that American manufacturing costs would rise proportionately to their wholesale prices. Moreover, with Canada within the orbit of the American economic system, and Australia and other Dominions jealous of any Canadian competitive advantage, there would be a danger of confusion spreading to the Empire exchanges, and to those of other parts of the sterling area. The attempt to follow the dollar might cause a similar confusion in the European exchanges; and it would be by no means a simple matter to follow the dollar, even if we desired to do so.

3. In this connexion, several points are worth noting. First there is the obvious one that there would be a serious risk of heavy ultimate exchange loss in buying dollars. Second, buying gold at a higher gold price, while it would lower sterling in terms of gold currencies, might fail to exert any effect on the dollar-sterling exchange, in view of the fact that there is at present no free gold market in the United States. This course might, therefore, give us the worst of both worlds, by precipitating the abandonment of gold by the present gold currencies with a consequential extension of the area of

[1] 23 June 1933.

exchange confusion, without contributing effectively to maintain stability with the dollar.

4. In addition to these practical points, there is a less definite but more far-reaching difficulty. . . .[1]

6. In view of the extremely disagreeable nature of the alternatives with which we thus appear to be confronted, I suggest that it is worth serious consideration whether we should not attempt to mitigate the depreciation of the dollar by buying not *valuta* but *commodities*. If the British Government were to buy American cotton or American wheat instead of dollars, it would buy something more likely to appreciate than to depreciate, but it would have precisely the same effect on the exchange that buying dollars would have, and so far from causing any possible American resentment it would be highly welcomed. If the British Government were to buy Canadian wheat, it would, because of the economic association of Canada with the United States, help to maintain the dollar, while helping to raise the price of wheat to the common benefit of all wheat producers and assisting Mr. Bennett in his pressing problem directly and materially. Generally, I take it that the sum of money voted for the Exchange Equalization Fund would suffice to buy up all the stocks of primary commodities in the world several times over. Thus we could certainly produce a marked effect on the prices of commodities by expending only a small portion of the sum which we had contemplated spending for the purpose of exchange stabilization, and at the same time go a long distance towards securing exchange stability as well.

7. The chief objection to this policy would be that agricultural commodities such as wheat deteriorate, and are therefore expensive to hold. Even allowing for this, however, most speculators today would probably take the view that it was better to buy commodities than to buy currencies, and it is not clear that the purchase of commodities by the Government would be intrinsically a more speculative proceeding than those contemplated in connexion with the Exchange Equalization Fund.

8. The suggestion that the Government should purchase commodities has occasionally been put forward simply as a means of raising prices. Regarded from this standpoint, it has been open to the objection that the British Government would be shouldering a

[1] The argument here omitted is reproduced in paragraphs 11–16 of the succeeding memorandum, pp. 114–17 below.

speculative risk in the interests of the producers of other countries, while suggestions for international schemes for the purchase of commodities are open to all the difficulties of international schemes of co-operation. But the present exchange problem has, I suggest, the effect of removing the first of these difficulties, for we should be running only the type of risk which we have been ready to run in the last year for the sake of exchange stability. Finally, the present trend of opinion in favour of schemes for restricting production diminishes the speculative risk entailed in buying commodities which may be subject to such schemes. The purchase of commodities would indeed form a natural complement to restriction schemes, and in some sense an assurance against the danger that they may be overdone.

12

INTERNATIONAL MONETARY PROBLEMS[1]

NOTE FOR DISCUSSION

1. HITHERTO the discussions of the Group have been mainly concentrated on questions of internal monetary and financial policy. The function of this paper is to open the discussion on the problems of an international monetary standard and of exchange policy.

2. The international monetary problem has been radically transformed by recent developments in the United States, including (*a*) her deliberate departure from the gold standard, (*b*) President Roosevelt's refusal during the World Economic Conference to subscribe to any formula looking, however demurely, in the direction of the stabilization of the foreign exchanges, and (*c*) the hectic experimentalism of American economic policy in general. These developments have put outside practical politics for the time being the possibility of restoring the gold standard, with whatever addition of new gadgets, as a common international system, and we must now expect a considerable period of exchange uncertainty and confusion, in which fresh disturbances of great importance, which may once again transform the whole perspective of the problem, are extremely likely to occur, before it will be possible to restore any sort of international monetary order.

3. The problem which the Group has to consider is, therefore, twofold in character:

   (*a*) What sort of exchange policy should Great Britain pursue during the difficult transitional period which lies ahead?
   (*b*) What sort of international system should we aim at re-establishing eventually, bearing in mind that much water will have flowed under the bridges in the meantime?

4. It is convenient to take as the starting-point of the discussion an issue which appears to be common to both the short-range and the long-range problems, the issue namely of exchange stability versus internal stability. Should the first consideration of our exchange policy under the conditions which now obtain be to secure

[1] 13 September 1933.

the largest attainable degree of stability in the foreign exchanges, or to contrive that the pound will move in such a way as is likely to be beneficial to British industry? Again, when the time comes to reconstitute some orderly international monetary system, should we seek a system which puts exchange stability first, with arrangements for securing what the Group has agreed to call 'continuity of values' in the second place, or a system which, without neglecting the former, gives priority to the latter objective? The similarity of the issue is, however, more apparent than real and is apt to cause confusion of thought and the coining of false slogans.

The Short-range Problem

5. So far as the short-range problem is concerned, the issue needs further definition. It is of the essence of being off the gold standard, as we have been for the past two years, that sterling is not rigidly linked to gold or to other currencies. Throughout this period, moreover, the British Government has refused warily and persistently, despite considerable pressure from abroad, to enter into any definite undertaking to return to a gold basis, insisting that all sorts of conditions, the fulfilment of which is necessarily remote, must first be satisfied. It is true that the Exchange Equalization Fund has been established with the object of steadying exchange fluctuations, an object which in itself is uncontroversial; and that this Fund was so administered over a prolonged period this year, in particular during the period covering the fall of the dollar and the World Economic Conference, as to keep the pound steady with the franc at a rate of from 85 to 86. It is further true that there were those, notably Lord Bradbury in his *Times* articles in July, who would have liked to continue this policy of pegging on the franc for some time longer. But the franc–sterling rate has been allowed to fall in recent weeks; and it has certainly never been our official policy to treat the maintenance of any sterling–franc rate as a sacrosanct principle which should be upheld even at the cost of intensifying domestic depression and deflation. Nor, I imagine, is there anyone who would recommend such a policy; Lord Bradbury's advocacy of a continued pegging on the franc was expressly related to the particular economic conditions which in his judgement existed, notably the fact that the gold-exchange value of sterling was well below its purchasing power in gold standard countries. In principle, it is common ground

that in present circumstances our hands in regard to exchange policy must remain free.

6. The immediate issue is thus not so much about the principle of exchange stability as about the exchange-level which is desirable for sterling under existing circumstances. Should we welcome and endeavour to bring about a further depreciation of sterling relatively to gold and gold currencies as a means to higher sterling prices and a consequent lightening of debt burdens and more active trade within the sterling area? Upon this issue there is a wide range of opinion. There are those who like Lord Bradbury would have kept the pound steady with gold currencies until sterling prices had risen sufficiently to restore purchasing power parity with those currencies; and it may be that on their left are some who would have desired a temporary pegging with the franc as a stepping-stone to a subsequent gradual appreciation of sterling towards its former gold parity. At the other extreme are those who would have wished from the time when the dollar fell to keep sterling moving downwards as near as possible in step with it. In between is a middle school, well represented by Mr. R. H. Brand, who, as he expressed it in his controversy with Lord Bradbury in *The Times*, 'would gradually release control of the sterling–franc exchange in order to indicate by facts our intention to pursue our own policy', expecting with equanimity 'that our cheap money policy will tend towards a further general rise of prices and therefore some depreciation of sterling as against the exchanges of those countries which pursue a wholly different policy'. Judging by subsequent events, it is Mr. Brand's policy which is actually being followed.

7. For the discussion of this issue it seems desirable to examine closely the way in which a further depreciation of sterling may be expected to assist in raising sterling prices or in improving British trade. When we were driven off gold in 1931, British industrial life received, in my judgement, an undoubted benefit from the fall in sterling which ensued. But the most tangible part of this benefit was not due to any rise in the general sterling price level, for there was no such rise, but to the improvement in the competitive power of our industries, both in the home market and in world markets, relatively to the industries of other countries. Now in 1931 the competitive position of our industries was extremely unfavourable. Ever since the return to gold in 1925 many of our exporting industries had been unable to approach the prices charged by their foreign

competitors, and had been gradually losing their hold on overseas markets as a consequence. When the world slump followed, this unfavourable position was greatly aggravated, wage rates being reduced drastically abroad while remaining comparatively rigid here. Indeed to secure a substantial amelioration of our competitive position by one means or another had become by 1931 an inexorable necessity of our economic life; and there were immense advantages in effecting this by means of an exchange depreciation rather than by a painful and perilous process of wholesale reductions in wages and every sort of money income.

8. In regard to this vital factor of competitive position, the present state of affairs is entirely different from that of 1931. At existing exchange levels, the pound, so far from being overvalued, is probably undervalued in relation to other currencies, with the important exception of the Japanese yen. It is almost certainly undervalued, as Lord Bradbury maintains, relatively to the gold currencies. How it compares with the dollar at the present moment it is more difficult to judge; and it is still more difficult to say how it is likely to compare with the dollar in a few months' time. But the United States is primarily concerned with raising her domestic level of prices and incomes; and it would be premature at any rate to assume that any serious weakening of our competitive position will emerge from the American experiment. It is true, of course, that the volume of our exports is still very low. But, subject to the Japanese exception already mentioned, this is not attributable to any competitive weakness, but to the continuance of depression throughout the world and to the trade impediments which that depression has called forth. In these circumstances it is, in my judgement, idle to suppose that any further improvement in our competitive position that might be brought about by a further depreciation of the pound could do any real good. On the other hand, it might do very serious harm. A favourable competitive position is one of those matters in which it is essential to be moderate, in which greed is sure to overreach itself. Your favourable position is someone else's unfavourable position. Attempt to push it beyond a certain point and you force the others to do their utmost to correct it. They may try to correct it by reducing further their wages and costs of production, a process prejudicial to general trade activity. They may try to correct it by raising their tariffs, by imposing exchange dumping duties, and by having recourse to quota schemes, a process

prejudicial to the revival of international trade. If pressed too far, they may be driven to follow suit along the road of exchange depreciation, with the result of reversing entirely the relative competitive positions.

9. The gold countries, under the pressure of the existing depreciation of the pound, have already done a good deal under the first two heads, and they are likely to do a great deal more if the pound continues to depreciate. If the pound were to fall to the level of, say, 60 French francs to the pound, which some would like to see, the possibility that the gold countries would abandon their existing gold parities would have to be reckoned with as a serious likelihood. The repercussions of such a development on world conditions generally represent a highly speculative question; but it would almost certainly destroy entirely the relative advantage which British industry now enjoys in world markets.

10. I conclude that the potential advantages of exchange depreciation to the competitive position of British industry have been fully exhausted by the depreciation that has already taken place. I have elaborated the foregoing argument to this effect at considerable length, not because I suppose that those who advocate a large further depreciation of the pound are thinking very much of improving our competitive position. I know that they are thinking mainly of raising the general level of sterling prices and incomes, a question to which I am now about to pass. None the less, I think that they are influenced at the back of their minds by a sense of the advantage which our industry derived from the fall of the pound in 1931, and it is important that it should be clearly understood that this is an advantage which cannot be carried any further. However that may be, the appropriate relationship between the values of different currencies is a factor of fundamental importance in the whole problem, which there is too great a disposition, as it seems to me, at the moment to ignore. I insist therefore that we must not lose sight of the fact that the pound, which was overvalued relatively to all currencies in 1931, is undervalued relatively to most of them today.

11. I pass now to the question of the way in which a further depreciation of the pound may be expected to assist in raising sterling prices. The fall of the pound in 1931 did not in fact secure a sustained rise in the sterling price level. It is, indeed, probable that it prevented sterling prices falling as much as they would have

fallen otherwise. But this conclusion is not certain; and no claim under this head can, I think, reasonably be pushed very far. For there is no doubt, in my judgement, that the depreciation of the pound was a powerful force tending to lower prices in gold-standard countries. In determining the world prices of many commodities, the British market is the decisive influence; the demonstration of that fact was one of the outstanding lessons of 1931. Over a considerable range of commodities, accordingly, it was gold prices rather than sterling prices that had to adjust themselves to the reduced exchange value of the pound. When we add to this the part which the fall of the pound undoubtedly played in inducing abnormal trade restrictions and thus in paralysing international trade, the contribution which it made to the lowering of gold prices must be regarded, I think, as a major one.

12. The depreciation of the dollar in the last few months has been, I think, a material factor in promoting the rise of prices which has occurred in the United States. But the question arises how far this is due to the fact that the depreciation of the dollar has meant a fall in its exchange value in terms of sterling. In so far as the British market is the determinant of world prices, it is natural that a fall in the dollar relatively to sterling should tend to raise dollar prices, just as the opposite movement of the sterling–dollar exchange in 1931 tended to lower them. Suppose, however, that instead of the dollar falling alone, sterling and the dollar had fallen together during the last few months, as some would have desired, could we be sure that either sterling prices or dollar prices would have risen, and if so why? Would they have risen because of the lower value of sterling and the dollar in terms of the franc and the lira, or merely on account of their lower value in terms of gold itself? These two possibilities need separate consideration.

13. It has become fashionable today to speak as though there were some direct and simple causal relationship between the gold content of a country's currency and its price level, entirely independent of the foreign-exchange ratios which that gold content may entail. This way of thinking is particularly widespread in the United States. Indeed, the common American apologia in connexion with the international discussions on currency stabilization ran very much as follows: 'We are not in the least concerned to snatch a competitive advantage by exchange depreciation. We are not interested in the foreign exchanges. We simply wish to lower the gold value

of the dollar as a means of raising prices. We have not the least objection to anyone else's doing the same: on the contrary, we should be delighted if everyone were to act in the same way as ourselves and then prices would go up all round.' There are many in Great Britain who accept this reasoning and would have us accept the invitation.

> If it be President Roosevelt's policy [writes Mr. Joseph Ricardo in *The Times* of 8 September] to raise domestic commodity prices to a remunerative level and keep them stable he should have no difficulty in realising his ambition without resorting to inflation.
>
> Gold is the measure of value of all commodities; domestic prices, apart from the effect of supply and demand, rise or fall with the gold value of the domestic currency. If the dollar were devalorized $33\frac{1}{3}$ per cent. it would cause a rise of 50 per cent. in the domestic price level, the effect of which would be to make the production of primary products profitable, increase employment and all-round ability to consume.

14. I know of no warrant either in theory or experience for this simple view of the relation between gold and prices. Why in the world should prices rise merely because the gold contents of currencies are reduced? They may, of course, rise because of a cheap-money policy, open-market operations, programmes of public works, recovery codes, and the like. That is another matter altogether. But apart from alterations in the foreign exchanges, the only relevant effect of depreciating the gold value of a currency is to increase the money value of the gold reserves of the central banks or other bodies or persons holding gold. This might be an important effect, if credit had previously been restricted owing to inadequate central bank reserves. Alternatively it is possible to imagine that the increase in central bank reserves might be put to constructive use as part of a general scheme of international stabilization in some such manner as that publicly suggested by Mr. Keynes. But such possibilities apart, it is difficult to believe that an addition to the already excessively large reserves of the principal central banks would exert any material influence. It is, of course, possible that the depreciation of currencies in terms of gold would raise prices by persuading speculators and others that they were likely to rise, but I am personally extremely sceptical of the durable efficacy of any purely psychological influence which has no basis in reality.

15. How far then would a further exchange depreciation of the

pound and the dollar relatively to the franc and other gold currencies be likely to raise sterling and dollar prices? Here we must remember that the countries still on gold represent only a small part of the world's economic activity and play a very minor part in determining world prices. There is something almost ridiculous in supposing that the powerful British and American economic systems could do much to hoist world prices by establishing lower rates of exchange with France, Holland, Italy, and Switzerland. It is far more probable that the effect would be a further serious deflation of prices in those countries, with the possible result of precipitating their abandonment of gold.

16. In the foregoing paragraphs I have been discussing the effects of a common depreciation of sterling and the dollar, the relation of the two currencies remaining unchanged. The prospect would be little more attractive, though it would be materially different, if we were to suppose a depreciation of sterling relatively to the dollar as well as other currencies. By a further depreciation of this kind, if it were practicable to effect it, we could probably secure some rise of sterling prices, because the United States is like ourselves an important world market. But against this would have to be set the likelihood of a set-back in dollar prices and a check to the hopes of American recovery. If, indeed, we were to set ourselves to bring back the sterling–dollar rate to something like the level prevailing six months ago, we should enter on an extremely dangerous course. The possibility which has often been mentioned in recent months of a campaign of competitive exchange depreciation would then acquire reality, and for reasons similar to those given above it is difficult to believe that anything but mischief could result from such a competition.

17. I conclude accordingly that under present conditions a lower exchange value for the pound is not to be desired; that it would not do nearly so much or so certainly to raise sterling prices or to improve sterling trade as is commonly supposed; and that on the other hand it would contribute materially to bedevil the international situation.

18. On the other hand, I share the view that a recovery of sterling prices is a vital condition of the restoration of economic health, in view particularly of the needs of the primary producers in the Dominions and other parts of the sterling area. I further share the view in principle that what may be loosely termed an expansionist

internal policy is desirable with this end in view. In so far as this policy achieves success, lower exchange rates for sterling relatively to the gold currencies and others might become appropriate, as they are not appropriate today. There would be no reason in my judgement to entertain the smallest regret if this were to happen, and we ought certainly not to allow the possibility that a further gold depreciation of sterling might become appropriate to fetter us or restrain us in any way in the pursuit of our internal policy. A few years ago a halo of prestige attached, as it still attaches on the Continent, to the maintenance of a high rate of exchange, irrespective of the background of economic circumstances. In recent years the wheel has swung so far round in Anglo-Saxon countries that the maximum degree of depreciation has almost come to be regarded as the key to prosperity. We ought, as it seems to me, to have no prejudice either way. Certainly in view of all that has passed it would be profoundly unwise to allow our policy to be influenced in any degree by the historic gold parity of the sovereign.

19. At the same time, I think it unlikely that circumstances will soon arise which will make a lower exchange value for the pound appropriate. This would only happen if there were to be a substantial increase not only in the sterling level of commodity prices but in wages and money costs of production. It is, of course, of the essence of the present American experiment to secure a recovery by means of raising wages and money incomes. The success of this experiment remains, however, to be seen, and it must in any case be remembered that the American position in respect of this matter is very different from our own, in that wages and money incomes have been drastically cut in America in recent years while they have remained more or less stationary here. On the whole, I am of opinion that recovery in Great Britain at all events is most likely to be reliable and sustained if it is allowed to proceed on the basis of substantially the present level of wages and other costs; and it seems improbable that on this basis there would be any justification for a lower exchange value of the pound.

20. As regards the short-term issue accordingly, I find myself in an intermediate position, if there is room for one, between Lord Bradbury and Mr. Brand. I see no sufficient advantage in seeking to maintain even for a limited period any precise ratio between sterling and the gold currencies, while there are substantial psychological disadvantages in doing so in the false impressions thereby

created in the Empire and at home. I am inclined, therefore, to welcome the fall that has taken place in the gold value of sterling in recent weeks, as disposing of the idea that the pound is in any way linked with the gold currencies. On the other hand, I do not consider that this fall is to be welcomed for its own sake or that it corresponds with the underlying realities of the situation. Nor do I think, as Mr. Brand appears to do, that we should encourage the idea that sterling is likely to depreciate further in the near future.

21. To complete the short-term picture, it is necessary to say a word on the technical aspects of exchange control. The Exchange Equalization Fund was formed in order to limit the fluctuations in the exchanges arising from purely temporary causes. It would be extremely difficult under present circumstances to use the fund so as to secure any stability with the dollar. Dollars would be too risky an asset to buy, and the absence of a free gold market in the United States excludes the possibility of checking any undue fall of the dollar by buying gold from there. By comparison it is a simple matter to secure stability with the gold currencies. In practice, the Fund has been used during the past year far more to prevent sterling from rising relatively to gold currencies than to prevent its falling. Notoriously there was for a prolonged period this spring an inflow of balances to London which but for the operations of the Fund would have sent sterling up. It was only natural, therefore, and only consistent with the avowed object of the Fund to eliminate fluctuations rather than to control the exchange level, that when the tide of balances turned round the Fund should have kept the exchange steady by releasing some of the assets it had recently acquired. This point is apt to be overlooked by those who criticized the actions of the control at this period. Most of them would have complained far more if the pound had been allowed to rise materially a little earlier. You can, of course, set out to control the exchanges with the deliberate purpose of lowering the value of sterling, but if this course is rejected, as I think it should be as a dangerous one, you have then only two alternatives. You can leave the exchange market entirely free, in which case you must not complain if every now and then sterling rises in a degree highly embarrassing to our export industries; or you can regulate the exchanges as the Fund purports to do, with the object of checking temporary fluctuations. In this case you must not complain if the

operations of the Fund are at times such as tend to prevent sterling from falling.

The Long-range Problem

22. I pass now to the question of what should be our ultimate objective. It is here that the issue of exchange stability versus internal stability properly arises. The great virtue of the gold standard was that it secured an almost precise stability of exchange rates between the currencies attached to it, for so long as they remained attached to it. But it offered no assurance for the maintenance of 'continuity of values' in any of the senses which may commend themselves to different members of the group. It did not even ensure a genuine 'neutrality' of monetary conditions. It required that prices in any country must move upwards or downwards as prices in other countries moved upwards or downwards; and the general movement in the world as a whole was dependent on a complex of essentially fortuitous circumstances, such as the discovery of new goldfields.

23. There can in my judgement be no doubt that the objective of securing a reasonable stability of economic conditions is of immeasurably greater importance than that of securing precise stability in foreign exchange. The present slump affords sufficient evidence of the havoc that may be caused by a formidable break in the 'continuity of values'. On the other hand, fluctuating exchanges, provided they do not fluctuate chaotically, are far from being a vital obstacle to international trade. Indeed, the fluctuating exchanges of the present time are definitely among the least important of the impediments to international trade which now exist. The chief importance of precise exchange stability lies in facilitating that part of international trade which represents the undertaking of capital contracts and in facilitating international lending, particularly of a fixed-interest form. The former function is certainly desirable, the latter is perhaps more open to question; but in any case these matters cannot compare in importance with the avoidance of serious trade depression.

24. This, however, does not settle the issue. In the first place, it is idle to hope to attain either objective if the other is completely disregarded. Exchange stability did not survive for long during the present slump. On the other hand, it would not be an easy matter

to secure healthy and steady trade conditions if the foreign exchanges were subject to chaotic changes. It is common ground, therefore, that we want to reconcile both objectives as far as we can. The question is which we should place first. Here the greater precision of the objective of exchange stability gives it a claim which has to be set against its lesser intrinsic importance. When an exchange is below parity there is no room for dispute about the fact, but there is plenty of room for disputing whether economic conditions at any time are tending towards depression on the one hand or towards inflation on the other. Furthermore, while there is no doubt under normal conditions as to the efficacy of certain well-tried expedients for correcting any movement of the foreign exchanges, profound doubts may be entertained, and are in fact entertained, as to the efficacy of any monetary devices for correcting a given trend of trade. Thus if the world makes exchange stability the fixed point of its system and seeks to add as much internal trade stability as is compatible with that condition, it can count on securing the exchange stability until at all events the system breaks down. If, on the other hand, it puts internal trade stability first, it may get no sort of stability at all.

25. It would not be profitable, I think, to pursue these general considerations further. It is better to examine in more detail the principal alternative possibilities, paying due regard to the feasibility of each as affected by the events of the present crisis and the movement of opinion in different parts of the world.

26. The restoration of the gold standard covers two very different possibilities which commend themselves to two very different schools of thought. We might aim (*a*) at a gold standard as much as possible like the pre-war one, essentially unmanaged so far as international action is concerned, or (*b*) at a gold standard conrtolled by a high degree of international co-operative action.

27. The former policy receives little overt support in Great Britain, but it has strong advocates abroad. It represents, at all events as things stand now, the real conviction of French financial opinion. Those who have talked with French financial experts will know how prone they are to argue that the monetary troubles of the last few years arise from the various attempts that have been made to manage currency instead of allowing the old automatic forces to have free play, and how they blame in this connexion the gold exchange standard system, open-market policy, and the tentative steps

in co-operation made by the central banks. So far from desiring more concerted international action in future, the exponents of this view would like a great deal less.

28. I shall not discuss this point of view on its merits. It seems to me obscurantist and perverse. From the standpoint of feasibility, the restoration of an old-fashioned unmanaged gold standard seems to me the most chimerical of all the possibilities that are theoretically open. It is chimerical both for objective and for psychological reasons. The comparative smoothness and stability with which the gold standard worked in pre-war days depended on the confidence that was felt in the absolute security of a short-term balance in a financial centre such as London. This confidence has suffered what must necessarily be a lasting blow from the failure of Great Britain to maintain the gold standard during the present depression. If, therefore, the gold standard were to be restored without effective international co-operation, we should have to reckon with the likelihood that foreign balances would be withdrawn from a financial centre abruptly at any period of difficulty. Under such conditions the stability of the system would be precarious in the extreme. Apart from this, there has now grown up in Anglo-Saxon countries a widespread opinion hostile to the gold standard and a disposition to attribute to the gold standard as such a large measure of responsibility for the present depression. This would make it impossible, at any rate for a long time to come, to secure a general return to an old-fashioned gold standard.

29. What then are the prospects of so controlling the gold standard by international co-operation as to ensure against a repetition of the recent disastrous experience and supply the monetary conditions necessary for steady trade development? If such a policy were feasible, there would be an immense amount to be said for it, but I am increasingly inclined to doubt its feasibility at the present stage of the world's history. The international co-operation that would be necessary would represent a task of great difficulty and delicacy. It would not carry us far to lay down the principle that central banks should in concert expand credit when world prices show signs of falling and restrict credit when there is evidence of an inflationary trend. Apart from the difficulty of interpreting the conditions in any country, conditions in one country often differ radically from those in another. But the crucial difficulty is that certain countries may be confronted with a dangerously adverse

balance of payments while other countries have an unduly favourable balance. How could the international co-operation of central
banks contribute to ease the strains resulting from such a situation?

30. There is in my opinion a crucial test for judging the feasibility
of effective international co-operation for the control of gold. The
logically appropriate and indispensable condition of a controlled international gold-standard system is the creation of an international
note-issue such as was publicly advocated by Mr. Keynes some time
ago, which would enable the supply of internationally accepted
purchasing power to be expanded or contracted as world conditions
might require. It is, however, the almost universal opinion that the
creation of such a note-issue would be quite impracticable.

31. It is therefore from the standpoint of extreme scepticism as
to the feasibility of restoring the gold standard either upon old-
fashioned or upon new-fashioned lines that I turn to consider the
alternative of endeavouring to build as much exchange stability as
is practicable on the basis of independently managed currency systems. It is obvious at the outset that a small and economically weak
country could maintain no sort of stability if it attempted to run
an independent currency system of its own: small countries must
necessarily attach themselves either to gold or to the currency
system of some stronger neighbour. But why should there not be
several different currency systems in the world independently
managed, say a sterling bloc, a dollar bloc, and a gold bloc? And
why should not these different systems maintain a degree of exchange stability with one another sufficient for the needs of most
forms of international trade? The degree of exchange stability
indicated might be supplied by giving the dollar and the pound
a parity with gold, only a parity that would be variable from time
to time as circumstances made it desirable.

32. I believe it is in this direction that we shall be carried by the
drift of events and of opinion, and I do not see why such a system
should not work reasonably well. It is necessary, however, to be
cautious in extolling its advantages. Some years ago in his *Tract on
Monetary Reform* Mr. Keynes suggested the device of variable gold
parities primarily as an instrument of securing stable prices. As gold
prices fell the gold parity of sterling would be lowered and vice
versa. I am sure that it would not be practicable to regulate the
movement of the gold parities by any simple or automatic reference
to this criterion. In the first place, there is the difficulty already

pointed out in connexion with the short-term problem that, when the number of gold countries is very limited, an alteration in the gold value of sterling might have a more powerful effect on gold prices than on sterling prices. Thus by altering the gold value of sterling in the way indicated, we might do more to upset trade and prices in the gold countries than to steady them at home; and it would offend international comity to attempt to secure our internal stability by exploiting the position of the gold countries in this manner. In the second place, we must bear in mind the possibility of large movements of short-term balances. One of the chief advantages of keeping the gold value of sterling variable for the future is the safeguard which this would afford against the possibility of such movements. We could, for example, check a large-scale withdrawal of balances by lowering the parity of sterling, so that further withdrawals could only be made at the sacrifice of an exchange loss. But if we are to be free to vary the parity of sterling for this purpose, it follows that we cannot commit ourselves to vary it in accordance with the movements of prices, which may bear no relation to the movements of short-term capital.

33. While, however, the device of a variable gold parity could not in my judgement be used directly as a means of securing internal 'continuity of values', it might serve indirectly to promote this end. For it would permit us to pursue a credit policy adapted to our trade requirements free from the restraints imposed by the movement of the exchanges under the gold-standard system. For this reason I should conceive the variable parities of a reconstructed system as something materially different from the *de facto* parities established in so many countries during the twenties as a prelude to the return to gold. The idea would be that the variable parities, though they would not be altered frequently or without good reason, would be altered readily and without shame if the course of prices in the sterling area and the gold area diverged so as to make an alteration appropriate.

34. I may sum up as follows the main principles which emerge from this memorandum:

> We should aim at pursuing an internal credit policy which will give us satisfactory and healthy trade conditions. We should not allow ourselves to be deflected from this policy by any movements in the foreign exchanges that may prove consequential. On the other hand, we must not expect that satisfactory trade

conditions can include a normal volume of exports so long as the world as a whole remains depressed, and we must not attempt to use exchange movements as a *means* of improving our internal trade. These principles should govern both our immediate exchange policy and the international system which we should seek later to re-establish.

13

INCREASING PRODUCTIVITY AND THE DEMAND FOR LABOUR[1]

A. INTRODUCTORY

1. I USE, in the above title, the phrase 'increasing productivity' rather than 'mechanization' or 'machinery'. From the standpoint of the question discussed in this memorandum, the significance of the introduction of labour-saving machinery is that it entails a reduction in the number of work-people required to produce a given volume of goods or services, or alternatively an increase in the volume of goods and services produced with the aid of a given number of work-people, i.e. an increase in output per head. But other developments may lead to the same result, for example, discoveries in the domain of biological or chemical science, which enable a given number of persons engaged in agriculture to produce an increased quantity of foodstuffs or raw materials, or improved methods of business management which result in the dismissal of employees found to be redundant.

2. Developments of these latter types differ from mechanization in the important respect that they do not necessarily entail, before their effective operation, a relatively large investment of capital. A labour-saving machine must be made before it can displace labour; labour must be employed in making it; and it must be an exceptionally profitable machine to the making of which there does not go a larger aggregate of man-hours of work than it will displace for some years after its introduction. On the other hand, there may be no such preliminary demand for capital and labour, or only a negligible one, in connexion with a biological discovery, or with improved methods of business administration. Prima facie it is the latter methods of increasing output per head which appear the more vulnerable to the charge of creating unemployment. Now it is sometimes argued that it is developments of the latter character, particularly in the field of agricultural production, that represent the special feature of the economic progress of the post-war period,

[1] 12 December 1933.

in contrast to that of the Victorian era. It will, therefore, be important to consider carefully in due course whether the demand for
labour is likely to be differently affected in reality by the two types
of development.

3. Before, however, this distinction can be usefully examined, it
is necessary to consider first the broad common issue that arises.
Mechanization and the other developments indicated share the
fundamental economic characteristic that they serve to increase
the amount of wealth that can be produced per head of the working population. Is it conceivable, and, if conceivable, is it reasonably likely that this will make for a reduction in the demand for
labour? More generally, and to extend the issue beyond the special
standpoint of labour, is it conceivable, or likely, that a marked increase in the world's power of producing wealth can be a cause of
general world impoverishment?

4. Such questions have often been raised before in periods of
severe depression; and a traditional economic answer has been
evolved, the broad effect of which is to exonerate mechanization
and other varieties of increasing productivity from any substantial
reproach. In recent years, however, and especially during the
present crisis, there has been a disposition, shared by some economists of repute, to question the validity, in the light of present-day
tendencies, of this traditional argument. In this memorandum the
attempt will be made, first, to restate the traditional argument,
second, to examine the grounds upon which it is now called in
question, third, to call attention to some new tendencies of which
comparatively little is heard in current discussion, but which
appear to have a vital bearing on the problem, and finally to offer
a positive judgement.

B. THE ORTHODOX ARGUMENT

5. The orthodox argument starts from the broad proposition that
the means of purchasing goods arises from production, and that an
increase in the volume of production tends therefore to be accompanied by a commensurate increase in the ability to buy them.
Every hundred pounds worth of goods sold to the ultimate consumer gives rise to £100 of income, distributed somehow among
the people who have contributed to their production and sale, and
this £100 of income represents purchasing power. (After all, one of
the recognized ways of computing the national income of a country

is to add up the 'net output' of the different industries and occupations; and this Census of Production approach squares reasonably well with the Inland Revenue approach.) If an increased volume of goods is produced and sold, there will be a corresponding increase in the aggregate real income of the community, a precisely corresponding one. If, owing to some labour-saving development, a given amount of some commodity can be produced with less labour, the commodity is likely to be sold at a lower price, in which case the consuming public will be able either to purchase a larger quantity of it, or to purchase more of other things, or to do partly the one and partly the other. If the commodity is not sold at a lower price those connected with its production will receive larger incomes per head, whether as wages, or salaries or profits, and *they* will be in a position to increase their purchases. However rapidly, therefore, productivity may be increasing, there is no fundamental reason why the growth of demand should not keep pace with it.

6. It is true, of course, the argument proceeds, that people may not choose to spend upon consumption the whole of the increase in their real incomes which arises from the greater productivity. On the contrary, it is probable that they will save a larger proportion of their incomes, as they become better-off. It might seem, therefore, at first sight as though part of the increase in real income which corresponds to the increase in production is withdrawn from the effective demand for goods and services. But in reality this is not the case, as a general rule. Normally people seek to invest their savings in some form that is likely to bring them a return. Now money that is invested is likely to contribute just as much to the demand for commodities and services as money that is 'spent' in the ordinary sense. Every £100 invested, for example, in the erection and equipment of a factory means in effect the purchase of bricks and mortar and machinery to the extent of £100. The investor is thus really buying one class of goods rather than another, producers' goods rather than consumers' goods. In short, saving, if accompanied by commensurate investment, does nothing to diminish the immediate aggregate demand for goods and services, while in the long run it helps to make the process of increasing productivity and increasing prosperity cumulative and progressive.

7. So far the orthodox argument is comparatively popular in its appeal, and is fairly widely known. At this point, however, it is developed along rather more academic lines in answer to an objec-

tion brought by critics who in Great Britain are mainly associated
with Left politics, though in the United States they include employers of the 'high wages' school. These critics say in effect:

Doubtless you may get on for a considerable time in the manner you
describe, using the money which well-to-do people don't want to spend
on consumption in employing workers to make more machines which
will still further enlarge productive power. But all the time you are
piling up trouble for the future. On your own admission the proportion
of its income which the public as a whole is spending on consumable
goods steadily diminishes, while the proportion which it devotes to
increasing the means of producing them steadily increases. That cannot
continue indefinitely. Sooner or later you are bound to find that the
power to produce consumable goods has outrun the demand for them,
and then there will be no return to be earned by erecting new factories,
there will be no outlets for the savings which well-to-do people are
withdrawing from current consumption, and you will get into a nasty
mess. That is what happens when a severe slump overtakes the economic
system, and it is bound to happen under our present system of society,
with its unequal distribution of wealth. The only remedy is to increase
the proportion of the aggregate income that falls to wage-earners and
comparatively poor people, who will spend it on consumable goods
rather than save it and invest it. In that way you may keep consumption
expanding as fast as productivity grows, but unless you do this the
increase of productivity is bound to cause periodic catastrophic crises.

8. To this the orthodox reply is as follows:

It is quite true that fluctuations in the volume of investment, that is to
say, in the output of capital goods, play an important part in the ups and
downs of trade. During a boom year there is apt to be an over-expansion
of constructional activity, followed during years of depression by a very
drastic curtailment. The difference between the output of the constructional industries in a good year and their output in a bad year is
very large, much larger than the corresponding difference in the case of
industries producing goods for immediate consumption; and the major
part of the unemployment that occurs during a severe depression is
attributable to this fact. But it is a complete mistake to infer from this
that the root of the trouble is a chronic tendency towards over-saving in
a capitalistic society. On the contrary, the trouble during the good years
is rather that the volume of real investment runs ahead of the money
savings of the community, so that the demand for goods and services in
the aggregate tends to exceed their supply and prices tend to rise. It is
an illusion, therefore, to suppose that the over-expansion of constructional activity during the boom arises from an excess of savings seeking

investment. It arises from over-optimistic calculations of the opportunities open for profitable capital enterprise; and poor communities with very scanty savings, such as Scotland at the time of the Darien enterprise or post-war Germany, are just as liable to make these optimistic mistakes as prosperous communities which save on a large scale.

9. In short, the argument proceeds, the trouble that underlies the occurrence of booms and slumps is not that the level of savings is normally too high, but that a serious lack of balance occurs from time to time between savings on the one hand and investment on the other. This maladjustment is sometimes in the one direction and sometimes in the other. At times there is a tendency to push new constructional activity in excess of the volume of money savings; that gives rise to a boom associated with a tendency towards inflation. At other times there is a tendency for new constructional activity to fall short of the volume of savings; that gives rise to depression associated with deflation of prices. But while these maladjustments occur, and while the damage that they do is immeasurable, they are essentially temporary maladjustments which natural forces are always working to correct. Just as, in the case of a particular commodity, any serious disequilibrium between demand and supply brings into play the corrective influence of changes in price, a lower price tending to diminish supply and to stimulate demand, so changes in the rate of interest correct maladjustments in the relation between savings and investment. If at any time the volume of savings exceeds the investment outlets for them, the rate of interest falls, and the effect of a lower rate of interest is, on the one hand, to discourage saving and, on the other hand, to stimulate capital enterprise. There cannot, therefore, be a *chronic* tendency towards excessive saving; for, if there were, the rate of interest would fall steadily towards zero, and, while it may be arguable that people would still save on a large scale even if they could only obtain a negligible return by doing so, it is not open to reasonable doubt that a trifling rate of interest would stimulate a vast additional demand for capital goods. It should be noted, in this connexion, that capital goods do not consist only of things like factories and machinery. There are, in addition, consumers' capital goods, of which houses are the outstanding instance, the demand for which would be very greatly increased if money could be borrowed on very easy terms.

10. The possibility of changes in the rate of interest has, more-

over, an important bearing upon the distribution of wealth. From every standpoint, it is very desirable that real wages should increase along with the growth in the prosperity of society, indeed that the lion's share of the greater prosperity should accrue to the poorer classes. But in any period in which the accumulation of savings grows faster than the investment outlets for them, natural forces tend to produce this result. For in such a period the rate of interest tends to fall, and a lower rate of interest is inevitably associated with a lower rate of business profits. The share of the total income accruing to the capitalist classes of the community is diminished and a larger share is available for other classes, including the wage-earners. There is thus no danger that the special interests of labour will suffer from an increase in productive power which increases the wealth of the community as a whole. Nor is any special menace to these interests found in any tendency towards oversaving on the part of the well-to-do; rather the contrary. Unfortunately it is untrue that over generations there is any prevailing tendency for the rate of interest to fall, because recurrent wars dissipate a large part of the savings which are accumulated in times of peace. This serves to hold back the improvement in the distribution of wealth which the increase of productivity would otherwise bring about.

11. Before passing from this statement of the orthodox argument to consider the modern criticisms of it, it is desirable to pause to note exactly what it claims and what it does not claim. The argument does not exclude the possibility that conditions of rapidly increasing productivity may make the economic system more unstable, liable to more extreme fluctuations of activity. It asserts that, as productivity increases, real purchasing power will increase proportionately; but it leaves open the possibility that the consuming public will not choose to spend the increment of their purchasing power in buying those particular commodities of which the output per worker has been increased. It leaves open the possibility accordingly that improved methods of production may lead to a surplus of productive capacity and to a redundant supply of labour in particular industries, entailing depression in those industries, with temporary adverse repercussions upon economic activity as a whole. It is, indeed, obviously easier to imagine perfect stability in a stagnant economic system in which productive methods and the incomes of consumers remain unchanged than in a society of rapid secular progress. Again the argument admits that fluctuations in

the volume of investment activity represent an important cause of the occurrence of industrial depressions, and such fluctuations are likely to be most marked in periods of widespread technological change. There is nothing, in short, in the orthodox argument to refute the view that an increase in the rate and range of improvement in productive methods is likely to make slumps more severe.

12. All that the argument really claims is that an increase in productive power will make in the long run for increased prosperity and that this increase in prosperity will be shared by all classes in the community. It claims that technological improvement, however much it may take the form of the displacement of labour by labour-saving machinery, will serve in the long run to increase and not to diminish the demand for labour. It disputes the nightmare view that the advance of science and the progress of invention are likely to render an increasing proportion of the teeming populations of the world functionless and permanently redundant. The claim so limited finds a powerful vindication in the history of the past century and a half, when technological development without a parallel in previous experience enabled Great Britain to find employment for a population which doubled itself and doubled itself again during the period at a standard of living which improved out of all recognition. This long experience affords a presumption of the truth of the orthodox argument which the bare fact of the occurrence of a depression of unparalleled severity, attributable in part at least to circumstances special to the aftermath of a great war, is clearly insufficient to rebut.

C. THE ROBOT ARGUMENT

13. What then are the new facts which are alleged today as reasons for doubting the applicability of the orthodox argument to the circumstances of the post-war world? The first contention to be examined may be conveniently described as the Robot argument. Mechanical improvements, it is pointed out, have a twofold aspect. They are, in part, rivals to labour, and, in part, tools for labour. Whether they will on balance exert an adverse or a beneficial effect on the interests of labour depends, it is argued, on whether their character as rivals predominates over their character as tools. An improvement which approximates in its type to the equipment of a labourer with a more efficient spade in place of a less efficient spade will prove an advantage. On the other hand, an improvement

which approximates in its character to the creation of a mechanical
Robot, which is capable of doing exactly what a labourer does, will
reduce the demand for labour and consequently the volume of
employment. Now the tide of mechanical invention is flowing, it
is claimed, in the Robot direction. The typical nineteenth-century
invention was the creation of a new, somewhat crude, instrument
which greatly increased the output of goods, but which gave rise
at the same time to a large demand for work-people to handle it
and use it. The typical post-war improvement is the introduction
of machinery so automatic in character that hardly any work-people
are required to run it.

14. This contention is rendered highly plausible to many minds
by the ocular demonstration afforded by a visit to a modern factory
equipped with highly automatic plant. There a succession of
amazingly ingenious machines, performing their functions with
flawless precision and served steadily by tireless mechanical con-
veyors, can be observed converting a raw material stage by stage
into a variety of highly elaborated products, without requiring
apparently the smallest assistance from the human factor. Such
spectacles impress the imagination strongly, and the effect is
heightened by stories which pass from mouth to mouth of how the
whole demand of a large community for this or that product can
be satisfied by a single plant employing a mere handful of labour.
These stories were the foundation of the case of the 'technocracy'
movement in the United States; and the following extracts from an
article entitled 'What is Technocracy?', by Wayne W. Parrish in the
New Outlook for November 1932, will illustrate their nature:

The ancient miller of Athens or Rome ground out in a day, between
his two crude milling stones, a barrel to a barrel and a half of indifferent
flour. A modern flour mill in Minneapolis produces 30,000 barrels a day
per man with a much shorter day and a much better flour. But for whom?

A shoemaker of ancient Rome took five and a half days to make a pair
of shoes. The 7,200 shoemakers in the Shoemakers Guild of Roman days
would make only 7,200 pairs of shoes in five and a half days. The same
number of employees in a modern shoe plant in five and a half days
would produce 595,000 pairs of shoes. But for whom?

The brickmakers for over five thousand years never attained on the
average more than 450 bricks a day per man—a day being over ten
hours. A modern straightline continuous brick plant will produce
400,000 bricks a day per man.

Even a century ago in these United States one man produced 25 tons of pig iron each year while it took another man a year to produce 800 tons of iron ore. In 1929 we mined on the Mesabi Range at the rate of 20,000 tons per man per year and in four weeks moved a greater tonnage than that of the Khufu Pyramid at Gizeh, while our modern blast furnace technique has made it possible for one man to-day to produce 4,000 tons of pig iron per annum.

A photograph of a modern steel rolling mill in full operation will show a large plant without a human being on the floor.

The implication is clear and plausible. Whatever may have been the effects of mechanization, when machinery was a clumsy, imperfect thing requiring men at every stage to feed it and tend it and check it, how is it possible to doubt that nowadays, when it assumes a highly automatic form, it must be detrimental to employment?

15. But the plausibility of this argument rapidly disappears when it is subjected to a critical examination. In the first place, it is not easy to attach any precise meaning to the distinction between mechanization which serves predominantly as a tool to labour and mechanization which is predominantly in rivalry with labour. It is of the essence of any profitable mechanization that it reduces the amount of labour required to produce a given output of goods. However imperfect, accordingly, the mechanization of the nineteenth century may have been, the labour required to work the machines that were introduced would not have sufficed to avert a net decline in the volume of employment. In order to account for the beneficial results which actually ensued in the nineteenth century, it is clearly necessary to include two other factors—first, the labour required to produce the machines in the first instance, and second, the increased demand for goods and services resulting from the lower costs of production which the mechanization made possible. The case of railway development well illustrates the fundamental importance of these factors. It was not the labour required to run the railways after completion but the labour required to build them and equip them that gave an immense stimulus to British economic life in the era of the railway boom. Again, the great advantage rendered by a completed railway to the community lay not in the number of work-people on its pay-roll but in the development of general economic life which resulted from cheaper, quicker, and more efficient transport. Indeed, if it had not been for this development, the numbers employed by the

railways would have been inconsiderable. Thus the main reasons which have always been assigned by economic historians for regarding railways as a key factor in the expansion of the Victorian era have nothing to do with the failure of railways to approximate to the character of Robots.

16. In the second place, it is very doubtful whether the allegation is really true that mechanization of the modern type entails a larger displacement of labour per unit of output than mechanization of the nineteenth-century type. Here again the example of the railways is pertinent. As compared with previous forms of transport, the railways entailed a huge net displacement *per ton-mile of goods carried or per passenger-mile*. It may be doubted whether any mechanization of the post-war period can show nearly as large a net displacement of labour per unit of output: certainly the modern change in transport from railways to motor transport on the roads can show no comparable result. Indeed, the revolutionary cheapening of transport costs which railways effected was attributable to the vast economy they secured in the amount of labour employed per unit of transport.

17. On the other hand, the economy of labour effected by the substitution of more automatic for less automatic machinery is often more apparent than real. Machinery is liable to become obsolete nowadays, and to require replacement, far more quickly than it used to do. This is, no doubt, partly attributable to the fact that technological improvements, effecting further, often comparatively small, economies, are constantly being made. It is also partly attributable to the fact that a highly automatic machine is specialized to the manufacture of a particular variety of product, for which the demand, in accordance with changes in taste and fashion, often proves short-lived. Whatever the causes, there is no doubt as to the general tendency to a more rapid rate of obsolescence. It is this that lies behind the complaints which come increasingly from the industrial world in Great Britain of the inadequacy of the income-tax allowances for depreciation and obsolescence. The more rapid rate of obsolescence diminishes the economy secured by the industrialist from a new labour-saving machine; and limits his power to reduce his selling-price. At the same time, since more rapid obsolescence implies more frequent replacements, it reduces correspondingly the net displacement of labour per unit of output. The labour employed to meet the additional replacement demand for

machinery must be set against the labour displaced in the factory using the machinery.

18. It must be borne in mind, moreover, that the evolution of automatic machinery is usually very gradual. Because very few people may now be employed in the actual operation of the machinery in a certain industry, it does not follow that large numbers of work-people have recently been displaced. On the contrary it will usually be found in such cases that for a considerable period past the numbers engaged in operating the machinery have formed a small proportion, and the numbers engaged in subsidiary processes, in the trading departments and in miscellaneous functions, a large proportion of the total employees of the factory. For this reason the final transition to the more advanced forms of mechanization often entails a much smaller percentage reduction in the numbers employed per unit of output than did the original introduction of mechanization of a cruder kind.

19. It is true, of course, that in some instances the progress of technological improvement has been extremely rapid. But, when these instances are examined, it will be found that they are the exceptions which prove the rule. The leading instance of the rapid triumph of modern mass-production methods is the motor-car. Within less than a generation from their first invention the methods of producing motor-cars had been carried to a high pitch of perfection, entailing a remarkable economy in the labour employed per unit of output. But this development was accompanied by so large and rapid an increase in the consumption of motor-cars, as to supply one of the chief impulses which have been given in recent years to industrial activity and to employment. When account is taken of those engaged in the manufacture of motor-cars, in the production of materials, like iron and steel and rubber, required for their manufacture, in the production of oil for their fuel and lubrication, in garages and other miscellaneous occupations connected with their use, it is obvious that the demand for labour associated with this industry is immense and far-reaching. But this result has only been made possible by the low prices at which motor-cars are sold, and these low prices are attributable in turn to the high economy of labour with which they are made. The motor-car, in short, supplies a striking modern vindication of the truth of the orthodox theory, a vindication, indeed, more striking than can ordinarily be expected. For, in this case, an increase in employment has demonstrably

arisen in the particular field of industry affected by the technological improvement, and not merely somewhere else, and this, of
course, is more than the orthodox argument claims as the normal
result. The case of the motor-car is, indeed, exceptional in many
ways. None the less it is not unfair to infer from it that in so far as
technological progress is relevant to the present crisis, the trouble
is more likely to lie in a dearth than in an excess of important
labour-saving discoveries. After all, as was pointed out in the introductory section, a labour-saving machine must be made before it
can be used, and the making of it will represent, as a rule, an
aggregate of man-hours of work many times larger than the annual
economy in labour which it will effect when used. At the worst,
therefore, an exceptional spurt in labour-saving development might
be expected to increase the demand for labour for a considerable
period.

20. Thus, for all its superficial plausibility, the Robot argument
appears, when examined, to be wholly devoid of substance. It is
both unsound in logic and untrue in fact. The distinction on which
it rests between mechanization which is in the main co-operation
with labour and that which is in the main competitive with it is
illusory, since all mechanization diminishes the amount of labour
employed per unit of output, while the inventions which have done
most in the past to stimulate economic activity have entailed an
especially large economy in this respect. If the orthodox argument
has ceased, for any reasons, to be applicable to modern conditions,
the Robot contention throws no light on what these reasons are.

D. THE ALLEGED 'AGRICULTURAL REVOLUTION'

21. It is often maintained that, while recent technological progress in the sphere of industry may not have been at all unusual,
there has been an altogether exceptional increase in productivity
in the sphere of agriculture, or, more generally, of the production
of primary commodities. It has become fashionable, indeed, to
speak of an 'agricultural revolution', a phrase which is designed to
convey by its implicit reference to the industrial revolution of a
century and a half ago, the impression of a big sudden leap forward
in the output per head of the agricultural population.

22. Now, in so far as it is true that there has really been an exceptional increase in agricultural productivity in recent years, this may
well enter as a material factor into the complex of circumstances

responsible for the present abnormal depression. A revolution in productive methods might easily give rise to a serious over-production of agricultural commodities. Owing to the well-known fact that agriculturists are much less prone than manufacturers to reduce their output, in face of an inadequate demand, a condition of serious agricultural over-production, once established, tends naturally to be obstinate and prolonged, entailing a severe and correspondingly prolonged fall in the relative prices of agricultural commodities. Agriculture, moreover, plays a predominant part in the economic life of a large part of the world. In many countries currency stability and governmental solvency are dependent on a reasonable level of prices for primary products. Any severe slump in agricultural prices must accordingly endanger the stability of the whole mechanism of international finance and exchange. There is, in short, no difficulty in understanding how a serious over-expansion of primary production might be a major cause of such difficulties as the world has experienced in the last few years.

23. How far this represents in actual fact the story of the present slump is a question that will be examined in a moment. Before this is attempted it is desirable to pause to note the bearing of the question on the main argument. Even if we could legitimately assign exclusive responsibility for the troubles of the last few years to the growth of agricultural productivity, this would not, speaking strictly, impair the validity of the orthodox argument, as it has been set out in this memorandum. That argument, as has already been pointed out, admits the possibility that the development of productivity may give rise to a condition of unbalanced production, and that this may give rise in turn to a general trade depression. Its claim is limited to the assertion that the long-run consequences must be beneficial, and this claim cannot be invalidated by anything that has happened yet. On the other hand, if we had to conclude that, with the extension of technological improvement to the domain of primary production, the economic system had acquired a new instability, rendering very probable the periodic recurrence of depressions like the present, the consolations of the orthodox argument would become decidedly less satisfying than they appeared during the nineteenth century. Certain special features of agriculture, notably the difficulty of curtailing excess production, suggest that this conclusion is *a priori* not unlikely. It is important, therefore, to examine closely the actual facts.

24. First, then, how far has there really been in recent years an increase in productivity in agriculture generally? The assertion that there has been a revolutionary improvement in productive methods can only be justified in the case of a very few commodities, of which the outstanding instance is wheat. In wheat-growing, unquestionably, mechanical improvements, in particular the use of the tractor, and biological discoveries, such as the evolution of drought-resisting and early-maturing varieties of wheat, have effected a remarkable increase in productivity, have greatly increased, that is to say, the amount of wheat that a given agricultural population can produce. It should be noted, however, that this increase in productivity is limited for the most part to the New World, and does not apply to the wheat-growing areas of the European Continent. When we turn to other important agricultural products the picture is very different. While there may have been certain minor economies, there has been no substantial lowering of the real costs of producing such crops as sugar, coffee, or tobacco. In the case of cotton, the main factor in the ebb and flow of productivity is the struggle with destructive pests such as the boll-weevil, and this struggle appears to be fairly evenly balanced. Certainly the main trouble in the case of cotton is not increased productivity, but diminished world consumption. There has been no marked improvement in the production of milk, which, taking the world as a whole, represents the most important of all agricultural products, or in the production of meat. Rubber is another instance of a primary commodity of which the costs of production have been substantially reduced; but rubber is a very special case, and the rapid cheapening of this commodity is essentially part of the story of the development of the automobile industry.

25. There has been, of course, in the post-war period a substantial increase in the volume of most forms of agricultural production; but in many cases this is attributable less to an increase in productivity per head than to an increase in the number of persons engaged in production. To an important extent the expansion of agricultural production has been fostered artificially by governments. This is especially true in the case of sugar. But, generally, European industrial countries have endeavoured to maintain or increase their agricultural populations by higher agricultural protection, while the countries of the New World have done their utmost to attract new settlers. In so far, therefore, as the present world troubles are

attributable to agricultural over-production, it by no means follows that increasing productivity is chiefly to blame.

26. This leads to the next question. To what extent has there really been a relative over-expansion of agricultural production? This question was examined in a pamphlet entitled 'Regulation of Supply' prepared by the Empire Marketing Board for the British Commonwealth delegations at the World Economic Conference. From the statistical evidence available, this pamphlet estimates that 'between 1913 and 1925, while world production of foodstuffs increased by 11 per cent., population increased by 10 per cent. and raw material production by 25 per cent.' For the years subsequent to 1925, the following table is given:

Indexes of Production and Prices. 1925 to 1932

	1925	1926	1927	1928	1929	1930	1931	1932
World production:								
Foodstuffs	100	100	103	106	106	104	102	..
Raw materials, agricultural	100	102	99	103	107	104	105	..
Raw materials, non-agricultural	100	102	111	117	127	112	96	..
Total, foodstuffs and raw materials	100	101	104	108	112	106	101	..
Commodity prices (end of year):								
United Kingdom	100	96	92	91	87	72	70 (a)	66 (a)
U.S.A.	100	95	94	94	91	76	66	60
Industrial production (10 countries excluding U.S.S.R.)	100	101	110	115	123	107	92	..

(*a*) Sterling price.

The conclusions drawn in the pamphlet are as follows:

From this examination of the statistical position four points emerge:
1. the production of primary products between 1925 and 1929 did not expand as fast as industrial production;
2. foodstuffs and agricultural raw materials did not increase as fast as non-agricultural raw materials;
3. industrial production has contracted more rapidly since 1929 than the production of primary products;

4. foodstuffs and agricultural raw materials have contracted less
rapidly than non-agricultural raw materials.
These conclusions suggest that agriculture has been the victim rather
than the cause of the world depression; that it is the falling off in demand
owing to diminished money incomes of consumers rather than an excessive increase in the supply of agricultural commodities which has brought
about the present position of over-production; and that the chief need
at the present time is to restore world demand rather than to restrict
production still further.

27. Statistics can never be conclusive upon such an issue; and it
may well be that an excess of supply over demand for agricultural
commodities played a more positive part as an originating cause of
the slump than the above summary admits. Evidence for this view
may be found in the widespread advocacy prior to the slump of
schemes for maintaining prices by holding stocks off the market,
leading to the creation of the Wheat Pools in Canada and the
Federal Farm Board in the United States. But this tendency, it
should be noted, was most marked in the case of wheat and was
confined to a limited range of commodities. No similar premonitory
symptoms of a consciousness of the difficulty of disposing of supplies can be discerned, for example, in the dairying industry or in
the production of meat. The general fall in the prices of agricultural
relatively to industrial commodities during the course of the slump
proves nothing. That is a familiar feature of every severe world-
wide depression, however it originates.

28. It seems fair to conclude, therefore, that though an over-
production of certain agricultural commodities may have contributed to the causes of the slump, it was a minor rather than a major
factor. In view of the further fact that the expansion of agricultural
production was only partly attributable to an increase in productivity, it seems impossible to sustain the contention that economic
stability has been greatly diminished by an agricultural revolution.

E. SURPLUS CAPACITY

29. Thus the two criticisms of the orthodox theory, so far considered, fail. But to demonstrate their failure will not suffice to
restore the orthodox theory to its former supremacy over the public
mind. Scepticism is widespread and deep-rooted that this theory
does not square with the facts of the post-war world. The two criticisms which have been rejected may be regarded as attempts to

explain why this has come about. The explanations may be bad ones; but to show this will not remove the impression of an irreconcilability between the theory and the facts.

30. But is this impression reasonable? It would be unreasonable, as has already been argued, to infer the unsoundness of the theory from the occurrence or the severity of the present slump; for the theory admits the possibility of slumps, and there is an abundance of special post-war circumstances to which the abnormal severity of the present one may be attributed. Yet, since the human mind is not completely reasonable, it is probable that these facts are responsible in very large degree for the scepticism which prevails today. A similar scepticism has been a normal feature of periods of depression in the past.

31. There remains, however, a ground for scepticism which cannot be so lightly dismissed. The more reasonable sceptics would base themselves not so much on the facts of the slump as on the facts prior to the slump. They would maintain that in the years when trade was good, and when consumption was sustained by various influences which we now recognize to have been inflationary in character, a tendency for supply to outrun demand was already clearly in evidence in many different sections of the economic field. They would point to the growth of schemes already referred to for maintaining the prices of various classes of primary commodities by holding supplies off the market. But, so far from regarding these schemes as evidence of an over-expansion of agricultural production relatively to other commodities, they would claim that there were even clearer indications of a tendency for production to outrun consumption in the sphere of industry. They would point to the growing preoccupation of manufacturers in the pre-slump years with the problem of selling, and to the elaborate attempts that were made, particularly in the United States, by such devices as high-speed advertising and the instalment-purchase system, to stimulate consumption sufficiently to carry off the growing product of industry. They would observe that despite these efforts the total number of persons engaged in manufacturing industry in the United States declined during a period of unexampled prosperity. They would call attention to the fact that it was actually in the United States during this period that the phrase 'technological unemployment' was first coined, and that Messrs. Foster and Catchings wrote their books and launched their propaganda based on

the idea of a prevailing tendency for unemployment to increase. Finally, they would point to the existence in industry after industry of a large excess of productive capacity.

32. The broad accuracy of these facts cannot be denied, and they represent a phenomenon that is in large measure new. As was stated in the careful survey on *The Course and Phases of the World Economic Depression*, published by the League of Nations in 1931,

> The existence of surplus capacity on a large scale is of course no new phenomenon; it existed before the war during certain phases of the business cycle. There is reason for believing, however, that surplus capacity during boom periods of the business cycle was in those days relatively small compared to its extent in 1928–29.

Thus we have a real distinction between the post-war period and previous periods of industrial expansion. Whatever bearing this change may have on the main issue discussed in this memorandum, it calls for explanation. To explain it, however, it is necessary to take account of other tendencies, the relevance of which to the present controversy is not usually recognized.

F. THE NUMERICAL INEXPANSIVENESS OF THE MARKET

33. The nineteenth century was a century of general expansion. Industrial invention and business enterprise led to an immense increase in the volume of goods produced by a given number of workers; but this technological progress was accompanied by a rapid growth of population throughout the world, and especially in the more advanced industrial communities, and also by a great extension of international trade. The economic development of the new world proceeded rapidly with the aid of the people and the capital of the countries of western Europe; while at the same time backward peoples were being brought increasingly within the range of international commerce. Accordingly the number of persons representing the effective market for a commodity grew rapidly and steadily throughout the century. Speaking generally, each individual industry in a manufacturing country like Great Britain found itself catering for a constantly increasing number of consumers, both in the home market as the result of the growth of population, and in the export market as the result of the development of international trade.

34. Now these conditions have undergone a complete transformation in recent years. In advanced industrial countries, birth-rates have fallen so far that the populations have ceased to increase rapidly, and must be expected in some cases, in Great Britain in particular, to decline in the near future. In the sphere of international trade, expansion has already given place to contraction, as the result of the exhaustion of the process of opening-up new areas to economic intercourse, and the growth throughout the world in the strength of the forces of economic nationalism. Both these changes, it should be observed, though they had their origin in earlier tendencies, have only become effective in the post-war period. Although the birth-rate in Great Britain has been falling for nearly two generations, the maximum annual increase in numbers was reached in the decade 1901–11. The volume of international trade, taking the world as a whole, continued to increase rapidly right up to the war.

35. Thus, within a very short space of time, a numerically stationary or contracting market has been substituted for a numerically expanding one. The consequences of technological progress are materially affected by this change in the environment in which it operates. When the number of consumers is growing rapidly, any reduction in the number of workers required to produce a given volume of goods is accompanied by a substantial increase in demand, not merely for goods and services in general, but for each particular commodity. But if there is no growth in the number of consumers, there may be no increase, or only a very small increase, in the demand for a large range of commodities. It is true that, in accordance with the orthodox argument, real incomes in the aggregate and consequently aggregate purchasing power, should increase proportionately to the increase in productive power brought about by technological improvement. But if the increment of aggregate income is entirely accounted for by a growth in incomes per head, and not by an increase in numbers, the increased consumption to which it will give rise will be very unevenly spread between different commodities. If numbers increase by 5 per cent., incomes per head remaining unchanged, we may expect an increase of roughly 5 per cent. in the demand for bread, for meat, for milk, for boots and shoes, for clothes, for houses, for each particular thing. But if incomes per head increase by 5 per cent., while numbers remain unchanged, there may be only a negligible increase in the demand

for many of the basic necessities of life, perhaps even a reduction in the demand for some of them, coupled with an increase of much more than 5 per cent. in the demand for goods or services of a luxury or semi-luxury character.

36. Thus when the numbers who constitute the effective market are stationary or declining, the demand for many commodities may fail to expand in as large a degree as labour-saving invention is reducing the number of workers required to satisfy a given demand. A condition of surplus capacity will then arise in those industries, accompanied by a redundant supply of workers who must be transferred to other occupations if they are to find employment. When, on the other hand, the number of consumers, both at home and abroad, is growing rapidly, the consequent increase in demand for every commodity will suffice in the great majority of industries to prevent an actual decline in the numbers employed. This certainly was the experience of the nineteenth century. So far as can be gathered from the available statistics, there were few industries in Great Britain which did not show a steady increase in the numbers employed from decade to decade right up to the war. There was, of course, a large change in the balance of productive activity. Some industries, notably the 'heavy' industries, coal, iron and steel, engineering and shipbuilding, increased their volume of employment in far larger proportion than others. But the industries where the numbers of employed declined were few and comparatively unimportant. This result was only possible in the environment of a growing population and expanding export markets.

37. The trend towards stationary populations and the decline in the volume of international trade explain, it is suggested, many of the phenomena which have been noted in the course of this memorandum. They explain, in particular, the widespread existence of surplus capacity in the years immediately preceding the slump and the decline in the United States during the prosperity period in the total number of workers engaged in manufacture. For, as wealth increases, it is inevitable that a diminishing proportion of the population will be engaged in producing commodities and an increasing proportion in supplying services, and when aggregate numbers cease to grow rapidly, this may well entail an absolute decline in the former case. The same tendencies help to explain the emergence of a condition of over-supply of certain agricultural products in the

pre-slump years. It seems probable that they also contribute to cause a more rapid obsolescence of plant in modern times.

38. What then is the bearing of these new tendencies upon the main issue? We must expect the following consequences:

(a) The irreducible minimum of unemployment, i.e. the unemployment that prevails in times of good and active trade, is likely to be materially higher than it was in pre-war days. There is likely to be at any time a larger number of persons who have been actually displaced from the industry in which their skill is specialized, by technological progress, and who, if they are beyond a certain age, will find it difficult to obtain alternative employment. In the environment of a numerically stationary or contracting market, increasing productivity will entail a greater degree of waste both of plant and of acquired skill than it did formerly.

(b) It seems probable that the economic system as a whole will be more unstable and more liable to sharp fluctuations in activity than it was in the last century. For it would be easier for a condition of unbalanced production, i.e. a serious over-supply of some commodities relatively to others, to arise when a steady, substantial increase in the demand for each particular commodity can no longer be assumed.

(c) Similarly, it is possible that the same change may make depressions when they occur more prolonged and obstinate than they used to be. The growth of numbers in the nineteenth century entailed a secular growth of demand which ensured that a depression could not be other than short-lived. It may prove less easy to escape from depressions without this natural resilience to help us out.

The two latter consequences, however, though probable are by no means certain, and it may be that one is led at the present time to exaggerate their likelihood and importance owing to the existence of certain other factors which will be mentioned later, making for instability. In any case it is important to observe that they are the consequences not so much of the growth of productivity as of the change in the environment in which increasing productivity now operates. Indeed, in view of the existence of other factors making for instability, it may be doubted whether much would be done to make trade steadier by putting an end to technological progress altogether, even if this were practicable.

G. UNPROFITABLE MECHANIZATION

39. The trend towards a numerically stationary or contracting market has had another consequence in the past decade which should be noted. The orthodox argument asserts that any profitable mechanization will increase aggregate real purchasing power sufficiently to avert any net displacement of labour. But not all mechanization proves profitable in fact; and in recent years there has been in some countries a tendency to carry mechanization further than economic considerations really warranted. This tendency was especially marked in Germany in the years after currency stabilization; modern labour-saving plant was installed in the German 'heavy' industries on a scale that has since proved to have been grossly excessive. This implied a miscalculation which was largely attributable to the tacit assumption that markets would continue to expand as they had done in the nineteenth century. In Russia also it seems probable that there has been much mechanization of an essentially uneconomic character. The reason in this case is different, namely the domination of a dogma that mechanization is the secret of progress applied with an almost complete disregard of considerations of profit and loss.

40. For uneconomic mechanization there is, of course, nothing to be said. If the result of introducing labour-saving machinery, when all factors are taken into account, is to increase and not to diminish the real costs of production, the interests of labour and of the community as a whole will be adversely affected. It seems probable that not a little of the modern reaction against the orthodox argument is really attributable to the fact that much of the mechanization of recent years has been uneconomic.

H. OTHER FACTORS MAKING FOR INSTABILITY

41. It is not the purpose of this memorandum to offer a systematic account of the causes of the present world depression. None the less, it seems desirable, if the main issue is to be viewed in proper perspective, to call attention to certain other factors which have made in the last decade for a high degree of economic instability. Prominent among these is the spread of the habit of speculation in

the stock markets among large sections of the community, particularly in the United States. The assumption that underlies the orthodox argument and also most monetary analysis is that individuals devote to the purchase of goods and services their incomes less a certain proportion which they save. But as regards large numbers of well-to-do persons in the United States, this way of looking at things is rapidly ceasing to correspond to the reality. Capital profits may go to swell the volume of expenditure in years of rising stock values, while when the tide turns round on the stock markets, expenditure may be curtailed as the result of capital losses far more than the reduction of income, in the ordinary sense of the term, warrants. It is suggested that an important part of the explanation of the special severity of the depression in the United States lies in the exceptional degree in which the habit of stock market speculation has spread in that country. But in Great Britain too the distinction between capital and income has lost much of the precision and sanctity which formerly attached to it, and this change undoubtedly makes for a liability to more extreme trade fluctuations.

42. The extraordinary fluctuations in the volume of foreign lending were another factor which made for instability in the post-war period. For some years the American investing public contributed largely, by means of loans which were often essentially uneconomic and which reached enormous aggregate figures, to sustain the purchasing power of the peoples of Central Europe and Central and South America at an artificially high level. Meanwhile the American investors regarded the interest on these loans as part of their spendable incomes. Later the flow of foreign lending ceased and gave place to an attempt to recall much of the money which had been lent. The result was to reduce the purchasing power both of the borrowing countries, and, by reason of the defaults which ensued, of the American public.

43. That these factors have played a large part in the economic story of recent years is, of course, generally recognized; but other peculiar circumstances of the post-war period have perhaps prevented us from appreciating fully how important this part has been. If the present abnormally severe depression is to be attributed mainly or largely to the factors described in the two preceding paragraphs, it would seem natural to expect that the depression would have been preceded by a boom of correspondingly exceptional extravagance. Yet, taking the world as a whole, such a

description cannot reasonably be applied to the conditions of the years 1924–9. Price levels, after all, remained fairly steady over this period.

44. The true explanation, it is suggested, is that this period was governed by the co-existence of superficial inflationary influences, such as have been indicated, with underlying deflationary conditions. These underlying deflationary conditions had their roots in the distorted balance of international payments, arising from the war, from reparations and war debts, &c. For a time the two sets of forces were fairly evenly balanced, the former predominating somewhat taking the world as a whole. But the superficial inflationary influences were in their very nature ephemeral and transient and subject to inevitable recoil. In 1929 the recoil came, and the weight of the superficial influences which had now become deflationary was added to that of the underlying deflationary factors. This, it is suggested, was the reason why a comparatively moderate type of boom was followed by a depression of unprecedented severity and range.

45. If this analysis is correct, it may well be the case that the forces of increased productivity, even in the environment of a numerically contracting market, have not contributed very much to post-war economic instability. After all, there is no fundamental reason why a need to shift productive resources from some industries to others should give rise to a trade depression. During the war, when aggregate demand was swollen by inflationary finance, an immense transference of productive resources was effected under conditions resembling boom rather than depression. If, on the other hand, we must expect in future large fluctuations in aggregate demand, in accordance with whether the stock markets have been moving upwards or downwards, it will be extremely difficult to maintain a reasonable measure of economic stability. While the large fluctuations in the volume of foreign lending may perhaps be regarded as an essentially transient phenomenon, part of the aftermath of the war, not likely to recur, it is less easy to be confident that this will hold true of the modern blurring of the distinction between capital and income. In this, therefore, rather than in technological progress, the chief menace to future economic stability would seem to lie.

I. CONCLUSION

46. The conclusions which emerge from this memorandum may be summarized as follows:

(i) The orthodox theory that improvements in productive methods work in the long run to the advantage rather than to the detriment of labour remains in all essentials true and applicable to modern conditions.

(ii) There is no substance in the objection that the character of mechanization has changed in modern times from a type which was mainly complementary to labour to a type which is mainly competitive with it.

(iii) An excessive expansion of certain forms of agricultural production probably contributed something to cause the present depression and to accentuate its severity. But the common allegation that an 'agricultural revolution' is in progress comparable with the 'industrial revolution' of the past two centuries contains only a small element of truth, which is quite insufficient to impair the validity of the orthodox theory.

(iv) The environment in which increasing productivity operates today has, however, been materially changed by the lower birthrates of advanced industrial countries, and the decline in the volume of international trade. These two developments have gone far to substitute a numerically stationary or contracting market for a numerically expanding one. In this altered environment, technological progress is likely to entail a much larger element of wastage, represented by redundant plant and a surplus of labour attaching to particular industries, than it used to do. It may also entail a greater liability to severe trade fluctuations.

(v) But future economic stability is menaced more seriously by other new tendencies, notably the spread of the habit of speculative investment.

(vi) Mechanization is, of course, only advantageous in so far as it effects a net economy in the costs of production, including a fair return on the capital expended. When it is carried beyond this point, either from miscalculation or from dogmatic principle, its results are harmful.

PART III

All Souls College

1932–9

1

DO WE WANT PUBLIC WORKS?[1]

LET me begin with a few remarks designed to avoid misapprehensions. Expenditure on public works, if the phrase is interpreted widely, must necessarily run into much higher figures nowadays than it used to do before the war. The tendency which is constantly at work to enlarge the economic functions of the State, together with certain fundamental technical changes, makes that inevitable. Road transport, for instance, has taken the place of railways as the expanding form of internal transport, and roads are built by public authorities, whereas railways used to be built by private enterprise. Similarly, electrical power is taking the place of steam power, and we have entrusted the business of the generation of electricity to a public board. The trend of social policy tells in the same direction. In the post-war period the State has concerned itself with encouraging by means of subsidies the provision of houses and it still continues to do so as regards slum clearance. A substantial volume of capital expenditure under the control of public or quasi-public authorities is an inevitable feature of the discharge by the State of these various economic functions, and of course there is always room for differences of opinion as to how far that expenditure should be carried in each particular sphere of activity on the merits of the particular case. Some people will say that our expenditure on roads in the post-war period has been grossly excessive and extravagant, while others maintain that it is inadequate merely from the standpoint of traffic requirements. Housing policy, again,

[1] Oxford Political Economy Club, 11 May 1935.

is a large controversial subject. Now so far as possible I want to avoid discussing questions of this sort. When I ask 'Do we want public works?' I do not mean to ask how far public works are likely to be desirable on their intrinsic merits. At various times during recent years a policy of forcing the pace of public-works expenditure has been advocated with the object of diminishing unemployment and giving a general stimulus to economic activity. This policy is widely advocated on these grounds at the present time, and this represents the issue which I wish to discuss tonight. There are really two questions involved: the first, under what conditions is a policy of this kind likely to be helpful, and appropriate, and the second, do these conditions exist in Great Britain at the present time?

Under what conditions then may a public-works policy designed to stimulate economic activity be appropriate and wise? There are various very different possibilities which it is necessary to consider. Public works may be advocated as a short-term remedy for a temporary period of depression. They may be advocated, that is to say, as a means of evening out the trade cycle, as a sort of tap which you turn on when trade is bad and turn off when it is comparatively good. That is the first possibility. Secondly, they may be advocated as a means of facilitating a large readjustment of the national economy. Great Britain, for example, has been confronted since the war with a serious problem of readjustment arising from the decline of her old-established exporting industries. Many of these industries are highly localized in character, so that we have to deal with the very difficult problems of surplus miners, surplus cotton operatives, and surplus shipbuilders. It is clear that if full employment is ever to be restored in Great Britain, it must be on the basis of a new equilibrium in which internal trade plays a larger part and external trade a smaller part than it used to do. Similarly it looks as though full employment can only be restored in the United States on the basis of a new equilibrium in which a diminished part is played by the production of agricultural produce for export markets. Now it can be argued that an active public-works policy might be of assistance in facilitating large readjustments of this character. If nothing is done, the argument runs, the depression in the groups of industry on which adversity has fallen may react so prejudicially on the economic life of the country as a whole as to create a prolonged general deflationary *malaise* which will serve to hold back the development of those branches of activity which are capable of expansion. Public works may be useful in preventing this, in substituting a prevailingly upward trend for a prevailingly deflationary trend, and thus in creating an environment in which the task of transfer can be better accomplished. That is the second argument, and you will note that it implies a public-works programme extending over a longer period of years than that implied by the trade-cycle tap idea, but still only for a limited period. It envisages using public works during a period of transition which may be long-drawn out but which it is hoped will sooner or later have an end.

But there is a third possible argument to be considered. A large-scale expenditure on public works may be advocated as a permanent policy to check a chronic tendency to disequilibrium. The growth of productive power, this argument runs, is constantly increasing the ability to save. The investment outlets for savings which are provided by ordinary industry and economic enterprise are inadequate to carry off this large annual volume of savings, and they are likely to be reduced in future by various factors such as the change from increasing populations to stationary populations and later on to declining populations. There arises accordingly the danger of a chronic tendency for savings to exceed investment (I know my terminology on this point is out of date): a tendency stronger (this is essential to the argument) than can be controlled by a normal corrective influence of a fall in the rate of interest. A large expenditure on public works may accordingly be necessary year after year indefinitely, and perhaps on an increasing scale, year by year, in order to provide investment outlets large enough to absorb the potential savings. Otherwise, the argument concludes, the aggregate demand for goods and services will always fall short of our powers of production, and unemployment and depression will be chronic.

We have then these three possible grounds on which public works can be advocated as a means of stimulating economic activity. As a short-term policy, as a trade-cycle tap; as an intermediate-term policy as grease for the wheels of transfer; and as a permanent policy as a sink for unwanted savings. In the post-war period they have in fact been advocated on all these grounds, but the emphasis has gradually shifted from the first argument to the second and from the second to the third. Immediately after the war, in the depression that began in 1920, the first was the only argument applied. There was then a serious depression which everyone hoped would speedily pass away. Now, it was said, was the time to press forward with the utmost possible energy with the construction of the roads and other public works which had been neglected during the war. In the years just before the great slump of 1929, the second argument, the transitional transfer argument, predominated. It is only in the last few years that the suggestion has been heard that large-scale public works may be desirable as a public policy, and this argument is still, I think, mainly confined to academic circles. It seems to me important to distinguish rather sharply between these different possible objectives of public-works policy, because they may be largely irreconcilable with one another. If you are using a public-works policy for either the second or the third of the purposes I have enumerated, you cannot use it as a trade-cycle tap as well. It is of the essence of the trade-cycle tap idea that during a comparatively good period you hold public works back as far as their actual execution is concerned, you hoard them up, as it were, in order to have something to throw in when the depression comes. But clearly you will not have anything additional to throw in if you are getting on with public works as fast as you know how all the time. The objective and the contemplated duration of the programme are always relevant to the question of the way in which it is proper to finance it, or at least to the claims that can legitimately be made as to the influence of the programme in increasing effective purchasing power. If you use public works as a trade-cycle tap you can not only borrow legitimately the whole of the money required to finance them, but you can fairly claim that virtually the whole of the additional money expended on them during the depression serves to increase effective purchasing power during that period. If, on the other hand, you are pressing year after year indefinitely a large programme of unremunerative public works, I am not sure that it is so legitimate to finance them in a way which will throw the burden of the works in the earlier years on the Budgets of later years, and in any case, apart from the pursuit of frankly inflationary methods of finance, sooner or later the Budget will have to carry the burden so that the purchasing power of the consuming public will be reduced to the extent that the works are unremunerative.

With those general observations in mind I turn to consider the three different possible objectives separately. The idea of using public works as a trade-cycle tap is a very old one which goes back to the days of the pre-war Poor Law Commission, and was first, I think, put forward by Professor Bowley. In principle the idea is uncontroversial and unobjectionable. But in practice I think that experience has shown that the idea is barren. Regarded as a tap public works are a most unwieldy and inefficient instrument. The extent to which you can hold them back in the comparatively good years is extremely limited. If they are intrinsically desirable, public works are required to meet some real need, and it is seldom possible to insist that this need must remain unsatisfied on trade-cycle grounds at a time when even though trade may be comparatively good, there is probably a considerable amount of unemployment. If it is difficult to hold them back in comparatively good years, the pace at which they can be improvised in the bad years in anticipation of future needs is also very difficult. It must always be remembered in this connexion that there are very few forms of public works which are under the direct control of the central Government. Most public works are in the hands of other authorities, and all that the central Government can do is to bribe and to harry them, possibly with opposite results from those which they desire. Moreover, apart from armaments, which can be ordered as it were in gross, and which therefore represent the one form of public works which is really susceptible to quick acceleration, public works represent essentially detailed transactions, each of which is related to some particular site which has to be acquired and to some particular purpose which has to be considered on its merits. There is, therefore, inevitably an immense time-lag between preparation and execution which tends to be longer the more important and desirable the public work in question is. As a trade-cycle tap, I am frankly disillusioned with public works from the practical standpoint, and in so far as we need a tap I think we should do better to look in other directions, to that, for example, of restoring the system under which unemployment benefit used to be financed, or was intended to be financed. Under this system the idea was that the Unemployment Fund accumulated surpluses during the good years which it dissipated during bad years, and in practice at all events it accumulated debt during the bad years at an altogether larger rate than that at which it accumulated surpluses during good years. These fluctuations were a far more powerful instrument in equalizing effective purchasing power over the trade cycle than public works had ever been, or could, I think, ever be.

But before passing from the trade-cycle tap idea, I wish to put my second question. From the standpoint of evening out the trade cycle, is this a time at which large-scale public works would be appropriate? To that question I think the answer is emphatically no. So far as the trade cycle is concerned, we have already reached a comparatively good phase. Our present unemployment is mainly a matter of the depression of our export trade: our internal trade activity has already reached a high level, and is continuing to increase at a very satisfactory rate. Moreover, the proportion of constructional activity to activity in the production of consumable goods is already, I think, very nearly as high as is consistent with a healthy state of affairs. One of the main features of the trade cycle on its industrial side is, of course, the large fluctuations that occur in the relation between constructional activity and the production of consumable goods, and this relation is one of the main criteria which we should apply in considering whether any given state of trade is approximating towards conditions of boom which are likely to be followed by a reaction. From this standpoint I do not say that the position is dangerous at present: I do not think it is. But the volume of constructional activity is at any rate increasing quite fast enough and public works are, of course, in essence a way of stimulating constructional activity. More shortly, public works cannot hope to improve our export trade, and there is nothing to be said just now for forcing the pace of the internal trade recovery which is quite satisfactory as matters stand. From the trade-cycle standpoint, therefore, there is nothing to be said for large-scale public works at the present moment.

I leave the second possible objective on one side for the moment and pass to the third, the idea of using public works as a sink for unwanted savings. The questions which arise in this connexion are very interesting. Personally I think it is true that in future, against a background of international peace, we shall have a lower demand curve for savings than we used to have—a lower demand, that is to say, at any given rate of interest, and that on the other hand the ability to save will tend to increase. And if this is true it follows that conditions of equilibrium will require a lower rate of interest than we used to have and possibly a lower rate than prevails today, but I am not convinced that the influence of a lower rate of interest will be insufficient to secure equilibrium. Of course one of the effects of a lower rate of interest will be that it will make a difference to the volume of public works which are intrinsically desirable. If it is a question, let us say, to take as colourless an example as possible, of building a new town hall in some municipality, it becomes more reasonable, regarding the matter from an ordinary conservative financial standpoint, to build a town hall, or to build a comparatively expensive and elaborate town hall, if the rate of interest is $2\frac{1}{2}$ per cent. than if it is 5 per cent. In that sense, therefore, and to that extent a permanent increase in the annual rate of public-works expenditure is an appropriate corollary of such a change in the conditions of the capital market as I have been discussing. But to secure this result there is no need to advocate public-works expenditure as a special policy. It will come about more or less naturally and if the proposition is pushed further than this and it is argued that we shall need public works which may not be justified on their intrinsic merits on a large scale and as a more or less permanent policy in order to absorb surplus savings for which there will be no economic use, I feel a profound distaste for it. I cannot regard it as a means of securing equilibrium at all. It amounts rather to saying that we can never hope to secure equilibrium by any means and we must deliberately waste a certain proportion of our savings every year. That is the counsel of despair which I am not ready to accept. I am not prepared to admit, as I have said, that the natural corrective of a lower rate of interest will not suffice to restore equilibrium if it is disturbed, and if this will not suffice then the sensible course in my judgement would be to take steps to check the excessive supply of savings by appropriate taxation or other means, a task which it is absurd to regard as one of insuperable difficulty.

But again under this head I wish to put my second question. Do the possibilities which I have been discussing of a change in the relationship between savings and investment strengthen the case for pressing on with public works at the present time? And again I answer certainly not. I agree as I have already indicated that the demand curve for savings, if we succeed in avoiding war or extravagant arms expenditure, is likely to be lower in the future than it has been in the past. I take this view for two reasons, which are to some extent connected. The first is that I think we have come to the end of the process of developing new continents overseas and opening up new countries to international trade which used to provide large outlets for international investment. My second reason is that I think the demand for capital at home will be reduced in various ways by the substitution of a stationary population for a rapidly expanding one. Now the former of these two influences is already in full operation. International investment can hardly be much lower than it is at the present time; but the latter influence has not really begun to operate. Take housing, which represents in itself a large part of the total demand for capital at home. The demand for new houses is, speaking broadly, a function of the number of new households and the number of new households is a function of the number of births a generation ago. Now a generation ago the number of births in Great Britain was at about its maximum, so that we still have today about the maximum number of new couples getting married and settling down and needing houses. This, I am convinced, is one of the factors which underlies the building boom that we have at the present time. But in another ten years or twenty years the number of new households will not be increasing but rather diminishing, and though, of course, there will still be a demand for new houses, in so far as housing standards rise or the geographical distribution of the population changes, I think it is very difficult to imagine that we can retain a volume of house-building activity anything like as great as we have now. Thus we have in any case before us the probability that our building industry will in another ten or twenty years find itself in a condition of surplus capacity and redundant labour, and this supplies an argument against deliberately swelling its capacity still further today by a large programme of State subsidies to housing. From the standpoint of economic equilibrium, as distinct from housing needs, we want to keep our State programmes for the time when ordinary private house-building activity falls off. Much the same thing applies to other forms of constructional activity. I have already referred to armaments which from the economic standpoint are simply a form of public works. We are likely to have in any case in the next few years a considerable volume of expenditure on armaments which will help to keep the constructional industries busy. It may be that long-run equilibrium will require a reduction in the volume of constructional activity relatively to the production of consumable goods, and if so we do not want to go out of our way to inflate constructional activity at the present time.

I turn accordingly to the second possible objective of a public-works policy, the intermediate term purpose of facilitating the solution of the transfer problem. This seems to me to supply by far the strongest and most cogent argument that can be put forward for a public-works policy in Great Britain. We have before us beyond any reasonable doubt a very formidable problem of adjustment. Our experience in the post-war decade before 1929 shows that the problem is capable of solution, but at the same time how formidable it is. We did in fact make considerable progress in those years in absorbing miners in other occupations, but a very large number of miners remained unemployed when the slump came. The slump has served to accentuate the difficulties of our export industries, and it is now unlikely, I think, that we shall restore our export trade even to the unsatisfactory level of 1929. The scale of our problem of transfer has in short been enlarged, and it is this problem rather than problems of the adequacy of purchasing power which represents the central economic problem for Great Britain. There is no doubt, I think, that an environment of prevailingly active trade makes the transfer problem easier to solve. That, as it seems to me, is one of the great morals of the economic experience of the war. From the economic standpoint the war was a gigantic boom: demand greatly exceeded supply in by far the greater number of occupations, and accordingly it was possible comparatively quickly and smoothly to effect a tremendous readjustment of economic activity, a large-scale transfer of work-people from one set of occupations to another, and though it would be rash today to attempt to create conditions of boom, I think in the interests of the transfer problem we should be wise to give the benefit of the doubt in that direction at the present time. We shall make much more headway in absorbing people from the distressed areas in the ordinary economic life of the community if demand is straining at supply than if the relationship is the other way round. In so far, therefore, as an active public-works policy pursued over a considerable though limited period of years would serve to create prevailingly active trade conditions, that represents a very substantial argument for pursuing such a policy. It is not necessarily a fatal objection that if the volume of public works is later diminished there will be a correspondingly depressing influence, for by that time, if the problem of transfer has been solved, the ordinary economic system may be stronger to hold its own.

But it is necessary to take account of the adverse considerations that I have mentioned earlier, namely that from the trade-cycle standpoint this would be a bad time to press forward with public works, and that construction activity will probably play a smaller part in our industrial life under conditions of equilibrium in future. The former consideration is a conclusive objection, I think, to forcing the pace of public works at the present moment. The latter consideration makes it desirable to be moderate in the extent to which we attempt to use public works in the interests of transfer over the next ten years. My broad conclusion, therefore, is as follows: that the transfer argument is strong enough to justify a policy of fairly considerable public works over the next ten years, though the present is not a time at which it would be appropriate to launch a new forward move. But that it would be unwise to rely mainly upon public works for our transfer purpose. As grease for the wheels of transfer I would look in the main in another direction, in a direction which in my judgement would harmonize more with other requirements of the economic situation, namely that of endeavouring to increase consumption. In so far as we can afford to place burdens on the Budget, I would rather impose them to finance a new move forward in the policy of social services designed to increase the consumption of the necessaries of life, and of foodstuffs in particular, than the financing of unremunerative public works for which there is only a very dubious case on their intrinsic merits. But that is another very long story into which I must not attempt to enter.

2

MR. KEYNES'S THEORIES[1]

To criticize the works of others is always an ungracious and usually a barren and unprofitable undertaking; and I have a special personal reluctance to criticize the works of Mr. Keynes. I have been closely associated with him in various capacities over a period of many years, and I owe him much. As an undergraduate and young don at Cambridge I derived an immense benefit, such as I am sure many undergraduates and young dons at Cambridge must still derive, from his intellectual eagerness and zest and above all from the appreciativeness and encouragement which he was always ready to extend to the immature. It seems a poor return to read such a very *un*appreciative paper as I'm afraid this must be.

But Mr. Keynes, by his latest book,[2] has made it impossible for anyone who wishes to do serious work in the field of economics, or who is concerned for the future of economics as a subject of study, and who disagrees with him as fundamentally as I do, to refrain from criticizing him. There is, of course, much in his book which is of value, much, for example, which is of real assistance towards the understanding of a severe slump which is complicated by a 'crisis of confidence', or which at least would be of real assistance if it were presented in a form appropriate to this limited purpose. But Mr. Keynes is not content with any such limited purpose. He invites the world to throw upon the scrap-heap a large part of the orthodox economic theory in which I still believe, to discard the methods of analysis which I intend to continue to employ, and to substitute a new theoretical system of his own which in my opinion asserts what is false and denies what is true, and is likely to cause an immense amount of intellectual confusion. His prestige is such that it is impossible just to ignore him and to proceed as though his book had not been written. For those of us who cannot accept what he says, it is necessary to combat what he says; and in the interest of economics I personally feel bound to combat what he says to the utmost of my power. I proceed, therefore, to the task of criticism with no

---

[1] Marshall Society, Cambridge, 2 May 1936.
[2] *A General Theory of Money, Interest and Employment* (London, 1936).

M

further introductory word beyond this, that if my language appears at any point unnecessarily polemical or even impolite, the impolitenesses are to be explained in the same way as the many that occur in Mr. Keynes's book. They are prompted, that is to say, by a desire for argumentative clarity and emphasis, and are not directed against him personally.

The central thesis of Mr. Keynes's book is that in the ordinary working of the economic system there is a chronic and general deficiency of effective demand, and that in this is to be found the main explanation of unemployment. It is of the essence of his case that the deficiency of effective demand is chronic and general. He is emphatic that it is not limited to periods of trade depression; he asserts that demand is usually deficient even in times of boom. He makes it equally clear that this deficiency is not limited to the special circumstances of our own country or of our own times, but existed in some degree even in the nineteenth century. He appears indeed to argue that there is no reason why the demand for labour should bear any relation to the available supply; and he pours scorn on the suggestion that there are natural forces which tend to establish such a relationship. Now it is remarkable that though this is Mr. Keynes's central theme, he makes no attempt whatever in his book to examine the actual facts of unemployment, or to analyse the various factors that contribute to it. He merely brushes on one side as 'frictional unemployment' those many varieties and forms which clearly spring from something else than a general deficiency of effective demand. He does not stop to consider whether unemployment of these types may not in certain circumstances be very large indeed. The impression that he conveys is that he believes that this so-called 'frictional unemployment' is always of trifling importance; and indeed, unless this is so, many of his arguments come tumbling to the ground. Yet, although the question of fact is really crucial, Mr. Keynes ignores it altogether.

His treatment entails a distortion of perspective which is so serious that I regard it as essential to start with a brief and necessarily inadequate survey of the more pertinent facts. The economic world in which we live is one of constant change. The demand for many commodities and services fluctuates from season to season, and in some cases from day to day. Work in a factory may be temporarily interrupted for a large variety of reasons, such as a breakdown of machinery, or a change-over from one variety of product to another. Even in an expanding industry there are usually to be found some firms which are losing trade to their rivals and discharging their work-people. Such ordinary fluctuations, interruptions, and shiftings of demand necessarily give rise even when trade is good to a considerable amount of unemployment. There is also, of course, on the side of supply a small margin of work-people of such poor industrial quality or such unsatisfactory character that no employer would willingly engage them, and a small margin possibly who do not wish to be employed. Items such as these, each of them individually small, account between them for a fairly considerable unemployment percentage, which we may call the percentage of 'minimum unemployment'. This percentage is certainly much higher under modern conditions of factory management and unemployment benefit than it used to be. Employers nowadays, faced with a temporary slackness of demand or interruption of work, perhaps in a particular department, do not hesitate to discharge or 'stop temporarily' work-people whom in former days they would have made shift to keep employed upon odd jobs. It will be observed that this doesn't necessarily mean a greater waste of productive power. The change means largely that what was formerly an imperfect utilization of labour within the factory or business is now translated into recorded unemployment outside it; and the greater the attention that is paid to the elimination of waste in industrial management the larger must we expect such unemployment to become. The system of unemployment relief is also of obvious importance in the same connexion. When unemployment insurance is extended to agriculture we must expect to find a large amount of seasonal unemployment among agricultural labourers. Thus the amount of recorded minimum unemployment depends *inter alia* on the technique of business management and the system of unemployment relief. Under the conditions which prevail in Great Britain today in those respects, I do not think that minimum unemployment can be estimated at less than 6 per cent. or three-quarters of a million persons for the country as a whole. Over about half the country, unemployment is not greatly in excess of this minimum level at the present time.

Unemployment of this kind does not greatly matter. I pass to a type of unemployment which matters very much indeed. The demand for the products of a whole industry, or for the products of the whole of an industry that is situated in a particular region or a particular country, may undergo a permanent decline. Alternatively the progress of invention and technical improvement may greatly reduce the number of work-people required to produce a given quantity of some commodity, and the demand for that commodity may fail to increase proportionately. In either case, employment in the industries in question will decline permanently; a portion of their work-people will be discharged and will remain permanently unemployed, except in so far as it is possible to transfer them to other industries. Now the transference of work-people from one industry to another is a difficult process, particularly if their skill is highly specialized, still more if they are middle-aged or elderly persons, and most of all if the industries which have discharged them are highly localized industries, concentrated in particular areas. Indeed when the industries in which the volume of employment is permanently curtailed are both important and highly localized, so that they represent a dominating factor in the economic life of the districts in which they are situated, the problem that ensues is formidable in the extreme. I have used general and hypothetical language; but, of course, this explains a large part of the heavy unemployment which has prevailed in Great Britain since the war. The surplus of labour attaching to the coal-mines, to the cotton industry, and to other industries such as shipbuilding, coupled with the reactions which the depression of these industries exerts on the economic life of the districts in which they are situated, is indeed today once more the real crux of the problem of unemployment in this country.

To this large and difficult problem of the adjustment of the supply of labour to a demand which has shifted its direction, Mr. Keynes pays no recognition whatever in his book. Or the only sentence in which it may perhaps be argued that he has it in mind is that in which he refers 'to the fact that the change-over from one employment to another cannot be effected without delay, so that there will always exist in a non-static society a proportion of resources unemployed between jobs'. Such is the light-hearted spirit in which Mr. Keynes disposes of the difficulty of absorbing an unemployed coal-miner of fifty in the Rhondda Valley, or a female cotton operative living as a married woman in Blackburn, in the manufacture of motor-cars or wireless sets.

It is no answer to this criticism to say that Mr. Keynes's book is a General Theory and that it is unreasonable therefore to expect him to consider the special facts of post-war unemployment in Great Britain. The plausibility of many of his sweeping assertions depends largely upon the fact that unemployment has been heavy in Great Britain since the war. Moreover, the problem which I have indicated is of a general character. It is true that the special circumstances of our post-war economic life, notably our loss of export trade and the exceptionally localized nature of the industries upon which that loss has chiefly fallen, have made the transfer problem peculiarly important and peculiarly difficult. But in some degree the problem is always there in a changing economic world; and its practical importance is likely to remain much greater throughout the twentieth century than it was in the nineteenth. The change in the population outlook is of crucial importance in this connexion. Rapid technological progress makes it virtually inevitable that it will become necessary to effect a radical alteration from time to time in the proportions in which the working population is distributed between different industries. Where the working population is growing rapidly, it is possible to effect a large redistribution of this character, without any transference of actual work-people, merely by directing the new recruits towards the more rapidly expanding industries. And that, speaking broadly, was what happened in the nineteenth century. But with a stationary working population, such a redistribution must entail a large contraction of employment in certain industries; and transfer problems are likely to prove in consequence more numerous and more formidable. In short, it was only the abnormally rapid growth of population in the nineteenth century which served to obscure the importance which must normally attach to transfer problems in a changing economic world. A theory of employment which ignores this class of problem or implies that it does not matter is, I submit, grossly out of focus.

Let me, for the sake of simplicity, give the name 'transfer unemployment' to unemployment which arises from this class of cause, and for which transfer to other industries or to other districts is often the only remedy. The normal course of trade is that which is commonly called the trade cycle, an alternation between periods of increasing activity and periods of depression. The periods of depression entail a further element of unemployment often called cyclical unemployment, which is large in proportion as the fluctuations of trade activity are severe. I suggest that there is no evidence whatever that there is any unemployment which does not fall under one or other of the three categories I have indicated, namely minimum unemployment, transfer unemployment, and cyclical unemployment. The last-named, cyclical unemployment, may certainly be regarded as an expression of a deficiency of effective demand, but not of a chronic deficiency; and the obvious remedy is greater steadiness of trade conditions. What of the other two categories?

The unemployment that I have called transfer unemployment is not, of course, an irreducible element. Death and retirement on the one hand, and the transfer of the comparatively young on the other gradually make an impression on it. The trouble is that the process is apt to be slow, and there is always the danger, a danger which exists in Great Britain at the present time, that before one transfer problem has been completely solved, another will make its appearance. Now undoubtedly a strong condition of effective demand helps to promote the process of transfer; and I personally agree that it should be an important objective of policy to keep effective demand strong, provided it is not made so strong relatively to existing supply as to cause prices to rise sharply or seriously.

But this proviso is in my judgement essential. Actually effective demand grows steadily during a period of increasing trade activity, and as a rule such a period culminates in what is called a boom, during which profits rule very high and prices and wage rates rise. Such conditions help temporarily to reduce the level of unemployment, since when profits are abnormally high, employers become more ready to engage work-people who for their purposes are comparatively inefficient. Unfortunately there are good reasons for believing that conditions of boom comprising inflated profits and rising prices and wages inevitably lead on to a crisis followed by a depression. I need mention only one of these reasons, which has an important bearing on the more theoretical parts of Mr. Keynes's book. Interest rates invariably rise during a boom. So long as prices continue to rise, the higher interest rates may not matter. But, unless the rise of prices is to be allowed to continue indefinitely, with a gathering momentum, to the point of a currency débâcle, it must be checked sooner or later, and when it is checked, a depression is bound to ensue. I do not believe therefore that the development of boom conditions is likely to be helpful in the long run to the reduction of unemployment.

Now what is Mr. Keynes's position upon this question? It seems to me incoherent in the extreme. The condition of effective demand that prevails in an ordinary boom is not nearly strong enough to satisfy him. He is not content to stop short of what he calls 'full employment'. The ordinary boom, he insists, does not give us 'full employment', and as he defines the term that is probably true. For, as I understand him, he would deny that there is full employment so long as there are any workers unemployed whom some employers might be induced to employ if there were a further intensification of effective demand, accompanied by a further inflation of profits. In any case he advocates creating a boom stronger and more prolonged than almost any of which we have had experience. Yet he recognizes that it is common enough in the booms that we do have, in the 'quasi-booms' as he calls them, for effective demand to prove strong enough to cause prices and wage rates to rise, often very substantially. At the same time, he advocates stability of prices. I cannot reconcile those different propositions. Possibly the explanation is that the stability of prices is only to begin after the full employment has first been secured. In that case, I ask two questions. First, what degree of inflation are we to contemplate as a preliminary before this goal is reached? Secondly, how would it be possible to bring the inflationary process to an end without causing a big reaction? Remember that during the inflation the expectation of abnormally high profits has induced employers to engage many work-people who are of low efficiency for their purposes. As soon as prices cease to rise the expectation of abnormally high profits disappears and the work-people in question cease to be worth their pay. Remember also that interest rates invariably rise during an inflation. The assumption that seems to underlie much of Mr. Keynes's argument that it is possible to stabilize employment at the top of an inflationary movement is nowhere argued or justified and is contradicted, I suggest, both by reason and by experience.

I turn to the theoretical structure of Mr. Keynes's book. I shall confine myself to what seems to me the crucial part of it, namely his treatment of the rate of interest, and of savings and investment. Mr. Keynes dismisses with scorn the orthodox theory that the rate of interest is determined by the relation between the demand for and the supply of savings. He calls this 'a nonsense theory', and he appears to deny that either the disposition of the community towards thrift or extravagance or the opportunities that exist for the investment of capital exert any influence on the rate of interest. His own theory makes the rate of interest depend upon two factors, and two factors alone, the first what he terms the state of liquidity preference, and the second the quantity of money.

Now in relation to the special problem of securing lower interest rates in a severe depression in a wealthy country, the factors to which Mr. Keynes calls attention are certainly factors of great practical importance. When you are in the depths of a depression, although a fall in interest rates may be an essential condition of recovery, you do not want people to save more, you rather want them to spend more. You do not want them to save more, because, as I should put it, it is probable that you already have a tendency for savings to exceed investment which is quite strong enough, unless it is overridden by other influences, to give you the lower interest rates that you require. But the fall in interest rates may be obstructed by other influences, notably by a development of what Mr. Keynes terms a preference for liquidity, or what is more commonly referred to as a tendency to hoard. It is of vital importance to overcome any such tendency to hoard. For this purpose it is necessary, as Mr. Keynes recognizes, to avoid any policies that are likely to upset confidence. But it is also true that an increase in the quantity of money made available by the central bank will help to counteract the effects of a tendency to hoard and thus to make possible the fall in interest rates which you want. With all this I cordially agree, though I would add that this does not mean that the more fundamental factors of the demand for and the supply of savings cease to operate during a depression, nor that Mr. Keynes's theory gives us an adequate explanation of short-period movements in interest rates.

But Mr. Keynes is not content to emphasize that *changes* in the quantity of money exert an important temporary influence on interest rates. He asserts a fundamental connexion between the quantity of money and the rate of interest as one of the central features of his system of analysis; and he enunciates this proposition with an air of mathematical precision, telling us that $M = L(r)$. Now if we are to talk of 'nonsense theories' I know of none to which the phrase can be more fitly applied than this. During and immediately following the war, we in Great Britain experienced a considerable inflation which has left us with a materially greater quantity of money (both currency notes and bank deposits) than we had before. Is that fact in any way helpful to the establishment of a low rate of interest at the present time? Suppose that our war-time inflation had been considerably larger and had left us with a quantity of money five or ten times as large as that which we actually have: would the rate of interest be any lower today on that account? In France the war and post-war inflation was in fact carried to much further lengths than here: does that help to give the French a lower rate of interest than our own? In Germany the inflation was carried to much greater lengths still, so that the quantity of money in terms of pre-war marks is still prodigious. Has that fact the smallest helpful effect on the rate of interest that rules in Germany today?

It is impossible to suppose that Mr. Keynes or any of his school would attempt to give an affirmative answer to any of these questions. What would be said, I suppose, is that in applying Mr. Keynes's formula to the long period, the quantity of money should be measured in terms of what he calls wage units. A wage unit in Mr. Keynes's terminology is the money wage of a unit of labour. It is, of course, a normal feature of an inflation that prices, money wage rates, and money incomes generally increase along with the quantity of money. Indeed the increase in the former sometimes runs ahead of the increase in the latter, so that even a colossal inflation may leave the quantity of money as reckoned in terms of wage units unchanged and may possibly even reduce it. Now I wonder how many of Mr. Keynes's readers, those at least who are unassisted by verbal explanations, would appreciate this point. When the quantity of money is first introduced into the story, there is no suggestion that it must be measured in terms of wage units. It is not until a late stage of the argument (p. 246 is the first instance that I have been able to discover) that Mr. Keynes first expressly mentions this proviso. Nor does he then call any attention to it; we merely find if we look carefully enough that at the end of a long sentence the phrase 'measured in terms of wage units' appears. Nothing is said to indicate that this entails the paradoxical consequence that a large inflation may leave the quantity of money unchanged.

With the aid of this eccentric definition it would be possible to reconcile Mr. Keynes's formula with the facts, though only at the expense of emptying it of all content and significance. His theory would become, to adopt an expression which he uses in criticism of Professor Pigou, a purely non-causative theory of formal relationships. But obviously Mr. Keynes does not intend to put forward a theory which means nothing. On the contrary, it is clear from the whole tenor of his book that he does mean to assert a causative and enduring relationship between the quantity of money, reckoned in terms of *money*, and the rate of interest. It is indeed one of his main contentions that the rate of interest can be brought down to as low a level as is desired and kept down by increasing the quantity of money sufficiently. It is with that contention that I am primarily concerned. I say that it is in conflict with the whole body of historical evidence; no increase in the quantity of money in the past has left any enduring influence of a helpful character upon the rate of interest. Nor is this just a matter of unfortunate coincidence: there are good reasons for it. But before attempting to develop them, I must consider first the short-period aspect of the question.

I pass, therefore, to the problems of the short period. Here, as I have already said, I do not question that the factors of the quantity of money and liquidity preference are important. But do these factors give by themselves an adequate explanation of short-period fluctuations in interest rates? I apply a broad and simple test. I take the generalization relating to the movement of interest rates that is most firmly established by experience, namely that interest rates, or at least short-term interest rates, fall during a prolonged depression and rise during a boom. I ask: does Mr. Keynes's theory account satisfactorily for these phenomena? The answer comes at once: it does not account for them at all. They cannot be explained by alterations in the quantity of money issued by governments or made available by central banks; for it is by no means generally true, certainly it has not been hitherto, that the quantity of money is increased during a depression and decreased during a boom. It is true that in the depression of recent years, steps have been taken or things have happened which have increased the quantity of money in many countries. But in this respect the recent depression has been unique; whereas the tendency for interest rates to fall during a prolonged depression and to rise during a boom holds good of every boom and depression of which we have a record. It holds good, for example, of the inflationary booms of the war and post-war periods, when the quantity of money was immensely increased, and yet interest rates rose continuously. Still less can the phenomena be explained by fluctuations in the state of liquidity preference. For these tell the other way. It is Mr. Keynes's contention that during a depression you are apt to get an increased preference for liquidity which prevents interest rates from falling as soon or as much as they otherwise would. This can throw no light on why it is that interest rates *do* fall in a depression. Thus the two factors which Mr. Keynes elevates to the role of the determinants of the rate of interest completely fail to explain not only the long-period but the most striking short-period phenomena relating to interest rates.

How then are these phenomena to be explained? The explanation can only be found in one or other of two influences, or in the two together. The first is that the demand for capital arising from investment declines during a depression and increases during a boom. This is one of the factors in the orthodox theory, the influence of which upon interest rates Mr. Keynes denies. The second influence is that the demand for money, not the quantity of money but the demand for it, declines during a depression and increases during a boom. During a depression employment declines, and the sums paid out by employers week by week in wages decline correspondingly. If wage rates fall, wage payments decline still further. Employers draw smaller sums each week from the banks in actual cash. If retail prices fall, the cash required to make retail purchases also declines. Thus money, actual cash, flows back to the commercial banks; their cash position is strengthened; and, without any increase in the quantity of money in the ordinary sense, there results an abundance of money in the money market which helps to reduce interest rates. In the case of a boom the opposite phenomenon appears; prices rise, wages rise, additional cash is withdrawn from the banks, so that the money market becomes tight, even though there may be a considerable increase in the total quantity of money. Indeed, this tendency is never more pronounced than during the course of a wild inflation. An acute shortage of cash, entailing the rationing of customers and queues at the banks, was a notorious paradox of the extreme phases of the inflation in central Europe. But a tendency towards monetary stringency is a normal feature of a boom, just as a tendency towards an abundance of bank money is a normal feature of a depression. There are occasional incidental passages in his book in which Mr. Keynes refers to these facts, but he leaves them entirely out of account in formulating his theory. His theory makes the rate of interest depend solely upon liquidity preference and the quantity of money, that is to say its supply; it ignores changes in the demand for money which in the short period often override the influence of changes in the supply of money.

I return from this explanatory argument to the broad proposition that interest rates fall during a prolonged depression and rise during a boom. I have said that Mr. Keynes's theory offers no explanation of this fact. Indeed, I imagine that any reader whose only knowledge of trade movements was derived from Mr. Keynes's analysis would be surprised to discover that this is what happens. But I am inclined to go further and to suggest that Mr. Keynes himself, though of course he must be perfectly well aware of the fact, is so bemused by his own theories as to forget it during a large part of his argument. For the fact is in my judgement fatal to Mr. Keynes's main position. It is fatal to the contention to which I have already referred, that by increasing the quantity of money sufficiently you can reduce the rate of interest permanently and indeed force it down to whatever level you think desirable, subject only to the resistances that are set up by psychology and convention. If such a policy were to lead to conditions of boom, or what Mr. Keynes calls quasi-boom, an overwhelming weight of experience shows that interest rates would rise and that the largest increases in the quantity of money would fail to prevent them from rising. The same fact is equally fatal to Mr. Keynes's contention that an increase in the propensity to save will do nothing, even in the long run, to increase investment or to reduce the rate of interest, that it will merely entail increased unemployment, and that there are no natural corrective influences which would prevent that increase in unemployment from being permanent. An important corrective influence resides in the very fact that interest rates invariably fall during a severe depression.

This brings me to the final stage of my argument. Is there any defect in the orthodox theory which maintains that the rate of interest is determined by the relations between the demand for and the supply of savings? This theory must be regarded, of course, as an equilibrium theory. It purports, that is to say, to explain the forces which determine the prevailing level of the rate of interest over a long period. It has always been recognized that other factors such as changes in monetary conditions may exert an important temporary influence upon interest rates, and particularly upon short-term rates. Mr. Keynes, oddly enough, complains of this as though it indicated a fundamental inconsistency in the orthodox theory.

It has been usual to suppose [he writes (p. 182)] that an increase in the quantity of money has a tendency to reduce the rate of interest, at any rate in the first instance and in the short period. Yet no reason has been given why a change in the quantity of money should affect either the investment demand-schedule or the readiness to save out of a given income. Thus the classical school have had quite a different theory of the rate of interest in Volume I dealing with the theory of value from what they have had in Volume II dealing with the theory of money. They have seemed undisturbed by the conflict and have made no attempt, so far as I know, to build a bridge between the two theories.

But there is no inconsistency or conflict whatever. Orthodox economic analysis draws a clear and surely useful distinction between long-period and short-period problems. The actual movements of the rate of interest are determined by the relations of demand and supply in what is sometimes called the capital market. Orthodox economic theory asserts that the fundamental factors that lie behind supply and demand in the capital market are savings and investment. This does not mean that they are the only factors that are ever operative. It is indisputable that the supply side of the capital market can be influenced by changes in the quantity of money and by a large range of factors which Mr. Keynes attempts to sum up in his concept of liquidity preference. But the orthodox position is that these latter influences are necessarily transient. If they cause the rate of interest to diverge materially from the level which is appropriate to the relationship of the fundamental factors, a tendency either towards rising prices and boom or towards falling prices and depression will be set in motion; and these tendencies will entail considerable changes in the demand for money which will send the rate of interest back towards its equilibrium position. This is a perfectly clear position which involves no inconsistency and which is supported by the facts relating to the movements of interest rates in times of good and bad trade.

As a long-run proposition the orthodox theory pictures the rate of interest as determined by the intersection of a supply curve of savings with a demand curve. This is what Mr. Keynes describes as nonsense, his essential criticism being that an increase of saving would lead to a reduction of employment which would result in a diminished ability to save. The answer is that it is not at all clear that there would be any more unemployment in a community in which people save much than in a community in which they save little. I compare two communities, with the implied assumption that their economic systems are habituated to the different rates of saving, because this seems to me the fair test to apply. If we are required to suppose a sudden increase of saving in a community which has been accustomed to saving upon a smaller scale, there is a qualification to be made which applies to every proposition in long-period economic theory, namely that short-term changes may in fact produce permanent results. A sudden increase of saving, unless investment were to increase simultaneously, would undoubtedly entail a period of depression and unemployment. A prolonged period of severe unemployment necessarily impairs the industrial quality of the population; it leaves many work-people less efficient for work for the rest of their lives than they were before; and for that reason I should not care to assert that after a prolonged depression we should be likely to get back in the subsequent recovery to as low an unemployment percentage as prevailed before the depression.

But this is not really germane to the theoretical issue. The essential point is that the condition of depression and abnormal unemployment that might result from a sudden increase of savings would not be permanent. Money would accumulate at the banks, interest rates would fall, as they always do fall during a prolonged depression; nor would this be the only corrective influence. There are many others, to which Mr. Keynes refers in his chapter on the Trade Cycle. The depression would not last for ever; a process of recovery, once it has fairly begun, is cumulative. As a rule it continues, gaining a gathering momentum, until it enters the phase of a boom in which profits rule high, prices and wage rates move upwards, and interest rates rise also, and various industrial maladjustments make their appearance. If the propensity to save is permanently higher than it was, this phase will not be reached until the annual volume of investment is on a materially larger scale than formerly, while interest rates will remain lower than they were previously. On the other hand, there is no reason why this phase should be reached until the resources of production are as fully employed as they were before, subject to the practical qualification I have already mentioned.

Let me add a few remarks to prevent possible misapprehension.

I do not wish to suggest that the process of severe depression and subsequent recovery which would be likely to follow from a substantial increase in the propensity to save would be easy and innocuous. On the contrary I would emphasize that it might be very long-drawn out and might entail an appalling amount of human hardship and economic waste. A transition from a higher to a materially lower level of interest rates is always likely to be lengthy, painful, and wasteful. The fact that we have had to accomplish a transition of precisely this kind from the very high level of interest rates which were the legacy of the war to the lower level which is appropriate to peace conditions forms an important chapter in the post-war economic story, and helps, in my judgement, to explain the otherwise puzzling phenomenon that the severest depression upon record followed upon a boom so mild that judged by the criteria of price and wage movements it was hardly a boom at all. I subscribe whole-heartedly to the view that an increase of saving which gives rise to a severe depression is an extremely disastrous thing, and I consider that it should be an important aim of economic statesmanship to avert developments of this character. I hope also that no one will suppose from my remarks about the existence of corrective forces during a depression that I am an advocate of *laissez-faire*. Natural economic forces work very clumsily indeed. By all means let us endeavour to bring deliberate policy to their aid, wherever we can do so with advantage, though I would add that deliberate policy is likely to be successful in proportion as it is based on a true appreciation of the working of the natural economic forces.

But all this has nothing to do with the question of the comparative merits of Mr. Keynes's theory and the orthodox theory of interest. To prevent the essential issue being lost in a maze of disputable detail, I shall conclude my argument by applying what I have already suggested is the really fair test. Let us compare two communities, in one of which people save on the average 5 per cent. of their incomes and in the other of which they save 10 per cent. Let us assume that in all other pertinent respects the conditions of the two communities are identical, that skill, knowledge, the technical opportunities for investment are the same, that their populations increase at the same annual rate, that there are similar systems of unemployment relief, and that in both communities the quantity of money is gradually increased at the same rate sufficient to keep pace with the normal growth of production. But in community *A* people save 5 per cent. of their incomes, while in community *B* they save 10 per cent. Now Mr. Keynes contends that the level of unemployment would be far heavier in community *B* than in community *A* and that the level of incomes would consequently be much lower. I am not prepared to admit that there is any truth whatever in that contention, regarded as a general proposition; but suppose that there is a measure of truth in it. No one, I imagine, will be bold enough to assert that more than half the population of community *B*, where they save 10 per cent., will be permanently unemployed, or indeed that unemployment would average anything approaching one-half. However full, therefore, employment may be in community *A*, it is obvious that its aggregate income will be nothing like double that of community *B*; and it follows that the aggregate volume of savings will be very much less in community *A* than in community *B*. If then you are to have, I will not say equality, but any approach to equilibrium between savings and investment, it is clear that the annual volume of investment in community *A* will have to be cut down to a far lower level than that prevailing in community *B*, and, if the technical opportunities for investment are the same in the two communities, this must mean a higher, and probably a much higher, rate of interest in community *A*.

It is equally clear that if we were to change the assumptions and suppose that the propensity to save was the same in the two communities, but that in the one case there were abundant opportunities for the profitable investment of capital in new technical developments, while in the other case practically no such opportunities presented themselves, a higher rate of interest would be necessary in the former community to preserve equilibrium. Thus the orthodox theory emerges from Mr. Keynes's criticism quite unscathed, while Mr. Keynes's own assertion that the rate of interest is an independent variable, independent that is to say of the propensity to save or to consume on the one hand, and of what he terms the schedule of the marginal efficiency of capital on the other, is perhaps the most extravagantly untrue proposition that has ever been put forward as a major contribution to economic theory by any serious economic writer.

I must apologize for the length to which this paper has run. Long as it has been, it has not been sufficient to enable me to develop my argument as fully as I should have liked. I should have liked to come rather more closely to grips with the details of Mr. Keynes's argument, and to trace some of his fallacies to their source which is to be found, in my judgement, in an unfortunate and artificial definition of the term 'investment'. I should have liked to comment on Mr. Keynes's Utopian speculations and on his historical generalizations, which convey a picture of the past which is perhaps no less distorted than is his picture of the facts of present-day unemployment. I should have liked also to try to disentangle some of the elements that are true and valuable in Mr. Keynes's book from the unfortunate theories in which they are embedded. But I have had to confine myself to a purely destructive task.

3

THE SIGNIFICANCE OF THE
RATE OF INTEREST[1]

FEW economic questions are of greater interest and importance today than that of the part played by the rate of interest in the working of the economic system, and the influence exerted by changes in interest rates on trade activity. The maintenance of cheap money has been a central feature of the economic policy pursued by the British Government since 1932; and this has undoubtedly been largely responsible for the marked reduction in the general level of interest rates that has followed. The fall in interest rates has made the Government's financial task of balancing the budget materially easier. There is thus a natural and strong predisposition in official circles to believe in the importance of low interest rates and to claim that the lower rates established have been a material factor in promoting general economic recovery.

For different reasons this predisposition is shared by the majority of academic economists. Withdrawn, as he is, from close contact with the details of the economic system, the academic economist is especially interested in those forces which are at work throughout the economic system as a whole, and the importance of which appears to be fundamental. The rate of interest is a force of this character. The movement in gilt-edged interest rates from the level of $4\frac{1}{2}$ per cent. or more which prevailed until 1932 to the level of 3 per cent. or less which was established in 1935 is to the detached student of economic affairs an event of great interest and intrinsic dignity, and his mind is ready to welcome the idea that it may have played an immensely important part in ways not easy perhaps to detect in detail, in the changes that have taken place in economic activity. This inclination is strengthened by the widespread preoccupation of economic analysis in recent years with the relations between savings and investment. While economists have been divided by abstract and complex issues as to the relative importance of the forces by which the rate of interest is determined, there has been little dispute as to the importance of its consequences.

[1] *Oxford Economic Papers*, No. 1, January 1938.

That a large part of the prolonged economic *malaise* of the post-war period might be attributable to a rate of interest markedly in excess of the level required for equilibrium is a doctrine agreeable to the instincts of economists of both orthodox and heretical leanings.

Thus both official circles and academic economists have a bias in favour of propagating the view that lower interest rates have been a major factor in recovery. Nor is the business community predisposed to quarrel with it. To the industrialist or trader, who works with borrowed money, lower interest rates mean a reduction in his costs. The reduction may not strike him as particularly important; none the less he welcomes it. Banks, insurance companies, and others who lend money for interest may be adversely affected, it is true, by lower interest rates, so far as their annual income is concerned; but owing to the consequential rise in security values many of them derive a compensatory benefit in the shape of a stronger balance-sheet position. Thus, up to a point at least, most lenders are not inclined to cavil at cheaper money. The investing public also welcomes the rise in security values. Low interest rates, in short, either are or seem to be to the material advantage of the great majority of the economic community. Add to this the natural tendency of the human mind to accept *post hoc* as *propter hoc*, and it is not surprising that the idea that cheap money has been one of the chief factors in economic recovery should have been accepted by public opinion in general as an established, if somewhat mysterious, truth.

Yet beneath this impressive harmony of outward acceptance there lurks a widespread bewilderment and detailed scepticism. If the question is put 'What is the *modus operandi* by which low interest rates stimulate economic activity?' there are few who are ready to offer a coherent answer, and they include hardly anyone who is intimately acquainted with the actual working of the economic system. Consider some of the difficulties that arise. Are lower interest rates really effective in inducing business men to undertake operations that they would not otherwise have undertaken? If so, what sort of business men and what sort of operations? Will manufacturers or traders be induced to purchase additional stocks of materials? There are obvious difficulties in supposing an affirmative answer to these questions. By increasing his stocks in excess of his requirements the manufacturer or trader will incur an unnecessary expense. Lower interest rates, it is true, will make this expense less than it would otherwise have been. But there will be an avoidable expense, and the question arises why either the manufacturer or trader should deliberately incur it. He may, of course, calculate that the prices of his materials are likely to rise or that the demand for his products will increase. If so, it is this expectation of higher prices or increased sales rather than the cheaper terms of borrowing that will constitute the real inducement. Moreover, in this event it is difficult to suppose that variations in interest rates will be an important factor in the calculation. No one is ever able to estimate with precision the magnitude and degree of probability attaching to an expected rise of prices. A man may form an opinion that it is more likely than not that prices will rise by anything from 5 to 10 per cent. or more in the next few months. His opinion will seldom be more precise than that. If, on such grounds, he decides that it is wise to purchase now in excess of his normal requirements, one would expect him to come to the same conclusion even if the annual charges for a bank overdraft were 1 or 2 per cent. higher than they are.

It may be, of course, that changes in interest rates constitute one of the reasons why business men expect prices to rise or trade to improve. There is little doubt, indeed, that this is true in some degree; for there is a fairly well-recognized tradition that a low Bank Rate helps to promote a rise of prices and greater trade activity. A rise in Bank Rate to a really high figure would undoubtedly be regarded by many business men as a warning signal enjoining a policy of caution, and, conversely, reductions in Bank Rate to a low figure probably serve as an influence inducing business men in a strong financial position to regard the business outlook more hopefully. It is clear enough, therefore, that changes in Bank Rate may, and probably do, exert some influence on business activity through the channel of psychology. But two observations suggest themselves. First, it hardly seems reasonable to suppose that this influence can be of major importance. There have been times when Bank Rate has remained low for a long period before any recovery in commodity prices has ensued. Most business men are concerned, moreover, not with the general movement of prices but with the prices of certain particular commodities which they buy or sell. It is difficult to suppose that they could give a very prominent place to reductions of Bank Rate in forming their view of the prospects of the markets in which they are interested.

Secondly, whatever may be the practical importance of this influence, it leaves the essential question unanswered. Presumably the expectation that lower Bank Rate will make for better trade or higher prices rests on some rational foundation; otherwise its influence would be precarious. What, then, is the solid basis for this expectation? The essential link in the chain of cause and effect has still to be discovered.

Let us pass then to another possibility. Is it reasonable to suppose that lower interest rates may stimulate long-term capital expenditure by business men, that manufacturers, for example, may be encouraged to extend their works or introduce new and improved machinery? At first sight an affirmative answer to this question seems more plausible; but when it is closely examined rather similar difficulties arise. We may suppose a manufacturer to be considering the question as to whether he should instal some new labour-saving machine which will entail a certain saving in his wages bill for a given volume of output. The annual saving thus effected may be estimated with some precision. There is no difficulty in supposing that it may be computed so as to represent some definite percentage of the capital cost of the machine. If the machine could be expected to last for ever or for a long period, such as 20 or 30 years, there would also be no difficulty in supposing that a difference of 1 or 2 per cent. in the long-term rate of interest might turn the scales of the calculation as to whether it was worth while to introduce the machine. In fact, however, most modern labour-saving machinery has a comparatively brief period of effective life. The same progress of invention which has given rise to the machine which the manufacturer is considering may, a few years later, produce a still better machine which will effect still larger reductions in the annual wages bill. In calculating, therefore, the profitability of introducing the machine a rapid rate of obsolescence must be assumed. In other words, the machine must be expected to pay for itself over a comparatively few years; not 20 or 30 years, but 7 or perhaps 5 or perhaps 3. This, however, makes it much harder to translate the problem into terms of a calculation of annual gain and loss in which the rate of interest is likely to be a material factor. For if such a calculation is made, the allowance for obsolescence or depreciation will inevitably be a much larger item on the debit side than the charge for interest. Yet the allowance for obsolescence must necessarily be of an arbitrary rough-and-ready character, and the event may diverge from it materially in the one direction or the other. The machine which is assumed to have an effective life at 5 years may actually be retained for 7 or, on the other hand, it may become obsolete in 3. Thus a high degree of uncertainty would necessarily attach to any calculation of annual gain or loss, and it is hard to suppose that a difference in interest rates, which could only represent a small item in the calculation, could play a material part in the decision reached. It is difficult, indeed, to suppose that many manufacturers would calculate the profitability of a new machine along lines which take account of variations in the rate of interest.

A large part of a manufacturer's fixed capital may not, of course, be of a highly obsolescent character. It will represent rather buildings and fixed equipment which will usually have a long period of effective life. But if it is easier in this case to calculate with precision the annual cost represented by the capital, it is much more difficult to calculate with precision the annual return which it is likely to yield. If a manufacturer is considering whether to put up new works which will enlarge his productive capacity, his dominating question, it is natural to suppose, will be whether he is likely to be able to sell profitably the extra output of goods. This is a question which seldom lends itself to precise calculation, and it is again hard, therefore, on general grounds, to suppose that many manufacturers would pay much attention to the prevailing rate of interest in deciding to enlarge their productive capacity. There remains the possibility that a manufacturer may choose a period of low interest rates to execute capital extensions which he has decided on other grounds to undertake before very long. But here again an awkward question suggests itself. Is this consideration likely to weigh for very much in practice as compared, for example, with the level of building costs?

There are, then, serious difficulties in supposing that a change in interest rates will exert any very important influence of a direct character on the capital expenditure of the ordinary trader or manufacturer, whether upon working capital or fixed capital. There remain other classes of capital goods, in respect of which these difficulties are less formidable. There are those capital goods the demand for which comes not from manufacturers or traders, but from private individuals, i.e. durable consumers' goods, the leading instance of which is a house or other dwelling. It is comparatively easy to see how a change in the rate of interest may affect materially the demand for houses. The utility of a house to its occupier does not depend, as a rule, on any uncertainty as to the profits he can make from living in it; he can therefore estimate directly the annual value to him of a house of a certain size and quality in a particular place. On the other hand, a house lasts for a long period of years and the interest on its capital cost is not, therefore, unimportant as compared with the allowance that must be made for its depreciation. There is no difficulty, therefore, in supposing that a substantial fall in the rate of interest may give a material stimulus to house building.

There are also durable capital goods which are owned neither by manufacturers, traders, nor private consumers but by public authorities, such as the state or municipalities. Capital goods of this character comprise a vast variety of types, and they account in the aggregate for a large proportion of the accumulated capital of the community. Here, as in the case of houses, the normal life of the capital goods is so long as to make the rate of interest a major factor in computing the annual cost. Their utility may be of a type which it is hard to measure in financial terms at all; but in such cases it is usually independent of necessarily doubtful calculations as to future earning capacity. On the other hand, where the capital goods are of a commercial character and represent the capital equipment of trading services such as gas or electricity, it is usually possible to calculate the probable demand for their services with a fair degree of precision. This last consideration applies also to public-utility concerns. It is therefore possible that such concerns in considering whether to modernize their plant or enlarge their capacity might measure the expected annual yield against the cost of the capital expenditure in a way that would take account of the prevailing rate of interest. There is thus no fundamental difficulty in supposing that changes in the rate of interest may exert a considerable effect on the amount of capital expenditure undertaken by public authorities and public-utility concerns.

The broad effect of the foregoing argument is to suggest that the influence of the rate of interest on capital expenditure is far less general and all-pervasive in character than is commonly assumed in economic discussion. There are only two types of capital goods on which it is plausible to suppose that expenditure might be appreciably stimulated by a lower, or appreciably retarded by a higher, rate of interest, namely (1) durable consumers' goods, and (2) the assets of public bodies and public utilities. These two classes of capital goods are both of very great importance; and over a period of years it is probable that they account between them for a very high proportion of our aggregate capital expenditure. If, therefore, the influence of the rate of interest were limited to these two spheres it might be a factor of great consequence; but it would be less automatic and reliable than is sometimes assumed. So far as the second category is concerned, the decision whether or not to undertake public works expenditure of a non-commercial character will seldom, if ever, be determined solely on financial grounds. Many considerations of policy, both local and national, will be taken into account. There is nowadays, for example, a growing advocacy of the view that public bodies and public utilities should regulate their capital expenditure systematically with the object of steadying the course of trade. In so far as this view is accepted, it appears at first sight as though the influence of the rate of interest would be weakened. As regards the other category, houses and other dwellings represent the only important type of consumers' capital goods likely to be affected materially by changes in the rate of interest. But the demand for dwellings is clearly dependent also on other factors, notably on the rate at which the number of families is growing in different sections of the community. In view of the trend of our vital statistics it seems probable that we are approaching a phase in which the number of families will cease to grow. It is difficult to suppose that under such conditions the demand for new private dwellings can remain at a very high level, however low the rate of interest may fall. This suggests that one of the major classes of capital expenditure which is susceptible to variations in interest rates may in future represent a much smaller part of our aggregate capital expenditure than it has done in the past. So far as the argument has gone the conclusion would appear to be that the influence of the rate of interest on capital expenditure is limited to certain particular directions, and that its continued efficacy in those directions is threatened by modern tendencies.

The argument, however, is not, as yet, complete. Changes in the rate of interest may affect economic activity through a channel different in kind from any that have hitherto been considered. A fall (or rise) in the rate of interest serves to raise (or lower) the Stock Exchange prices of fixed-interest securities, and has a considerable effect on the prices of most ordinary shares. This may affect the

willingness of large sections of the public to purchase goods and
services in general. When prices are rising on the Stock Exchange,
dealers and speculators make profits, whereas as a body they are
apt to make losses when Stock Exchange prices are falling. Many of
them expect to make profits over an average of years and regard
these profits as a part of their spendable income. When, accordingly, the trend of Stock Exchange prices is upwards, dealers and
speculators will feel better able to spend money than when times
are bad. Under the heading of speculators in this connexion may
be included not only professional speculators but a large number
of persons who habitually buy and sell shares with a view to capital
profits. People who do this are much more numerous nowadays
than they used to be, and they probably account for an appreciable
fraction of the aggregate purchasing power of the community.
Moreover, even people who seldom change their securities are
influenced in their state of mind by a rise or fall in their capital
value and would be more likely to feel that they can afford a certain
piece of expenditure when security prices are rising than when
they are falling.

There are grounds for supposing that this particular influence is
of considerable and growing importance. It is notorious that a
slump or boom on the Stock Exchange quickly affects the demand
for certain luxury goods, e.g. the more expensive types of motor-
cars. It is fairly well established, again, that the Wall Street crash
in 1929 led directly to a substantial curtailment of consumers' purchases. Indeed, this chain of cause and effect supplies one of the
most probable explanations of the fact that trade movements are
normally more violent in the United States than in Great Britain;
for the distinction between income and capital still retains in Great
Britain a far greater degree of sanctity than it does in the United
States. Thus, in the influence of the rate of interest on security
values, and the influence of the level of security values on effective
purchasing power, we have a channel of connexion which is consistent both with common-sense considerations and the broad facts
of recent experience.

A rise in security values, it should be added, may affect businesses
as well as private individuals. It will improve the balance-sheet
position of a business which holds marketable securities; and it
will also make it easier for companies to raise new capital without incurring prior charges. In these ways, businesses might be

encouraged to undertake extensions to which a certain risk attached. Conversely, a fall in security values may be an influence making for more cautious business policies.

The minds of many economic students have been feeling their way in recent years towards the tentative conclusions which have been set out above. But it has seemed desirable to some of us at Oxford that a more systematic effort should be made than hitherto to ascertain whether these conclusions, positive and negative alike, are well founded. There has been in existence for some years among the tutors engaged in teaching economics at Oxford a research group which has been investigating the factors affecting the course of economic activity. These investigations cover a considerable range of problems, and the methods include both statistical analysis and interviews and discussions with business men. One of the questions examined has been that of the effects of changes in the rate of interest, and a number of leading business men, representative of different branches of industry, commerce, and finance, have been closely questioned by us as to the way in which, as they see it, their activities are affected. [The results were summarized in *Oxford Economic Papers* I.] Broadly, it will be observed, the opinions of the business men whom we have examined are in conformity with the argument developed above. The majority deny that their activities have been, or are likely to be, directly affected in any way by changes in interest rates. Of those who take the view that they might sometimes be affected, few suggest that the influence is an important one. This applies, it should be observed, with some qualifications, even to the representatives of the building industry whom we consulted. In at least the majority of cases the negative character of the answers given cannot be attributed to prejudice. It was common to find witnesses who denied that their activities were in any way affected by changes in interest rates, but who, none the less, held the view that the rate of interest is an important factor in the economic situation for reasons not easy to ascertain. Still less can the nature of the answers be attributed to misunderstanding or confusion of thought. Our questions were closely pressed and reiterated in different terms, and they covered every possible reaction. Frequently, moreover, in response to our questions, the methods of calculation actually employed in weighing projects of capital expenditure were precisely explained; and these were such as to disregard altogether variations in interest rates.

Our investigations in the Oxford Economists' Research Group have been intensive rather than extensive, and the 'sample' of firms consulted is small. Moreover, the sample may be said to be biased in one important respect. The majority of business men we have consulted represent prosperous firms in a strong financial position. It may be that changes in interest rates have a greater influence on the actions of businesses which are in financial difficulties. Certainly on general grounds one would expect that such businesses would be more likely to be affected by changes in the ease or stringency of credit conditions, i.e. in the abundance or scarcity of bank money as distinct from the rate charged for it.

It seems fair, however, to claim that our investigations, though not amounting to a conclusive demonstration, confirm with a high degree of probability the negative conclusions which have been tentatively advanced on grounds of common sense, i.e. that the direct influence of variations in the rate of interest on the actions of the majority of businesses of an ordinary industrial or commercial character, either in purchasing materials or in undertaking capital expenditure, is not likely to be very great. Indeed, they go somewhat further than this, and suggest that the influence exerted indirectly through the change in the level of security values and consequently in balance-sheet positions, though of some importance, is not of great importance so far as the actions of businesses are concerned.

Though these conclusions are essentially negative, we think that their publication may contribute, if only by way of clearing the ground, to the constructive development of economic thought. It is of interest, therefore, to consider some of the corollaries which appear reasonable if these conclusions are accepted.

In the first place it would be very rash to infer that the importance of the rate of interest in the working of the economic system has been exaggerated. The economist's presumption that great importance must attach to a factor so fundamental as the rate of interest remains, and should not be lightly dismissed. What emerges is that the role played by the ordinary business man in the transmission of the effects of interest changes is an essentially passive role. The active agents in the process must be looked for elsewhere; and the directions in which they may be found have already been indicated. Possibly the suggestions conveyed by the general trend of economic analysis in the past have under-estimated these other effects of interest changes as much as they have over-estimated the direct reactions upon the ordinary business man.

It was suggested above that the growing vogue of the idea of regulating public works with a view to trade stability might seem calculated to weaken the influence of the rate of interest on the volume of this type of capital expenditure. It may well be, however, that this is a superficial view. One important aspect of all projects of public works expenditure is the budgetary aspect. This is an aspect which is apt to receive only slight attention in economic discussion, largely because of the spread in recent years of the idea that unbalanced budgets may be a useful instrument in recovery from depression. But the necessity for governments to balance their budgets over a period of years remains inexorable. Two powerful tendencies are at work today which are likely to make this task increasingly difficult. There is first the unprecedently heavy expenditure on armaments which is being undertaken in many important countries. Secondly, there is the movement from rapidly growing towards declining populations which is in progress throughout the western world, and which is likely in various ways to aggravate budgetary difficulties. In these circumstances it is to be expected that governments in many countries, including particularly Great Britain, will be increasingly preoccupied in future years with the problem of budgetary equilibrium. It follows that the financial aspect of projects of public works is likely to be of crucial importance. Schemes of public works which would entail substantial charges on the national exchequer or on local funds would encounter formidable resistance on financial grounds.

The rate of interest may, therefore, play an extremely important part in determining the volume of public works expenditure which it proves practicable to undertake. There are many types of public works or public utility expenditure which yield an appreciable financial return, which, however, may be insufficient at the prevailing level of interest rates to cover the service of the loan required. If a materially lower level of interest rates could be established, the range of public works which were commercial propositions would be enlarged, and the range which could be undertaken without imposing serious burdens on the budget would also be enlarged. Moreover, a low rate of interest by facilitating a reduction in the annual charge for the national debt contributes directly to balancing the budget, and thus makes it easier to undertake public-works schemes, which are not fully remunerative but are desirable on general economic grounds. For these reasons it may well prove that a low rate of interest will be of vital importance in the years that lie ahead. It may represent the only means of reconciling the conflict between considerations of economic activity and considerations of financial solvency, neither of which can be disregarded without disaster.

The influence of the rate of interest on the expenditure of private individuals may prove equally great. It has already been suggested that the direct effect of changes in interest rates on the purchase of consumers' capital goods may prove of diminishing importance in future; but that, on the other hand, the indirect effect on general expenditure exerted through Stock Exchange prices may be of increasing importance. If this conclusion is sound, the problem of securing a reasonable stability in Stock Exchange values becomes of central importance in the working of the economic system, and deserves more systematic attention than it has hitherto received.

But there is another aspect of this question which is of great interest to the analytical economist. A generation ago there was much discussion of the question whether a fall in the rate of interest was likely to increase or decrease the volume of saving. The traditional view was that a lower rate of interest would diminish saving, and vice versa. But discussing the question exclusively in terms of the ability to save and the incentive to save, economists found it increasingly difficult to reconcile this assumption with common sense and general experience, and the discussion ended in a prevailing agreement that the effect of a change in the rate of interest on the volume of saving was about as likely to be in the one direction as the other, and was not likely to be important in either case. The reactions of the rate of interest on security prices have, however, an important bearing on this question. As we have seen, there are substantial grounds for believing that an important section of the public is induced by an upward movement on the Stock Exchange to spend more freely, and consequently, other things being equal, to save less. Indeed, the importance of the rate of interest in the working of the trade cycle may, perhaps, lie as much in its reactions on saving and consumption as in those on investment.

This, however, is a short-period transitional influence, associated with falling rather than with low interest rates. Is it possible that as a long-period proposition also the old-fashioned assumption that a lower rate of interest will check saving and vice versa is more soundly based than economists in the past generation have felt able to assume? This is a question that is likely to prove of great importance to the economic stability of society. For a period which may be fairly prolonged we have before us the prospect of large and increasing armament expenditure. But it seems inevitable that sooner or later we shall be confronted with the necessity of effecting a transition to a new economic equilibrium in which capital expenditure plays a substantially smaller part than it does today. Loan expenditure on rearmament must come to an end eventually. The expenditure of the public on houses cannot be expected to continue at anything like the level of recent years when the number of families has ceased to grow. It is impossible to suppose that expenditure on public works will be undertaken on a scale that will compensate fully for the probable decline in capital expenditure under these two headings. But if the demand for capital goods must be expected to diminish it will be essential, if a prolonged period of economic *malaise* is to be avoided, to secure a corresponding increase in the demand for ordinary consumers' goods. Indeed, the central economic problem of the next generation may be how this can be effected against the background of difficult budgetary conditions. The problem is formidable in the extreme. The difficulties in the way of an adequate solution are immense. But a solution would become much easier if it could be assumed that the establishment of a materially lower rate of interest would exert an enduring influence on the habits of a large section of the public in regard to expenditure and saving.

PART IV

Memoranda Written while at the Treasury during the War
1940–5

1

THE PRINCIPLES OF THE BEVERIDGE PLAN[1]

The following essay was written by Sir Hubert Henderson when Sir William Beveridge was working on his report on the social services and was discussing it with representatives of the Treasury.

I⊤ is important not to overlook one remarkable feature of the *Beveridge Report*, namely the lack of correspondence between diagnosis and remedy. The governing object of the Plan is declared to be the 'abolition of want'. This, indeed, is the central theme of the *Report*. The claim is repeatedly made that the abolition of want is a practicable post-war aim, on the ground that Mr. Rowntree's *Survey of York in 1936* showed that the aggregate deficiency of purchasing power in working-class households with incomes below the poverty line was less than one-eighth the aggregate 'surplus' of those with incomes above this line. We are told at the outset that 'the Plan for Social Security . . . starts from a diagnosis of want'. This diagnosis is to the effect that 'from three-fourths to five-sixths' of want before the war 'was due to interruption or loss of earning power', and that the remainder was mostly due to 'failure to relate income during earning to the size of the family'. The conclusion is drawn that 'abolition of want requires a double redistribution of income through social insurance and by family needs'.

So far the argument is coherent, the generalizations of fact seem reasonable, and the conclusion that for the complete abolition of want some system of children's allowances is necessary follows

[1] 4 August 1942.

logically enough. But when we pass to the other and larger part of the problem, namely to the proposals made for meeting want attributable to 'interruption or loss of earnings' all real connexion between diagnosis and remedy disappears. We already have in this country extensive schemes of social insurance, supplemented by other forms of provision, for meeting want arising from causes under this head. The *Report* pays the following tribute to the existing system: 'Provision for the immense varieties of need through interruption of earnings and other causes that may arise in modern industrial communities has already been made in Britain on a scale not surpassed and hardly rivalled in any other country of the world.'

It would be natural to expect that before proposing to replace this system by a new and immensely more expensive one, the *Report* would first consider where and how it is defective for the purpose of 'abolishing want', and that it would relate its proposals to the deficiencies thus ascertained. The outstanding paradox of the *Report* is that it makes no attempt whatever to do this. It bases its proposals on 'six fundamental principles' which are either irrelevant to the objective of abolishing want, or, as is true of the more important of them, in conflict with it. In general, the six principles are proclaimed as though their desirability were self-evident.

It seems important to subject these principles to a critical examination; for the proposals follow (for the most part) from the principles, and the enormous financial cost follows inexorably from the proposals. They are arranged in the following order:

1. Flat Rate of Subsistence Benefit.
2. Flat Rate of Contribution.
3. Unified Social Insurance.
4. Adequacy of Benefit.
5. Comprehensiveness.
6. Classification.

I. ADEQUACY

It is convenient, however, to consider them in a different order, and to commence with what is really the key principle, namely the fourth, termed 'Adequacy of Benefit'. This would be better named 'Adequacy of Benefit without reference to Needs'; for the *Report* makes it clear that it means that the rate of benefit should be sufficient to support the recipient without any means test, that is to say, on the assumption that he or she has no other source of income or means of livelihood, and obtains no help from relatives. In its own words: 'The flat rate of benefit proposed is intended in itself to be sufficient without further resources to provide the minimum income needed for subsistence in all normal cases.'

If this principle is accepted, the *Report*'s application of it cannot be condemned as excessive. It proposes a benefit rate for adults of 20*s.* a week, at pre-war prices, to be written up to 25*s.* a week, on the assumption that post-war prices (other than rents) are one-third higher than pre-war, and that there is no increase in rents. This may be fully sufficient to supply the minimum needs of an adult living in a cheap cottage with a vegetable garden in a country district. It is almost certainly insufficient for the majority of the people in large towns if every possibility of aid from other sources is disregarded. Moreover, the cost of living has already risen by more than 25 per cent. above pre-war; and we shall be fortunate if the post-war level is not at least one-third, rather than one-quarter, above pre-war. For these reasons, it would almost certainly be necessary to concede materially higher rates of benefit (with a consequent increase in the financial cost of the Plan), if this principle were to be adopted, expressly or implicitly, as its basis.

On what grounds does the *Report* put forward this principle? In paragraph 8 of Part III the principle is proclaimed without any attempt to justify it; and it is necessary to search the body of the *Report* for incidental supporting arguments. In paragraph 18 of Part I it asserts that 'benefit in return for contributions rather than free allowances from the State is what the people of Britain desire'; and it refers to 'the strength of the popular objections to any kind of means test' which it suggests 'springs not so much from a desire to get anything for nothing as from resentment at a provision which penalizes what people have come to regard as the duty and pleasure of thrift, of putting pennies away for a rainy day'. These observations seem to comprise the case for the 'adequacy without means test' principle. They include, it will be observed, three elements; namely (*a*) the incompatibility of a means test with the idea of insurance, (*b*) popular objections to any means test, and (*c*) the undesirability of penalizing thrift.

The first consideration, however, is not relevant to the question of 'adequacy'. It is fully met if, as is already the rule, insurance benefits themselves are not subject to a means test; and it has no real bearing on the question whether the level of benefits and contributions should be high or low. Means tests are undoubtedly unpopular; but so are many other things, including compulsory contributions at the rates that would be necessary to finance the Social Security Plan; and it is by no means clear that the former is more unpopular than the latter would prove to be. This consideration clearly cannot be regarded as disposing of the issue.

The essential argument is presumably the last; namely that a means test which takes account of the past savings of the recipients penalizes thrift. There is undoubtedly some force in this objection; though it is now met in practice, to a considerable degree, by arrangements which disregard savings up to a certain amount. But again, a 'means test' is not the only thing that penalizes thrift. High rates of taxation may do so; indeed, some such penalization is an almost inevitable feature of any large-scale attempt 'to redistribute purchasing power'.

These are the only arguments, or suggestions of argument, in favour of the principle of 'adequacy without means test' that can be traced in the *Report*. What are the arguments that can be urged on the other side? The central objection, is, of course, that it adds immensely to the cost of the Plan. What is perhaps less obvious is that it multiplies the cost without doing anything (except perhaps incidentally) to promote the objective of abolishing want. Indeed, this is to understate the case. The principle of 'adequacy of benefit' without means test and the principle of 'abolishing want' through the redistribution of income, are mutually contradictory.

It is important to appreciate clearly how fundamental this contradiction is. It is apt to be obscured by a very natural confusion of thought. It is easy to understand that the idea of a 'means test' is unpopular. The phrase directs attention to the *method*; it evokes the picture of an offensive inquisition, conducted by individuals, themselves comfortably off, into the detailed family circumstances of the poor. It is equally easy to understand that the idea of 'abolishing want through the redistribution of income' makes a strong appeal. The phrase directs attention to the *result*; it conjures up the vision of a fairer society, in which no one has too little, and fewer people have much too much. None the less, the two ideas are fundamentally similar, being rather like the two sides of the same shield. If we are to redistribute income more fairly or more equally, we must first ascertain how much different people have. This implies an inquiry into means; and when the State raises money by direct taxation (which is by far the most potent instrument we have evolved for redistributing wealth more equally), it does in fact undertake an increasingly rigorous inquisition into means. If it is right that the State should apply the test of means when it takes money away from people, it seems equally right that it should apply the test of means when it gives money to people. There is no justification in *principle* for applying a means test to one part of the redistributive process, and refraining from applying it to the other. There may be practical reasons which make it wise to draw such a distinction, at any rate in part; but, if this is argued, these reasons must be considered on their merits, on the strictly practical plane, in the light of all the relevant circumstances. They can derive no legitimate support from appeal to general principle.

It is interesting, in this connexion, to note the repeated references which the *Report* makes to the results of the *York Survey* as proof of the feasibility of abolishing want completely. It stresses the fact that the total surplus of wage-earners' incomes above a defined poverty line is eight times the total deficiency of those below it, and concludes that it is certainly practicable to abolish want by redistributing income, since it could be done by a redistribution among the wage-earners themselves. This argument is cogent, and indeed conclusive, if all that is meant by abolishing want is the raising of those family incomes that are below a bare poverty level up to that level, and not beyond. In other words, the *Report* would be entitled to use this argument if it was proposing to relieve want solely by the method of public assistance with a strict means test. But in fact it is proposing an entirely different plan under which most of the additional money that is to be spent will go to persons whose incomes are already above the defined poverty line. It is obvious that the statistics of the *York Survey* throw no light on the question of whether such a plan is economically feasible or not. The *Report* is using a calculation which assumes a means test to show that we can afford to do without a means test.

This criticism must not be taken to imply a desire for a more extensive adoption of the means-test technique. Want, in the sense of an income insufficient for the minimum requirements of subsistence, is not the only evil that follows from interruption or loss of earning power. There is much hardship that falls short of want in this sense; and, if it were not for our system of social insurance, there would be a great deal more. It is a hardship to find oneself unable to maintain the essentials of an accustomed standard of life, which may be considerably above subsistence level, and to have to fall to a definitely lower standard, even though this may still exceed subsistence level. The desire to have some safeguard against hardships of this kind, in the event of contingencies which are sufficiently common to enter into the apprehensions of the ordinary man, is natural and deep and widespread; and this had given rise to an extensive system of voluntary insurance covering classes far removed from the likelihood of actual want, long before the foundations of the compulsory insurance system had been laid. There is a strong case for arrangements which fulfil a similar function to the mass of wage-earners; and this was the primary object of the national insurance system.

In other words, the system of national insurance was designed not so much to abolish want as to *help* to maintain accustomed standards of living, by supplying benefits which are of substantial value. For this purpose, a means test would be quite inappropriate; but equally, since there may be no question of want, there is no reason why the benefits should be high enough to provide the full needs of minimum subsistence. In order to abolish want, on the other hand, the essential condition is that the incomes of those in want should be raised to an adequate level, and it is unnecessary that they should be raised above this level. For this purpose, there is nothing inappropriate about a means test. On the contrary, it is only through a means test that it is possible to secure that the money is really directed to the object of abolishing want.[1]

Thus the principle of adequacy of benefit without reference to needs is a less logical approach to the problem of abolishing want than that of our existing arrangements, under which a system of national assistance based upon a means test is added to the system of national insurance directed primarily to other purposes. The practical consequence follows that by far the greater part of the additional money which the scheme would cost would not go to persons who are in want under our existing system. The payments which *can* be made to destitute individuals under national and public assistance are fully as large as the scale of benefits which the *Report* proposes. It is thus only in so far as the present system is

[1] Sir William Beveridge states that 'the benefits . . . will continue indefinitely *without means test, so long as the need continues*'. This is very like a contradiction in terms.

faultily administered that any destitute persons would receive more money under the Plan than they do at present.

It is important to note another aspect of the principle under examination. It is not really proposed that the benefits should be paid without *any* means test. So far as *earned income* is concerned, the means test is still to be retained; indeed, it is to be made somewhat more rigorous than it is at present. An insured person who reaches the old-age pension age can earn today as much as he chooses and still continue to draw his statutory pension without deduction. Under the Plan he could not do this. He would receive no pension until he 'retired'. After retirement he would have to make a 'periodical declaration of earnings' and half his earnings might be deducted from his pension.

The *Report* defends this proposal by the following argument:

> To make retirement from work a condition of a pension is a logical consequence of giving adequate pensions. There is no sense in giving adequate pensions for anything but retirement, i.e. in giving them to people who are in full work, merely because they have passed a particular birthday. This is a waste of resources which the nation, with its rapidly growing proportion of men over 65 and women over 60, should not attempt to afford.

This may be a cogent, but it is a means-test argument. The prospect of a growing proportion of elderly persons of pensionable age should undoubtedly make us pause before we decide to make large additional payments to such persons without considering whether they need them or not. But this applies just as strongly to unearned income as to earned income. Why is it contrary to 'sense' to pay 25s. a week to an elderly man who is earning £2 or £3 a week, but not contrary to sense to pay this sum to another elderly man who is getting as much or more from interest on dividends? Why should the former be termed 'a waste of resources', and the latter termed 'the abolition of want'?

What arguments can be advanced for drawing this sharp distinction between earned and unearned income? The *Report* objects, as has been seen, to an unearned-income means test on the ground that it 'penalizes thrift'. But it is equally clear that an earned-income means test penalizes effort. A man who has retired will be less likely to supplement his income by work if half his earnings are deducted from his pension than if (as now) he is allowed to retain them all. Is it more important to avoid discouraging thrift than to avoid discouraging effort? There are undoubtedly those who would answer this question in the affirmative. To the reasons quoted above for making pensions conditional upon retirement, the *Report* adds the following sentence: 'The desirability of paying pensions in old age only to those who were no longer earning was urged on the Committee from many quarters, including the Trade Union Congress General Council.'

But this view, as becomes clear a few lines lower down, was based on a diagnosis of unemployment which Sir William himself expressly repudiates. He tells us that the representatives of the T.U.C. 'took the view that men should be given an incentive to retire from work as early as they could *so as to leave employment for others*'. He points out that this 'assumes a limited total of employment which should be reserved for younger men'; and so far from accepting this view he maintains that 'there is no such limit to the total of employment, while, on the other hand, there is a danger that the large and growing proportion of older people in the population may depress the standard of life for all if they cease work before they need. . . . So far from wanting to hasten their retirement they should be encouraged to remain at work.'

Upon this issue, there is little room for doubt that Sir William Beveridge is right. The argument he uses is reinforced by two further considerations. First, it is prudent to assume that for a considerable period to come the Armed Forces will continue to absorb a larger number of men in the prime of life than they did before the war. Second, our loss of overseas-investment income entails the consequence that we shall have to produce substantially more than before the war in order to regain our pre-war standard of living. It would seem reckless and irresponsible in these circumstances to go out of our way, by discouraging the elderly from work, to increase the number of 'idle mouths'.

How, then, does the *Report*, holding the same view upon this issue, justify the proposal to make pensions conditional on retirement? The answer appears to be that it hopes to avert any stimulus to earlier retirement by a further proposal to make the age of retirement 'flexible'. It hopes to induce men to postpone retirement by increasing their eventual pension by 1s. a week for each year they continue to work after reaching pensionable age. That this would *diminish* the inducement to retire early may be readily conceded. That it would eliminate it, or as it appears to claim, reverse it, must be regarded as extremely doubtful. The *Report* does not propose to make the increase of pension, in the event of postponed retirement, equivalent in value to the pensions rights forgone. On the contrary, it expressly states that 'the addition to basic pension where retirement is postponed should be substantially less than the actuarial value of the postponement', and it claims an important economy under this head. Thus, from an actuarial standpoint, the inducement of the higher pension to remain at work would only *partly* offset the inducement to retire early supplied by the rule that the pension would only be payable on retirement. It is difficult to suppose that for psychological reasons the actual compensatory inducement would be worth *more* than its actuarial equivalent. The disposition to prefer a bird in the hand to two in the bush, the consideration that, after all, a nominally retired person could retain as a matter of right half any earnings he made in addition to his pension, the hope that he might be able, in practice, to retain considerably more, would all tell in the opposite direction.

After a man had decided to retire, it is indisputable that the proposal to deduct half of any earnings he made from his pension would supply a discouragement to work which does not exist under our present arrangements. Altogether, therefore, there is a clear presumption that the proposed Plan taken as a whole would tend to discourage work by persons of pensionable age. In view of the importance it rightly attaches to avoiding this result, the *onus* of proof rests on the author to show the contrary.

However this may be, the main argument is unaffected. The *Report* regards it as an unjustifiable 'waste of resources' to pay 25*s.* a week to elderly people who remain in full work. It does not tell us why it thinks this wasteful; but the reason can only be that such people are not 'in want'. This, however, is equally true of those who have substantial incomes from investments or other sources; and it is impossible to understand why the *Report* does not regard it as equally wasteful to pay 'adequate pensions' to such persons. It calls attention to the important fact that 'of those who are in receipt of the statutory pension of 10*s.* a week only one-third have applied for supplementation'. Moreover, by proposing to make his plan 'comprehensive' and to bring the higher income-ranges within its scope, it would make the greater number of comfortably off and wealthy people eligible for pensions. Yet in this it apparently sees no waste of resources. To this objection it is no sufficient answer to say that these well-to-do people will have established a claim to pensions by virtue of their contributions. In the first place, the Security Fund is to be heavily subsidized, partly by the contributions of employers, and partly by the State. Secondly, the man of pensionable age who remains 'in full work' has also paid his contributions, so that an arrangement under which pensions were given to everyone of pensionable age, whether retired or not, would be equally justifiable on insurance grounds. None the less, the *Report* calls this 'a waste of resources' and, by so doing, it implicitly accepts the view that expenditure from the Fund must be justifiable on its intrinsic merits, and not solely by reference to insurance principles.

In short, it is not too much to say that the sentences in which the *Report* denounces the wastefulness of paying adequate pensions to persons who remain at work comprise a logic which is fatal to the principle of Adequacy of Benefits without Means Test.

II. COMPREHENSIVENESS

It is convenient to consider next the fifth fundamental principle, namely Comprehensiveness. This means that the national insurance system is to be made practically universal by including:

(*a*) persons who are now wholly or partially exempted because they belong to particular occupations such as domestic service, or the Civil Service;

(*b*) persons in non-manual occupations who are paid at a rate in excess of £420 a year.

Some incidental comment has already been made upon the effects of extending the scheme to persons of the latter class. These persons are seldom in 'want', and their inclusion would do little or nothing accordingly to abolish want. On the other hand, it would greatly increase the 'waste of resources' entailed in paying 'adequate benefits' to persons with adequate incomes.

The *Report* sets out the arguments in favour of this extension. They are mainly arguments of administrative convenience; e.g. the avoidance of difficulties which arise 'through persons passing out of the insurance field in middle life' and of 'troublesome questions as to the rate of remuneration in fluctuating occupations'.

It is impossible, of course, to draw any line without giving rise to certain difficulties in regard to borderline cases. But there is no reason to think that the existing difficulties referred to are of any serious importance. On the other hand, the proposed extension would give rise to new administrative difficulties which seem likely prima facie to prove far more formidable, and which the author does not appear to have considered. For example, the existing problem of 'miscellaneous earnings' by persons in receipt of benefit would take on a new character, if the insurance system were extended to persons who receive from time to time literary earnings of a miscellaneous character. A journalist, let us say, or a lecturer, or the secretary of a propagandist organization, loses his salaried employment, and devotes himself for some months to writing a book, which may or may not yield him an income in royalties subsequently. Is such a man entitled to receive unemployment benefit while he is writing this book, unless he is offered and refuses salaried employment similar to that which he held before? This is only one of many similar conundrums that would arise; and whatever answers were found for them, the anomalies and arbitrary distinctions would probably be at least as great as those involved in our present arrangements.

Indeed, this criticism is perhaps more fundamental than the above statement of it may suggest. The idea of providing benefits in case of 'interruption or loss of earnings' rests on the assumption that the interruption of earnings is a definite and clear-cut affair. As regards manual wage-earners, for the great majority of whom the weekly wage is the sole source of earned income, this assumption corresponds sufficiently to the facts. But in more highly remunerated non-manual occupations, it is far more common for the earned income to be derived partly from salaried work, and partly from other work, in which a considerable interval may elapse between the effort and the reward. In such cases, the notion of 'interruption of earnings' is vague and blurred; and the idea of providing benefits for such a condition is fundamentally much less appropriate and consequently much more difficult to apply.

The presumption is, therefore, strong that extending the scope of the insurance scheme to the higher income ranges will serve on balance to increase the administrative difficulties and anomalies involved.

It is partly on similar grounds of administrative simplification that the *Report* defends the proposal to abolish the exception of particular occupations; but again it takes no account of the new administrative difficulties that would be created. It points out that 'where one section of domestic service, namely indoor domestic servants in private houses, alone are excluded, while all other domestic servants, such as those in establishments and institutions are included, anomalies and passages into and out of insurance are unavoidable'. This is true. On the other hand, as the *Report* points out elsewhere, 'the only satisfactory test of unemployment is an offer of work'; and it is likely to be more difficult to apply this test to indoor domestic servants than to other work-people, since the question whether it is fair to expect an unemployed servant to accept service in a particular house will depend largely on the temperament and personality of the particular mistress, which cannot easily be judged from outside. Here again, therefore, there are disadvantages which need to be weighed against the advantages. The *Report* confines its attention to the latter.

It cites, however, another reason for seeking to bring the excepted occupations within the scope of the insurance system, namely that occupations with a low or negligible risk of unemployment ought to 'stand in' with others and contribute to the relief of unemployment in other occupations. 'The principle underlying unemployment insurance today', it says, 'is that industries cannot to any substantial extent control their own volume of unemployment, and that no industry, accordingly, should contribute less to unemployment insurance because its normal rate of unemployment is below the average.' There is no doubt that much can be said on practical grounds in support of the *Report*'s view upon this question, just as there is much that can be said against it. But the principle to which it appeals in the above sentence is illogical, being indeed inconsistent with the fundamental idea of an insurance system.

It is possible to hold that the cost of relieving unemployment should be borne by society as a whole, and that those who work in secure occupations should not, on this account, contribute less than others. But if this view be taken, it follows that it is wrong in principle to use the insurance method in order to relieve unemployment. The essence of insurance is that premiums are paid to secure cover against certain risks, and the first condition of a satisfactory insurance system is accordingly that the premiums, the benefits, and the risks should be properly related to one another. The *Report* appeals frequently to this principle. In arguing, for example, against making children's allowances part of the contributory system, it refers to

the 'difficulty of principle, that while most people contributing for
unemployment, disability, or retirement will be paying with a prospect of some return, very many people will contribute for many
years before they have any prospect of children; many will contribute for years after it is clear that they will have no children'. But
why should it be objectionable in principle to require persons who
are unlikely to have children to contribute to children's allowances
and yet be positively desirable in principle to make persons who are
unlikely to be unemployed contribute to unemployment allowances?
Here again the *Report* uses an argument which appears to be fatal
to its main contention.

This inconsistency of argument is emphasized by inconsistency
of recommendation. Having turned the essential principle of insurance out by the front door, so far as unemployment is concerned,
the *Report* immediately readmits it by a back entrance. It proposes
that persons who reach pension age without having drawn as much
in benefit as they have paid in contributions should have part of
their excess of contributions repaid to them. This proposal, it says,
has the objects:

(i) To meet the strong objection that will undoubtedly be felt by men
with little or no risk of unemployment or complete alternative
provision for disability to being forced to pay contributions on the
same terms as everyone else.
(ii) To give an incentive to avoidance of unnecessary claims to benefit
in the hope of qualifying for refund.

It proceeds to remind us

that under the social insurance scheme liability to contribute will be
extended to large numbers of persons with very secure positions, in
the public service and other pensionable employments, to agricultural
workers, and to private domestic servants whose availability for work it
may be difficult to control. To give to such classes an incentive to avoid
unnecessary claims is very desirable.

By making this proposal, and defending it thus, the *Report* implicitly admits that it is unfair to make persons engaged in occupations which have little or no unemployment risk contribute as much
as others to the cost of relieving unemployment. It admits, in other
words, that it is right from the standpoint of insurance principle
that industries should be allowed 'to keep the advantage' of a low
rate of unemployment. Why, then, deny them this right in the first

instance and compensate them subsequently for this denial? It might conceivably be defensible on practical grounds, if 'comprehensiveness' brought with it great administrative advantages; but, as has already been shown, the administrative losses would probably exceed the administrative gains; and the latter part of the passage just quoted suggests that Sir William Beveridge is himself aware of this.

Thus we are still left without any argument in favour of the principle of comprehensiveness which can be accepted as valid, or which the *Report* itself is able to sustain consistently. By contrast, the arguments against this principle seem overwhelmingly strong. Its adoption would greatly increase the proportion of the benefit expenditure that would be paid to persons who are in comfortable circumstances. For most people in the higher-income ranges, the benefits would be too small to be a real safeguard against the contingencies for which they wish to provide; and they would still have to rely mainly, as Sir William contemplates, on voluntary insurance and personal savings. Thus there would be no real administrative simplification, but, on the contrary, a vast and essentially purposeless duplication. There is, indeed, something inherently absurd in collecting a few shillings a week from men with four-figure salaries, with the idea of returning them 25s. a week in certain circumstances. This absurdity might perhaps be accepted with tolerant amusement, if it was believed that the comparatively well-to-do were paying into the Fund far more than they were drawing out, and were thus being in effect taxed for the benefit of others, though even then the question would remain whether this was a sensible or economical way of taxing them. But there would probably be many cases of persons who ended their careers as wealthy men or women, actors or film-stars, for example, after having drawn out from the Fund far more than the actuarial equivalent of what they had paid in; and an arrangement under which such persons appeared to be receiving pensions at the expense of severely felt exactions from the wages of railwaymen, domestic servants, and agricultural labourers would be extremely difficult to defend.

In the last analysis, the principle of Comprehensiveness, when taken in conjunction with the principles of a flat rate for benefits and contributions, is exposed to the objection that it does not fit the facts of social life. The burden represented by a given rate of weekly contributions, and the value represented by a given rate of benefits, differ widely as between different sections of the community; and it seems unrealistic to proceed as though these differences did not exist. Apart from this, there is the important point that the conception of interruption or loss of earnings has a definiteness in respect of those who are insured today, which it would not have in respect of many of those now outside the scope of insurance.

III. FLAT RATE OF CONTRIBUTION

This principle is closely connected with that of comprehensiveness; and the main issue which it raises, namely whether it is really desirable as a matter of principle, and whether it is consistent with the technique of insurance, to fix premiums on a basis which disregards large ascertainable differences in the risks which are covered, has already been sufficiently discussed. On practical grounds, such as those of administrative convenience, there is undoubtedly much to be said for a uniform rate of contribution for those within the scope of a national-insurance scheme. This is today the general rule; but certain exceptions from it are permitted, namely two 'special schemes' for banking and insurance respectively, which were allowed to 'contract out' of the general scheme in its early days, and the separate treatment of agriculture. The main effect of this particular principle would be to abolish the exceptional treatment of these three occupations.

This is not a matter of very great importance. To require bank clerks, insurance clerks, and agricultural labourers to come within the scope of the main scheme would doubtless inflict no great hardship on them. On the other hand, nothing much would be gained. So far as agriculture is concerned, the fact that agricultural labourers have hitherto received lower wages than most industrial labourers, and on the other hand enjoy the lower cost of living which is associated with rural life, goes to justify a lower level of benefits and contributions. It is true that the wages of agricultural labourers have now been raised, and that other workers, such as roadmen may enjoy an equally low standard of living. None the less, it is not clear that there will be any net advantage in assimilating the agricultural scheme to the general scheme.

In insisting on this change as a matter of principle, the *Report* displays a tendency which perhaps underlies much of its thought, to derive a general principle from what are really practical difficulties which limit the application of an opposite principle. The

chief argument for a flat rate of contribution is that when unemployment insurance was first introduced it was contemplated that
'contracting out' might be permitted more freely than has in fact
been allowed. Since the course of development has been in the
direction of greater, rather than less, uniformity, it infers that the
maximum uniformity is right in principle. This, however, is to place
'events in the saddle' to a greater extent than is surely justified.[1]

It is worth observing that the *Report* does not propose in practice
to apply this principle without important qualifications. It proposes
lower rates of contribution for women than for men, on the ground
that part of the latters' contributions must be regarded as paid 'to
provide for marriage needs'. Here we have another appeal to the
principle of insurance proper, which it throws overboard in its
application to unemployment. Nor, inasmuch as women get married
as much as men, is this particular appeal very convincing. The
practical reason for charging women a lower rate of benefit is that
their rate of pay is normally lower; and this is obviously the reason
which leads the *Report* to suggest the further proviso that 'the
employer may not deduct more than 2s. from any wage payment
not exceeding £2, and more than 1s. from any wage payment not
exceeding £1'.

IV. FLAT RATE OF SUBSISTENCE BENEFIT

This is the principle on the strength of which the *Report* proposes to pay benefit at the same rate in respect of unemployment,
sickness, and old age. In this application, which is the only one that
matters, it is a logical corollary of the principle of Adequacy of
Benefit without Means Test. As a principle, therefore, it stands or
falls with the arguments that have been considered under that
heading. It may be agreed that it is anomalous to pay lower rates
of benefit for sickness than for unemployment. It is far from clear
that it is desirable to pay equally high benefits (apart from evidence
of want) for old-age pensions. Here, again, however, it is observed
that the *Report* does not apply this principle consistently. For it
proposes to pay pensions for disability on quite a different basis,
e.g. 'two-thirds of estimated full-time earnings' for total disability,

---

[1] The more so, since the Report tells us that the suspension of 'contracting-
out' was attributable to the heavy general unemployment of 1921 and succeeding years, and since it expressly bases its new Plan on the 'assumption' that
heavy unemployment will not occur in future.

and it proposes to defray the costs partly by 'a special levy on employers in industries scheduled as liable to substantially more than the normal risks of industrial accident or disease'.

V. UNIFIED SOCIAL INSURANCE

This principle again calls for little discussion. Unified administration is certainly an advantage, though an advantage which belongs to the nature of practical considerations rather than of principle. The essential question is how far the *Report*'s scheme is likely to realize this advantage. As against rather doubtful simplifications within the national-insurance system, there must be set a great increase in duplication and overlapping as between national insurance and voluntary insurance.

VI. CLASSIFICATION

This principle is essentially a qualification of the others. It is intended as a label for the idea that 'social insurance while unified and comprehensive must take account of different ways of life or different sections of the community'. In some respects, notably, for example, in the proposals to meet the special needs of housewives, the *Report* undoubtedly makes a real attempt to give practical effect to this idea. It is of the essence of the above criticisms that several of its other principles do not 'take account of different ways of life or different sections of the community'.

CONCLUSION

The task of this paper, namely to examine the six fundamental principles on which the *Report* bases its plan, is now completed. No attempt has been made to consider the proposals in detail, except in so far as they arise directly from, or are relevant to, one or other of these principles. The Plan contains various attractive features and interesting suggestions, which undoubtedly deserve to be considered on their merits.

None the less, the general character of the Plan is, as it claims, derived from these six principles, which in their turn are really summed up in those of Adequacy, Comprehensiveness, and Flat Rates of Benefit and Contribution. It is a remarkable fact that, as was observed at the outset, none of these principles has any relation, other than a contradictory relation, to the proclaimed objective of abolishing want. The more important of these principles are, moreover, arbitrary in themselves; they are in conflict with some of the arguments which the *Report* itself employs, with some of the proposals which it is driven to make, and with the essential principle of insurance to which it frequently appeals. The *Report* writes as though it were proposing to substitute a simple and logically coherent Plan for an existing jungle of anomalous confusion. But it is fairly open to question whether a scheme founded on its principles would not introduce more anomalies, more complications, and more illogicalities than it would remove. It would certainly cost immensely more, and it would do nothing, that could not be much more easily done otherwise, to diminish want.

2

GREAT BRITAIN'S POST-WAR COMMERCIAL POLICY—A POSITIVE STATEMENT[1]

I. THE PROBLEM OF OUR BALANCE OF PAYMENTS

1. WE recognize that if the problems of post-war commercial policy are to be wisely handled, they must be approached in a broad spirit of international co-operation, and that worries and anxieties arising from special national difficulties should not be allowed to inhibit constructive action. None the less, the fact that our means of paying for imports have been seriously reduced as a consequence of the war is necessarily a source of anxiety to us; and we are bound to have regard to that fact and to its implications in considering what commercial arrangements may be possible for us when the war is over.

2. One consequence that seems to us quite inescapable sooner or later is a large-scale readjustment of our import-export balance. We have hitherto been accustomed to import commodities to a value greatly exceeding our exports, the balance being defrayed partly by receipts for various 'services' such as shipping, and partly from the large income due to us from overseas as interest or dividends on past capital investments. These means of purchasing imports will be greatly reduced in future, as the result of the sale of part of our overseas investments during the war, the new indebtedness that we are incurring towards other countries, and the uncertainties attaching to our future net income from shipping services.

3. During the war of 1914–18 our overseas income from such sources was affected in a similar way, though not in so serious a degree. This, however, did not give rise to any inexorable need to change the balance between our imports and exports of merchandize, because we entered that war with a large favourable margin in our balance of payments on current account, which we were accustomed before 1914 to reinvest overseas. The last war did not do more than reduce this favourable margin for fresh investment,

[1] 6 January 1943.

and accordingly no large readjustment of our economy was forced upon us, though a continued readiness on the part of our financial institutions to undertake fresh overseas investments on a scale larger than our reduced resources warranted may have played a part in the international financial troubles that led to the world crisis of 1929–32. So far from there being any decline in the excess of our merchandize imports over exports, this excess increased throughout the inter-war period, in consequence of the loss of markets by our old-established exporting industries. The result was that we entered the present war in 1939 with no favourable margin left in our balance of payments, indeed with a balance that had already become slightly adverse.

4. It is possible that new international financial or monetary arrangements may be devised which may help in the solution of the general international economic difficulties which are to be expected when the war is over. A large proposal of this character has been put forward from the British side. An improved international monetary mechanism would be of assistance in two ways. First, it would supply countries which emerge from the war with a temporary stringency of foreign-exchange resources with a breathing space, in which they can turn round and restore their external economies to equilibrium. Second, it might help to supply an expansionist stimulus to international trade in general, which would make it much easier for countries to correct an adverse balance of payments by means of an expansion of their exports rather than a contraction of their imports.

5. But no monetary or financial arrangements can be expected to achieve more than the above. It is not to be supposed that as part of a normal peace-time system exporting countries will be willing to supply their goods to importing countries without material payment in some form, or that the principle of 'from each country according to its ability; to each country according to its means' could be made the basis of international economic relations. Certainly we in Great Britain feel bound to assume as a long-run proposition that we shall only be able to import to the extent to which we can find the means of paying for our exports. Nor can we think that it would be right to encourage any country to base its policy on any other assumption.

6. Moreover, whatever temporary financial assistance we may need to obtain in order to overcome the exceptional difficulties of

the early post-war years, the United Kingdom is not a country which can prudently become a continuing borrower. We are not a country with undeveloped resources or means of communication, representing an appropriate outlet for international investment. On the contrary, our industrial structure is such that it would be more appropriate that we should continue to play a part in financing the development of other countries. This, however, will only be possible in so far as we can reconstitute a favourable margin in our balance of payments on current account. It is clear that our position will be fundamentally unsound, until we can succeed in eliminating any adverse margin.

7. For these reasons, a drastic alteration in our pre-war balance between merchandise imports and exports will be for us a fundamental and inexorable necessity; and it will be important that we should accomplish this, when the war is over, without undue delay. We regard this as constituting, even upon favourable hypotheses, an extremely formidable task. For a short period, which may last perhaps for two or three years, we do not anticipate any great difficulty in finding markets abroad for goods that we are able to produce and make available for export. But during this initial period our exports will be limited by considerations of productive capacity. Subsequently we must expect our export trade to be affected by the widespread desire, stimulated as it must be by war experience, in the less-developed regions of the world, to foster industrialization, and also perhaps by keener international competition. Similar developments led after the last war, as has been mentioned, to a loss of export markets which we were never able to recover.

8. An environment of expansion in the sphere of international trade would, of course, make it much easier for us to secure an increase of our export trade. For this reason, we shall gladly cooperate in any measures which seem to us well-designed to create such an environment. We cannot, however, afford to assume lightly that this condition will be easily fulfilled, or that this would suffice to ensure us not merely the maintenance but the very large expansion of our export trade above its pre-war level that would be necessary to avert a reduction of our imports. We are bound to take into account, as a very serious possibility, that our export trade may not be large enough to provide us with the means of paying for imports on the pre-war scale. If this should happen, the question

as to how we could best use limited foreign-exchange resources so as to maintain as fully as possible the standard of living and the employment of our people would inevitably arise. We should regard it as out of the question in such circumstances either to allow an unbalanced situation to develop to an extent which might threaten us with a currency débâcle, such as overtook the currencies of central Europe after the last war, or to allow limited foreign-exchange resources to be used for the importation of luxuries to the detriment of essential living needs.

9. The above in brief outline and in general terms is the British balance of payments problem. It is a problem which we cannot affect to disregard or to treat wishfully. It is against this background that we necessarily approach the problems of post-war commercial policy.

II. TRADE BARRIERS

10. Our economic development for two centuries past has depended on international trade in a very large degree. For nearly seventy years preceding the last war our commercial policy was one of unqualified Free Trade; and the Free Trade tradition still makes a wide appeal to the British people. Our economic structure has taken its shape from this experience. We have become dependent on large-scale imports of food and raw materials; and no expansion of our domestic agricultural produce could serve to reduce this dependence more than slightly. On the other hand, our industries have been accustomed to rely very largely upon export markets. In many of them, indeed, our peace-time productive capacity is greatly in excess of the absorptive capacity of the home market.

11. In these circumstances, we naturally are in full sympathy with the aim of promoting the expansion of international trade. We should greatly prefer as a broad proposition to bring our balance of payments into equilibrium by means of an increase in exports rather than by a reduction of our imports. Beyond a limited point, indeed, we could not hope to achieve the latter, except in ways which would be liable to injure our living standards as a nation.

12. For this reason, the objective of securing a general lowering of trade barriers makes a strong appeal to us. None the less, this is not a matter on which we feel in a position to take a leading part. As we see it, the essential problem is to reconcile the aims of an

expansion of international trade and equilibrium in the balance of payments. For this purpose what is chiefly needed is that those countries which are otherwise likely to have an unduly favourable balance of payments should be willing to do most to reduce import duties and to remove other impediments to imports. Countries which are likely to be faced with an adverse balance of payments should not be expected to respond in an equivalent degree. Indeed, it is only in so far as an expansion of their exports serves to bring their balance of payments towards equilibrium that measures likely to increase their bill for imports could be reconciled with ordinary prudence.

13. It must clearly be for the United States, as one of the countries which is likely to emerge from the war with a strongly favourable balance of payments, to decide how far she is prepared to go in the direction indicated. We recognize that questions of tariffs and commercial policy, partly because of the history attaching to them, partly because they affect the interests of particular sections of the community in a palpable manner, are apt to prove among the most controversial of internal political issues. Every government is bound, accordingly, to shape its policy with reference to prevailing public opinion. We welcome and appreciate the various statements that have been made from time to time by members of the United States Administration seeking to lead American opinion in the direction of readiness for a more liberal commercial policy.

14. The question for us is how far we can assist a movement in this direction by a readiness to make reciprocal concessions. Our power to make concessions which would be likely to result in practice in a material increase in our imports is unfortunately narrowly limited by the considerations already set out. To restore our balance of payments to equilibrium within a reasonable time must be an essential objective of our post-war policy; and arrangements calculated to increase our imports and our exports in roughly commensurate degrees would be of no assistance towards this goal.

15. This does not mean that we should be unwilling to consider a substantial lowering of the rates of duty in our tariffs as part of an arrangement with the United States, or as part of a wider multilateral agreement for the reduction of tariffs. As a country to which a large-scale export trade is in any case essential, we are conscious of the importance of keeping our costs of production at a level consistent with effective competition in world markets. We are

therefore averse in general to forms of protection that are likely
to enable our manufacturers to obtain in the home market prices
materially in excess of those prevailing in the outside world. Any
arrangement, therefore, and more particularly a multilateral agreement, providing for lower tariffs, either by cuts in existing rates of
duty, or by imposing a maximum ceiling to tariff rates, which was
likely to be acceptable to others, would be agreeable to ourselves.

16. It would be necessary, however, for us, so long as we have
to correct an adverse balance of payments, to reserve the right to
limit the volume of our imports by other means, such as some form
of quantitative import control. This might also be necessary for
other countries faced with similar difficulties. It is obviously open
to doubt whether a readiness on our part to make reciprocal tariff
reductions, which is subject to this very important reserve, would
be found helpful or the reverse by the United States Administration in its efforts to promote a more liberal commercial policy. That
is a question which we are not in a position to judge. To prevent the
possibility of subsequent misunderstanding, however, we think it
essential to make it clear that we see no likelihood, in the best of
circumstances to be expected, of being able to dispense with quantitative import control, as a means of correcting our adverse balance
of payments for a considerable period after the war is over.

17. It is possible, moreover, that there will be a growing disposition in future to use the method of quantitative regulation in preference to tariffs for a variety of other purposes. The tendencies
making in this direction, and the special international problems
which are raised by the use of this method are considered subsequently.

III. IMPERIAL PREFERENCE

18. We recognize that United States opinion takes exception to
the system of Imperial Preference, as developed at the Ottawa
Conference. It has never been the object of that system to create
anything in the nature of a self-contained economic unit. On the
contrary, both we ourselves and the Dominions require markets for
our products much wider than the Empire can supply. We both
accordingly desire to see the development of international trade
on a multilateral world-wide basis, and wish in particular to promote closer economic relations with the United States. We are

anxious, therefore, that our preferential system should not be such as to be a source of legitimate grievance to American interests; and we are ready to do our best, subject to the overriding requirements of our balance of payments problem, to meet American wishes in particular connexions to which importance is attached in the United States.

19. We cannot, however, accept the view that our preferential system is objectionable in principle, on the ground that it entails discrimination. In a certain sense of the term, it is true, of course, that any tariff involves a 'discrimination' in favour of the traders belonging to the individual State or Customs Union imposing it against traders belonging to other countries. But discrimination in this sense is universally regarded as an entirely fair and legitimate expression of the corporate unity implied by membership of the same State or Customs Union. The political structure of the British Commonwealth is far looser than that of most unitary or federal political systems; and because the political structure is looser, a lesser degree of fiscal solidarity than is implicit in a Customs Union is appropriate. That is the main justification in principle of our preferential system. In our view, the possibility ought not to be excluded that it may be desirable in post-war Europe to permit, and even to encourage, similar preferential systems between neighbouring groups of States, whose political solidarity it may be important to foster, but who may not desire to go so far as a complete Customs Union.

20. We cannot, therefore, accept a philosophy which would condemn as discriminatory preferential arrangements between members of a common political system, while accepting as legitimate Customs Unions between independent States. There are doubtless arguments which can be urged for preferring Customs Unions to preferential systems. But these arguments belong to the plane of practical convenience and cannot form the basis of sharply contrasted moral judgements.

21. A concrete illustration may help to make clearer our general position on this issue. We accord a substantial preference on sugar to the British sugar-producing colonies, which include many islands in the West Indies. The withdrawal or even the substantial reduction of this preference might have disastrous results on the standard of living of the inhabitants of these islands, for whose welfare we cannot, and do not wish to, disclaim responsibility. In fact,

however, the preferential price which we pay for colonial sugar is far below the price which Porto Rico, a very similar West Indian island, receives by virtue of the free entry of her products into the United States. A principle which would require us to reduce our price to Jamaica or Barbados, but permit the continuance of the higher United States price to Porto Rico seems to us to be fundamentally unsound.

22. There is, moreover, another aspect of the preferential question, which in certain contingencies might become important. Membership of the British Commonwealth is associated in a large degree, though by no means wholly, with membership of a common monetary system, sometimes described as the 'sterling area'. Each country in this area is entitled to call on the monetary authorities in London to supply it with the foreign exchange required to defray its imports. If, accordingly, there is, or threatens to be, a shortage of foreign exchange at the disposal of the Bank of England, the question whether a particular sterling country obtains its imports from within or from without the sterling area cannot be regarded as a matter of indifference. In such circumstances precisely the same considerations that may compel a particular country which is in a weak exchange position to curtail the volume of imports may make it important to reduce the purchases made by countries within the sterling area from countries outside it.

23. For these reasons we cannot agree that the system of Imperial Preference can be regarded as a species of discrimination; and we took pains accordingly to reserve our position on this issue during the exchange of messages which preceded the signature of the Mutual Aid Agreement. On the other hand, as has been indicated, we are anxious to promote the expansion of trade between ourselves and the British Commonwealth on the one hand, and the United States on the other, provided that this is of a character which is calculated to assist rather than to hamper a solution of the balance of payments problem. Informal discussions have been taking place in Washington for some time past as to the possibility of mutually advantageous reductions of tariff rates and preferential margins. We are disposed to think it is by means of concrete negotiations of this character that progress can best be made on this particular matter; though we recognize that when it comes to embodying the result of such negotiations in trade agreements on the model of the Anglo-American Trade Agreement of 1938, diffi-

culties may arise in connexion with other problems, notably that of quantitative regulation which has still to be discussed.

IV. QUANTITATIVE REGULATION

24. In any consideration of the problems of post-war commercial policy, it seems to us important to have regard to the possibility that there may be an increasing disposition to use methods of quantitative regulation for a variety of purposes. When a country is faced with the necessity of correcting an adverse balance of payments, quantitative regulation may be by far its most satisfactory means of conserving limited resources of foreign exchange for essential needs; and, as already indicated, we contemplate the probability that we shall have to use it ourselves for this purpose. Apart from this, the method of quantitative control has been used by many countries to protect particular branches of industry; and though it has its disadvantages and possibilities of abuse, it has decided advantages, as compared with tariffs wherever the object is to maintain a certain volume of home production, at reasonably stable prices. As a safeguard against 'dumping', for example, it is arguable that import restrictions are a more satisfactory technique than anti-dumping duties.

25. Similarly it is impossible to exclude the possibility that there may be an increased use of methods of 'State trading', so far as bulk lines of trade are concerned. During the war, for example, the greater part of our imports of food and feeding-stuffs are purchased centrally through the Ministry of Food; and the continuance of part at least of this system is advocated in several different quarters on a variety of grounds. We do not wish to express, or to be taken as implying, any opinion as to the desirability of such a policy, which represents, indeed, a possible source of internal political controversy. But this consideration would make it impossible for us to give any undertakings which could be regarded as debarring developments in the direction indicated.

26. Quantitative import control and State-purchasing arrangements possess the common feature that under either the question of how much a country will import of a particular commodity is settled as a matter of deliberate policy, instead of being determined by the play of market forces, as affected by tariffs. This substitution of deliberate choice for the chances of market competition is closely associated with the idea of 'planning' to which public opinion tends

increasingly to incline. Moreover, the principle involved, namely that of quantitative regulation, is the principle that underlies commodity regulation schemes, such as that for wheat.

27. It is true that commodity regulation schemes rest on an international basis, whereas quantitative import control is imposed by a particular State. But this difference seems to us an insufficient ground for condemning the principle in the latter application, while approving it in the former. It may fairly be urged that the fundamental problem is the same in both cases, namely that the operation of market forces cannot be relied on to correct in a satisfactory manner large disequilibria, whether in the international balance of payments or in the relations of demand and supply for particular commodities; and that to secure equilibrium in either case, deliberate quantitative regulation may have a useful part to play.

28. For these reasons we are convinced that it would not be practicable or fruitful to attempt to forbid or to check the extension of the methods of quantitative import control or State trading. On the other hand, these methods are capable of being used, and have in the past been used, in such a way as to cause serious injury to the legitimate interests of other countries; and we recognize the importance therefore of endeavouring to devise satisfactory rules for regulating them.

29. The Anglo-American Trade Agreement of 1938 contains clauses representing a first attempt to formulate such rules as between Great Britain and the United States. These provisions cannot, however, be regarded as appropriate to the conditions likely to prevail in future. It is to be observed in the first place that they attempt to apply radically different principles to the two branches of the problem. As regards quantitative import control, the governing principle is that where imports from different supplying countries are determined by means of quotas, these quotas are to be based on imports 'in past years'. As regards State purchasing, the governing principle is that the purchasing authorities must be guided solely by 'commercial considerations'. The application of the former principle would tend to stereotype rigidly the distribution of imports between different sources of supply; the application of the latter might involve violent shifts as between one source and another.

30. In our view, State-purchasing arrangements must be regarded as an extreme form of the method of quantitative import control;

and it seems desirable accordingly that the guiding principles of international fair-dealing should be similar for both branches of the problem. The true principles should, we suggest, be intermediate between the sharply contrasted principles just indicated. Neither through the mechanism of State purchasing nor that of quantitative import control should an importing country shift its purchases suddenly, drastically, or without good cause, from one source of supply to another. Under neither system, on the other hand, should the distribution of purchases be determined on a rigid, unvarying basis. In both cases the importing country should be ready to discuss the allocation of its purchases with the principal supplying countries. It should be an essential principle of international good behaviour that a country employing either of these methods of regulation would conduct its policy with a view to ensuring a reasonable degree of steadiness both as regards prices and as regards the flow of trade for all parties concerned.

31. We are ready for our part to undertake that, in so far as we may use quantitative import control or State trading methods, we should observe these principles in our treatment of imports from the United States.

3

NOTES ON THE PROBLEM OF MAINTAINING EMPLOYMENT[1]

I. DIAGNOSIS

1. THE analysis of unemployment under the three broad headings of minimum unemployment, structural unemployment, and cyclical unemployment is an essential preliminary to any understanding of the problem, and particularly of the British unemployment figures. There is a danger, however, that this method of approach may lead to an unduly abstract treatment of the constituent parts of the problem, involving in effect an evasion of what will almost certainly be our main difficulties in the post-war period. This applies particularly to the third category, namely cyclical unemployment.

2. This phrase is used to describe the unemployment that arises from time to time owing to a general deficiency in the effective demand for goods and services; in other words, the unemployment attributable to trade depression. The word 'cyclical', however, is apt to suggest that one depression is so much like another that it is needless to consider closely the particular circumstances in which depression is most likely to occur after the war is over. The problem is regarded accordingly as one of preventing trade depressions in the abstract; and conclusions are apt to be drawn and policies recommended which ignore some of the main factors in the post-war problem.

3. The diagnosis of the problem, which results from general trade-cycle analysis, may be shortly stated as follows. Fluctuations in the volume of capital expenditure play a major part in the ups and downs of trade. It follows that in order to avert trade depressions the chief need is to stabilize as far as possible the aggregate demand for capital goods. It is difficult to stabilize the investment expenditure of private industry. Public-works expenditure should therefore be used as an equalizing factor so as to offset the variations in private investment.

[1] 20 May 1943.

4. Now up to a point this diagnosis is sound. It is true that the demand which falls off first and most in a depression is the demand for capital goods, such as machinery, ships, and buildings. Indeed, the comparatively slight decline that is apt to follow in the demand for consumers' goods and services is essentially a consequence of the loss of income resulting from reduced activity in the capital goods industries. But the inference that we should try to stabilize the total demand for capital goods does not follow. The suggestion provokes, or should provoke, the question: What is the level of demand for capital goods which we should seek to stabilize; by what criteria should this level be determined? The answer *implied* in the above diagnosis is: The level that happens to exist, whatever it may be, or, alternatively, the level which will absorb the productive capacity of the capital goods industries, whatever that may happen to be. It may be doubted whether this would be a satisfactory answer in any circumstances, though in ordinary times it might serve well enough for practical purposes. In relation to the immensely complex problem of changing over from a war to a peace economy it is palpably inadequate.

5. One of the chief features of war-time economy is that it involves a large expansion of industries that produce, or are capable of producing, capital goods; engineering and shipbuilding in particular. Similarly the demand for capital goods will be abnormally large in the early post-war years, owing to the accumulated arrears of renewal and replacement work throughout industry, and in the public-utility field, as well as housing. In this phase of the post-war period there will be no 'cyclical' unemployment. Structural unemployment may even then constitute a formidable problem, and together with minimum unemployment, under new conditions and higher rates of benefit, may conceivably result in fairly substantial unemployment figures. None the less, the supply of effective purchasing power is likely to remain during this phase far in excess of the supply of goods and services, so that inflation rather than deflation will be the danger.

6. The 'cyclical' problem will arise later, when the demand for capital goods begins to decline substantially. When this second phase is reached, what should be the aim of policy? Should it be to maintain the total demand for capital goods at a level as near as possible to what it was in the first phase by means of a lavish expenditure upon public works? That is what facile trade-cycle

theory is apt to suggest. But surely it is fundamentally wrong. There is not the smallest reason to suppose that the particular relation between the production of capital goods and the production of consumers' goods, which will serve the purposes of post-war reconstruction, will suit equally well the normal needs of peace. On the contrary, as has just been said, war and the phase of post-war reconstruction both require a swollen volume of capital goods production, and this implies that normal peace conditions require a smaller volume. To try to retain indefinitely in the capital goods industries as large a proportion of our labour and productive capacity as we need there during war, or as we shall need there for a few years subsequently, would not be good sense. If it could be done, it would represent a most wasteful use of our productive resources. Sooner or later, we must effect a transition from an economy based on a large proportion to an economy based on a materially smaller proportion of capital-goods production. That is the essence of the long-run problem of maintaining full employment. It is only when we recognize this clearly that we are in a position to appreciate how difficult that problem is, and it is only in so far as we appreciate its difficulties that we are likely to succeed in solving it.

7. The great difficulty of this transition, it may be agreed, is to maintain the aggregate demand for goods and services at an adequate level. In assessing this difficulty, three points must be noted. First, capital goods, whether they are ordered by private individuals, private industry, or public authorities, are ordinarily financed by borrowing or from capital resources; consumers' goods and services are paid for out of income. Second, the production of capital goods generates income just as much as does the production of consumers' goods. Third, so long as the capital goods are being made, their production adds nothing to the supply of consumers' goods and services on which the income generated can be spent. These are the reasons why inflation is the danger during a period of abnormally high investment expenditure. They are equally reasons why it is difficult to effect a transition to a materially lower level of investment expenditure without heavy 'cyclical' unemployment.

8. The problem can perhaps be understood more clearly if we state it in illustrative concrete terms. Let us suppose that towards the end of the initial post-war reconstruction phase our national production is as follows:

	£ millions
Consumers' goods . .	6,000
Capital goods . . .	1,000
Total production . .	7,000

Suppose that this represents a state of reasonably 'full employment', subject to 'structural' difficulties, and suppose also that substantial economic equilibrium has been achieved, i.e. that inflation is not at work, that rationing has been done away with, and that consumers can buy what they want in shops. Disregarding minor complications, the above production position will then correspond to the following income and expenditure position:

	£ millions
Current expenditure . .	6,000
Savings	1,000
Gross national income .	7,000

9. Now arises the problem. The demand for capital goods begins to fall off, and we are required to adjust ourselves to a position in which, say, the total output of this category of goods may decline over a few years to an annual level of, say, £600 millions. If we disregard structural complications, there has been no decline in our national productive power. This will rather have grown as the result of technical progress; but disregarding this too, or setting it off against the structural difficulties, it is clear that what we want is to achieve the following position as regards production:

	£ millions
Consumers' goods . .	6,400
Capital goods . . .	600
Total production . .	7,000

To correspond, we want the following position as regards income and expenditure:

	£ millions
Current expenditure . .	6,400
Savings	600
Gross national income .	7,000

This is what we want; and if we could achieve it we should be living better to the tune of £400 millions per annum, apart altogether from technical progress. This is the great paradox of the problem. The transition which presents such formidable difficulties offers at the same time the potentiality of a higher standard of life. Unfortunately, if we leave matters to chance, this is not what we are likely to get. It is probable, first, that the gross national income will fall fairly quickly by nearly the amount of the decline in the output of capital goods. Next, it is probable that the amount of savings will fall only slowly and partially and as a consequence of business losses and unemployment towards the level indicated. Finally, it is probable that expenditure on consumers' goods will decline rather than increase, and that we may find ourselves temporarily in some such position as the following:

Production			*Income and expenditure*		
		£ millions			*£ millions*
Consumers' goods .	.	5,900	Current expenditure	.	5,800
Capital goods	. .	600	Savings . .	.	700
Total products	. .	6,500	Total income .	. .	6,500

In other words, a waste of £500 millions per annum of productive power, in cyclical unemployment and depression; a diminished output of consumers' goods, despite the increased resources available to produce them, and yet an output which exceeds the current demand for them, so that there is much talk of the satiation of demand in modern industrial communities; and a piling up of stocks so that we have as yet reached no resting-place, but are still caught up in the cumulative progress of depression.

10. How are we to avoid this result, and to attain or approximate towards the ideal result? The crux of the problem is to contrive that the demand for consumers' goods and services increases as the production of capital goods declines, and by much the same amount. Since there is a natural tendency for aggregate incomes to become less as capital expenditure falls off, this is obviously not an easy thing to do; and we must not make the mistake of supposing that the economics of war, or of intensive rearmament, throw any light on how to do it.

II. PUBLIC WORKS

11. What help then may we get from the various policies that it is fashionable to prescribe as remedies? First, what of public works?

A sensible policy of trying to time their execution with reference to the trend of employment and trade activity may be useful as a palliative or mitigating factor. We are hardly likely to make a success of the difficult job of switching over our economy from capital goods to consumers' goods unless we can tackle it gradually. If it were to come upon us suddenly in its full magnitude, a disastrous depression might be unavoidable. Public-works policy may be of great help in ensuring the necessary gradualness.

12. It cannot, however, do more than this. To regard public works as a sort of sovereign remedy is to misconceive the problem altogether. The problem is to readjust ourselves to an economy based on a smaller annual volume of capital works. This, sooner or later, unless our hopes of peace are disappointed, we have got to do. To try to use public works to make the task of readjustment more manageable is a sensible aim. It would be another matter to try to use them so as to escape the readjustment indefinitely. That would be to shirk the essential problem; to put off the evil (or rather the difficult) day at the expense of adding to the difficulties later on. It would be analogous to attempts in the international economic sphere to treat borrowing or international credits as a device for avoiding the need to correct an adverse balance of payments, instead of as a means of securing a breathing space in which to correct it.

13. To illustrate the point and drive it home, let us take what is perhaps the most promising possibility within the field of public works, namely, house-building. Our post-war housing programmes are expected to be large, and, what is even more important, to last for a long time. It is recognized that to build houses on the scale required, the labour force in the building industry will have to be increased by special training arrangements; and a White Paper has been issued on Training in the Building Industry (Cmd. 6428, 1943) explaining what is contemplated. 'It is considered', states this White Paper, 'that a post-war construction programme designed for ten to twelve years will require the labour force in the industry to be built up over a period to about 1,250,000 men.' A subsequent passage suggests that the period of building up the labour force should be about three or four years. This then is the picture; the numbers in the building industry to be increased for three or four years, and then to be held steady at a high level for from six to nine years more. What after that? It is implicit in all discussions of post-war

building problems that a decline is inevitable in the second post-war decade.

14. Suppose that, in consequence, say, of a decline in engineering and shipbuilding activity, 'cyclical' unemployment makes itself felt three or four years after the end of the war, when building employment is approaching the contemplated maximum. The prospect that employment will be maintained at a high level for several years more in the building industry will help greatly to avert the danger of a major depression, and to make our problem manageable. But would it be right in such circumstances to attempt to absorb much larger numbers of men in the building industry and to speed up the housing programme with this in view? Conceivably, yes, in a mild degree, by way of immediate palliative; but not surely in a large degree. For in proportion as we did this, we should be aggravating the problem of downward adjustment which will arise in any case in the second post-war decade; we should be gaining immediate relief, at the expense of making our subsequent problem more unmanageable. To stick to a steady programme, speeding it up somewhat, perhaps, but not very greatly, would seem to be the wisest course, quite apart from the practical difficulties with the building operatives which would arise if a policy of rapid acceleration were attempted. This means that we could not use an expansion of building to counter a decline in engineering and shipbuilding in the circumstances supposed.

15. If we could not use building for this purpose, still less could we hope to use other normal forms of public capital investment. Over most of the field of public enterprise there will be the same tendency in the post-war reconstruction phase towards an abnormally heavy capital expenditure, as there will be in private enterprise, and for the same good reason that there will be arrears to be made up and urgent needs to be met. But most of this work will not take so long as the housing programmes to accomplish. In general, therefore, it is idle to speak as though we might counter a decline in private capital expenditure by an offsetting increase in public capital expenditure. A decline in the latter may be an important element in the problem we shall have to face.

III. FISCAL DEVICES TO MAINTAIN TOTAL INCOME

16. The next type of remedy to be considered is that which advocates trying to increase the effective purchasing power of the

community, when depression threatens, by some fiscal device. The budget should be deliberately unbalanced when trade is bad, by remissions of taxation. This will leave the public with additional purchasing power and so help to increase the demand for goods and services generally. To meet obvious objections on the score of sound finance, it is further proposed as a corollary that the budget should be overbalanced when trade is good, a surplus being then collected which will serve to cover the depression deficits, and also act as a brake on booms.

17. This is the simplest form of this proposal. There are many variants; for example, it is suggested that this technique should be applied not to the budget as a whole, but to employers' and workers' insurance contributions.

18. It can fairly be claimed for proposals of this type that they would do something to meet the essential objective of increasing the demand for consumers' goods as the output of capital goods declines. But there are strong objections to them. First it is difficult to believe that they could be reconciled in practice with the essential requirements of sound finance. Here again we must avoid the danger of treating the problem in unduly abstract terms—as that of the general phenomenon of the 'trade cycle'. The trade depression, the 'cyclical' unemployment to which we should address our minds is that which may come upon us after the post-war reconstruction phase. Now during that phase, though it may be marked by many of the features of boom, we shall certainly not be accumulating surpluses in the budget, or repaying debt. We may be making progress towards a balanced budget, but having regard to the force of the arguments in favour of reduced taxation, to the many inescapable needs and deserving causes on behalf of which increased expenditure will be urged, and also to the general loss of faith in the supreme importance of a balanced budget, we shall be very lucky if we have achieved it. The practical significance of the proposals under examination would therefore be, not that of an evening out of taxation between good years and bad, but that of a further widening of a budget deficit which has not yet been closed.

19. Second, if we were to attempt to base our finances (or the finances of a social security fund) on the principle of an evening out between good years and bad, it is important to have some clear criterion for determining what years are bad, and, as would matter more, what years are good. It is commonly suggested that

the unemployment figures should be taken for this purpose. But the unemployment figures cover not only cyclical unemployment, but structural unemployment and minimum unemployment. The numbers in these latter categories are liable to large variations in accordance with changing circumstances, and changing policies, indeed in accordance with what may fairly be called different ways of reckoning the unemployed. It is difficult to assess objectively the numbers to be expected under these headings in peace conditions. Moreover, if the task were attempted it would not be done objectively; the force of politics would be thrown on the side of under-estimating them.

20. The objections to this type of remedy from the standpoint of a sound public finance are, therefore, serious. On the other hand, it seems unlikely that the remedies, even if they were applied at the right time, would be very efficacious. They would, it is true, leave the public with an increase of spendable income (in a sense and balanced in theory by equivalent subsequent commitments) on a scale which could not prudently be made very great. How far would this be translated in practice into an effective and immediate increase in the demand for consumers' goods? To some extent, no doubt; but there are many reasons for doubting whether the increase in expenditure would be nearly as large as the increase in spendable income.

21. In considering the efficacy of the remedy another aspect of the problem must be considered. Though the distinction between cyclical and structural unemployment is convenient, and has been adopted in these notes, we should never forget that the phenomena are apt to be mixed up in practice. On the one hand, if trade is depressed it becomes much more difficult to deal with structural unemployment; but equally the existence of the latter greatly reduces the power of a global financial remedy. Shipbuilding, let us say, is active for some years after the war; and then so many ships have been built that a reduction of work in the shipyards is unavoidable. On the labour side, the problem is to transfer shipyard workers to other industries. This is not an easy thing to do; but the difficulties can be overcome to a large extent if there are other industries in the same neighbourhood which are calling for more labour. Unskilled labour can move fairly easily; the absorption of new entrants into the expanding industries can help as regards skilled labour.

22. Shipbuilding, however, is localized in certain areas; and its depression tends to depress all activity in those areas. A small increase in purchasing power over the country as a whole would not be likely to increase the effective demand for goods in these particular areas. It might do so elsewhere, perhaps a long way off. But the process of moving from one area to another is very difficult indeed, if the number of those who must move is large. That is the lesson of our experience of the 'transfer' problem in the inter-war period; and it is superficial to suggest that the war has shown that this difficulty can easily be overcome.

23. So far as possible, we want to find work in the shipyard districts for those who will no longer be needed to build ships. There seems no really fundamental reason why we should not succeed in doing this, at any rate in a very large degree. This, therefore, should be our aim; and remedies which would not help to achieve it can only be regarded as second-rate. Thus, the idea of countering a depression by fiscal remedies, when we consider it on the background of the conditions which we must expect to prevail in the post-war period, has very serious disadvantages. On the one hand, it is peculiarly objectionable from the fiscal standpoint. On the other hand, its remedial power is weak; it may hit the outer rings but it does not go near the bull's-eye of the target.

IV. ORGANIZED UTILITY PRODUCTION

24. Is there not a more excellent way? I suggest that a more promising line of approach may be found in the development of our war-time system of the organized production of utility goods, followed possibly at the appropriate time by a reduction of the hours of work. In what follows I shall confine myself to an attempt to bring out the broad principles of the sort of policy that I think might be appropriate. The ways in which these principles would best be applied in practice might vary from one part to another of the field of utility production.

25. The heart of the problem, once again, is to secure an increased demand for consumers' goods, as the production of capital goods declines. In the long run, of course, this demand can only come from the individuals who compose the consuming public, and will depend partly on their incomes, and partly on their habits of expenditure. In the first instance, however, what affects employment and trade activity is the volume of orders placed with manufacturers;

and these orders are placed by traders, wholesale dealers, and retail shopkeepers. Accordingly, the first principle that suggests itself is this: when the time comes to switch over from capital goods to consumers' goods, let the State place the orders, or let it see to it, at all events, that the orders are placed. Let the State, if necessary, over a wide range of commodities entering into mass consumption, assume the functions of a wholesale dealer ordering from the manufacturers, selling to the retailers, and taking the risks of accumulating unsold stocks.

26. If the State were to act upon these lines, there seems prima facie to be a good chance that the purchases of the consuming public would increase both quickly and substantially. Total purchasing power would be sustained just as effectively by the placing of increased orders with manufacturers as by any of the fiscal devices considered previously. But it would be much more likely that potential purchasing power would be translated into an actual demand for goods. For it is of the essence of the idea that the State would be offering good value to the consuming public, supplying commodities of the kinds most required, of good quality and at low prices.

27. The maintenance of employment would indeed not be the only object of the policy suggested; perhaps it should not be the main object. The governing idea should be to use our productive resources as fully as possible to improve the standard of life. There is an important element of truth, mixed up though it may be with many exaggerations, in the popular view that the magnitude of war production is evidence of a waste of productive power in time of peace. Nor does this waste arise solely, or even mainly, from unemployment. The chief waste, I suggest, is connected with *marketing*. More precisely, it lies partly in the excessive portion of our labour power which we devote to advertising, salesmanship, and the like, in contrast to production; and partly in the fact that of most commodities we produce an excessive number of types, and change those types too frequently, so that we fail to make adequate use of the potentialities of mass production.

28. This is one of the true lessons of our war experience. In many different branches of industry it has been shown how greatly the costs of production can be reduced by standardization. It is also the chief lesson taught before the war by those marketing portents, Woolworth's and Marks & Spencer. It is confirmed by the marked

success, in face of adverse conditions, of many of the utility goods experiments that have been organized by the Board of Trade.

29. It will be clearly desirable to retain and to extend these utility schemes during the phase of continuing shortage immediately after the war. It would surely be unfortunate if they were to be abandoned later. It is just when we have emerged from the state of shortage, and have productive resources to spare, that they may have their most useful role to play. It is then that they might be developed so as to be a means of securing that these spare productive resources are used to raise the standard of living instead of being wasted.

30. If the State were to arrange, as the demand for capital goods falls off, that staple lines of consumers' goods are offered to the public of rising quality and at lower prices, and were to support these offers by a suitable publicity campaign, it can hardly be doubted that a substantial increase of consumption would ensue. If, therefore, the State incur the risk, where necessary, of itself placing increasing orders in advance with the manufacturers, it might well prove that the stocks of unsold goods which accumulated on its hands were not unduly large.

31. None the less, unsold stocks might accumulate. If this were to happen, what would it signify? A lack of desire on the part of the public, despite the maintenance of their spendable incomes, to purchase as large a volume of consumers' goods as our industries were capable of producing. In this contingency the moral seems clear. Since we could do with less production, reduce the hours of work. If possible, reduce the hours of work throughout industry without reducing the weekly wage. In this way the supply of goods made available would be reduced, while the purchasing power represented by money incomes would be maintained. It is true, on the assumptions made, and on the further assumption that the scheme was being run without subsidies, that the prices of the commodities offered would be increased, so that a given money expenditure would not buy so large a quantity of goods as previously. But, partly for this very reason, partly as a psychological consequence of greater leisure, individuals would be likely to spend a larger and save a smaller proportion of their incomes; and this, in the last analysis, is the fundamental readjustment that would be needed.

32. If the above policy were pursued to the stage of reducing hours, various complicating problems would arise, notably, for

example, that of the effects on international competition. It would
be premature, however, to carry the argument into these complications. It seems preferable to return to the earlier stage of the programme, namely the placing of orders for utility goods, and to note
one important advantage which this technique has to offer. The
orders could be distributed among the different areas of the country
in such proportions as seemed desirable. To revert to a previous
illustration, if shipbuilding activity was on the decline, large orders
for utility goods could be placed with manufacturers in, or near,
the shipyard districts. In this way we could avoid geographical
transfer, with all its formidable attendant difficulties, except in so
far as geographical transfer was really necessary or desirable. As
compared with the policy of fiscal devices for maintaining aggregate
income, the method of utility orders hits the centre of the target.

33. It will be seen that it is not an essential part of the idea that
the State should incur any financial loss from its organization of
utility production, as distinct from the financial risks of assuming
the role of a giant wholesale dealer. But there might be good
reasons why the State should subsidize the supply of commodities
of especial importance to the standard of life. Already in the inter-
war period, the State subsidized housing and the supply of milk for
schoolchildren; and it did these things with a view to health and
well-being, rather than to employment. It may be that there will be
a valid case for extending the scope of such subsidy schemes; and,
if so, the organization of utility production might enable this to be
done more easily and with greater effect. It would certainly be
desirable that any developments along these lines should be timed,
where possible, to assist the maintenance of employment, or, as I
prefer to put it, should be introduced when our available productive
resources enable us to afford them. This might (though it need not)
entail some unbalancing (or some increased unbalancing) of the
budget at the time when depression threatened; and this would
serve to enhance in some degree the employment-sustaining power
of the utility schemes at the expense of some danger to the maintenance of sound financial principle. How far a temporary budget
deficit would be desirable in such circumstances is a question which
may reasonably be left open. In any case, this financial feature
would be a subsidiary feature of the policy; and the State would
be incurring the deficit for a definite, concrete purpose of social
value, not just for a hope.

V. THE STATE AS ENTREPRENEUR-IN-CHIEF

34. The argument must be broadened, if a false impression is not to be conveyed. I do not wish to suggest that the production of utility goods can play more than a fairly limited part in the economic system, or that a more abundant supply of consumers' goods is what is chiefly needed to raise the standard of life. On the contrary, I am inclined to suggest that one of the true lessons of our war experience is how easily, and with what small loss of real welfare, we can get along, if put to it, with greatly reduced quantities of miscellaneous manufactured goods. Of course, there are very many things which we need to have in reasonable quantities, but the things upon which we cannot, without something approaching hardship, materially reduce our peace-time expenditure are chiefly food, house-room, heating and lighting, transport, and certain other services. Similarly, if we look forward to the future and consider objectively what would do most to raise the general standard of living of the British peoples, the answer, I suggest, is chiefly better food, better housing, more and better facilities for recreation, holidays, and travel, more and better services of various kinds directed to improving culture, health, and amenity. Cheaper or more abundant supplies of consumers' goods, at least on a narrow interpretation of that term, rank in importance after these.

35. The scope of utility production might well be made wide enough to help to meet some of these more important needs. It might include certain types of foods; it should certainly cover the main things needed for furnishing and running a house. None the less, a policy which set out to organize the use of our productive resources so as to secure the maximum human welfare would be lopsided and incomplete, if it were framed solely in terms of commodities, as contrasted with services, and were to overlook such vital elements in welfare as culture, health and amenity; recreation, holidays, and travel.

36. In my view, there is as large and constructive a role for the State to play in organizing the supply of services for such purposes, as in organizing the supply of commodities. I believe, moreover, that the organized provision of such services offers possibilities of greatly cheapening their cost analogous to the economies of the mass production of manufactured goods.

37. The proposals made above with regard to the production of

utility goods should, therefore, be regarded as a particular (and comparatively easy) application of a larger policy, covering a much wider field. In connexion with utility goods, it was suggested that the State should assume, in a sense at least, the role of a wholesale dealer. But this phrase does not bring out the essential idea. What I really suggest is that the State should assume the role of entrepreneur-in-chief, directing the flow of productive resources to the employments in which they can best serve human needs. In our economic system at present that post is vacant. But if hazy talk about a more 'planned' society means anything, it surely means that the State should fill it.

38. Of course, this would mean a new departure in the economic functions of government, to which many might object on broad political grounds. But if there is a danger that the policy suggested might be entangled in fundamental political controversy, there is perhaps an equally good possibility that it might supply a means of controversy that may otherwise rage fiercely upon the issue of Socialism versus Private Enterprise. It has long been the paradox of that controversy that the main claims made on either side do not meet. Opponents of Socialism are on strong ground when they argue that the State would be unlikely in practice to run complicated industries more efficiently than they are run at present. Socialists are on strong ground when they argue that reliance on supply and demand, and the forces of market competition, as the mainspring of our economic system, produces most unsatisfactory results. Might we not conceivably find a *modus vivendi* for the next decade or so in an arrangement under which the State would fill the vacant post of entrepreneur-in-chief, while not interfering with the ownership or management of particular businesses, or rather only doing so on the merits of the case and not at the behests of dogma?

39. But it is with the economic side of the problem that these notes are primarily concerned. From this standpoint there are three points implicit in the foregoing argument which it may be desirable to stress. The first is something of a paradox. We are more likely to succeed in maintaining employment if we do not make this our sole, or even our first aim. Perhaps employment, like happiness, will come most readily when it is not sought for for its own sake. The real problem is to use our productive powers to secure the greatest human welfare. Let us start then with the human welfare, and con-

sider what is most needed to increase it. The needs will change from time to time; they may shift, for example, from capital goods to consumers' goods and to services. Let us think in terms of organizing and directing our productive resources, so as to meet these changing needs; and we shall be less likely to waste them.

40. Second, the problem is one of the structural organization of our industrial and economic system; and this is a task which we must treat as such and attack directly in a concrete way. We must not suppose that the readjustments needed can be satisfactorily made as the indirect consequence of global financial stimuli.

41. Thirdly, we must never forget that for a period that may amount to several years after the war the prevailing economic conditions will be those of a shortage of goods and services rather than those of a surplus of productive power. That phase of shortage will present many problems and grave dangers. It is true that it may help us in various ways to handle those problems rightly, if we allow our minds to leap ahead to the different problems which will arise later. None the less, it is the problems of the immediate reconstruction phase which deserve priority in our post-war thoughts.

4

INTERNATIONAL ECONOMIC HISTORY
OF THE INTER-WAR PERIOD[1]

I. THE LEGEND

IT is evident that opinions on issues of post-war economic policy are greatly influenced by the view that is generally held both here and in the United States of the course of events in the inter-war period. In its cruder forms, this view runs somewhat as follows:

1. The last war was followed by an outbreak of economic nationalism, involving a general heightening of tariff barriers, and the introduction of new and more disastrous obstacles to international trade, such as import restrictions, exchange control, clearing agreements, and bilateral bargaining.

2. There ensued as a natural consequence a huge decline in the volume of international trade, which spelt unemployment for the industrial population of the depressed areas of Great Britain, ruinous prices for the farmers of the New World, and impoverishment throughout the world. It entailed a shocking waste of resources, illustrated by international restriction schemes, and the organized destruction of certain surplus crops.

3. The bilateral and discriminatory character of many of the new forms of trade restriction worsened the international political atmosphere. The development of Imperial Preference entailed the closing of the open door in the British Colonial Empire. The system of clearing agreements destroyed the multilateral character of international commerce, and led towards the formation of rival economic blocs. All this supplied the 'have not' countries with a valid grievance, and helped to spread the view that more 'living space' under their direct control was essential to them. In this way the growth of trade barriers and discrimination was an underlying cause of the present war.

4. These deplorable tendencies developed in face of the advice

[1] 3 December 1943.

and admonitions of the far-seeing and the internationally minded, expressed in resolutions adopted at a series of international conferences at Geneva and elsewhere, directed to the lowering of trade barriers. But these resolutions were not embodied in binding international agreements; nor were there any international economic institutions sufficiently comprehensive and powerful to ensure that they were followed up. Thus, although the wisdom of international economic liberalism was so manifest that most governments were constrained to pay lip-service to it, the forces of economic nationalism, backed by selfish interests, prevailed.

5. The moral is that after the present war we must be more resolute and whole-hearted than we were last time in our efforts to lower tariffs, to eliminate discrimination, and to extirpate the more vicious types of trade impediment; and that these efforts must be embodied in binding international agreements and supported by appropriate international institutions.

The view which is thus summarized commands a remarkably large measure of uncritical assent. It may be taken as representing for practical purposes the quasi-official view of the present United States Administration. Indeed, the references to commercial policy made from time to time by leading American statesmen consist largely of the enunciation of most of the propositions set out above. The same point of view is widely shared in Great Britain, where minds are predisposed to accept it partly by the old Free Trade tradition and partly by the newer devotion to the League of Nations idea.

The above is to be understood, of course, as a statement of the generally accepted view in its cruder and more popular versions. There are many who are in general sympathy with this view but who would regard the above statement of it as out of focus and who would think it essential to qualify it or to add to it. Two of the additions which would be most commonly made should be specially mentioned. Many, both in the United States and here, would attach a special degree of responsibility to the high-tariff policy of the United States, arguing that it is especially incumbent on a country which has acquired a strong creditor position to take the lead in the direction of greater freedom. Others would add that the increase of trade barriers was partly attributable to a defect in the international monetary mechanism, which failed to provide enough purchasing power to sustain aggregate world demand at a sufficiently high level. These would draw the conclusion that a general reduction of trade barriers must be accompanied by new arrangements designed to create 'expansionist' monetary conditions, both internationally and in the internal economies of the leading countries.

Subject to these refinements, the view that has been described has attained the position of an established legend, by which current ideas on post-war policy are profoundly influenced. It is desirable, therefore, to consider how far it is supported by the facts.

The inter-war period comprised four different phases:

1. the phase of *inflation and foreign exchange confusion*, lasting from 1919 until about 1925;
2. the phase of *expansion and large-scale American lending*, covering the later 1920's;
3. the phase of the *world economic crisis* from 1930 to about 1933;
4. the phase of *partial recovery* from 1933 until the outbreak of war.

It is important to distinguish these various phases clearly from one another. It is particularly important to distinguish the first two, which cover roughly the 1920's, from the second two which make up the 1930's.

II. THE NINETEEN-TWENTIES

(a) General Characteristics

During the first phase international trade, particularly European trade, was adversely affected by the conditions which have been designated as the essential characteristics of the phase, namely inflation and foreign exchange confusion. Foreign exchange rates were subject to frequent and violent changes which imposed heavy risks on either the importer or the exporter. Mr. Lloyd George, when Prime Minister, likened trading under these conditions to 'playing billiards on an Atlantic liner'. Still more serious was the fact that the runaway inflations which developed in several important European countries entailed, while they were in progress, a sharp decline in the foreign-exchange resources of the countries affected, and consequently in their capacity to pay for imports. The fall in exchange rates during the course of these inflations kept far ahead of the rise in internal prices and incomes; so that imported commodities became prohibitively expensive to the peoples of, for example, Austria, Poland, Germany, and later France.

It was upon finding a remedy for these conditions that contemporary opinion and contemporary constructive effort were rightly concentrated. Apart from the special case of German Reparations, there was as yet no consciousness that the balance of payments might have become a serious problem. It was taken for granted that the traditional mechanism of international exchange, if it could be set going again, had sufficient strength and elasticity to effect any quantitative adjustments that might be needed, provided only that Germany's Reparation liabilities were kept within the bounds of reason. The accepted prescription was that governmental expenditure must be curtailed and budgets balanced, that exchange rates must be stabilized, and that, to make this possible, Reparation obligations must be reduced, and external loans made available to countries which needed assistance. It was no easy task to carry out this programme; many formidable obstacles stood in the way. But eventually after a lengthy series of efforts, which were marked by the close and cordial co-operation of the Governors of the Bank of England and of the Federal Reserve Bank of New York with one another, and with the economic and financial organization of the League of Nations, the obstacles were surmounted one by one. The problem of German Reparations was provisionally settled by the adoption of the Dawes Plan; in addition to the Dawes Loan, which formed part of this plan, a series of reconstruction loans were raised for Austria, Hungary, Bulgaria, Greece, and other European States; the internal finances of some of the more embarrassed of these States were brought under some degree of external control; budgets were balanced; and exchange rates were fixed by placing currencies again on a gold basis, so that an effective 'multilateral' system of external payment was restored. The process was a gradual one, but in central Europe it had been accomplished by about 1925, though there were subsequent sharp depreciations in the currencies of France, Belgium, and Italy.

There followed the second phase—namely that of expansion and large-scale American lending. In Great Britain the essentially expansionist character of the later twenties was to some extent obscured by difficulties resulting from the over-high parity at which the gold standard was restored and from the failure of our old-established exporting industries to regain their pre-war markets. None the less, even in Great Britain, the volume of industrial production increased by 12 per cent. between 1924 and 1929, business profits were generally good, and the standard of life improved materially. In the United States these were years of such rapid and sustained expansion in all forms of economic activity that the idea that the secret of continuing prosperity had been discovered, and that slumps were things of the past, and unemployment a disease of effete dole-giving countries, became extremely widespread. Incidentally, this idea contributed not a little to the final excesses of the Wall Street boom. In other countries, also, production and economic activity went ahead. Expansion, in short, in the late 1920's was a world phenomenon.

This expansion, it should be added, was by no means confined to increased production for *internal markets*. The volume of international trade also increased rapidly. According to the League of Nations *Review of World Production, 1925–32*, the quantum of world trade increased by about 20 per cent. between 1924 and 1929, while the production of industrial goods rose by about one-quarter, and that of primary products by rather more than 10 per cent. This increase in international trade was associated with international financial conditions of a highly 'expansionist' character. It had been one of the hopes of the Central Banking authorities and the League of Nations experts that the success of their efforts to stabilize European currencies would pave the way for a revival of large-scale international lending, in which it was recognized that the American public must play a much larger part than hitherto. These hopes were realized, though with consequences which were eventually as disconcerting as those which are proverbially apt to follow on the fulfilment of human wishes. The Dawes Loan and the League Reconstruction Loans served their purposes of 'priming the pump'; the American investor was induced to buy foreign bonds by the most up-to-date methods of high-speed salesmanship; and financial institutions both in the United States and Great Britain lent substantial sums on short term to central Europe.

Thus the international financial conditions that prevailed in the late 1920's were such as to supply an 'expansionist' stimulus to international trade; and the temporary increase in world trade that took place was doubtless partly attributable to this cause.

(b) Trade Restrictions

What influence did tariffs and other trade restrictions exert on the course of international trade during the two phases that have been described? A country which is undergoing a runaway inflation, with exchange depreciation leading the way, will, of course, try to stop the rot by curtailing its imports. For this purpose tariffs are a clumsy instrument. The *ad valorem* equivalent of a specific duty is reduced by each fresh inflation of the price level; and it is impracticable to adjust the rates of duty sufficiently frequently to keep pace with a continuous inflationary process. Moreover, apart from this, the effects of duties on the volume of imports are always uncertain unless they are raised to prohibitive heights. A more precise and effective instrument lay ready to hand in an adaptation of the system of import licensing, which, together with export licensing, had been introduced during the war for various war-time reasons. During the inflationary phase of the early 1920's accordingly, import restrictions and import prohibitions were extensively employed by countries which were actually undergoing, or which felt themselves in danger of, a serious exchange depreciation.

It would be palpably misleading to describe this development as a manifestation of economic nationalism or of a desire for 'autarky', or even as an indication of insufficient faith in the virtues of economic liberalism.[1] No country threatened by a disastrous fall in its rate of exchange can afford to allow its limited reserves of foreign exchange to be dissipated on unnecessary imports. The adoption of the technique of import restrictions was a matter of elementary self-protection, almost, as it were, a reflex action to exchange difficulties which could not be ignored. Indeed, the valid criticism which can be brought against the governments which imposed import restrictions during the early 1920's was that they did not sufficiently appreciate the need for more drastic action. They controlled their imports by new and more effective quantitative methods; but they shrank from the idea of exchange control. No effective restriction was placed on capital movements; private individuals were left free to put their money abroad; and speculative 'bear' transactions in exchange markets soon assumed a magni-

---

[1] 'It is a fact that all Governments without exception were opposed to quantitative restrictions in principle and were anxious to return to pre-war trading methods as soon as possible.' (*Quantitative Trade Controls*. League of Nations, 1943.)

R

tude which rendered futile the attempts that were made to control the more tangible transactions of international trade.

This failure to introduce exchange control is attributable to a number of causes. First, the establishment of an effective system of exchange control is an extremely difficult administrative task. Second, the inevitable difficulties were aggravated by the political conditions of Europe in the early post-war years. The authority of many governments was uncertain or weak; while, in the case of Germany, there was a special difficulty arising from the occupation of the Rhineland by Allied troops which created what Germans came to call the 'hole in the west'. But a third factor which undoubtedly played a part was the spell cast by the tradition of economic liberalism, to which the idea of a State monopoly of foreign-exchange transactions was then, and for long afterwards, peculiarly repugnant. Free-trade theories, which were still dominant in Great Britain, found, it is true, only limited support in Continental Europe; but a belief in freedom of enterprise, in free markets and in economic liberalism generally made a much wider appeal, and formed part of the workaday philosophy of European governments. This, it may be observed, was one reason why it was so easy in the inter-war period to persuade international conferences to pass resolutions strongly condemnatory of the newer types of trade impediment.

None the less, the logic of events was not without its effect on responsible opinion in the countries which experienced runaway inflations. The conviction took root that in times of monetary crisis it is no less essential to control the movements of money and capital than to control the movement of goods. This was to bear fruit later. In the meantime the remedy was found, as indicated above, in the policy sponsored by the League of Nations and the central banks, and in the large-scale international lending that ensued.

During the second phase, when there was no longer an atmosphere of exchange crisis, the import restrictions which had been imposed earlier were either removed altogether, as in Germany and Hungary, or greatly relaxed.[1] Poland was the only country to intro-

---

[1] 'In the course of the next three or four years (after 1925) restrictions of this kind were gradually whittled down. They no longer represented the main obstacles to international exchanges in Europe, and were mild compared with the restrictions that developed in the '30s. But they were still far from being inconsiderable or unimportant.' (*Quantitative Trade Controls.* League of Nations, 1943.)

duce new import restrictions during this phase, and inasmuch as her currency and exchange position was still precarious, she may be regarded as the exception which in the strict sense 'proves the rule'. Nor were any other new types of trade impediment introduced in this phase. The gold standard was restored throughout the greater part of the world. Thus in the later 1920's the essential features of the 'free' international economic system, as it existed before 1914, had been largely restored. There remained, it is true, the time-honoured impediment of tariffs; and, in the words of the Report of the World Economic Conference of 1927, tariffs were 'higher and more complicated, less stable and more numerous than in 1913'.

This Conference was the most important and impressive attempt made in the 1920's to secure freer trade by international agreement. It recommended the complete suppression, subject to minor exceptions, of all forms of quantitative trade regulation. But it concentrated its main attention upon tariffs, as the chief remaining trade impediment. Its recommendations were summed up in the following declaration, which won considerable renown at the time: 'The Conference declares that the time has come to put an end to the increase in tariffs and to move in the opposite direction.'

The proceedings of the 1927 Conference were exceptionally harmonious, and its resolutions unusually unqualified and vigorous in tone. Its recommendations were adopted unanimously by the League Assembly, and endorsed by no less than twenty-nine governments in specific declarations. They were also blessed by the International Chamber of Commerce, with a call to governments to act upon them. Tariffs were not reduced as a consequence; on the contrary, in a few countries tariffs were further increased. None the less, as is said in the League of Nations Survey of *Commercial Policy, 1919–39*, 'the Conference was in fact followed by a certain stabilization of the world tariff position'. In other words, the trend towards higher tariffs was virtually checked—until the occurrence of the world economic crisis. It is not every international conference that achieves as much. Alike in the vigour of its resolutions, and the cordiality of their reception, the World Economic Conference of 1927 represented the high-water mark of economic liberalism in the inter-war period.

Two other points should be noted. First, the trend towards higher tariffs until 1927 represented in part the adjustment of specific duties to higher price levels; and the effective increase of tariffs was not as great as is sometimes supposed. Second, by virtue of the most-favoured-nation clause, which was a feature of most commercial treaties, tariff systems were, speaking broadly, non-discriminatory, in the sense which that phrase usually carries. Imperial Preference had not in the 1920's been introduced to any important extent into the fiscal system of the United Kingdom. Thus the commercial arrangements of the later 1920's gave substantial effect to the principle of non-discrimination.

(c) Summary

To sum up the story, so far as it has been carried, the difficulties of international trade in the first post-war phase were chiefly due to the collapse of currencies and the confusion of exchanges. The import restrictions that were then imposed were imposed reluctantly and as a matter of elementary self-protection by governments which disliked them. In the second post-war phase, when the atmosphere of exchange crisis had been temporarily removed by international loans and credits, these import restrictions were largely removed or whittled down. Although tariffs were higher than before 1914, their upward movement was virtually checked by 1927, and they paid substantially full regard to the principle of 'non-discrimination'. Apart from tariffs and the import restrictions that remained, there was no other serious trade impediment. Expedients such as exchange clearing systems, payments agreements, and 'barter' trade agreements were unknown. Exchange rates were stabilized. A system of multilateral payments had apparently been effectively re-established, with the aid of large-scale international lending which served to supply an 'expansionist' monetary environment. The later 1920's were emphatically not a phase of economic nationalism or of contractionism. On the contrary, they were marked by a serious and sustained effort to re-create an expanding international trade on the basis of a freely working multilateral system.

For some years all seemed to go well. A large expansion of international trade in fact took place. International hopes ran high in the political, no less than in the economic sphere. The Locarno Pact was signed, and the Rhineland was evacuated. These hopes were dashed as a consequence of the world economic crisis which ushered in the third post-war phase. It was then that the trend towards economic liberalism was reversed, that international trade was seriously curtailed and was subjected to all manner of new im-

pediments. But these developments were the direct outcome of
the world economic crisis; and the foregoing narrative reveals no
reason for attributing the crisis to economic nationalism or to trade
restrictions.

III. THE WORLD ECONOMIC CRISIS

(a) The Monetary Breakdown

It is unnecessary to attempt a comprehensive diagnosis of the
causes of the troubles which began at the end of 1929, or to assign
to each of the various factors its due importance. Trade depressions,
of greater or less severity, have occurred periodically throughout
modern economic history, and a large literature has been devoted
to attempts to elucidate their causes. But this particular depression
was catastrophic beyond all precedent. For this it can be argued
that much responsibility attaches to particular developments in the
internal economic life of particular countries; notably to the un-
restrained Stock Exchange speculation in the later 1920's in the
United States, which accentuated the fluctuations in effective purchasing power. From the external economic standpoint, however,
the outstanding fact was the collapse of the whole mechanism of
the international gold-standard system which had been laboriously
reconstructed a few years earlier; and the question which has here
to be considered is why this collapse occurred.

Its immediate cause was that, when the flow of American lending
ceased, most countries in central and eastern Europe and Central
and South America became unable to meet their financial obligations to the outside world. At the root of this inability lay the fact
that these countries had been living during the second phase with
a balance of payments on current account which was persistently
and heavily adverse. The sums, that is to say, which they were liable
to pay to other countries in respect of their imports, interest on
loans, or in some cases for Reparations obligations, greatly exceeded the sums that were due to them in respect of their exports.
They had been meeting the difference by borrowing. The large-
scale international lending had thus served for the time being to
cover up their unbalanced position. It had supplied a breathing-
space; but this had not been used to restore equilibrium.

The difficulties of the debtor countries of Europe in meeting their
external financial obligations were greatly aggravated by attempts

on the part of creditors abroad to withdraw their money, by attempts on the part of their own nationals to put money abroad and by 'bear' movement against their currencies in the foreign exchange markets. 'Runs' were made upon the currency of one country after another, rather like the runs on banks that used to cause an internal banking crisis. During 1931 these runs gained a strong momentum; and the countries on which they were made found themselves faced with an imminent danger that their reserves of gold and foreign exchange would be completely exhausted.

Countries in this position had to choose between two courses; exchange depreciation or exchange restrictions. They could suspend gold payments, and allow their currencies to be bought and sold on the foreign exchange markets for what they would fetch. In that event they must be ready to see their currencies depreciate to an extent which could not be measured in advance. Alternatively they could restrict dealings in foreign exchange, and continue to supply gold or foreign exchange for their currencies for 'approved' transactions only. In that case they must develop an elaborate system of exchange control. In either case, international trade was likely to suffer. That, however, could not be helped. The dilemma was inescapable. No degree of enlightened broadmindedness could have enabled a government or central bank to supply gold freely in exchange for its domestic currency when all its gold was gone. Nor would it have been prudent to wait until its reserves were actually exhausted before taking action, though this was very nearly what Great Britain did in 1931.

It was only natural that European countries which had undergone runaway inflations during the early 1920's should regard exchange control as the lesser of the two evils. An outstanding feature of those inflations, as observed above, was that the fall of the exchange rates had led the way, keeping well ahead of the rise in internal prices, and making further internal inflation unavoidable. In Central European eyes, accordingly, inflation and exchange depreciation had become virtually synonymous terms of terrible significance. In 1931 the danger that what happened before might happen again was real and pressing. The same forces were at work; money was flying abroad in panic, and speculators were 'bearing' currencies with gusto. It seems improbable in these circumstances that another phase of runaway inflation would have been avoided if dealings in foreign exchange had remained unrestricted.

of the Inter-war Period247

For exchange control, on the other hand, the inflationary ex-
periences of the first post-war phase had done much to prepare the
ground. They had shown that a currency rot cannot be stopped
without controlling the external movements of money; and they
had stimulated thought upon the most effective means of controlling them. Meanwhile, the Allied evacuation of the Rhineland had
removed the special German difficulty of the 'hole in the west'.

It was no less natural that Great Britain, when the pound in due
course became the subject of a powerful 'bear' attack, should prefer
the other horn of the dilemma. The traditions of London as a financial centre, in which foreigners were accustomed to deposit large
balances on the understanding that they could withdraw them
readily on the shortest notice, were enough in Great Britain in
September 1931 to make the idea of exchange control unthinkable.
On the other hand, we had not suffered before from a runaway
inflation, and our international financial position was still strong
enough to make any such development most improbable.

The fall of the pound was, of course, a painful shock to public
opinion. Nothing could be farther from the truth than to suppose
that a sense of the competitive advantages which our industries
might obtain in world markets from exchange depreciation played
any part in Great Britain's departure from the gold standard. We
went off gold because we were driven off. In the attempt to remain
on, we had borrowed as much money as we could from the United
States and France at high rates of interest, and we had adopted a
policy of budgetary retrenchment so drastic as to provoke a political
crisis, the formation of a National Government, and a General
Election. At this election, the menace of inflation was one of the
leading themes; and for a few months the possibility that the
chances of the exchange markets might cause the pound to fall
indefinitely remained a matter of genuine anxiety to the British
financial authorities. But such warnings and worries were quite
different from the Central European sense of the imminence of
catastrophe.

In several countries, especially in South America, both expedients
were employed. They allowed their exchange rates to fall, and when
this fall went so far as to become alarming, they had recourse to
exchange restrictions as well. Meanwhile some countries, notably
the United States, France, Holland, Belgium, and Switzerland, had
no difficulty in maintaining their exchange parities; for it was to

them that the funds moved that were being withdrawn from other countries.

There thus grew up a great diversity in the international monetary sphere, in place of the essential uniformity which was secured by the gold standard. In 1932 the countries of the world could be classified from the foreign exchange standpoint under four broad headings:

1. the genuine gold standard countries;
2. the 'pseudo-gold' countries, i.e. those which maintained their nominal parities with gold by an elaborate system of exchange control;
3. the sterling area, which strictly covered only those parts of the British Commonwealth which kept their monetary reserves in the form of sterling balances, but which could be regarded more loosely as including various foreign countries, notably in Scandinavia, which had decided to 'peg' their currencies on sterling;
4. the remaining countries, where heavy exchange depreciation was combined as a rule with exchange restrictions.

(b) The Growth of Trade Restrictions

This foreign-exchange situation was detrimental in various ways to international trade as hitherto conducted; and it gave a powerful impetus to the erection of fresh trade barriers. In countries which adopted exchange control, the system was usually such as to constitute in itself a formidable impediment to imports. An importer could only obtain foreign exchange to pay for foreign goods at the discretion of the exchange-control authorities; and in practice foreign exchange was only made available for a greatly reduced volume of imports. This is not in all circumstances an inevitable feature of exchange control. Under the arrangements that have been evolved in Great Britain and the sterling area during the war, exchange control is used in order to regulate capital movements only; foreign exchange is supplied freely for commercial transactions, and imports are regulated by other means. But the shortage of monetary resources in the countries that had recourse to exchange control round about 1931 was such that it was not enough for them to prevent a flight of capital. They had also to correct an adverse balance of payments on current account, and to correct it quickly; and they used exchange control as the most efficient and most flexible instrument for this purpose.

In short, under drastic systems of exchange control in their earliest phases, the extent to which foreign exchange was made available to defray imports was determined by arbitrary, *ad hoc*, day-to-day decisions in the light of the resources available. Gradually, as it became possible to look further ahead, import programmes were planned on a basis corresponding more nearly to a system of import restrictions; none the less the regulation of imports was still treated as a subordinate branch of exchange control. This, it may be suggested, is in principle the proper way to treat import restrictions that are imposed for exchange or balance of payments reasons, as distinct from those designed to protect particular industries.

In countries which underwent exchange depreciations, the fall of exchange rates served as an impediment to imports; and it was usually followed by higher tariffs. As has already been said, the British authorities were worried about their capacity to check an undue fall of sterling for several months after our departure from the gold standard. To improve the balance of payments seemed in those circumstances an urgent objective of policy; and this consideration was an important factor, though not the only one, in the introduction of a general tariff in 1932. This step led on to others. The ban which the Free Trade tradition had hitherto imposed on the extension of Imperial Preference was removed, and there followed the arrangements of the Ottawa Conference of 1932, and the introduction in large parts of the colonial empire of preferences in favour of British goods, and 'quotas' designed to check the increase of imports from Japan. It should be noted in passing that the Japanese had invaded Manchuria long before this development occurred.

The intensification of trade restrictions in the phase of the world economic crisis was, however, by no means confined to countries which had an adverse balance of payments or which were short of monetary reserves. On the contrary, the two countries which absorbed most of the gold that other countries were losing, namely the United States and France, played a leading and early part in the process. In 1930 the United States adopted the Hawley–Smoot Act, which raised the American tariff to the highest level in its prevailingly high tariff history. Early in 1931 France introduced a system of import licensing, covering cereals and certain other food-stuffs, and a few months later took the lead in extending this system to non-agricultural products. Stimulated by these examples, tariff increases soon became the rule throughout the world, and quantitative import restrictions became widespread throughout Europe.

The Hawley–Smoot tariff, following the reversal of the flow of American lending, and adopted in despite of a strongly favourable United States balance of payments, was a glaring example of an action diametrically counter to world needs. This is fully recognized in retrospect by American opinion. Perhaps, indeed, the sense that this measure was indefensible from the standpoint of international good behaviour may have encouraged some exaggeration of the influence which it exerted. 'Our people', said Mr. Cordell Hull in 1940, 'are not likely to forget the contribution which the enactment of the 1930 Tariff Act made to the intensification of economic warfare among nations, to the growth of trade barriers, to the vicious spirals of resentment, ill will and retaliation.' Undoubtedly the Hawley–Smoot tariff aggravated the difficulties of other countries. But, before it became operative, the world depression, though it had not yet reached its nadir, had already assumed catastrophic proportions; and it is improbable in the extreme that the international monetary breakdown could have been avoided, or that the subsequent story would have been materially different, if the American tariff had been left unchanged.

Moreover, the Hawley–Smoot tariff, though it was quite unjustified by any balance of payments reasons, was none the less an outcome of the depression. Its object was to check the growth of unemployment and the formidable fall of commodity prices in the United States. Similar considerations were responsible for the raising of tariffs and other trade obstacles in other countries which could plead no international financial difficulties. From the international standpoint such actions were undeniably 'self-regarding'. In retrospect it has become common to describe them as attempts 'to export unemployment'. It is certainly to be desired, and perhaps it is not extravagant to hope, that a greater regard for the general world interest will exercise a restraining influence on such acts in future. Even here, however, due measure should be observed in passing censures and prescribing rules. It may be illegitimate and anti-social for a country to attempt to 'export' its unemployment; but it cannot reasonably be expected to 'import' it uncomplainingly.

In practice, under conditions of depression, it is difficult to define the point at which protective measures pass from an attempt to check the import of unemployment to an attempt to force its export.

Until the fall of the pound in September 1931 the United Kingdom studiously refrained during the world depression from placing any fresh obstacle in the way of imports. Under the prevailing conditions of falling prices and wage reductions in competing industrial countries, this led not only to a serious weakening of our national balance of payments, but to the importation of unemployment on a substantial scale. Only the still potent force of the free-trade tradition made it possible for us to acquiesce in this state of affairs as long as we did; and having regard to the increasing importance attached to stability, economic security, and 'full employment', it seems very doubtful whether any country could be expected to 'import unemployment' so unresistingly in future.

Measures of agricultural protection were especially prominent among the trade restrictions imposed for reasons of internal stability. It was, indeed, mainly agricultural commodities that were the subject of the quantitative import restrictions that were so widely imposed during 1931 even by countries which were in no international financial difficulty. This development sprang from the fact that an abnormally severe slump of agricultural prices was an outstanding feature of the world depression, and threatened the stability of the agricultural systems of food-importing countries. The collapse of agricultural prices was important in another way. It played a considerable part in the disequilibrium in the balance of international payments, the causes of which have still to be examined.

(c) The Balance of Payments

The disequilibrium in the balance of payments, as has already been suggested, lay at the root of the international monetary breakdown. It was concealed for some time by the large-scale flow of international lending, but became apparent when this flow was reversed.

A major factor in the disequilibrium was the radical change which the war of 1914–18 had brought about in international debtor-creditor relations. The United States, hitherto a debtor country, emerged from the war as a substantial creditor. Her nationals had acquired a large portion of the American securities previously held by foreigners. Her government had large debts owing to her from the governments of the European Allies, together with a claim to a share of German Reparation payments. Germany was stripped of her capital assets overseas and of her mercantile marine; her position was further weakened by territorial losses, and she was made subject to heavy Reparation liabilities. Great Britain's overseas investments were materially reduced, though they still remained large; and her government had contracted a substantial war debt to the government of the United States. France, though victorious in the war, emerged in an economically weak condition. Traditionally, she had been one of the great lending countries, but her loans in the generation preceding the war had been directed preponderantly to financing her ally Russia, and with the advent of the Soviet Government to power, these securities became worthless.

The war also left a lasting mark on the structure of international trade which aggravated the consequences of the change in debtor-creditor relations. The Lancashire cotton industry lost ground in Far Eastern markets, which it was never able to regain, partly to Japan and partly to local Indian production. In the automobile industry, at a critical phase of its development, British manufacturers, who had already got somewhat slowly off the mark, were put several years behind by the diversion of engineering to munitions. Thus, alike in old and in new lines of trade, the war dealt enduring injury to British exports, which in the later 1920's had to carry the handicap of an overvalued pound. In Germany and central Europe broadly similar disadvantages (except for the overvalued pound) were accentuated by the dislocating effects of defeat, revolution, and the currency confusion of the early post-war phase. On the other hand, the war opened out new opportunities for Japan, and gave a stimulus to the export industry of the United States, which had already been making significant progress on the basis of the solid advantages of inventive pre-eminence and the largest home market in the world.

These influences combined to produce the following broad results on the international balance of payments during the 1920's. At the one end of the scale, the United States had a large favourable balance. At the other end, Germany and central Europe had a heavy adverse balance. In the middle was Great Britain with a balance which remained on the right side until the world economic crisis, but without the huge favourable margin which had previously enabled London to act as the chief centre for new loans.

The general disequilibrium of the international balance of payments comprised, however, another major factor of profound significance. Those countries which specialized in the production of agricultural commodities for world markets were among the first to undergo an exchange crisis. Prominent among them were Argentina, Brazil, and indeed most of the South American communities, Australia and New Zealand in the British Commonwealth, and in the Old World the countries of east-central Europe. Their exchange difficulties were a consequence of the abnormally heavy fall of agricultural prices which marked the onset of the world depression. This served to derange the balance of payments of countries whose exports consisted mainly of agricultural products, and led inevitably in many cases to exchange depreciation and financial default.

The severe slump of agricultural prices thus played an important part in the international monetary breakdown. It was some time before the significance of this development was fully appreciated; indeed it is doubtful if it is generally appreciated even yet. Trade depressions had always been recurrent phenomena; and in every trade depression the prices of agricultural commodities had fallen more than those of manufactured goods. This made it natural to assume that the unusually heavy fall round about 1930 was merely an indication of the abnormal severity of the depression as a whole.

(d) Agricultural Surplus Capacity

In the nineteenth century, however, though gluts of agricultural commodities might occur from time to time, they were only temporary, and soon gave place to conditions of excess demand which led to the opening up of new productive areas. The essential fact before 1914 was that the world demand for most agricultural commodities increased, year in and year out, more rapidly than could be met, under the existing conditions of agricultural technique, from the existing areas of supply. But in the 1930's it became apparent not only that new productive areas were no longer needed, but that the existing areas could sustain an output which for many commodities was far larger than the world's demand, and which tended under the influence of technical progress to increase at least as fast. A prevailing excess of supply over demand had indeed become evident in the 1920's. It was 'taken care of' for a time by pooling schemes, and other devices for holding surplus stocks off the market, in the vain hope that the condition of over-supply might prove only temporary. This, of course, aggravated the trouble later.

There emerged, in short, the essentially new phenomenon of a persistent excess of productive capacity in many branches of world agriculture. There are many who would dispute the view that the persistence of this excess was in any sense inevitable; they would attribute it mainly to the growth of agricultural protection in the importing countries of Europe. In the light of the actual sequence of events, this diagnosis seems both inadequate and somewhat superficial. The accumulation of agricultural surpluses and the collapse of agricultural prices preceded any marked general increase in agrarian protection. It was in order to safeguard their agricultural systems from the dislocation which the slump in world prices seemed to threaten that European countries, other than Italy, first introduced new protective measures. Once this movement had begun, indeed, it went further than the original purpose warranted; many continental countries cut down their agricultural imports drastically; and the world problem was thereby gravely aggravated. Vicious circles of this kind often complicate the course of economic development, and make it more difficult to disentangle cause and effect.

It is clear, however, that behind the excess of world agricultural capacity lay other and more fundamental factors. The rate of technical progress in agriculture, which throughout the nineteenth century was far less rapid than in manufacturing industry, was rapidly speeded up in the present century. In successive branches of agriculture, output per acre, and output per individual increased significantly, as the result partly of discoveries in the fields of chemical and biological research and partly of mechanization. This development served, of course, to reduce costs of production, and thus enabled farmers to sustain a substantial fall in the relative prices of agricultural commodities. But it also helped to create conditions of excess supply, which drove prices down below a remunerative level. This quickened rate of technical progress was accompanied by another trend, which told in the same direction, namely the slowing-down of the rates of population growth in the Western industrial countries, which were the chief importers of agricultural commodities.

The redundancy of agricultural capacity exerted far-reaching

repercussions on the international economic system. It was probably an important independent cause of the world depression, as
well as of the international monetary breakdown that ensued. It
set in motion, as has been suggested, the trend towards increased
agricultural protection and self-sufficiency in Europe. It played a
special part in the evolution of the Ottawa system of Imperial
Preference. It led directly to attempts to maintain remunerative
prices by means of international commodity regulation schemes.
It gave new strength and insistence to the desire for greater industrialization in countries which had hitherto specialized in export
agriculture. Finally it was a major cause of the collapse, in default,
fraud, and universal disillusion, of the system of large-scale international lending.

(e) The Collapse of International Lending

In the freely working economic system of the nineteenth century,
international lending played a prominent role. Indeed no part of
that system received so much praise from contemporary observers,
or seemed to supply so good an illustration of the favourite theme
of a natural harmony between enlightened self-interest and the
common good. It was not suggested that a man who subscribed to
an overseas loan did so out of public spirit; none the less the consequences were of benefit to the whole world. By means of such
loans, machinery or railway equipment was exported from Great
Britain, where it could be produced most cheaply, to new countries
where it could be put to the most advantageous use. The annual
output of food and raw materials in the new countries was thereby
largely increased; and these commodities were then exported to
Great Britain, partly by way of loan interest and partly in exchange
for manufactured consumers' goods. This was to the advantage of
the mass of people in the borrowing and the lending countries alike.
It gave the former a share in the benefits of the industrial revolution.
It opened out for the latter a way round the barriers which the law
of population and the law of diminishing returns from land had
seemed in the age of Malthus to place in the path of social progress.

Thus international lending bore a good name; and it did not
seem unreasonable in the 1920's to hope that it might play a helpful
part in post-war reconstruction. The revival of international lending
became accordingly one of the main objectives of economic states-

manship. It was recognized, as has already been noted, that the
lending must be related to a favourable balance of payments on
current account, and that the United States must therefore step
into the foremost ranks of the lending countries. This object was
attained in a degree which for a time surpassed the most optimistic
expectations.

The methods by which it was attained were open, however, to
much criticism; and it became common to lay the blame upon these
methods when disaster overtook a large proportion of the foreign
bonds which American investors had been induced to buy. Americans, in particular, are prone to attribute the trouble to their
national lack of experience in foreign lending. Here again, however,
it is open to question whether their self-censure is not excessive.
Many of the foreign bond issues which in the light of our after-
knowledge seem most unwise did not seem so in the 1920's even to
cautious financial minds.

The main causes of the trouble lay much deeper—in the disequilibrium of the balance of payments which has been analysed
above. An essential condition of the tolerably smooth functioning
of international lending in the nineteenth century was that it facilitated an increased output by the borrowing countries of commodities for which there was a rapidly expanding world demand. So long
as this condition was fulfilled, the subsequent payment of interest
and sinking-fund charges gave rise to no 'transfer' problem or
foreign exchange difficulty. But the international lending of the
1920's did not fulfil this condition. It was to cover a heavily adverse
balance of payments that the European borrowing countries raised
loans abroad. The capacity of the South American borrowers to
discharge their obligations was destroyed by the saturation of the
world market for agricultural commodities.

It is not surprising, therefore, that a substantial proportion of the
European bonds and a much larger proportion (reaching about 90
per cent.) of the Latin American bonds raised in the United States
during the 1920's should have gone into default. This experience
killed stone-dead the short-lived vogue of American foreign lending; and for several years after 1931, through the medium of the
purchase of American securities in Wall Street, the United States
became a substantial net importer of long-term capital. British
foreign investments also suffered seriously from default; and the
consequential reluctance of London to undertake new foreign

issues was reinforced by the anxieties of the British monetary authorities about the stability of sterling.

If the results of the international lending of the 1920's were unpalatable to the lenders, it must not be supposed that the borrowers found them satisfactory. The role of a defaulter is invidious; and most debtor countries struggled hard to avoid it, some successfully; all were concerned to defend their currencies against undue depreciation. The obligation to pay large sums across the exchanges as interest on their external debts was an important element in their exchange difficulties; and the sense of the burden of such obligations grew accordingly. This feeling added fuel to the resentment which had long been latent in borrowing countries against the control of public utilities or other important local enterprise by foreign capital. Thus the world economic crisis left behind it in lending and borrowing countries alike a state of mind profoundly antagonistic to international lending, at any rate of the traditional types.

The broad question arises whether the good name of international lending in the nineteenth century did not depend largely on conditions which have now passed away, on the slow rate of progress of agricultural technique and on the rapid rate of growth of the populations of industrial countries, which together made the opening up of new food-producing areas one of the world's vital needs. There will doubtless be scope in future for international investment in new forms and directed to the purpose of the industrialization of the less developed countries. It seems improbable, however, that such international investment could supply, as did the lending of the nineteenth century, the main lubricant of an automatic, self-adjusting system.

(f) Summary

Under the strain of a severe trade depression which began in the latter part of 1929, the international economic system which had been laboriously re-created in the 1920's broke down. The multilateral payments system provided by general adherence to the gold standard, the comparatively liberal trend of commercial policies, the lubricant of large-scale international lending, all disappeared. The quantum of world trade fell by about one-fourth between 1929 and 1932.

The chief moral to which this breakdown points is the essentially fair-weather character of an international economic system based on the free play of market forces, qualified by tariffs. When equilibrium already exists, market forces may suffice to correct small departures from it. In the 1920's, however, there were large maladjustments to correct; maladjustments in the international balance of payments, maladjustments between demand and supply for important agricultural commodities. In part these maladjustments were the result of changes brought about by the war of 1914–18. In part they may have reflected more deep-seated changes, which deprived international lending of its historical *raison d'être*. In either case, they called for readjustments in production and in the flow of trade, which proved to be beyond the compass of the automatic responses of an unregulated system.

IV. THE GROPINGS OF THE NINETEEN-THIRTIES

(a) *Deliberate Exchange Depreciation*

The bottom point of the depression, taking the world as a whole, was reached in 1932; but for some time thereafter recovery was extremely slow. Bad trade, unemployment, and agricultural distress were the main preoccupations of public opinion throughout the world, and they carried an obvious threat, which actually proved fatal in many countries, to the stability of the social structure and the political régime. Different governments accordingly felt constrained to experiment with various new types of policy in the effort to stimulate recovery, without paying much regard to the repercussions of their actions upon their neighbours. It was in these circumstances that many of the practices which are now the subject of particular censure were evolved.

One of the most startling of these experiments was the deliberate depreciation of the dollar by the United States in 1933. The gold-value of the dollar was forced down by more than 40 per cent. by means of a series of measures which included an increase in the buying price offered for gold at the mints. This policy, adopted in face of the vast American gold reserves, was something entirely new in monetary history. The first announcement of it fell with shattering effect upon the World Monetary and Economic Conference which had just opened its proceedings in London, and which had been called to consider, among other problems, the stabilization of currencies. It seems to have been largely inspired by a crude statistical generalization to the effect that the price level varied proportionately to the price of gold, which received at the time great publicity in the United States, and commended itself to President Roosevelt as an hypothesis worth testing. But another important influence was a sense of the advantages which Great Britain and other sterling countries had derived from the fall of the pound in 1931, coupled with a suspicion that we were trying to transfer our share of the burden of depression on to American shoulders by means of our newly instituted Exchange Equalization Fund.

The idea that the British departure from the gold standard was influenced by a desire to devalue the pound is entirely baseless. We were driven off gold, despite strenuous efforts to remain on. None the less, we soon found that the fall of the exchange brought substantial compensations with it; and the sense that the over-valued pound of the later 1920's had been an incubus of which we were well rid became general. For several months, as has been seen above, the weakness of the pound was a source of serious anxiety to the British monetary authorities. But early in 1932 the tide of market forces turned, and the pound began to recover rapidly. When this happened, British opinion was quick to realize that greatly as it had disliked the original depreciation, it would dislike even more a return to the former parity. It was in these circumstances that the Exchange Equalization Fund was established, with the object of mitigating the fluctuations of exchange rates.

Inasmuch as the Fund accumulated substantial reserves of gold and foreign exchange over the next few years, it is clear that it was used predominantly to keep the pound down rather than to keep it up. This does not mean that the British authorities were pursuing a policy of competitive exchange depreciation, a purpose which they consistently disavowed. There were solid grounds for the belief that the pound had been overvalued between 1925 and 1931; and during the depression wage rates had been cut far more drastically in competing industrial countries than in Great Britain, both before and after September 1931. In these circumstances, a return of the pound to its former parity could have afforded no stable basis for international trade. The same largely speculative market forces which had pulled the pound down and were now pushing it up again might at any moment pull it down once more. To try for some sort of stability at a lower level seemed, therefore, the course of wisdom. Nor did it seem unreasonable or anti-social that we should take the opportunity to replenish our monetary reserves, which had been virtually exhausted when we suspended gold payments.

In the meantime, however, other countries had observed with different feelings the fact which had so impressed British opinion, namely that the fall of the pound had been a positive relief to us. During the 1920's a fall of a country's exchange rates had been the signal for the commencement of an inflationary process, involving the vicious spiral of prices and wages chasing one another, and sometimes culminating in an uncontrollable *dégringolade*. Many Continental observers expected that the fall of the pound would be followed by a similar inflationary process in Great Britain. The sequel was disconcertingly different. British prices rose hardly at all; prices in gold-standard countries underwent a sharper fall, and there could be little doubt that the depreciation of the pound was in part responsible for this. In Great Britain and the sterling area trade ceased at any rate to get much worse. Elsewhere depression deepened alarmingly. The British seemed to have contrived to transfer its brunt to other shoulders; and having regard to the indisputable fact that the Exchange Equalization Fund was used predominantly to keep the pound down rather than to keep it up, it was only natural that the British policy should arouse suspicion and resentment and the impulse to retaliate.

The memories of inflation were too vivid in the principal Continental countries to tempt them to follow our example; but it was otherwise in the United States, where there were no such memories and where monetary heretics always find a ready ear. The desire to counter the depreciation of the pound was therefore one of the main influences which prompted the intrinsically very different policy of the deliberate devaluation of the dollar. It may be noted that in authorizing the President to devalue the dollar, Congress declared that the extent of the devaluation should be such 'as he [the President] finds necessary from his investigation to stabilise domestic prices or to protect the foreign commerce against the adverse effect of depreciated foreign currencies'.

The devaluation of the dollar exerted disastrous reactions upon the economies of those countries which still maintained their gold parities, on the basis of free, or largely free, convertibility. These countries were now reduced to France, Belgium, Holland, Switzerland, and Czechoslovakia. The exchange rates of their currencies with the dollar were forced up by two-thirds, and their exchange rates with sterling, since the British authorities strove to avert a similar appreciation of the pound, also increased materially. Thus the currencies of the gold bloc became heavily 'overvalued'; their producers were placed at a serious disadvantage in international competition, and it became necessary for them to choose between devaluing themselves or undertaking a severe deflation. Despite the manifest difficulties attendant on the latter course the former was ruled out for the time being by an overwhelming force of public prejudice, which was especially strong in France. Belgium fell out of the ranks fairly soon, but the remaining gold countries continued to cling to their parities for more than three years after the devaluation of the dollar.

Meanwhile internal deflation, though insufficiently drastic to restore equilibrium, was carried far enough to provoke increasing discontent; and this was an important factor in the electoral triumph of the Popular Front in France in 1936. M. Blum assumed office with a programme of social experiment, which was clearly incompatible with the maintenance of an overvalued franc; French citizens put their money abroad in increasing volume; and after a few months of vacillation the decision to devalue the franc was taken in September 1936. The realignment of the remaining gold currencies soon followed.

The devaluation of the French franc was accompanied by simultaneous declarations by the governments of France, Britain, and the United States, which became known as the Tripartite Agreement. In fact, these declarations contained nothing of substance beyond a general assurance that the devaluation of the franc would not be made the occasion for a fresh depreciation of the dollar or the pound. There was no arrangement for positive co-operation. None the less, the assurance mentioned was of some significance as marking an agreement to avoid for the future any competition in exchange depreciation.

In the preceding years there had seemed at times to be some danger that a competition of this sort might go far and spread wide. It was evident that if two countries were to set out to regulate the exchange rate between their currencies by unilateral action, each being resolved to avoid an overvalued currency for itself, any difference of view between them as to what the exchange rate ought to be would logically involve a collision of policy from which a competition in depreciation might easily result. The positions of the United States and the United Kingdom did not seem very different from this after the deliberate depreciation of the dollar; and there were frequent speculations in other countries as to the possibility of open warfare between the British and American Exchange Equalization Funds. It was further evident that any such downward rivalry between the two principal world currencies must sooner or later make it impossible, as in fact it did, for other countries to maintain a fixed parity with gold; and there was an obvious possibility that if these other countries were forced to abandon orthodoxy, they might, like the puritan who turns rake, throw over all restraint, and intensify the competitive scramble. The Tripartite Agreement of 1936 marked the removal of these dangers. It recorded a *modus vivendi*, vague, but none the less effective.

The path to this *modus vivendi* was smoothed by the growth of disillusionment in the United Kingdom, and still more in the United States, about the power of exchange depreciation to promote national recovery. The Americans found that the devaluation of the dollar opened no royal road to the restoration of agricultural prices and prosperity; their attention turned to the problem of excess production, and to the internal experiments of the New Deal. British manufacturers discovered that the additional export trade that could be obtained by a lower pound was, in the prevailing world circumstances, limited and insecure. In short, the weapon of exchange depreciation proved in practice somewhat blunt, and this made it easier to secure a 'gentleman's agreement' not to use it.

It should be noted that the bluntness of this particular weapon was due largely to the fact that most of the world's trade was now subject to exchange clearings, import restrictions, commodity regulation schemes, barter arrangements, international cartels, preferences, and high tariffs. Only a small sector remained in which there was an open field for price competition. To use a common terminology, international trading conditions had been rendered 'rigid' by the development of new types of trade restriction. Under these conditions the competitive advantages of an undervalued currency, or the disadvantages of a slightly overvalued one, ceased to count for very much. Thus, the rigidity of the trading system, upon which such sweeping censures have been passed, perhaps helped not a little to avert exchange depreciation war.

(b) Managed Money

From the Tripartite Agreement of 1936 until the eve of war, exchange rates remained comparatively steady. But there was no definite stabilization, no return to the fixed parities which were a central feature of the old gold standard. Despite strong pressure that was brought to bear from time to time, the British Government persistently refused to restore any definite link between the pound and gold. We had adopted a policy of cheap money, believing that this would assist internal trade recovery. If this policy were to have a fair chance, it must be pursued uninterruptedly. It was doubtful, however, if this would be possible in face of the ever-present possibility of adverse capital movements, if we had a definite gold parity to defend.

The British refusal to return to gold was thus largely attributable to the desire to pursue an autonomous credit policy, to regulate our internal credit conditions in accordance with our view of the needs of trade. It is important to note that the idea of an autonomous, or, indeed, of a deliberate credit policy, was quite new. It was of the essence of the old gold-standard system that money rates, and the abundance or scarcity of credit, were determined by the movement of the exchange rates and the inflow or outflow of gold. The system was praised as being essentially 'automatic' and thus free from the danger of political manipulation; and the function of management was supposed to be limited to that of registering correctly the pressure of forces which no one attempted to control. In the United States, in the 1920's, the superabundance of gold reserves had made it possible to experiment with the deliberate regulation of internal monetary conditions; but these experiments were tentative, and any ambitious purpose of maintaining a steady price level was emphatically disclaimed. No such freedom of action on a gold basis had seemed open to countries which had not large surplus stocks of gold.

The pursuit by Great Britain of an autonomous credit policy entailed another important consequence besides the absence of definite exchange parities. The volume of internal currency was divorced from the volume of the gold reserve. Under the gold standard they had been linked rigidly together; an outflow of gold caused a corresponding reduction of the currency available as a basis for bank credit, and this, if the outflow was substantial, led to credit restriction and set in motion a deflationary process. This, it should be noted, was an essential link in the chain of automatic reactions by means of which international equilibrium was maintained under the gold-standard system. The internal deflation resulting from an outflow of gold did something to stimulate exports by reducing costs, and still more perhaps to curtail imports by reducing purchasing power. In these ways, it served to improve the balance of payments.

The link between internal currency and the gold reserve was broken as an incident of the creation of the Exchange Equalization Fund. This fact received less attention at the time than the instability of foreign exchange rates and the dangers of competitive exchange depreciation; and it is doubtful if its full significance is yet appreciated. For it meant that the main regulator of the old freely working international economy had been removed. International trade was then so widely controlled that this did not seem to matter much. If, however, the attempt should be made to re-establish a freely working system, it might matter a great deal more. For it is certain that the old regulator has been removed for good. The trend of ideas in internal policy, the insistence in particular on the maintenance of 'full employment' would make it impossible for any major country to leave the volume of its internal purchasing power to be determined in future by blind external forces. In this respect there can be no return to the automatism of the gold-standard system.

(c) Exchange Clearings and Dr. Schacht

While the exchange rates of the free-exchange countries were undergoing the vicissitudes that have been described, developments of great significance had been taking place in central and eastern Europe. Germany, in the crisis of 1931, had introduced an increasingly effective system of exchange control as the only alternative to a renewal of depreciation. This did not suffice, however, to solve her problem, which was aggravated when the pound sterling fell and Britain adopted a general tariff. Still shrinking from exchange depreciation in the belief that German opinion would regard this as a signal for inflation, the Brüning Government set themselves to restore equilibrium by deflating costs and prices, and persisted in this course until the strains it caused swept away the Republican régime and brought Hitler into power. It has already been seen that a similar deflationary policy was to prove largely instrumental three years later in bringing M. Blum into office in France. There was no surer prescription for the defeat of governments during the inter-war period than persistence in deflation.

Hitler was no less determined than his predecessors to avoid an open depreciation of the mark. But his general policy was hardly reconcilable with a continuance of deflation; and the overvaluation of the mark was materially increased in 1933 when the dollar was artificially forced down. A means of escape from this *impasse* was provided by the expedients of Dr. Schacht, who became President of the Reichsbank under Hitler. The mark was kept nominally at its parity with gold; but materially lower exchange rates were in effect permitted for approved trading transactions. Complex arrangements were made under which there were various classes of mark accounts with different degrees of convertibility and different effective exchange values. The attention of the outside world was caught by the anomalies incidental to these expedients; but their chief importance in the story is that they helped to give a peculiar form to the exchange clearing agreements which Dr. Schacht proceeded to negotiate with other countries.

Germany, it is important to note, did not initiate the exchange-clearing system. The first exchange-clearing agreement was made between Switzerland and Hungary as early as November 1931; and this was followed by a series of similar agreements between European countries. Their purpose was to facilitate the continuance of mutually advantageous trade despite the impediments resulting from the collapse of the gold standard and from national systems of exchange control. Though the form may vary, and though the technical details are often complex, the essential principles of an exchange-clearing agreement can be stated simply as follows: The individuals who are parties to a trading transaction between the two countries concerned receive payment from, or make payment to, their own central bank, in their own currency. The two central banks 'clear' these and other transactions, i.e. set inward payments off against outward payments, at an agreed rate of exchange; and any resulting balance is represented by a credit accruing to the one central bank in the books and in the currency of the other.

This arrangement carries the automatic consequence that the country with a favourable balance lends the difference to the country with an unfavourable balance; and, if the latter country maintains a strict system of exchange control, this loan can only be liquidated by the purchase of its goods or services. Thus under the conditions which prevailed in the 1930's, exchange-clearing agreements were apt to lead on to 'barter' trade agreements, designed to keep the clearings in reasonable equilibrium. This meant in effect an attempt to adjust the trade between countries on highly bilateral lines, and a sacrifice of the advantages of 'triangular' or multilateral trade. On the other hand, it did much to enable countries which had got into trouble through a heavily adverse balance of payments to restore equilibrium without curtailing their imports unduly.

These are consequences which must ordinarily be expected to result from an exchange-clearing system, adopted in conditions of disorganized international payments and world depression. But Germany gave a peculiar turn to this system by incorporating in her agreements the expedient of the overvalued mark, qualified where necessary by differential exchange rates. In her clearing agreements with the Balkan countries, Germany insisted that the mark must be reckoned at its nominal gold parity. In return for this, she was willing to make long-term contracts for the purchase of the Balkan cereals, pigs, and tobacco, at prices that were materially higher, in terms of the Balkan currencies, than the market prices ruling. One effect of this arrangement was to keep prices up in Germany and the Balkans alike. In the Balkan countries, for example, the agricultural producers obtained higher prices for their exports than they could otherwise have done, while manufactured goods or machinery, which had to be obtained from Germany, were correspondingly dear. Under the prevailing conditions of depressed prices, and especially of depressed agricultural prices, this feature had decided attractions as a safeguard against internal unrest.

Another consequence, or another aspect of the same consequence was, however, more equivocal. The high prices which the Balkan agricultural producers obtained in the German market cut them off from other markets. To German manufacturers, exports to the Balkans became similarly an especially remunerative branch of trade. The German share of the import and export trade of the six Balkan countries (including Turkey) rose from roughly one-fifth in 1933 to roughly one-half in 1938. Thus the Balkans fell into a condition of substantial economic dependence upon Germany which assisted Hitler's political and strategic aims.

From a strictly economic standpoint there is no reason to suppose that Germany derived any advantage from her insistence on the overvalued mark or from the large geographical diversion of trade which it caused. The difficulties of her traders in competing in free-exchange markets were increased thereby; and she found it necessary to adopt various roundabout and only partially effective expedients for subsidizing exports in order to obtain the foreign exchange which she required. But from the standpoint of preparation for war it was of great advantage to Germany to reduce her dependence on sources of supply which would be cut off during war and to extend and deepen channels of trade which she could protect and command. Under cover of apparently makeshift and ramshackle commercial expedients, she was forging a weapon to counter the blockade. To the rulers of Germany this consideration was paramount.

Germany negotiated clearing agreements with many other countries, besides those of south-eastern Europe. In 1932, it is worth noting, France, Holland, and Switzerland entered into clearing agreements with her, hoping to ensure that the proceeds of Germany's export surplus to them would be earmarked for the payment of debt charges to their nationals. This hope was quickly disappointed; the German authorities saw to it that their export surplus was replaced by an import surplus, and thereby converted the clearings into a means of borrowing more. In 1935 Dr. Schacht proceeded to negotiate a series of agreements with the South American republics which, like those with the Balkan countries, were intended to develop trade. Here, however, he was unable to get his point accepted that the mark should be reckoned at its nominal gold parity. The South American agreements were based on special *ad hoc* rates of exchange which represented varying rates of discount for the mark. The particular rate embodied in a particular treaty was determined mainly by economic bargaining strength. Dr. Schacht was prepared to concede a comparatively low rate for the mark to countries whose products Germany urgently desired to buy. He stuck out for a comparatively high one in his negotiations with countries which had no alternative outlet for their products.

Thus Germany used the technique of differential exchange rates as a means of securing favourable 'terms of trade'. She took the different South American countries one by one, and tried, like a 'discriminating monopoly', to charge in each case what the traffic would bear. This was something quite new in international commerce; it seemed unfair; and the indignation of other countries was the more readily aroused because third parties were liable to suffer in their export trade from the 'barter' element in the clearing agreements. Gradually it became evident that the German foreign-trade policy, taken as a whole, was proving markedly successful from the German point of view. It was natural, in these circumstances, to attribute the success to the peculiar Schachtian expedients, and to conclude hastily that Germany had succeeded by a ruthless exploitation of her bargaining strength in obtaining exceptionally favourable terms of trade at the expense of poor agricultural-exporting countries.

This belief is still widely prevalent; but it is a complete illusion. Germany's terms of trade were not more favourable but less favourable than those of free-exchange industrial countries. The relation between the prices of primary products and the prices of manufactured goods, which prevailed throughout most of the 1930's, was, of course, extremely unfavourable to countries which specialized in the former. But Germany seems, on the whole, to have given as good terms as any other country to her agricultural suppliers. In her dealings with the Balkan States, it is doubtful if Germany attempted to exploit her bargaining position to the full. Her governing object there, as has been seen, was to develop channels of trade on which she could rely during war, as well as to build up a position of political domination; and for these purposes it was desirable that the trading arrangements should be manifestly to the economic advantage of the Balkan peoples. In her dealings with the South American States, Germany was restrained by no similar scruple and undoubtedly tried for the most favourable terms she could get. But in this she does not seem to have achieved any conspicuous success.

This is not to say that the exchange-clearing system was not economically advantageous to Germany. This system enabled her, despite her external indebtedness and her lack of monetary reserves, to maintain and to increase the *volume* of her trade. It enabled her, in other words, not to buy cheap and to sell dear, but to buy *more* and to sell *more*. It is a mistake to suppose that her Nazi rulers set out to reduce Germany's external trade to a minimum. They aimed doubtless at self-sufficiency for commodities which could be produced in sufficient quantities at home. But this was in order to make possible increased imports of other commodities, notably war materials. Actually, Germany's foreign trade increased by about 20 per cent. between the low point of 1932 and 1938; and though during this period there was a substantial recovery of world trade, the German share of world trade increased slightly. The significance of this increase is heightened by the fact that it was accompanied by a huge increase, largely represented by armaments, in German production for the home market, which would tend under unregulated conditions to reduce a country's capacity to sell abroad.

The moral which this part of the German story suggests is that a sufficient volume of trade is much more important than favourable terms of trade to a country in a weak international financial position but possessing a large industrial capacity. Production for export is only a comparatively small part of the total production of an industrial country. Even in Great Britain the pre-war proportion was only 15 per cent. From the standpoint of production, therefore, an adverse movement of the terms of trade by as much as 10 per cent. would mean only that we should have to increase our total production by 1·5 per cent. in order to purchase an undiminished quantity of imports. This is an increase which the ordinary process of technical improvement gives us in a single year. It represents only a small part of the productive power which industrial countries normally waste in unemployment. Such countries have therefore no good reason to adopt a grudging attitude upon the terms of their trade with agricultural countries, *if* they can be assured of selling enough to defray their imports. To be able to sell enough may, on the other hand, be of vital consequence.

The advantage of selling more as a means of buying more, which Germany derived from the clearing agreements, did not depend on the special Schachtian expedients; it sprang from the esssential principles of the exchange-clearing system as defined above. It was not an advantage which accrued to Germany alone; it was automatically extended to the agricultural countries in the Balkans and in South America, with whom the clearing agreements were made. To the Balkan countries in particular the economic gain was great. Their agricultural technique was backward, and their marketing organization rudimentary. Their products were therefore of poor or uncertain quality, not easy to sell in world markets under conditions of excess supply. Yet, lacking for the most part industries of their own, they urgently needed to export in order to obtain the wherewithal to buy manufactured consumers' goods. Their clearing agreements with Germany met this need, and rescued them from the apparently irremediable confusion in which they had been plunged by the world depression. Germany's attempt to acquire political preponderance in the Balkans was helped by the fact that her economic relations with them were relations of reciprocal advantage rather than of exploitation.

This at least was broadly true until 1938. As the war drew near Germany turned to her advantage another feature of the exchange-clearing system, namely that the country with a favourable balance of payments automatically lends the difference to the country with an adverse balance. With her industrial capacity increasingly concentrated on armament production, Germany cut down her exports to the Balkan countries, and the latter were obliged accordingly to sell part of their produce not for goods but for credits. During the present war, with Germany in a position to dictate her terms, this process has, of course, been carried much further; and Germany's satellites have been forced to supply an increasingly large portion of their output in return for mark balances which may be worth little when the war is over. Apart from the question of their eventual value, these accumulating mark balances are, of course, fundamentally similar to the accumulating sterling balances by which Great Britain has financed a large part of her war-time purchases. The British system of payments agreements and indeed the arrangements of the sterling area provide automatic borrowing facilities which closely resemble those of the exchange-clearing system.

The moral of this part of the story is that these automatic borrowing facilities are a help and a protection to countries in a 'debit' position, i.e. with an adverse balance of payments which they cannot speedily adjust. The borrowing country does not have to approach the lending country with a request for accommodation; the *onus* is upon the lending country to refuse the accommodation, if it chooses, by curtailing its exports. This transfer of the initiative is a great advantage to a country which needs to borrow. The advantage can be put to good ends or to bad. Germany used it to increase her power for aggression. We have since used it to increase our power to resist aggression. The advantage is subject to the limits set by the complaisance of the lender; and it should be noted that the credits which Germany obtained through the mechanism of her exchange clearings amounted to only a small fraction of the loans which she raised during the 1920's and subsequently repudiated. It is not clear, therefore, that the automatic borrowing facilities of exchange clearing are more open to abuse than the traditional forms of international lending, organized with the aid of an hypnosis of wishful thinking. Nor is it clear that the former facilities, related as they are to the actual flow of trade, might not provide in less warlike times a more efficient lubricant for a balanced system of international commerce.

The chief significance of the main story of the exchange-clearing agreements is that they served to increase rather than to decrease the aggregate volume of world trade. They enabled both Germany and her agricultural customers to buy more and to sell more than they could have done otherwise. Nor were these mutual economic benefits obtained at the expense of any commensurate injury to the trade of other countries which were financially strong enough to maintain a free-exchange system. These countries had no desire to increase their imports of either Balkan and South American agricultural products or of German manufactures. Yet, unless they did so, neither Germany nor the Balkan and South American countries could afford to buy more from them.

(d) Selective Import Control

Germany combined her exchange-clearing agreements with an elaborate system of selective import control. By means of the former, she maintained and increased her external purchasing power; by means of the latter she put this purchasing power to the most effective use. The governing object of her policy was to develop her strength for war; and this she did with a rapidity and a completeness which confounded all the calculations based on previous experience with which the democracies lulled their misgivings for several years. Starting from a position of decisive military inferiority in 1933, Germany had attained by 1938 the overmastering ascendancy which enabled Hitler to dictate the terms of Munich. Never in history had the balance of power been so suddenly reversed. Never had so little resistance been offered to the rearmament of a State whose dangerous designs were only perfunctorily concealed. Behind this lack of resistance lay many factors, among them the perverse purblindness imposed on the democracies by their favourite formulas. But also among them, it is clear, was the quite unexpected rapidity with which the rearmament was accomplished.

The development of German strength for war rested on the solid basis of the large productive capacity of German industry, together with its high technical skill. This, however, would not have been sufficient in itself. Germany needed to import materials to a large aggregate value, both for her ordinary industries and for her armament production. She wanted also to lay in large stocks of these materials as a war reserve; and, in fact, it was with large stocks of petroleum, bauxite, manganese, &c., that she entered the present war. To finance these purchases it was important for her to increase her external purchasing power as much as possible. As has been seen, she did this to a fairly substantial extent by means of her clearing agreements. None the less, these agreements left Germany with a much smaller external purchasing power than she had enjoyed in the later 1920's. Moreover, many of the more important of the materials she needed could only be obtained from free-exchange markets, in which the self-imposed handicap of the over-valued mark, and in some degree the Jewish boycott, made it difficult for her to sell.

Default on her external loans and the later seizure of the monetary reserves of Austria and Czechoslovakia helped her somewhat. But selective import control was the instrument upon which Germany mainly relied. She cut down ruthlessly her imports of commodities which her people could do without or could produce for themselves, and by this means she made more foreign exchange available for the materials she wanted for her war preparations. For imports essential to the standard of life she continued, however, to find sufficient foreign exchange. Indeed, the proportion of food in her total imports increased between 1933 and 1938, though this increase doubtless represented the accumulation of war reserves. It was widely believed at the time that Germany was developing her strength for war at the expense of her standards of living. That was true in the sense that her people worked harder and for longer hours without very much additional real reward. But, when all factors are taken into account, it seems a mistake to suppose that the standard of living fell; certainly it did not fall materially.

In other words, the German policy of intensive rearmament and the accumulation of war supplies raised two distinct problems, a production problem and an import problem. The production problem was solved easily enough by the absorption of the unemployed, the taking up of industrial slack, the increased employment of women and longer hours of work. The import problem was solved partly by means of clearing agreements, which enabled Germany to export and import more than she could otherwise have done; but mainly by a systematic selection of imports, on the basis of an efficient system of exchange control. There was nothing magical about the results which Germany achieved. During the war we have used largely the same methods, and have obtained essentially the same results. None the less, these results were in sharp contrast to the tribulations which Germany had endured in the 1920's. They contrasted no less sharply with the contemporary experience of France, where the power and even the will to strengthen the national defences was paralysed by economic confusion.

In these contrasts, it is true, the fundamental factor was the existence or the absence of effective control over capital movements; and the first lesson that emerges is the importance of this control to almost any country which wishes to assure itself against dislocating disturbances in its economic life. But the German achievement also indicates how great is the relief which a country that is short of international purchasing power can obtain from a deliberate and systematic selection of its imports.

The items that make up a country's import-bill, when imports are unregulated and subject only to the impediment of old-established protective tariffs, are extremely miscellaneous. They include necessaries and luxuries; commodities of which the people consume too little, and commodities of which they consume more than enough, for a satisfactory standard of life; commodities that might have been, and commodities that could not have been, produced at home. There is also what is sometimes called the 'invisible' import of expenditure on foreign tours or travel, which makes a call on the foreign-exchange resources of the tourist's country. Great Britain, for example, in times of peace spends her foreign exchange upon a wide range of purposes, which includes wheat, meat, fruit, and tobacco; cotton, wool, iron-ore, and newsprint; motor-cars, wine, foreign films, and holidays at Monte Carlo. Under unregulated conditions, the amount of foreign exchange which a country spends upon each of these diverse purposes is determined as the aggregate result of the decisions of its individual citizens and business men, in accordance with the length of the purse which each happens to command.

That is well enough for a country that has plenty of foreign exchange. But it is not a satisfactory arrangement, or lack of arrangement, for a country that is suffering from an acute shortage of external purchasing power. This, as has been seen, was the condition of many countries during the inter-war period, as it may be the condition of many after the present war. A country in this condition must strive to limit its annual expenditure by reference to its international income. If it neglects to do this it will incur a steadily increasing international indebtedness, with a serious exchange crisis as the probable sequel. But if it must curtail its imports below the level that would result from an unregulated demand, it seems only right and reasonable that it should endeavour to cut down first the 'fat' which is contained in every country's peace-time import programme, and to maintain its essential imports as long as it can in undiminished volume.

This was the purpose of many of the import prohibitions and import restrictions that were introduced so widely during the 1930's. The world economic depression, and the collapse of agricultural prices which accompanied it, left many countries, notably those of eastern Europe and South America, with an external income which was insufficient to meet their accustomed import bill. It was no longer possible for them to meet the deficiency by borrowing, and a reduction of imports was forced upon them accordingly as an inexorable necessity. They were faced with the problem of laying out a shrunken international income to the best advantage, a problem essentially similar to the problem of domestic economy which arises from time to time in many private households. For solving this problem, for cutting the national import-bill substantially with the minimum of hardship, the method of quantitative restrictions and prohibitions had manifest advantages over that of tariffs. Thus countries in exchange difficulties had recourse increasingly to the quantitative method. Germany, as has been seen, used it with scientific thoroughness, as a means of developing her strength for war. Long before this, Soviet Russia had selected her imports equally systematically by means of her State monopoly of foreign trade. But most of the countries which selected their imports by quantitative regulation during the 1930's did so without any predisposition in favour of this method, acting rather under the urgent pressure of events.

All types of import restrictions were naturally unpalatable to exporters elsewhere, who found their goods excluded. The United Kingdom and the United States were prominent among the exporting countries which suffered or appeared to suffer from these restrictions; and it is not surprising, therefore, that the first reaction of public opinion in the English-speaking world should have been to condemn import restrictions generally as a new type of trade impediment, more objectionable than tariffs. But it is doubtful whether the volume of international trade was diminished by import restrictions that were imposed to meet exchange difficulties. The countries that were suffering from a shortage of foreign-exchange income had no desire to cut down their total imports more than was necessary for equilibrium; and by and large they did not do so. They imported one thing rather than another, necessaries rather than luxuries; but they imported in the aggregate as much as they could afford to buy.

Undoubtedly the curtailment of their imports was a *pis aller*. It would have been more satisfactory to them to increase their exports, and thus to obtain the wherewithal to import more. This they tried to do by exchange-clearing agreements, by barter arrangements, by every means open to them. The fact remained that their international income had been reduced. The corollary remained that they must reduce their external expenditure. The practical inference remained that they could reduce their external expenditure with the least injury to their standard of living by selecting their imports deliberately by quantitative means.

(e) The Varieties of Quantitative Regulation

Import restrictions were introduced during the 1930's for other purposes besides the one that has been indicated; and there were other types of quantitative regulation besides import restrictions. Indeed; the evolution of quantitative arrangements of various types and for diverse purposes was a significant feature of the decade. Several of them have already been mentioned in the course of this narrative.

The principal forms of quantitative regulation were as follows:

1. *Selective Import Control*; that is to say, import restrictions or

prohibitions designed to lay out a limited external purchasing power to the best advantage.

2. *Protective Import Restrictions*; i.e. restrictions designed to protect particular producing interests in the countries imposing them. Many countries used import restrictions during the 1930's to protect agriculture.

3. *Preferential Import Restrictions.* Quota restrictions were imposed in many British colonies on imports of textiles and certain other goods from foreign countries. These restrictions were so framed that they applied in practice only to imports from Japan, which had previously been increasing with quite exceptional rapidity. Their object, of course, was to safeguard the share of the Lancashire cotton trade and other British exporting industries in colonial markets. Quota restrictions were also imposed by the United Kingdom on imports of meat and bacon, partly with the object of giving an effective preference to producers in the Dominions.

4. *Barter Trade Arrangements*; that is to say, the provisions in many trade agreements by which one country undertook to import not less than so much of certain products from another. As has already been seen, such barter arrangements were a common supplement to exchange-clearing agreements. Similar arrangements were a feature of the trade agreements which the United Kingdom made with various countries, e.g. Denmark and Argentina. Their object was to safeguard or to extend the mutual trade of the parties concerned.

5. *Commodity Regulation Schemes*; that is to say, schemes for regulating the production or export of certain primary commodities by agreement between the chief producing countries. The object of these schemes was to keep the prices of the regulated commodities from falling to unremunerative levels as the result of excess supply. The method employed was that each producing country agreed to restrict its exports and often its production within the limits of an assigned 'quota'. These schemes were usually organized by governments, and were backed by local legislation. The principal commodities that were so regulated were rubber, tin, sugar, and tea; and the British colonial empire was a major participant and beneficiary in all of them.

6. *International Cartels*; by which the business interests of different countries allocated export markets in certain lines of trade by mutual agreement.

7. *State Trading*; by which the purchase of certain imports (or the sale of certain exports) was centralized in a single agency. The quantity of the goods imported was made the subject of deliberate decision as an incidental feature of this system which could, of course, be used as a means of selective import control, of domestic protection, or for any other purpose. This system has been carried to its furthest lengths by Soviet Russia.

The variety of purpose and of character which these arrangements cover will be apparent. Some were designed to defend currencies, some to protect industries, some to promote self-sufficiency, some to develop foreign trade, some to maintain prices. Again, some were set in a national, some in an imperial, some in a bilateral, and some in an international frame. Yet all of them embodied the common principle of deliberate quantitative regulation which before 1914 was virtually unknown. It is stupid to sweep away all this variegated development with schoolmasterly disapproval as something which should not have occurred and must not occur again.

The unity of principle underlying so much diversity is the more impressive in that the development proceeded for a considerable time without any conscious recognition of the principle, and certainly without any predisposition in its favour. Import restrictions, for example, in their early days had no friends. They were condemned equally by the exponents of traditional economic doctrine and by those of fashionable nostrums. They were repugnant to individualists, to collectivists, and to business men; and the governments that imposed them did so at first reluctantly. Most of the quantitative expedients that have been enumerated were introduced, not as applications of a new constructive idea, but as *ad hoc* remedies for pressing evils; and they were chosen because no other remedies seemed likely to be equally efficacious.

The drift towards quantitative methods came from the increasing failure of the price mechanism to discharge the functions that had been entrusted to it. Hitherto it had been thought unnecessary for economic policy to concern itself with quantities, or volumes, or gross concrete facts. It was assumed that any readjustment that might be needed could be brought about by a change in some price or rate. Was some commodity in excess supply? A fall of price would reduce production, stimulate demand, and the excess would disappear. Had some country an adverse balance of payments? A lowering of its costs and income-level, or alternatively a lowering of its exchange rates, would put the matter right. Was capital flying abroad? Higher interest rates would bring it back. Were there too many work-people seeking employment in a depressed industry? Reduce their wages and they would move elsewhere. Did a country wish to protect its peasant agriculture from foreign competition? It was easy to calculate the necessary scale of import duties or of subsidies. Economic theory was almost exclusively devoted to analysing the working and the inter-connexions of the different parts of the price system. To a very large extent, moreover, this outlook was common to the advocates and to the opponents of *laisser-faire*. Their difference was that the former maintained that the price system would work best if left to itself, while the latter held that active intervention was often needed to get the rates or prices right.

In the conditions that prevailed after the world economic crisis, the price system failed to justify the faith reposed in it. Producers of primary commodities found that prices might fall to disastrous levels, and still supply might greatly exceed demand. Importing countries that wished to ensure a reasonable livelihood to their farmers were unable to judge what rates of import duty would be sufficient for the purpose. Countries in serious exchange difficulties found higher discount rates futile as a check to a flight of capital, and deflation disastrous as a means of adjusting current payments. In one sphere after another it became evident that there were dis-equilibria too large and too deep-seated to be adjusted indirectly by the manipulation of a price or rate. There was no alternative but to grapple with them directly, that is to say, by concrete quantitative means.

In most of its applications, of course, the technique of quantitative regulation raised problems and difficulties of its own. In applying import restrictions, for example, how should the permitted volume of imports be shared between different exporting countries or between different importing firms? The former question might be affected by a bilateral trade agreement or preferential arrangement, but, subject to this, the usual answer to both questions was to assign 'quotas' on the basis of past performance, that is to say, by reference to the exports or imports in a particular year or longer period, selected as a base. The same principle was used in allocating export quotas under commodity-regulation schemes. It was the obvious principle to adopt; it met the desire for fair-play in an intelligible manner; and so long as the quantitative arrangements could be viewed as emergency measures, it seemed reasonable enough. It is clear, however, that it would be seriously defective as the basis of any continuing arrangement, and though provisions were made under some quantitative schemes for revising the original allocations from time to time, it cannot be said that any satisfactory means of doing this had been evolved.

When the problem of allocation had been settled, another difficulty arose. If the permitted volume of imports of some commodity was materially less than the competitive demand, the natural consequence would be to raise the price in the importing country but to reduce it in the exporting countries. There was thus a potential gap between the import price and the export price, with the possibility of large profits to traders on one side of the frontier or the other. From this it followed that import licences might have a substantial cash value and thus offer new temptations to corruption. For reasons such as these quantitative restrictions have been described in the booklet on Quantitative Trade Controls, published by the League of Nations in 1943, as a 'non-conformable' type of interference with the individualist economy.[1]

This, however, is to use the phrase 'individualist economy' in a strict, or rather an extreme, sense in which it no longer corresponds to the facts of a large part of the economic system. It assumes that international trade in any commodity is the result of a multiplicity of small individual transactions between competing private traders in the importing and exporting countries. In modern times, how-

---

[1] The following is the passage in which this phrase appears: 'Quantitative restrictions constitute a much more serious interference with the individualist economy based on the price mechanism and free enterprise than the other type of regulation. We may characterise them as a "non-conformable" type of interference, a foreign substance, as it were, in the body of the free economy which necessarily leads to dangerous ulcerations and suppurations and threatens to weaken or undermine the individualist economy altogether. On the other hand, Customs tariffs, even high ones, are "conformable" interferences which do not destroy the price mechanism on the functioning of which a private economy must depend.' It seems hardly appropriate, however, to describe central marketing organizations for agricultural commodities as 'ulcerations and suppurations'.

ever, countries that produce agricultural commodities for export
have tended increasingly to organize their marketing through some
central selling agency. This has enabled them to grade their products scientifically, and by ensuring that their exports are of reliable
quality to win 'goodwill' for them in export markets. There is no
doubt, indeed, that this development marks an improvement in
technical efficiency. The Danish bacon trade owed much of its
successful expansion to the fact that it had long been organized
upon this basis.

Where central selling arrangements exist, the potential gap
between import and export prices under quantitative regulation
need not be either an objection or a difficulty. It is possible for the
importing country, if it is so disposed, to allow the selling organization of the exporting country to obtain the whole benefit of the
higher price in the import market resulting from the reduced
volume of sales. In this way producers in the exporting country will
receive compensation in the form of higher prices for the reduction
in their volume of business.

It was in this spirit that the United Kingdom Government administered the restriction of bacon imports, which they imposed
in 1933. They had decided to build up a bacon industry at home;
and at first indeed contemplated carrying their policy to extreme
lengths. But they wished to do this with the minimum injury to
Denmark and other exporting countries. The price of bacon, like
those of most agricultural commodities, had fallen very low; and
there was a widespread and somewhat crude disposition to regard
the fall of commodity prices as the *fons et origo* of the evil of the
world depression, and to welcome accordingly any recovery of
these prices, anywhere, however brought about. British Ministers
were also influenced by the consideration that the Danes would
be able to buy more British goods if they got better prices for their
products. In these circumstances they quite genuinely thought it a
merit of the quantitative method of protection that it would enable
the Danes, through their central organization, to get the benefit
of a higher price and the further benefit of planning their future
production on the basis of knowledge rather than guesswork. Other
exporting countries shared in these benefits, and the fact that the
system stimulated them to develop similar central marketing agencies was certainly no disadvantage to them.

It is obvious that the interests of Denmark and other bacon

exporters would have been far more seriously injured if the United Kingdom had tried to establish a bacon industry at home by protective tariffs. The duties would have reduced the prices received by the Danish farmers; and, if they were to fulfil the object of making room for home production, they would have had to be put high enough to reduce the volume of Danish exports. Thus the producers of bacon would have suffered a double loss, whereas under the plan adopted the total payment they received was actually increased. In short, the use of the quantitative method enabled the British Government to show far more consideration for the established trade interests of the supplying countries than would have been possible if they had used tariffs instead; and it seems only fair to remember this fact when quantitative restrictions are contrasted with tariffs as a more objectionable form of 'economic nationalism'.[1]

From the British point of view the quantitative method had the advantage that it was a more accurate means than tariffs of achieving a moderate protective end; that is to say, ensuring a limited volume of home production, without raising prices unduly to the consuming public. The bacon scheme, as it happened, was not particularly successful, and the result makes it doubtful whether it is wise to aim at developing pig production in England as a major livestock industry. But on the question of method the experiment showed that for agricultural products at any rate quantitative regulation may be more 'conformable' than tariffs with modern marketing arrangements. It should be noted in this connexion that

[1] Yet paradoxically enough the fact is treated by some critics as an additional offence. The League of Nations booklet on Quantitative Trade Controls gives the following version of the story: 'In many cases quotas were allocated not only to home importers but to foreign exporters, or only to the latter. Foreign interests were thus given a part of the spoils and induced to acquiesce in the situation, creating further vested interests and removing possible opposition. The whole benefit, indeed, sometimes went to the exporter. . . . Similar results ensued from the imposition of the quota restriction on Danish bacon imports into the United Kingdom in 1933. The Danish exporters, who were organised, were able to raise bacon prices so that they were more than compensated for the cut in the quantity of their exports.' This passage is significant as indicating how deeply intellectualist criticism of quantitative methods is influenced by nostalgia for the price system rather than by genuine concern for the well-being of any of the human beings affected. Arrangements designed to mitigate injury to exporting countries are described as though they were a sinister sort of bribery. The use of the word 'spoils' implies a tacit assumption that the price which would result from unregulated supply and demand, even under severe depression, represents the *justum pretium*.

all the statutory marketing schemes introduced during the 1930's as a principal feature of British agricultural policy were accompanied by the quantitative limitation of imports, as an obviously appropriate counterpart.

Of the international regulation schemes, several worked in practice better than might have been supposed. The *a priori* predisposition was to regard these schemes as illegitimate conspiracies of producing interests to exploit the consumers. The Stevenson rubber scheme of the 1920's, which attempted to maintain the price of rubber at a highly profitable level, had indeed been fairly open to this charge; but the speedy collapse of that experiment taught the lesson that it was impossible to obtain and to enforce an agreement to limit production on a sufficiently comprehensive basis, if the price offered a strong temptation to increase output. The regulation schemes of the 1930's were accordingly marked by moderation of aim. Persistent efforts were made to induce governments that were chiefly interested as consumers to participate; and the objective of stimulating and diversifying demand was pursued as well as that of limiting supply. Production was not restricted by more than was clearly essential in order to raise prices gradually to a modest target price; no complaint could reasonably be made of the prices that were in fact reached under any of the schemes for agricultural commodities.

It may be added that the subsequent wartime experience of these schemes went to show that there was substance in the claim that regulation might prove as helpful when it was desired to increase production as when it was desired to restrict it. The huge increase in the American demand for rubber which occurred in 1941, and which the lack of prescience incidental to a free market had deferred unwisely until then, would hardly have been met with such a moderate rise of price, if production had been unregulated, and the estates had been left to scramble with one another for labour without restraint. It is doubtful, moreover, whether so large a productive capacity would have been available in Malaya and the Dutch East Indies with which to meet this demand if nothing had been done to maintain the price of rubber after 1932.

The instance of rubber serves to illustrate one of the fundamental reasons why the automatic adjustments of the price system fail to work satisfactorily nowadays for most agricultural products. The period of agricultural production is often very long. It takes from

five to seven years after planting for rubber trees to become productive. It is possible, therefore, under unregulated conditions, for excessive planting to persist for several years under the stimulus of a
comparatively high price, and for the productive capacity to continue to expand after the price has fallen heavily. This characteristic
is shared by other plantation industries, such as tea and coco-nuts;
and in a lesser degree or in a more complex form (e.g. through
systems of crop rotation) it holds good of a wide range of agricultural production. Other factors contribute to the same result, i.e.
a large proportion of the world's agriculture is in the hands of
peasants or small farmers who respond to a fall in their receipts by
increasing their exertions. It was only because of the continuing
need for additional productive capacity that serious trouble did
not arise from these causes before 1914. But now that agricultural
technique has caught up with the expansion of world demand, the
need to regulate production deliberately, if disastrous fluctuations
are to be avoided, presents itself with a practical force that cannot
be ignored.

International regulation schemes were one of the attempts of the
1930's to meet this need; and it seems probable in the light of this
experience that for a limited range of commodities such schemes
may have a useful role to play in future.

The attempts of industrial cartels to allocate markets among competing countries were open to more serious objections and were less
clearly justified, though it would be rash to infer that they can
never be justified. More generally, the experience of the 1930's suggests that quantitative methods of regulation are less satisfactory
for industrial than for agricultural products. But this does not mean
that import restrictions upon manufactured or semi-manufactured
goods may not be a sensible expedient for a country with a heavy
adverse balance of payments. In such circumstances, the theoretical
difficulty of the gap between the import price and the export price
may be overcome either (when the goods are luxuries) by coupling
the quantitative restrictions with substantial import duties, or (when
the goods are more essential) by combining them with measures of
price control. Again, as has been seen, trade agreements of a barter
character may be useful in enabling countries that are short of
international purchasing power to maintain a larger external trade
than would otherwise be practicable.

The war-time development of central purchasing is closely related to the question of quantitative methods. During the war the greater part of Britain's imports are bought centrally through the agency of the Ministry of Food and the Ministry of Supply. For several commodities these departments enter into bulk contracts for the purchase of the output of certain countries, and these arrangements have advantages from the standpoints of both the importer and the producer. How much of this system of central purchase will be retained when the war is over is, of course, uncertain. Similar arrangements were evolved during the last war for a number of foodstuffs and materials, and were swept away quickly afterwards. Upon this occasion, however, there will be many arguments for retaining part of the war-time mechanism for at least a considerable period. It is possible that in other countries systems of central purchase may be retained or introduced in order to deal with pressing post-war difficulties. As already indicated, such arrangements may be regarded as a special, and indeed extreme, variety of quantitative regulation.

The broad impression that emerges from a review of the quantitative experiments of the 1930's is that they served on the whole to help rather than to hinder international economic recovery. They brought much-needed relief to hard-pressed sections of producers and to hard-pressed countries. They provided an area of firm ground amid the quagmire of disordered price levels and exchange rates. They facilitated constructive efforts to improve marketing arrangements and made it easier for all concerned to plan ahead. They showed themselves a useful, if not an indispensable auxiliary of internal policies designed to meet the widespread desire for greater economic security, including, in particular, steadier employment.[1]

This record compares favourably with that of most of the other devices by which the economic statesmanship of the 1930's tried to grope its way out of depression. Especially striking is the contrast with the results of exchange depreciation which, as has been seen, were disappointing to the countries that attempted it, yet caused

---

[1] These advantages, it is worth noting, are tacitly admitted by the critics, under cover of the name 'temptations'. Thus the League of Nations booklet on Quantitative Trade Controls observes: 'It is easy to understand the temptation to cling to a method offering such precision in the control of foreign competition and such a degree of certainty in the regulation of foreign trade.' It says further: 'Never again—such was the argument current among European Governments in the middle 'thirties—must the country's economic life be at the mercy of fluctuations coming from abroad.'

disastrous disturbance to the economies of other countries. By the test of results, as distinct from *a priori* preconceptions, the quantitative technique must be judged far more consonant with international comity.

It has, of course, been subjected to much international criticism on the ground that it provides a way round the obligations of the most-favoured-nation clause, and may entail 'discrimination'. But before the justice of this criticism can be appraised, it is necessary to consider another remarkable development of the 1930's, namely the challenge to the most-favoured-nation clause itself which came from the countries with the most consistently liberal traditions of commercial policy.

(f) Preferential Systems and Low-tariff Clubs

Under the most-favoured-nation clause a country is bound to give equally favourable tariff treatment to all countries with which it has treaties containing this clause, whether their tariffs are high or low, increasing or diminishing, 'negotiable' or 'non-negotiable'. It was widely believed in the early 1930's that this served to hamper the reduction of tariffs on a basis of reciprocity. Countries A, B, and C might agree that it would be to their mutual advantage to admit one another's goods more freely; but they could not do this under the most-favoured-nation régime unless each of them was willing to reduce its duties also on imports from another country D, which might have just increased its tariffs on their goods from a high to a prohibitive level. This seemed unfair, particularly after the Hawley–Smoot tariff; and for countries with limited monetary reserves it might be dangerous. Several attempts were therefore made to modify the clause, or to obtain agreed 'derogations' from it, so as to remove what had come to be regarded widely as an indefensible injustice.

One of these attempts was a proposal which was blessed by the Stresa Conference of 1932 that the Danubian countries should be allowed to grant tariff rebates to one another, other countries being asked to waive their most-favoured-nation rights so as to make this possible. Another was that known as the Ouchy Convention. In 1932 Holland, Belgium, and Luxembourg agreed to reduce their duties on each other's goods by 10 per cent. annually up to a total cut of 50 per cent., provided other countries would waive their most-favoured-nation rights. They further agreed that any State that wished could accede to the Convention and obtain its benefits on the same terms.

Both these projects proved abortive. The chief obstacle to the Ouchy Convention was the opposition of the United Kingdom; and this opposition was directed against the principle, which, it was feared, might lead to serious complications, of extending the privileges of the Convention to unspecified countries. On the other hand, the British Government, though reserving the right to judge each case on its merits, did not offer any general objection to preferential arrangements between countries connected by 'historical and geographical ties'. In other words the British Government opposed the idea of 'low-tariff clubs', but not that of regional preferential systems. In practice, the latter idea was equally barren of results.

None the less, the movement of opinion in favour of these ideas in the 1930's was impressive. The lead in the movement towards 'low-tariff clubs' was taken, as has been indicated, by Belgium, Holland, and Luxembourg, i.e. by countries with a low-tariff reputation. Resolutions in favour of new permanent exceptions to the most-favoured-nation clause were passed by a series of international conferences, including the Conference of American states at Montevideo in 1933. Recommendations in the same sense formed part of the so-called 'Van Zeeland plan' of 1938. The insistence on the need to modify the most-favoured-nation clause became part of the current internationalist ideology. The failure of this movement of opinion to achieve any tangible results was mainly a reflection of the extreme difficulty of achieving practical results through the method of multilateral agreements.

Meanwhile, in the British Commonwealth, Imperial Preference was developed from rudimentary beginnings into the comprehensive arrangements of the Ottawa Conference. The results proved somewhat disappointing to the Dominions who had previously been the chief protagonists of Imperial Preference. The output of some of their major agricultural industries, notably wheat in Canada, and wool in Australia, had attained dimensions which far exceeded the aggregate demand of the United Kingdom. Whenever this was true, preferential tariffs were bound to prove nugatory. For a preference in the United Kingdom could do nothing to increase the price obtainable for that part of the Dominion output which had to be sold in other markets, and the pressure of competition forced down the price in the United Kingdom to the same level that could be obtained elsewhere. The gradual recognition of this fact led to a reaction of opinion in the Dominions against the preferential idea, and towards the view that their interests lay in the direction of freer world trade.

None the less, some important sections of Dominion agriculture derived material benefits from the Ottawa arrangements. The most substantial benefit, it is worth noting, was that which resulted from the preferential treatment of Dominion imports under the quantitative restrictions imposed by the United Kingdom on imports of meat.

The preferential system was extended to the colonial empire, though some colonies were unable to grant preferences owing to their obligations under the Congo Basin treaties. The same difficulty, namely that a large excess of Empire production over Empire demand renders preferences nugatory, applies to many colonial products, e.g. cocoa. Thus the benefits and sacrifices of the preferential system were unevenly spread, some colonies giving much more than they got, and others getting much more than they gave. But the fact remains that the sugar colonies in the West Indies and elsewhere were rescued from probable disaster by the substantial preference on sugar granted by the United Kingdom and by Canada.

The British preferential arrangements aroused growing resentment in the United States. The mutual preferences between Canada and the United Kingdom were especially objectionable in American eyes, since they seemed to entail an unnatural diversion of trade which conflicted with the manifest destiny of the economic unity of the North American continent. But dislike of this particular application was broadened into a general disapproval of the preferential system, and led to a disposition, which has found insistent expression since the war began, to demand its abolition in the name of 'non-discrimination'.

The story of the 1930's is pertinent at several points to the issue of policy that arises. On the one hand, it is certainly wise to go as far as possible in modifying those parts of the preferential system which constitute a practical grievance of the United States; and the disillusionment of the Dominions with the potentialities of the British market, and their desire for freer access to the American markets, are additional reasons in favour of this course.

On the other hand, the revolt of opinion against the most-favoured-nation clause in the 1930's should warn us against regarding 'non-discrimination' in the narrow sense which the phrase usually carries, as synonymous with justice or fair-dealing. The traditional rules for non-discrimination involve distinctions which are far from equitable. It has always been customary to allow exceptions from most-favoured-nation in favour of Customs Unions. In other words, the States that form a Customs Union are allowed to discriminate in favour of each other against the rest of the world in what may be an extreme degree. But small neighbouring countries may have good reasons for seeking to cultivate closer economic relations without wishing to go so far as a complete Customs Union. Mutual preferential concessions may often represent their most practicable road towards greater unity. To insist that they must do all or nothing, to bless Customs Unions but to condemn preference, is doubtful policy. The distinction can be defended by various arguments on the plane of practical convenience; but it cannot be justified by any clear or compelling principle of ethics.

The application of the doctrine of non-discrimination to Imperial Preference involves similar anomalies. In some empires the tariffs of the colonial territories are integrated with those of the metropolitan countries in a common customs system. This arrangement is permissible under the non-discrimination formula, though in fact it may entail the virtual exclusion of foreign traders from these colonial markets. But if this is to be treated as legitimate, it would be palpably inequitable to forbid the less exclusive preferential relations which Great Britain has developed with her colonies.

Thus the doctrine of non-discrimination is far from being the simple matter of justice which it is sometimes made to appear. On the other hand, complex systems of differential tariff rates have practical disadvantages. Among them is their tendency to distort the price structure, and thus to make it more difficult for countries which rely on preferential duties in certain markets to compete effectively in other markets. For this among other reasons it may perhaps prove that quantitative arrangements, conceivably on the basis of central purchase, may play a larger part, and preferential duties a smaller part, in future attempts to develop trade between countries which wish to draw nearer together.

V. THE MORALS OF THE STORY

(a) *The Falsity of the Legend*

In the foregoing pages the attempt has been made not only to describe the principal developments of the inter-war period, but to bring out their significance. Many of the more detailed lessons which emerge from the story have accordingly been sufficiently indicated during its course. It seems desirable, however, to attempt a summary of the major conclusions which constitute the central theme.

In the first place, the legendary view, defined in the opening section, which is so widely and so uncritically accepted by British and American opinion, is false in all essential respects. It can only be made plausible by inverting the sequence of events, or by kaleidoscoping essentially different phases. The key event in the story is the monetary breakdown of 1931. That represents, as it were, a watershed dividing the 1920's from the 1930's. After that breakdown it was inevitable that international trade should be drastically reduced and that new measures to defend currencies and protect industries should be widely adopted. But the world economic crisis which led up to the monetary breakdown was preceded by persistent and apparently successful attempts to restore a freely working international system, to reduce tariffs or to check their increase, and to revive international lending. It cannot be attributed to an orgy of economic nationalism or trade restrictions. As Macaulay once said, '*post hoc, ergo propter hoc* may be bad reasoning; but *ante hoc ergo non propter hoc* is unanswerable'.

For the same reason, it is false to attribute the Axis will to war to trade barriers or measures of discrimination. Whether economic factors played any material part in causing the present war, or whether it is not sufficiently explained by the deep-rooted political ambitions of the Axis States combined with the doctrinaire pacifism of the democracies, is a question upon which it is not easy to pronounce. In so far as any share of responsibility is attributable to economic policies, it belongs to the policies that led up to the world economic crisis and not to those which followed it. Had it not been for that crisis it is conceivable that Hitler would never have gained power in Germany, and that the subsequent course of world history would have been radically different. But to suppose that Hitler might have pursued a peaceful policy, if foreign trade had been easier for Germany, is surely to persist beyond pardonable measure in the illusions of the 'appeasement' years. As for Japan and her grievance against the colonial quotas, the decisive fact is that she invaded Manchuria long before there were any such quotas, and before the Ottawa Conference was planned.

It is more to the point to appreciate how greatly the Axis States were helped, in developing their strength for war, by the continuing attachment of the democracies to liberal commercial ideas. It was mainly from sources controlled by countries with which they intended or expected to be soon at war that both Germany and Japan obtained the materials which they laid by as an indispensable war reserve; and it was after the prospect had become so menacing that only the most wishfully minded could seriously hope that peace would be maintained that they imported these materials in the largest quantities. The significance of this traffic was indeed unmistakable; yet it seemed impossible to interfere with it because this would have offended those principles of the liberal commercial code which still inspired respect. Thus there is better reason for holding that the remains of economic liberalism helped the Axis States to make war than that economic nationalism provoked them to it.

(b) The Unwisdom of Repeating the 1920's

The history of the inter-war period provides no support for the view that we should attempt once again to reconstruct a war-shattered world on the basis of a freely working economic system, international credits, the reduction of trade barriers, and the outlawry of quantitative regulation. To attempt this would be not to learn from experience but to fly in its face. It would be to repeat the mistakes made last time in the name of avoiding them. It would be to invite the same failure, and the same disillusionment; the same economic chaos and the same shock to social and political stability; the same discredit for the international idea.

This is not to imply that those who threw their heart and energies into this attempt in the 1920's, whether in central banks, in the League of Nations organization, or elsewhere, have any cause to reproach themselves. They would have needed almost superhuman insight and prescience to have discerned clearly that the conditions essential to the smooth working of the system they were rebuilding had passed away and could not be reproduced. The task they set themselves seemed feasible, and they brought to it perseverance, judgement, and expert skill. No other policy was practicable in the circumstances of the time.

Stripped of their institutional trappings, the schemes which are emerging from the Anglo-American expert discussions closely resemble the policy pursued in the 1920's. Indeed, there are only two differences that seem material: the first is that it is proposed for the future that countries should be allowed, and in certain circumstances required, to control capital movements. This undoubtedly is a helpful change and a welcome concession to the teachings of experience. If, however, it is proper to regulate capital movements it becomes more difficult to see why it should be improper to regulate anything else. After all, the capital movements of the inter-war period were not the ultimate source of trouble. They sprang from deeply rooted maladjustments in the balance of international payments. It must be expected that the present war will leave behind it maladjustments on a still larger scale, which the control of capital movements will do nothing to correct. Moreover, since the line between capital and current transactions is often blurred, it may be doubted whether a flight of capital could be effectively prevented in the contemplated *laissez-faire* environment.

The second difference is that it is proposed in effect to replace deflation by exchange depreciation as the regulating spring of the international mechanism. That deflation can no longer serve this purpose is clear enough. Few countries would be willing in future to make the volume of their internal purchasing power depend on the magnitude of their gold reserves. It follows that it is also right to make provision for altering exchange rates so as to avoid large overvaluations or undervaluations of particular currencies. But the experience of the inter-war years does not support the idea that exchange depreciation might provide an efficient substitute for deflation as the regulator of a quasi-automatic system, still less the idea that the alterations of exchange rates which are to serve this critical purpose might be made the subject of amicable international decision.

Of the various expedients which different governments employed in the 1930's, none produced more unfortunate results than deliberate exchange depreciation. It was the least helpful to the countries which tried it, and the most harmful to other countries. It is true that this was largely because the expedient was intended in its most sensational use, namely the devaluation of the dollar, to serve as an instrument of internal recovery rather than of international equilibrium. None the less, to suppose that it could be used effectively for the latter purpose, and for that purpose alone, through a procedure requiring general international accord, is to expect a great deal. It has been seen above that the *modus vivendi*, by which the danger of an indefinite continuance of competitive depreciation was avoided in the 1930's, was facilitated by the 'rigidity' of the international trading system. If, however, conditions were established under which the postulates of abstract price theory were fulfilled, and export markets could be quickly swung away from country *A* to country *B* by an alteration of exchange rates, it is difficult to imagine that the assent of country *A* to the adjustment would be readily obtained. Nor, if such major economic consequences were involved, would the issue lend itself to quasi-judicial decision by a new-born international authority.

The force of this criticism, it will be observed, turns on the extent to which the idea of a return to a liberal commercial system is realized. If the volume of internal currency cannot in future be made to depend in most countries on monetary reserves, it is clear that exchange rates may have to be changed from time to time; and a procedure for securing that such changes are made so far as possible by international agreement is certainly to be desired. It is not unreasonable to hope that this procedure might work with sufficient smoothness if exchange rates can be varied without affecting radically and decisively the flow of trade, the stability of important industries, and the livelihood and employment of large masses of men and women. But if this condition is to be satisfied, it is essential that the postulates of abstract price theory should *not* be fulfilled, and that human welfare should be protected by a reasonable degree of 'rigidity' against violent change.

In other words, inter-war experience suggests that exchange-rate alterations cannot serve as the mainspring of a self-adjusting system. Once it is granted that deflation must be thrown on the scrap-heap, the self-adjusting international system is destroyed, and it may become necessary for the individual country to regulate its balance of payments by deliberate action. Moreover, this may be necessary, not only in occasional emergencies, but as a continuing policy, so that equilibrium, once re-established, may be maintained.

(c) *The Conditions of International Economic Order*

This leads to the positive lessons which are to be learnt from inter-war experience. Some measure of support can be drawn from it for many conclusions and many courses of action, the truth or wisdom of which may yet be doubtful. The following catalogue is confined to the lessons that seem reasonably clear:

1. The first lesson is the fundamental importance to any orderly international economic life of the objective of equilibrium in the balance of payments. In the long run, no country can expect in peace to import from outside more than it can pay for by means of its exports of goods and services or as interest on its investments. Hazy notions that the international economic system might be based on some different assumption are illusory, and attempts to base policy upon them can only lead to harm. The world is not nearly ripe for any application of the principle of Communism as between countries; the principle, that is to say, of 'From each country according to its ability; to each country according to its needs.' This principle can be applied in some degree between allies during war, united by the common purpose of the defeat of a common enemy, and with varying capacities to contribute to this task by military and economic means. It is chimerical as a basis for peace-time international relations.

2. The second lesson relates to the uses and abuses of financial aid. It may be of great help to a country, which is short of international purchasing power and faced with a large deficit on its balance of payments, to obtain credits or financial accommodation in some form either from a strongly placed country or from an international institution. This assistance may relieve the intensity of the immediate pressure on the country in difficulties, and supply it with a breathing-space in which it can adjust its import-export balance gradually, and thus cause less hardship to its own population and less damage to the trade interests of others. But whatever form the assistance takes, it will do mischief if it is used to evade the task of adjustment. If, therefore, it is given subject to conditions which seriously fetter the power of the country receiving it to bring its import bill within its international income, it is a doubtful blessing. One of the chief economic duties which a country, like an individual, owes to its neighbours is to live within its means; and in

general no country should be restrained or discouraged from taking any step which in the opinion of its responsible authorities is essential for this purpose.

3. Next, the marked trend towards an increasing degree of collective organization and State intervention in internal economic affairs must necessarily exert a far-reaching influence on external economic policies. The idea of greater economic security is fundamentally incompatible with that of an unregulated external economy. If a country's economic life is to be rendered reasonably stable, it may be essential to safeguard it against extreme disturbance from the vicissitudes of foreign markets. No country which makes the maintenance of full employment one of its major aims can abdicate its authority to check an abnormal flood of imports which threatens to disorganize employment. Nor can a food-importing country which contemplates new ambitious social policies, e.g. for improved nutrition, divest itself of the right to give essential imports a first claim on its exchange resources.

4. Although quantitative methods of regulation have their defects, limitations, and dangers, they are appropriate and useful for a large range of purposes. Whenever economic security is the object, or whenever the problem is to effect a large-scale readjustment with the minimum of disturbance, quantitative regulation is far superior to tariffs, subsidies, or the manipulation of exchange rates. It can provide a reliable safeguard against violent change and a considerate means of effecting gradual change. It is in harmony with the trend of modern development, e.g. in agricultural-marketing technique, and with the idea of planning. It is in harmony also with the deeper human urge to set reasonable limits to the arbitrary power of money over economic life.

5. Finally, the task of statesmanship is to build a new international economic order on the basis of freedom for individual countries to regulate their external economies effectively. The old international order of the nineteenth century was based on *laisser-faire* and has broken down for good. Nothing but failure, futility, and frustration can come from the attempt to set it up again. The problem is to devise a code of international good behaviour which will fit the conditions, the needs, and the aspirations of the modern world. There is no fundamental reason why we should not gradually evolve a working solution of this problem if we recognize it for

what it is. But we shall greatly increase the difficulties of doing so if we persist in associating the idea of international economic co-operation with the subordination of human welfare to the absolute rule of market forces, under the influence of doctrinaire abstractions, misplaced idealism, and nostalgia for the past.

5

NOTES ON PLANNING AND ON THE LAND VALUES PROBLEM[1]

1. It is common ground that, in order to facilitate housing and physical reconstruction after the war, adequate powers should be provided for the compulsory purchase of land by public authorities at reasonable prices. There is also agreement that these powers must enable land to be acquired with reasonable speed, and that the prices payable should be based on the general principle of the '1939 ceiling'. None the less, before these agreed aims can be carried out, many important and difficult questions have to be settled; for example, the application of the principle of the 1939 ceiling raises issues that are decidedly controversial. It is obviously important that these questions should be settled as soon as possible if the work of reconstruction is not to be impeded. Unfortunately their consideration seems to have become entangled with that of quite different issues about the 'development rights' of land which public authorities will not wish to acquire. The Ministry of Town and Country Planning evidently take the view that these issues are also urgent; and discussion has proceeded on this assumption.

2. In view of the *impasse* to which the attempts to solve them has led, it seems desirable to consider whether this assumption is well founded. The object of these notes is to suggest that the advantages of settling the Uthwatt issues quickly may not be very great, and that on the other hand the disadvantages of settling them prematurely may be very serious indeed.

I. THE QUESTION OF URGENCY

3. What is the case for regarding the Uthwatt issues as urgent? It rests on the assumption that it is important to speed up planning schemes and to bring them into full operation at an early date. In order to facilitate this, it is contended that it is necessary to compensate owners whose land would become 'sterilized' and that compensation can only be provided as part of a general settlement of

[1] 26 January 1944.

the problem of development rights. In fact, however, it is clear that it is already possible to prohibit any building development which is regarded as undesirable on planning grounds without paying any compensation. The exact legal position has been set out by the Inland Revenue in a Note, the effect of which is to bear out Sir Malcolm Eve's dictum that 'it is already the law of the land that, generally speaking, no one can change the use of his land without the consent of the appropriate planning authority'.

4. The existing powers of control are, however, expressly 'interim' powers; and it may be admitted that it would be unsatisfactory to rest content with them, if private building development were to be expected in an early future upon a very large scale. Landowners who were precluded by virtue of 'interim development control' from realizing their development rights during a prolonged phase of rapid development, which might prove to be the period during which these rights could have been used most profitably, would have strong grounds for complaint if they were denied any compensation. On the other hand, if development on privately owned land is likely in any case to be limited to fairly small dimensions for a long time to come, it would not be unreasonable to use the powers of 'interim development control', without compensation, to prevent undesirable development in the meantime. The question of urgency seems, therefore, to turn largely in practice on the prospects of development.

5. For some time after the war the capacity of the building industry will be insufficient to meet the large demands that will be made upon it; and it is generally agreed that in these circumstances it will be necessary to subject building operations to control in order to avert an inflationary trend of building costs. The claims of essential repairs and renovations on the one hand, and of the rehousing of the populations of 'blitzed' areas on the other, will presumably receive first priority. Generally, it seems fair to assume that the building of new houses in the early post-war years will be virtually confined to public housing schemes. In other words, the houses will be built on land which is acquired by some public authority. It may well be that in deciding where to build, and therefore what land to acquire, the local authorities will be greatly assisted by comprehensive planning schemes that were slowly evolved before the war, or are being drawn up now. But it is quite unnecessary to bring such schemes into full operation and to arrange compensation for

sterilized land. All that is necessary is to enable the local authorities to acquire the sites of their choice at reasonable prices.

6. This proposition is in no way weakened by the possibility that where the central areas of towns have been blitzed it may often be desirable to rehouse the population, or a large part of it, somewhere else. If the rehousing is undertaken by public authorities, it will presumably be done on publicly owned land, whether inside or outside the town itself. Moreover, it would seem much the best course from the standpoint of good planning that the 'blitzed' central areas which are to be replanned should also be purchased outright.

7. Other types of public building, e.g. the erection of schools, which seem likely to absorb a considerable part of our building capacity, will also be on publicly owned sites; and the same conclusion holds good.

8. In this early phase, therefore, there is not likely to be much development on privately owned land. It may be hoped, however, that the phase during which building demand is strictly controlled will be comparatively brief; and if there were good reason to suppose that a large-scale private building boom would follow, as soon as the capacity of the building industry is sufficient to permit the substantial abandonment of control, a case might still perhaps be made out for attaching some urgency to the Uthwatt issues. It is desirable, therefore, to survey briefly the later prospect. For undeveloped land the private development demand may be divided into two broad categories: (*a*) the concentrated demand, which affects large areas, such as that which arose from the housing-estate development of the inter-war period, and (*b*) the scattered demand for sites of limited extent, e.g. that for agricultural labourers' cottages in villages. This distinction, it will be seen, becomes even more pertinent when the financial side of the problem is considered.

9. There are various considerations that make it doubtful whether housing-estate development will be renewed on anything approaching the scale of the 1930's. First, it was the opinion of most competent judges that this development, though it had not yet reached saturation point, showed signs of approaching it when the present war began. Second, the housing-estate boom reflected the rapid increase in the number of family units of what may be called a middle-class income range. It is very doubtful if this increase will be maintained in future. Thirdly, the boom depended on a low level

of building costs relatively to middle-class incomes, the continuance of which is also doubtful.

10. Upon the second of these points the altered population outlook resulting from the fall in the birth-rate is highly pertinent. The increase in the number of middle-class family units, which supplied the scope for the housing-estate development, was the product of two factors:

1. changes in the structure of industry and business which increased the proportion of the salariat in the total population;
2. the high birth-rates of twenty or thirty years earlier which entailed an increase in the total number of persons getting married and wishing to establish households.

11. The former influence may still continue to operate. On the other hand, the number of persons of age-groups round about 25 has already passed its peak. It will be observed that a change in the birth-rate does not exercise its influence on the demand for housing until a generation has passed. The number of persons wishing to establish households is a function of the number of persons born from twenty to thirty years before. In the 1930's this number was still increasing, because the annual number of births reached its maximum in the first decade of the present century. It will now begin to fall appreciably and before long fairly rapidly. The demand for new houses is bound to be materially affected. It would be foolish to overlook or to minimize the fundamental importance of the population factor, because its influence is so delayed that it has not hitherto made itself felt. Clearly the huge increase in population over the last 150 years was a major factor in the huge increase of land values.

12. For a considerable period, however, the question of costs may be of even greater importance. By the 1930's a combination of low building costs and low interest rates made the building of small houses for sale a practicable economic proposition. On the most favourable hypotheses we must expect that the level of building costs will be materially increased as a consequence of the war. It is far from clear that net middle-class incomes will be increased in proportion. For several years, therefore, high costs may prevent any large-scale resumption of the building of houses for sale. Afterwards the population factor may exert an increasingly important influence.

13. Despite these considerations, the arrears of demand that have

accumulated during the war will doubtless suffice to ensure a demand on a fair-sized scale, as soon as the relaxation of control permits. It does not follow, however, that there will be a corresponding demand for new building land. It must be remembered in this connexion that the housing-estate development of the 1930's had purchased or leased land in anticipation of future demand well in advance of actual development. In other words, there is substantial scope for additional private building within the estates already bought or leased and laid out. It is far from clear that the post-war private housing demand will be much larger for a long time to come than can be satisfied within these limits.

14. Apart from housing-estate development, the only purpose for which it can seriously be claimed that it might be important to speed up planning schemes for undeveloped land is to prevent the country-side from being further defaced by haphazard industrial development. This will not be an imminent danger so long as building demand is subject to control; and it may quite possible be rendered still more remote by the adoption of new policies, aimed at directing the location of industry so as to avoid concentrated unemployment in depressed areas. The demand for sites for private residences or labourers' cottages carries no serious threat. Existing legislation seems to provide sufficient safeguards against a renewal of 'ribbon development'.

15. Altogether, therefore, it is far from clear that any serious harm would be done if the question of the development rights of undeveloped land were left unsettled for several years.

II. THE DANGER OF A BAD BARGAIN FOR THE STATE

16. The objections to a hasty treatment of the problem seem far more weighty. In the first place, it is an admitted fact, which forms the basis of all the alternative proposals for compensation, that the prospective building value of land, as valued in accordance with current practice, is in the aggregate enormously inflated. The Uthwatt Committee recorded their opinion that if the State were to acquire the development rights of undeveloped land at prices determined by piecemeal valuation 'between two and three times too much would be paid'. This estimate is entitled to respect. It is understood to have been based on a careful inquiry by the Inland Revenue Department, in which the individual properties over a large area were valued, as they would be valued for compulsory

purchase, and the aggregate result compared with a computation which had regard to the rate of development to be expected in the light of past experience and the current value of developed land.

17. It is a paradox at the outset that the State should be expected to buy something at a time when it is computed to be so greatly overvalued; and the paradox carries with it the danger that the State may have to pay far too much. It is true that the Uthwatt Committee sought to provide against this danger by proposing that a fair global sum should be assessed for the aggregate of the development rights to be acquired, and that this should be divided among the different landowners in proportion to the valuation of their separate properties. But this suggestion contains an obvious defect which inevitably reduces its value as a safeguard.

18. If the individual valuations are so unreliable as to produce a total sum which is from twice to thrice what it ought to be, they cannot provide a satisfactory criterion for distributing the proper total among the individual claimants. There is no reason to suppose that the overvaluation will be roughly uniform as between 'dead-ripe' land, and land where the prospects of building is comparatively remote. 'Dead ripe' land can hardly be greatly overvalued since for it current transactions provide a comparatively reliable test. On the other hand, if the diagnosis of the Uthwatt Committee were to be accepted, which attributes the overvaluation entirely to the phenomenon of 'floating value', and which comes near asserting that all land which *may* be built on one day is valued as though it certainly would be built on within a measurable period, the inflation of the more remote and uncertain building values may be proportionately very large. As will be suggested, this diagnosis is in fact open to serious criticism; but for other reasons, the conclusion to which it points, that the main relative overvaluation must be for the more remote building values, seems highly probable.

19. Thus the plan of fixing a total sum for compensation, which might be from one-third to one-half the aggregate of the individual valuations, and distributing it in proportion to these valuations, would almost certainly lead to very serious injustice to individuals. This consideration sets going a natural process to diminish this injustice by raising the compensation. In his latest scheme the Minister of Town and Country Planning proposes to pay 50 per cent. of the individual valuations 'by way of interim settlement',

and to give certificates which would carry a further payment if the State should profit from the schemes as a whole. This has led to the suggestion that it might be better for the State to pay 60 per cent. firm and have done with it. Now 60 per cent. is very nearly twice the lower limit of the Uthwatt Committee estimates of the proper global sum. We are thus led back to the danger that the State may pay far too much, while still leaving the owners of 'dead ripe' land with a valid and substantial grievance.

20. This danger is greatly increased by a further and perhaps more important consideration. There is reason to think it probable that the current trend of valuations overestimates the building value of undeveloped land even *more* seriously than the Uthwatt Committee supposed. Their calculations were based, as has been indicated, on the assumption that private building development will proceed in future at much the same rate as hitherto. This, however, is extremely doubtful for the reasons that have been set out above in Section I, i.e. the effects on housing-estate development of high post-war building costs, followed later by the delayed effects of the fall of the birth-rate. Now the return which the State will derive from the development rights which it is asked to purchase will depend upon, and will vary in proportion to, the rate of development. If development should proceed at only half the rate which the Uthwatt Committee assumed, the revenue which the State will receive will be reduced by one-half. Thus the question of the rate of development is of vital importance to the finances of the scheme.

21. The purchase of the development rights of undeveloped land would indeed be, from the standpoint of the Exchequer, a highly speculative gamble on the prospects of future development. It is doubtful if this aspect of the problem is sufficiently appreciated. The Uthwatt Committee seem to have concealed it from themselves under cover of a false analogy. The technique of assessing a global sum for compensation, without regard to individual valuations, and distributing it in accordance with these valuations was used for the State purchase of coal-mining royalties in 1938. Its use for that purpose was generally and rightly regarded as a reasonably safe arrangement for the Exchequer; and this seems to have led the Uthwatt Committee to infer that it must be almost equally safe for the purchase of the development rights of land. They wrote accordingly:

In our view it is possible fairly to ascertain the proper amount of the Fund. That such a sum is a matter of estimation and not of arithmetical computation is obvious. That the real matter to be taken into account is the economic future of the country is equally obvious. It may be in some respects more difficult to quantify than the sum ascertained for the purposes of the Coal Act, 1938. But the general future economic conditions of the country had to be considered in estimating the value of coal royalties, for royalties largely depend on output. Matters such as the future of the export trade in coal, the prospects of increased efficiency in the use of coal, the prospects of competition of oil as a source of heat and power, the demand for more comfort in housing leading to an increased demand for fuel and light, the possibility of new legislation such as the royalty levy affecting royalty owners only, had, we apprehend, to be taken into review.

22. This passage contains signs of recognition that the analogy is not altogether perfect. But it does not bring out the radical nature of the difference. Under the Coal Act, the State bought all the mineral rights, developed as well as undeveloped. Its revenue is proportionate to the annual output of coal, not to the rate at which that output increases. The analogy would be more to the point if the State had decided during the latter part of the last war to purchase the right to any increase in royalties that might ensue from additional coal production, and had agreed, moreover, to pay for this right a sum to be assessed by reference to the fact that coal production had increased steadily and fast right up to 1914.

23. The human mind instinctively disbelieves that any trend which has continued for a long period is likely to be reversed. The fact that the aggregate building value of land has risen uninterruptedly for hundreds of years suffices with almost everyone to create a strong presumption that it will continue to rise indefinitely. Moreover, there is always a tendency to underrate the practical influence of fundamental long-run changes, such as the revolution in the population trend, until it has become actual and apparent. These predispositions conceal how heavily the dice would be loaded against the State in the speculative gamble which it is asked to undertake. It is necessary, therefore, to emphasize that the development value of undeveloped land depends in the long run more upon the growth of the adult population than on any other single factor. Undoubtedly there are other factors that will ensure the continuance of some substantial new building demand. It is not suggested that development will come to a dead stop. But, having

regard to the importance of the population factor, it does not seem at all an extreme hypothesis to suggest that the rate of the future demand of land for development may be only about half that of the past.[1] If this happens the State will incur a loss of 50 per cent. from this cause alone.

24. So far, then, as the argument has gone, there are two reasons why the State is likely to lose money, if it buys the development rights; first, in order to mitigate palpable injustices, the total payment may be fixed above what may be termed the Uthwatt level; second, the Uthwatt level may prove in fact to be far too high. But under the latest proposals of the Minister of Town and Country Planning there would be yet another source of loss. Under the original Uthwatt Plan the State would have obtained the full value of the development rights which it purchased, when, and in so far as, these rights eventually matured. Under the latest plan it would not do so. This, it is true, purports to treat it as an open question whether the 'suitable charge' which the Planning Authority is to make should amount 'to the whole or part of the increased value of the land'. But the general character of the scheme would make it quite impracticable to charge the full value. This is, in fact, the conclusion reached, though not very clearly emphasized, in the paper.

25. There are, moreover, reasons, which are developed in the following section, for doubting whether the State could attempt in practice to charge on the average anything like 80 per cent. of the value—this being what the paper implies would be a reasonable proportion. Accordingly, the suggestion that the administration of the development rights should be entrusted to a Land Commission, which should have discretion as to the fees it should charge for each transaction, carries with it a further danger of heavy financial loss.

---

[1] In judging the likelihood that this will happen, it is important to keep clearly in mind the distinction between the amount of building to be expected and the amount of additional land that will be wanted for the purpose. Current ideas about housing policy make it reasonable to assume that house-building will be undertaken on a large scale for a considerable period of years. But the greater part of this house-building will be designed to improve housing standards, i.e. to replace inferior dwellings by better ones, as in slum-clearance. This does not entail a demand for additional land, except to the extent that the new dwellings are less densely concentrated. Moreover, this house-building will be undertaken mainly on publicly owned land, and there seems no good reason why most of the land needed should not be purchased in the early post-war years by an enterprising use of powers of public acquisition.

This danger is not removed by the perfunctory proviso that the exercise of this discretion should be made subject to general direction by 'the Minister (or the Treasury)'; for the danger is rooted in the fundamental fact that fees calculated to go anywhere near recouping the Exchequer for the cost of purchase would make the scheme unworkable. For most undeveloped land, indeed, it is by no means clear what effective rights the State would obtain under the new scheme in return for the money it would pay.

III. THE CAUSES OF BUILDING VALUE

26. The question raised in the last paragraph above is so important both from the financial standpoint and because of the doubts which it throws on the feasibility of the latest plan, that it seems desirable to consider it more closely. The original Uthwatt scheme, though based on the unsatisfactory principle of 'dual ownership' of land, would none the less have given real effect to the State's acquisition of development rights. It contemplated that a would-be developer would negotiate with the Planning Authority. The landowner would not come into the picture until development had been 'decided upon', when he would be required to sell his land to the Planning Authority for its agricultural value. The Planning Authority would then lease it to the developer for a period of years for a rent or a premium, or a combination of both, equivalent to the full value of the land in its new use. In other words, the State would become the absolute owner of all land that passed into development, and could use its position as landowner to ensure that it obtained full value for the development rights.

27. This plan is open to obvious criticisms. It would be difficult to take land away from agriculture without even considering what the landowner might have to say. On the other hand, the landowner would have no incentive to facilitate the transaction, and must be expected to do his utmost to obstruct it. Thus the original Uthwatt plan opens out a vista of representations, appeals, and administrative delays; and the new plan has presumably been devised with a view to meeting this objection. The question is whether the baby may not have disappeared with the bath-water.

28. The new plan is based on an attempt to secure the willing assent of the landowner to each transaction for development. It leaves him as one of the principals to the transaction. The assent of the Planning Authority would be required, of course, for any

change of use of land; and for this assent the Authority would charge a 'suitable' licence fee. But, having obtained his licence, or a promise of it, the would-be developer would approach the landowner much as he does now, and bargain with him for the purchase of the land. At no time would the State become the owner.

29. What sort of licence fee would be 'suitable' under this procedure? The idea which seems to underlie the plan is that the landowner would not be willing to sell if he was offered no more than the agricultural value, but that he would become glad to sell if he were offered only slightly more than this. On the other hand, it is assumed that the price which the developer would be willing to offer would be reduced to the full extent of the licence fee which he has to pay to the Authority. Both these assumptions are extremely doubtful. They can best be considered in the light of illustrative figures.

30. Suppose that there is an area of agricultural land, worth £50 an acre in agricultural use, which has some prospect of attracting a building demand, and which is scheduled as eligible for residential building in a planning scheme. Suppose that these facts would cause it to be valued today at £100 per acre. Under the new plan, then, compensation to the extent of £25 per acre, or £30 (if a 60 per cent. basis were adopted) would be paid forthwith for the restrictions imposed on change of use; and this would be paid, of course, both for land which may be and for land which will never be developed.

31. Suppose, then, that a few years hence some part of this land is actually wanted for building, and that this part, under our existing arrangements, would be sold for £200 an acre. The idea seems to be that the Planning Authority would impose a charge of about 80 per cent. of the excess of £200 over the agricultural value, that is to say, a charge of £120 per acre, and that the would-be purchaser would then say in effect to the landowner: 'This land is worth £200 per acre to me; but I have to pay £120 per acre to the Planning Authority; I can therefore only offer you £80 per acre.' It is then assumed that for £80 per acre the landowner would be glad to sell.

32. The question whether the loss incurred by the State in respect of this particular feature of the scheme would be limited to 20 per cent. of its money depends on whether this last assumption is valid. Conceivably it may be true of land which becomes the object of

what has been termed above a concentrated demand; in other words, it may be true of transactions affecting a large compact acreage, though even this is far from certain. But, as regards the more scattered demand, it seems quite unrealistic to suppose that a landowner would willingly accept a price of the order of £80 per acre for small parcels of good agricultural land, two or three acres here, or three or four acres there, if he retains the option of keeping them in agricultural use.

33. Here we reach what is surely a most pertinent fact. As things are today, an agricultural landowner is seldom anxious to sell odd parcels of his land for building purposes. To do so will often upset the layout of his farms. It may, therefore, seriously reduce their value, or, alternatively oblige the landowner to incur expenditure in the erection of new farm buildings. His reluctance to sell, will, of course, be increased by the force of inertia. The transaction will cause him some time and trouble; and he will have to arrange matters to the satisfaction of the tenants affected, who may feel aggrieved. Sentimental considerations, e.g. the desire to maintain an estate intact, or considerations of amenity, may increase his reluctance still further. Where the land is farmed by an owner-occupier, who is in financial difficulties, the force of these considerations may be diminished; on the other hand, they may be felt even more strongly by an owner-occupier who is doing well.

34. The point may be summed up by saying that the *marginal* agricultural value to the landowner of an odd two or three acres of his land is usually far in excess of the average value per acre of the agricultural estate of which it forms part. It may be suggested, indeed, that this marginal value is usually far nearer £200 per acre than £80 per acre; and that that is the main reason why the landowner would be offered a price of the order of £200 under our existing arrangements. Alternatively, it may be said that the price paid for odd parcels of agricultural land today includes an important element of compensation for disturbance to the landowner. If, as the new plan contemplates, the landowner retains the option to keep the land in agricultural use, it will still be necessary to compensate him for disturbance. Nor is there any good reason to suppose that the price required for this purpose would be reduced by the operation of the plan.

35. To revert then to the statistical illustration, the landowner would in most cases refuse an offer of £80 per acre made by a

would-be developer for a small parcel of good agricultural land. The consequence would be either (*a*) that the negotiation would break down and the development be frustrated, or (*b*) that the developer would increase his offer to the landlord, raising it perhaps to as high as the full £200 per acre,[1] despite the fact that he had also to pay the charge of £120 to the Planning Authority. In either case, it is worth noting, the significance of the State charge or licence fee would be that of a tax upon development. Its character as a tax would not be altered, nor would the objections to such a tax be diminished by reason of the fact that the State had previously paid substantial sums of money to landowners, irrespectively of whether their land would or would not be developed subsequently.

36. The proposition that the State charge would have the effect of a tax upon development holds true also of its application to land which may become the object of a concentrated building demand. It is true that for such land the practical outcome of the scheme would probably be less glaringly in conflict with its intentions, since there would be better reason to expect that the *incidence* of the tax, in so far as it did not choke off development, would be mainly upon the landowner. On the one hand, the minimum price *per acre* required to compensate the landowner for disturbance would be much less when a large compact acreage was sold. On the other hand, the purchaser, e.g. a development syndicate, would have to consider more carefully whether the payment of a materially higher price (including the State charge) might not absorb an undue part of the computed margin of profit. Even here, however, it seems optimistic to suppose that landowners would sell freely for anything like £80 per acre. For, although the element of compensation of disturbance would be less, there is another factor that has to be taken into account. The same process of urban development that brings a new area of land within the scope of a concentrated building demand is apt to increase its value *in agricultural use* by bringing the farms nearer to an urban market.

37. It is not easy, in short, to calculate with precision what the effects of a tax on development would be. What is fairly certain is that no one would think a tax on development a good tax, if it was

---

[1] This extreme result might occur quite frequently. The price of the land bought for development, high though it may be, relatively to an ordinary agricultural price, is none the less small in comparison with the cost of the buildings erected on it.

put forward as such; and it is not easy to see how the objections to it are diminished if its proceeds are used, or anticipated, to make payments to landowners by reference to the existing valuation of their properties. The force of the objections would speedily become apparent if the plan were adopted. There would be a demand, which could hardly be resisted, to give the State effective possession of the development rights upon which it had laid out so much money. Thus the probable sequel would be a reversion to the technique of the original Uthwatt scheme, that is to say, the compulsory acquisition by the State of land that passed into development at its agricultural value.

38. This, however, though it would remove one of the three sources of probable financial loss to the Exchequer, would do nothing to meet other pertinent objections. The effect of the above analysis is to suggest that the main principle of the Uthwatt Report is seriously defective. In so far as the price paid for agricultural land that is bought for development represents fair compensation for disturbance to the landowner, the landowner has an equitable claim for compensation when, and only when, his land is actually taken for development. On the one hand, it is absurd and profligate to pay him compensation for forbidding a change of use, which would be barely profitable to him, or at any rate barely attractive to him on a balance of considerations. On the other hand, it is unjust to take away from him for an average agricultural price land that is in fact worth much more to him in its agricultural use. To an important extent, under the Uthwatt Plan, the State would pay what it ought not to pay and leave unpaid what it ought to pay. Some landowners would be hardly treated, in order to pay unnecessary largesse to others.

39. The force of this objection is increased by the point made earlier, that the admitted fact of the overvaluation of development rights can only be explained by attributing it to land with a remote and uncertain building prospect rather than to 'dead-ripe' land. In so far as this is true, the application of the Uthwatt principle would result in paying too much to the owners of the more speculative, and too little to the owners of the more solid building values. It seems important, therefore, that the question how far this is true should be examined carefully. It is alleged that the preparation of planning schemes has had the effect of raising the valuation of land which is coloured on planning maps as eligible for building. It is easy to

believe that this may happen, although, of course, the fact that land is so coloured creates no real presumption that it will actually be wanted for building purposes. This explanation seems much more probable than the doctrine of 'floating value', upon which the Uthwatt Committee lay such stress, which is discussed separately in an Annex to these notes.

40. Essentially the same objection applies to the proposals made for restricting the redevelopment of developed land. These proposals raise, however, so many special difficulties of their own, notably that of defining what constitutes a redevelopment, that it seems best to confine these notes to the simpler problem of undeveloped land.

IV. CONCLUSIONS

41. Altogether the danger seems great that any scheme framed along the Uthwatt lines will result in heavy losses to the Exchequer, and in legitimate grievances to many landowners, and also in impeding desirable developments. Nor is it clear what advantage it would bring sufficient to outweigh these formidable objections. It would be designed, of course, to facilitate the progress of planning; but the question arises whether our ideas about town and country planning do not call for readjustment in the light of the new prospects that are now before us.

42. These ideas have hitherto been based on the assumption that by far the greater part of building development will be undertaken by private enterprise on privately owned land. For this reason most planning schemes are essentially negative in character. They are mainly directed, that is to say, to prohibiting building or particular classes of building in particular districts. But planning, to be worthy of the name, should have a more positive character than this.

43. Reasons have been given above in Section I for believing that in future development public housing schemes and other forms of public building may well preponderate. Furthermore, there are strong arguments for holding that where the replanning of large areas of bombed cities is desirable, it would be best that the land to be replanned should be publicly acquired. These possibilities open the way to planning of a much more promising sort than that contemplated in our Town and Country Planning Acts; planning that will determine what shall be built, and how and where, in accordance with a genuine architectural design, rather than what

shall not be built in particular districts by private enterprise. The sensible corollary seems to be that we should do wisely to concentrate our minds for the time being on all the various measures (which are complex and difficult enough) to facilitate the planning of public development.

44. It is not unreasonable to suggest that the areas of land to be acquired for schemes of public development should not be narrowly restricted, but should be sufficiently extensive to include land which was clearly likely to acquire a materially higher value from the public development. The same facilities might also be given where land is acquired by public utilities. Arrangements along these lines would meet every substantial purpose connected with the idea of 'betterment', and it would be foolish to worry unduly because a few agricultural landowners might still make a profit by selling pieces of their land for private building. The arrangements would involve a considerable financial investment by the State; but it would be a fundamentally sound investment, in contrast to the 'wild-cat' speculation implied in a wholesale purchase of development rights.

ANNEX

THE DOCTRINE OF FLOATING VALUE

THE doctrine of 'floating value' plays a large part in the analysis of the Uthwatt Report. It constitutes their explanation of the fact that the aggregate of individual valuations of undeveloped land greatly exceeds any reasonable 'global' valuation. They are able to cite much authoritative opinion in its support, including the evidence of a professional body. None the less, when it is closely considered, it becomes difficult to accept it as satisfactory.

The Uthwatt Committee state the doctrine in the following terms:

Potential value is necessarily a 'floating value', and it is impossible to predict with certainty where the 'float' will settle as sites are actually required for purposes of development. When a piece of undeveloped land is compulsorily acquired, or development upon it is prohibited, the owner receives compensation for the loss of the value of a probability of the floating demand settling upon his piece of land. The probability is not capable of arithmetical quantification. In practice where this process is repeated indefinitely over a large area the sum of the probabilities as estimated greatly exceeds the actual possibilities, because the 'float', limited as it is to actually occurring demands, can only settle on a proportion of the whole area. There is therefore overvaluation.

The suggestion, it will be observed, is that the overvaluation arises from uncertainty as to where the 'float' will settle. This becomes more explicit and emphatic in the extract which they quote 'from the evidence of one of the professional bodies':

One of the reasons for this overvaluation is that when any single piece of land is being considered, the prospect that building development may come its way and none other must be taken into account. This 'floating value', as it has been called, may attach to many pieces of undeveloped land on the outskirts of a town when they are considered as separate units. When considered together or 'globally' each and every unit cannot in fact secure this 'floating value' to itself, because that would assume that the demand for building land would settle upon all the units simultaneously. Such demand, however, is in fact neither 'global' nor simultaneous; it settles upon different pieces of land at different dates. Hence the 'global' method of valuation cannot assume, at the date on which the valuation is made, the possibility that demand will settle upon all the units at that date. Therefore the 'global' valuation must be less than the aggregate of the individual valuations when considered separately.

This passage, in which the last sentence, with its unqualified 'must be' should be noted, relates to 'undeveloped land on the outskirts of a town'. But the same doctrine is applied in a more extreme form to land in a rural zone in an extract from a Report on the Preservation of the Countryside by the Minister of Health's Town and Country Planning Advisory Committee which the Uthwatt Committee quote with apparent approval:

If all building except agricultural is permanently prohibited over wide areas, compensation must be paid for the loss of potential building value over these areas. It may be that on any reasonable estimate that can be formed not more than 100 houses are likely to be built in a 100,000-acre rural zone in the lifetime of the scheme, so that over the whole zone the loss of 'potential building value' on prohibition of any building would be only 100 houses. But potential building value is necessarily a 'floating value' and it is practically impossible to predict where it will settle. Hence, if the 100,000 acres are held in many ownerships, and claims by individual owners for loss of potential building value come to be separately adjudicated (as under the present system they must be), the total resulting bill for compensation is likely to be enormous, and greatly to exceed in the aggregate the amount of the real loss.

The use of the word 'enormous' clearly implies that land which has only a small chance of being built on is ordinarily valued as though it certainly would be built on. It is further worth noting that this passage suggests that the overvaluation is increased when the land is 'held in many ownerships'.

This diagnosis provokes two questions. First, why should land which only may be built on be valued as though it almost certainly would be built on? Why should the 100,000 acres on which 100 houses may be built be valued (if that really is the practice) as though they would be covered with houses? This is not the practice with other things the value of which depends on where a 'float' may settle. A man who draws a horse in a Derby sweepstake may decide to sell his ticket before the race is run. He does not expect a price based on the assumption that his horse will win the race, but merely one appropriate to the chance that it will win the race. In practice he is usually content with a price well below the true actuarial equivalent of his chance. The shares of a company engaged in a speculative enterprise are bought and sold on the Stock Exchange at prices dependent on the prevailing estimates of its chances of making profits; but here again the usual tendency of the market is to put the price below rather than above that which would correspond to an exact balancing of the chances of gain or loss. More generally, the business world is well used to paying definite prices for things of uncertain future value; but as a rule it inclines to pay for them too little rather than too much.

Why then should the practice in valuing land be so radically at variance with the general business practice? Upon the question of principle, it seems only reasonable to suppose that the last of the above extracts must do the land valuers an injustice. It is impossible to believe that they set out to value land, which only may be built on, as though it was certain to be built on. They *must* pay regard to the chance as they compute it that it will actually be wanted for building within a reasonable time. It is far easier to believe that they may greatly overestimate the chance that it will be wanted. Why they should overestimate has, however, still to be explained. The phenomenon of floating value supplies, in itself, no good reason for their doing so.

The main influences which it would seem natural to suppose may cause a general tendency to overvalue are twofold; first, the actual rate of building development during the 1930's, and second, the false significance that may be attached to the scheduling of land, as available for building, in planning schemes. As to the first point, the Uthwatt Committee seem to have assumed the continuance of fairly active development in their attempts to compute a reasonable global figure; so that it seems difficult to attribute to this cause anything like the overvaluation that is alleged, though it may well account for part of it. It seems difficult to resist the conclusion, to which this process of elimination points, that the major influence must be that of the false significance attached to planning schemes.

The second question provoked by the exposition of 'floating value' contained in the Uthwatt Report is why, for agricultural land, which is unlikely to be the object of a concentrated building demand, there should be any very large building value to 'float', and ultimately to settle. Why, when a piece of land, which is remote from any town, is purchased for some form of development, should the price paid so greatly exceed its agricultural value? The possible sites are many, the likely bidders few. Why then cannot a prospective purchaser play one landowner off against another, especially if the sites are 'held in many ownerships', until he obtains the land at only slightly more than its agricultural value? To revert to the illustration about the 100,000 acres on which in all 100 houses may be built, why should there be any appreciable building value to 'float' among these acres?

It is not easy to explain the phenomenon otherwise than by reference to two facts stressed in these notes. First, the marginal value in agricultural use of an odd parcel of agricultural land is much greater to the landowner than the average agricultural value, so that there is in practice no eager competition of landowners to sell land even at the prices that are offered. Secondly, the cost of the land is usually a comparatively minor factor in the calculations of the purchaser. He has, therefore, no pressing inducement to drive a hard bargain with the landowner; and on the other hand he has usually some reason for preferring one site to another. As a rule, therefore, he will fix on the particular site which seems to suit his purpose best, and make an offer which he hopes will prove attractive to the landowner, rather than engage in a meticulous comparison of the prices at which he might obtain alternative sites which would suit his purposes almost equally well.

The proposal to acquire 'development rights' rests on the assumptions that the price paid for land that is bought for development approximates to the maximum which the purchaser could afford to pay, and that the whole amount by which it exceeds an ordinary agricultural value represents sheer profit to the landowner. If the above analysis is correct, neither of these assumptions holds good of agricultural land which may become the object of a scattered building demand. It seems probable that for such land the price paid often corresponds more nearly to the landowner's minimum than to the purchaser's maximum.

If this is the true reason why even land that is remote from towns usually fetches a considerable figure when it is sold for building, it seems not unlikely that this may combine with a prevalent mis-interpretation of the significance of planning schemes to produce a quite anomalous result. Much agricultural land, which has some remote prospect of becoming later the object of a scattered building demand, which would not really be particularly advantageous to the landowners if it should occur, may none the less be valued because of that prospect at far more than the agricultural value.

The chief moral, indeed, which emerges from an attempt to examine the doctrine of floating value is the need for a radical revision of the principles and methods of land valuation.

6

LORD KEYNES AND EMPLOYMENT POLICY[1]

LORD KEYNES adopts towards this report the tone of an authoritative exponent of Scientific Truth dealing with the fumbling efforts of the half-educated. He recognizes a praiseworthy groping towards the light, but deplores an undue timidity attributable to muddled thinking and the tenacity of error. He implies that his own point of view, which would prescribe more boldly, and claim much more, is that not of an eminent individual or of a particular school of thought, but of 'theoretical economic analysis', and that it is really not open to challenge by anyone who understands what he is talking about.

Now it is quite true that the currents of abstract economic thought have been flowing in recent years in the direction of sympathy with the doctrines to which Lord Keynes is attached. This enhances the danger that Lord Keynes's confident claim that these doctrines are covered by the mantle of unchallengeable scientific authority may be accepted as valid. It is important, therefore, to emphasize at the outset that this is very far from being true. In the first place the currents flowing in this particular direction are mainly in the stream of *abstract* economic analysis; that is to say of the method which starts with highly simplified assumptions, or even with identical propositions, and builds on this foundation an elaborate structure of quasi-mathematic reasoning. Such analysis cannot possibly justify sweeping conclusions upon the concrete problems of the actual economic world. It may be useful in *suggesting* generalizations which must be tested by other means. But it can prove nothing; and the suggestions which it throws up, while they may be helpful, may equally be false or misleading, as in this instance I believe they are.

Secondly, despite the current trend of fashion, the implication that all reputable economists would accept these doctrines is a grotesque exaggeration, unless indeed their acceptance is taken, as perhaps it is by Lord Keynes, to be the criterion and hall-mark of a reputable economist. In my opinion these doctrines are unhistorical,

[1] 1 March 1944.

unimaginative, and unscientific. That is to say, they ignore the lessons of the past, or give a superficial and distorted picture of them; they give an equally superficial and distorted impression of the conditions and problems to be expected in future; and they are based on the *avoidance* of any serious systematic study of the facts of industry and of employment or unemployment, preferring to rely on crude, sweeping, abstract assertions which miss the crucial points.

This report is in my view far too much under the influence of these doctrines. It contains, it is true, various passages of reservation or qualification, which indicate some recognition of the essential factors in the problem. But these are introduced so incidentally, and so deprecatingly that they are perhaps likely to convey to others as well as to Lord Keynes the impression of over-timidity in accepting the logical conclusions of the argument. They are not developed in such a way as to bring out the unreality of some of the main propositions advanced.

A lengthy paper would be required to deal fully and systematically with the points of controversy. I must content myself with an attempt to indicate summarily what seem to me the chief defects of the momentarily fashionable approach to the problem; though in order to correct current misconceptions I think it necessary to dwell rather more at length on the inter-war facts.

1. *The central issue.* After the last war we combined a policy of austere financial orthodoxy with a general return to economic *laissez-faire*. The central prescription for the future of what Lord Keynes calls 'theoretical economic analysis' is to combine an eventual return to economic *laissez-faire* (after a transition period during which it is recognized that many controls will be necessary, but which it is hoped will be very brief) with throwing financial orthodoxy to the winds. As a recipe for full employment, I believe that both parts of this prescription are mistaken. I certainly think that financial orthodoxy can be carried too far, and was actually carried too far upon two occasions during the inter-war period. But it is a dangerous exaggeration to suppose that full employment or 'aggregate demand' can be maintained by the instrument of financial profligacy, that is to say by deliberately reducing taxation or social security contributions, or by pouring out public money on public works, whenever unemployment is in excess of an assumed average level. Under conditions of great external weakness, such as we must

expect, the more probable result of such a policy would be a currency collapse. In order to secure full and steady employment, it is the economic *laissez-faire* rather than the financial orthodoxy that *chiefly* needs to be altered. The latter calls only for minor modifications; the former for more radical changes.

2. *The inter-war facts.* Unemployment in Great Britain throughout the inter-war period was mainly due to *external* causes; that is to say, either to the loss of export markets, or, as was true to a marked extent in 1930 and 1931, to the displacement of labour in the home market by competing imports. Upon two occasions an unduly austere budgetary policy served in my view to aggravate the trouble, namely during the 'Geddes Axe' retrenchment phase of 1921–2 and *after* the fall of the Labour Government in 1931. Upon neither of these occasions, however, was this over-austerity a major factor. The slump of 1920–1 was essentially a slump in international trade; and it was comparatively short-lived.

Between 1923 and 1929 we suffered in Great Britain from concentrated unemployment in highly localized industries, such as coal and cotton, whose loss of pre-war export markets proved to be permanent. The return to the gold standard at an over-high parity in 1925 was partly responsible for the loss of our export trade, though the trends towards the more economical utilization of coal on the Continent, and the increasing international competition resulting from growing industrialization in the Far East and elsewhere were probably more important influences. In any case an overvalued exchange rate is best regarded as a factor within the sphere of *external* economic policy. During these years there was no internal deflation or deficiency of aggregate purchasing power. There was never before a period of such rapid expansion in the south of England. The process of 'transfer' from the depressed areas to others made considerable progress, though it was slow as such a process (in the absence of compulsory labour direction) must always be. Financial conditions were sufficiently 'expansionist' to give rise to an unhealthy boom in new 'mushroom' issues.

The heavy increase in *general* unemployment between September 1929 and September 1931 was due wholly to a further loss of export trade as a consequence of a severe world slump, and to the displacement of home production by a rapid increase of imports under conditions in which wage rates were being cut abroad, and maintained at home, while tariffs were *taboo*. By September 1931 unemployment had already practically reached its highest level. Up to then there was no financial austerity. Mr. Snowden abstained in the interests of industrial recovery from increasing taxation in April 1931, despite the clear prospect of a budget deficit; the Unemployment Fund was piling up debt at a heavy rate; housing and road subsidies were largely increased; and the Labour Government was striving to the best of its ability to improvise fresh schemes of public works. It will be remembered that in the summer of 1931 the May Committee calculated (exaggeratedly as I have always thought) that if all factors were taken into account the magnitude of the true budget deficit was enormous; and the publication of their report precipitated the political crisis and the subsequent reversion to extreme financial austerity.

There followed the second occasion on which it can reasonably be suggested that undue financial orthodoxy aggravated unemployment. In September 1931 the budget was balanced on the basis of defraying out of taxation not only current expenditure, but a good deal of capital expenditure, such as new trunk-road construction which had hitherto been met by borrowing. To attempt this at the bottom of an unprecedentedly severe depression is in my view fundamentally unwise; and although the argument that it was essential to restore 'business confidence' carried much weight, I cannot believe that so extreme a policy was either necessary or helpful for this purpose. On general grounds I am satisfied that its adoption served to retard the recovery which began slowly to ensue. None the less the significant fact remains that recovery did begin despite it.

The prima facie morals of this experience are twofold; first, that for a country like Great Britain the most important condition of maintaining employment is to secure a reasonable degree of stability and steadiness in that vulnerable part of its economy which is exposed to disturbance from external causes; and second, that attempts to compensate for heavy unemployment in this sector by means of public works or unbalanced budgets are in practice ineffective. If these morals are well founded the key to a successful policy of full employment must lie in the external rather than in the internal sector of economic policy. It would seem, therefore, to be of primary importance that in considering international projects, particularly for commercial policy, critical scrutiny should be given to their probable effects on the steadiness of employment.

3. *Investment and public works.* There is no doubt that fluctuations in the volume of investment rank next to, though a long way after, external disturbances among the causes of unemployment; and I agree that it is important to try to regulate the rate of public investment, so as to contribute to stability of employment. But so far from agreeing with Lord Keynes that the report underestimates what might be done by this means, I am convinced that it errs in the opposite direction. There are three points here which I wish to emphasize.

First, though the report rightly calls attention to 'four main obstacles' which make it difficult to control the rate of public investment, it makes no reference at all to the possibility that the attempt to stimulate *public* investment, when unemployment is high, may *cause* a decline, and perhaps a larger decline, in the rate of *private* investment. This is no mere theoretical possibility. One of the outstanding features of the course of house-building activity during the inter-war period was the fact that the total volume of house-building was lowest when the most insistent efforts were being made, by subsidies and administrative pressure, to press forward with public housing schemes. Indeed the complete abolition of housing subsidies, except for slum-clearance, after 1931, led immediately to a spurt forward in house-building, although trade was still in the depths of depression, which developed into the sustained housing boom of the 1930's. Since house-building activity is likely to be one of the major forms of public investment after the present war, this experience is pertinent; and though I do not wish to base any sweeping or dogmatic judgement upon it, I do urge that the possibility that the stimulation of public investment may react adversely on the volume of private investment is a major difficulty which ought not to be ignored.

Second, if the originating cause of the unemployment which it is sought to cure is a loss of export trade, or a displacement of home production by imports, which entails an adverse balance of payments, an attempt to absorb the displaced labour in public works would be an inappropriate and dangerous remedy. For this must serve to aggravate the adverse balance through its tendency to maintain or to increase imports; and it would retard the process of reducing costs of production which may be essential in order to restore equilibrium. Nothing could be more dangerous in such circumstances than to couple an increase in public works with exchange depreciation. Confidence in the currency, both at home and abroad, would quickly be destroyed if this were attempted.

Third, the fact that public-investment activity is likely to be at an abnormally high level for a prolonged period, perhaps for more than ten years after the war, must necessarily reduce its efficiency throughout this period as a trade-cycle 'tap'. This point is mentioned in the report, but it is insufficiently emphasized; for its significance is to render quite unreal the statistical computations that precede it of the extent to which public investment might be varied between good years and bad. If a depression should occur in the first post-war decade at a time when public investment is falling away from an extremely high level, but is still at a substantially higher level than it would be sensible to maintain permanently, it would be very doubtful policy indeed to try to push it up again in such circumstances. If this meant trying to speed up the rate of public house-building at the expense of aggravating a subsequent inevitable decline, it might be open to very serious objections.

It is highly desirable, I think, to provide for a systematic review of public investment programmes, as suggested in the report; but for the reasons indicated I think it dangerous, and likely to prove a source of serious future embarrassment, to prescribe a policy of varying the aggregate volume of public investment as a cure to be applied to unemployment in general, in advance of and without regard to the actual circumstances of the problem. The statement in the report that 'it is not too much to say that the broad success of the Government's policy of maintaining employment will depend in the main upon the contribution which the field of public investment can make to stabilizing the total aggregate demand' seems to me absurdly out of focus, and calculated to invite a repetition of previous disillusionment.

4. *Deficit financing.* The report appears to accept the general doctrine of 'deficit financing' as the best means of stimulating consumption in depression, and, while indicating the need for caution in applying it, gives a general blessing to the proposal that Social Insurance contributions should be varied in accordance with the state of unemployment. Here again, while Lord Keynes regards the report's suggestions and analysis as absurdly over-cautious, I regard them as over-profligate, and likely to prove dangerous in practice in the difficult post-war years.

I have never believed that financial orthodoxy should be carried to the point of increasing taxation in years of cyclical depression in order to avert a deficit, which there are fair grounds for believing would disappear when trade recovered. But there is an immense practical difference between refraining from increasing taxation in such circumstances, and deliberately widening the deficit by reducing either taxation or the revenue of extra-budgetary funds. I think that this is an unwise and inappropriate idea for three main reasons.

First, the deficits may easily become very large. The criterion adopted for normal or average unemployment may be far from the mark; yet since the element of prediction over a long period is involved, it will always be open to dispute whether matters may not come right in the end; the process of revision would entail action in the opposite direction to the general prescription of the plan; and politics would add to the difficulty of undertaking it in good time, except possibly under a wave of revulsion towards excessive financial orthodoxy. Apart from this possibility the tendency would be to urge a stronger dose of the same medicine; and there would doubtless be many, under the influence of Lord Keynes's doctrines, who would do so with conviction. Once more, if this policy were applied, when the real cause of the trouble was a loss of export trade, entailing an adverse balance of payments, the repercussions on the stability of our currency might, I believe, be very serious indeed.

Second, as a remedy for unemployment, the policy is fundamentally inappropriate. It can be argued with some force that a sinking fund may be a deflationary influence, because by its means the State withdraws more purchasing power from the public than it lets out again. For this reason I agree that sinking funds can properly be suspended when there is clear evidence of cyclical depression. But if the State is spending as much as it is collecting, it is not withdrawing purchasing power; and if productive resources are none the less being unused, that indicates a defect of economic organization, not of financial policy.

Third, in practice, the effects on unemployment would in my view prove extremely disappointing. The report accepts the assumption that 'most of the additional income accruing to the workers (as a result of lowering contributions) would be spent immediately and not saved' and that 'this would give rise to increased output and employment, and so to a further increase in the demand for goods and services and so on'. But the second part of this assumption begs a very large question. Part of the additional money spent would be spent on things like seats at cinemas. This would have no *early* effect on the demand for labour. Cinemas would be somewhat better filled, and as a consequence the date when new cinemas would be built might be advanced. But the time-lag involved would be indeterminate and might be large. A further part of the additional money spent would be spent on imported goods, such as food or tobacco. This would do more to increase an adverse balance of payments than to increase the demand for British labour. Next, even as regards that part of the additional expenditure which was directed to British manufactured goods, the first effect would be a decline in the stocks held by shops, and again there would be an indeterminate time-lag before more persons were set at work in making these goods. Finally, if the unemployment were mainly localized in particular districts, a slight addition to the flow of expenditure throughout the country as a whole would not even eventually be in itself a very efficacious remedy. For these reasons, I cannot agree that the instrument of varying social insurance contributions would be likely to prove 'powerful'.

5. *The national-income approach.* Behind the above there lies a more fundamental question to which I must refer. From the perfectly true proposition that it is important to maintain 'aggregate demand', there is in the fashionable doctrines, reflected in the report, an unwarranted jump to the conclusion that the key to maintaining the demand for labour in consumption goods industries is to maintain by fiscal means the aggregate national income. This diagnosis is in my view defective in two important respects. First, the decisions of consumers to incur expenditure do not depend solely on their incomes. It is notorious that a Stock Exchange boom entails a large increase in current expenditure by a large variety of individuals (whose expenditure is important in the aggregate), e.g. speculators, who have made capital profits, and shareholders who have merely noted that their shares have risen in value. Conversely it is notorious that a Stock Exchange slump, such as that in Wall Street in 1929, may exert a paralysing influence both on national and world economy. As a means of securing steady trade and employment, I believe that the problem of diminishing the range of Stock Exchange fluctuations is as important as any other within the

sphere of internal economic affairs. It is a pity that the national-income approach results in ignoring such problems altogether.

Secondly, it ignores the fact that in determining the demand for labour, the decisions of the entrepreneur, the manufacturer, and the wholesale dealer, are no less important, and *immediately* are more important than the decisions of the ultimate consumer. It is true, of course, that the former depend in the long run on the latter. But since time-lags are of the essence of the problem of the 'trade cycle' it is important not to forget that the crucial dynamic factor in the economic system is the volume of orders that is placed with manufacturers. If workers are set at work producing goods, their incomes as consumers are increased or maintained as a consequence. On the other hand, if workers are once discharged through lack of orders, the deflationary vicious circle may become so wound up that attempts to correct matters subsequently by fiscal devices may prove ineffective. In my opinion, accordingly, the idea of trying (when desirable) to influence directly the volume of orders, and also the localities in which those orders are placed, offers a far more promising approach to the problem of maintaining employment than the idea of maintaining consumers' incomes by fiscal devices after unemployment has already reached abnormally high dimensions. This idea might be applied in a large variety of ways.

6. *The multiplier.* The above has a bearing on the doctrine of the 'multiplier' on which Lord Keynes lays such stress. This doctrine as formulated is far too static to be applicable to the actual conditions of the world. It ignores the vital time factor. Behind the doctrine there is the important element of truth that trade movements, both of boom and slump, are cumulative. But it is of the essence of the problem that these cumulative forces take time, and gather strength with time. It follows that the most essential condition of success in maintaining aggregate demand is that the measures adopted for this purpose should be *timely*. The essential weakness of all 'automatic' schemes is that they begin to operate too late.

7. *The regulation of the external economy.* Finally, I return to the dominating importance for the problem of maintaining employment of securing satisfactory and steady conditions in the external sector of our economy. To treat the problem of employment as predominantly a question of internal economic policy; and to treat issues of external economic policy as a matter of removing 'trade

restrictions' and 'discrimination' is to approach both in false perspective. Personally I find it extremely difficult to imagine that reasonable security of employment could possibly be obtained on the basis of international plans of which the central idea is to put the flow both of imports and exports as much as possible at the mercy of the chances of unregulated market forces.

PART V

Post-War

1945–51

1

THE USES AND ABUSES OF
ECONOMIC PLANNING[1]

THE idea of economic planning has become very popular in recent years. It is widely agreed, by many with enthusiasm and by others with a more reluctant acquiescence, that in Great Britain today we need a central economic plan. What is meant by this phrase is not always perfectly clear. It seems to mean somewhat different things to different minds. That, however, is more or less inevitable with a phrase which has acquired a sudden vogue; and, allowing for that, there is perhaps more reason to be surprised at the apparent measure of agreement as to what it means or should mean. But an idea may be incoherent, although there is little apparent dispute as to its content; and if an idea is incoherent, it may become mischievous when the attempt is made to apply it unconditionally to practical affairs. It is high time, in my view, to subject this particular idea to close analysis.

Evidently economic planning includes the idea of regulating by deliberate policy many matters which were formerly left to the laws of supply and demand, of relying less on impersonal economic forces and more on conscious organization than has been customary in the past. The idea of economic planning must comprise that as a minimum; and there are some who seem to mean by it not much more than that. They however are, I think, a small minority. Indeed, if that were all that the phrase 'economic planning' were intended to convey, it would perhaps be more appropriate to use quieter if

[1] The Rede Lecture, Cambridge, 9 May 1947.

longer words and to speak rather of the need for more State intervention and direction in our economic life. A second element forms
an essential part of the content of planning as it seems most generally
to be interpreted; that of quantitative programmes, the formulation
in terms of precise statistics of the main objectives of economic
policy. That is laid down as of the essence of central planning and
control by Sir Oliver Franks in the lectures which he delivered in
London on this subject and which have just been published in
pamphlet form.[1] 'I think', he says, 'the essential elements are plans
consisting of decisions of policy, quantitatively expressed in the
form of programmes and such measures as in particular circumstances may be necessary to ensure the performance of these programmes.' Again, in the rather curious disquisition upon economic
planning which forms the introduction to that best-seller White
Paper, which appeared last February, known as the *Economic
Survey for 1947*,[2] stress is laid on quantitative programmes and
what are called 'economic budgets'. And there are phrases which
imply that this White Paper, with its tables on Distribution
of Resources and Distribution of Man-Power containing columns
headed 1947 or December 1947, itself sets out at least a short-term
plan.

But this raises another question as to the content of the idea. If
ever we speak of making a plan in our personal affairs, we usually
mean that we shall make definite arrangements for a longer period
ahead than we might otherwise do. This 'looking ahead' is of the
essence of the idea of planning in everyday life. It is natural, therefore, that many critics of the Government's White Paper should
complain that a central economic plan, which is worthy of the
name, cannot be limited to the current year, but must cover a period
of years, four years or five years, on the analogy of the plans of
Soviet Russia or Nazi Germany or of the Monnet Plan in France.
The White Paper contains an apologetic paragraph in anticipation
of this criticism:

The main emphasis so far has been laid upon comparatively short-term
planning—planning for the next year ahead. This was the most urgent
need—a guide to the vast number of decisions which had to be taken
in the short-term allocation of resources. But exactly the same approach
can be and is being applied to the longer-term problem, in order to

[1] Sir Oliver Franks, *Central Planning and Control in War and Peace*. Long-
mans, Green & Co.   [2] Cmd. 7046.

secure a balanced development of the economy as a whole. It is too early yet to formulate the national needs over, say, a five-year period with enough precision to permit the announcement of a plan in sufficient detail to be a useful practical guide to industry and the public. There are still too many major uncertainties, especially in the international economic field. But a considerable amount of work is being done on these lines, in order to clarify the national objectives for a longer period ahead than is covered by this Paper, and to provide a framework for the long-term decisions of Government and industry.

I have quoted this paragraph in full, because of the light which it throws on the difficulties of the idea of economic planning, as currently interpreted. It is all very well to say that it is too early to formulate a statistical plan for five years because of 'major uncertainties, especially in the international economic field'. Have we any good reason to assume that those uncertainties will become materially less as time goes on? Is it likely to be easier to forecast the volume and value of our export trade even for a year or two ahead, when the present sellers' market has disappeared, and when the chances of international price competition may again exert a dominating influence on the flow of trade? And even if that question were to be answered Yes, on the ground of a vague belief that somehow things will gradually settle down, so that one year will be more like another than it is today, is it not for the unsettled times when matters cannot be expected to run smoothly of their own accord, that planning is said to be especially important? Evidently there is a conflict between the desideratum that economic planning should relate to a considerable period ahead and the desideratum that it should consist largely of quantitative programmes. Yet, as we have seen, both these desiderata play a part in the idea of planning that is prevalent; and the idea which includes these warring elements makes a wide and strong appeal.

The strength of this appeal springs mainly from the belief that our economic and industrial achievement under war conditions was phenomenal. During the war, a very large part of our productive resources, more than half according to the accepted reckoning, was devoted to war purposes, to manning the Armed Forces and to supplying them with an immense range of costly equipment. Yet we succeeded somehow, with the remaining half of our productive power, in maintaining a tolerable standard of living, and for the poorest classes one that was higher on balance than they had known during peace. This suggests the moral that our productive resources were used far more fully and effectively during the war than they were previously, and the further moral that we might obtain a more satisfactory return from our exertions in time of peace, if we would apply to our peace-time economy methods of organization resembling those which served us so well in the war. Now much central direction by the Government, entailing the use of quantitative production programmes, was the outstanding feature of our war-time economic organization. This then is the principle (so runs the conscious or subconscious argument) which we should strive to apply, with suitable modifications, to the problem of securing increased prosperity in time of peace.

I shall not stop to inquire how far the belief which forms the basis of this argument is well founded, how far, that is to say, the apparent over-all achievement of war-time economic organization was a reality, or an illusion reflecting *inter alia* the quantitative importance of two branches of economic activity, which could be drastically curtailed for the duration of the war, but which are indispensable in the long run, namely production for export and the production of fixed capital goods, such as houses and generating stations. Upon that issue, I merely record my personal view that the apparent achievement was, in the sense indicated, largely an illusion, but did contain a significant element of reality. I am concerned at the moment with the psychological fact that by the end of the war, belief in the value of economic planning had taken root. At that time, moreover, this belief was accompanied by an optimistic assumption that the technique of planning was comparatively easy.

On the latter point, as distinct from the former, there has been a marked change of opinion over the last two years, and especially during the last few months. It has gradually become appreciated that there are greater difficulties in planning for prosperity in peace than in planning for efficiency in war; and in current pronouncements on the subject, insistence on the importance of economic planning is matched, and sometimes it seems overmatched, by stress upon these difficulties. First, it is pointed out that in peace the objects of planning are not so clear and simple as they are in war. 'In war', said the Lord President of the Council recently, 'there were two simple tests and two only: the needs of the fighting forces and the minimum needs of the civil population. Today, there is a whole complex of needs, short-term and long-term, with the need to export cutting across all the others.' Therefore, it becomes more difficult to formulate clear plans. Secondly, the community is not bound together by the same unity of will and purpose, the same readiness to make sacrifices or to accept compulsion in the general interest; so that various methods which were used in war to aid in the carrying out of central economic policy, methods such as the direction of labour, the restriction of engagements, and industrial concentration schemes, are scarcely practicable in peace. Therefore, it is more difficult to execute any plans that may be formulated. These are the differences between the problems of war-time and those of peace-time economic planning on which attention has been chiefly focused in recent public discussion. They are important differences, undoubtedly. But I am not sure they are the most important ones; or at least that so stated they go to the root of the matter. There are two other differences, associated to some extent with those that I have mentioned, but deserving separate recognition, which have, in my view, an even more crucial bearing on questions as to the feasibility of planning and the type of planning that is appropriate in a peace-time economy. And it is to these two further differences, and to the implications which they carry, that I am chiefly anxious to invite attention.

The first of these differences is that during the war, the Government was the final purchaser, the effective consumer, of the munitions and war equipment which were wanted and were produced in greatly increased quantities; and the primary object of economic planning was to satisfy, as effectively as possible, this expanded Government demand. It was a practicable, though a highly complex task, to formulate the various Government requirements with precision, and to break them down, with increasing accuracy as time went on, into terms of the labour and materials which they would absorb. The supplies of labour and materials which could be made available set limits to the extent to which these requirements could be met, and among the requirements which had to be brought into the reckoning, though often as a very minor item, were the minimum needs of the civil population. These needs were therefore included within the scope of the elaborate programmes of quantitative allocation that were evolved.

But the impact of these allocation programmes upon the civilian market was simply that of a rationing of scarce supplies, a rationing that was often both drastic and rough and ready. For commodities that are still in scarce supply, both raw materials and consumer goods, rationing systems are retained today with general acquiescence. This is what we term control. It is the sort of control, the need for which we all hope, not perhaps very confidently, will become progressively less extensive in future years. It is certainly not what enthusiasts mean by central economic planning. 'A real national plan', declares Mr. Morrison, 'must be far more than a plan to ration scarce goods in the most sensible and far-sighted way; not a plan to make the best of poverty, but to increase prosperity.' The glowing hope which the idea of planning arouses in so many breasts is that it will prove an efficient instrument of expansion.

It is precisely here that the war-time analogy may be most deceptive. The plausibility of the notion that the technique of quantitative planning may help us to obtain increased prosperity in peace is derived from the success of this technique in promoting a great and rapid increase of war production. But this success depended on the fact that the Government was itself the consumer of the war products. The programmes of quantitative allocation were mainly concerned with the sorting out and satisfaction of Government requirements. Accordingly, to quote Sir Oliver Franks again:

> These programmes were not estimates of need made by the intellect reviewing a situation, nor were they targets of aspiration springing from the heart; they were acts of will. Estimates of need were taken into account and attention was given to what was desirable, but the plan of allocation for a period was a directive to action.

I submit that it is only for commodities of which the State is the chief consumer that quantitative programmes can have this quality of 'acts of will' or 'directives to action' for purposes of increased consumption.

Today, the State is the effective consumer or final purchaser of a considerable and increasing range of commodities which satisfy civilian needs—notably for the houses which are built under local authority housing schemes and for the plant required for the coal-mines and other public utilities which are being nationalized. These are mostly fixed capital goods; and in the demand for such goods, the production of which forms the chief element in what is sometimes called investment, the State may now have come to play a predominant part. Therefore, in this section of our economy, there is scope and need for quantitative planning. It is certainly important that the Government should frame definite programmes of the houses, the schools, and the generating stations which they intend to build. It is important that they should compute as precisely as possible the calls which these programmes will make on manpower, materials, and productive capacity, and that they should determine the magnitude of these programmes in the light of the economic situation as a whole, including the urgency of the need for consumer goods and services. There is scope, therefore, not only for detailed programmes relating to house-building, school-building and so forth separately, but for an overall programme or budget for expenditure on fixed investment.

Here, however, I would interpolate a reservation. I have used the term 'fixed investment'. In my view, it is inexpedient for this purpose at least to lump long-term capital goods, such as I have been considering, in a common category with the machinery which is purchased by an ordinary industrial concern. That, of course, is what is usually done in economic analysis. A broad distinction is drawn between capital expenditure and current expenditure, which rests ultimately on the fact that the goods belonging to the former category yield their utility only gradually over a period of years and are therefore ordinarily financed from capital resources or borrowing, whereas the objects of current expenditure are consumed more quickly and are paid for out of income. Even from this standpoint, the distinction drawn is somewhat crude. A house, a school, or a generating station lasts for a very long time; let us say for forty years or more. Much of the machinery used in industry becomes obsolete and is replaced after about seven years; and it must therefore earn a return sufficient to cover its cost comparatively soon. Some of the consumer goods which we regard as objects of current expenditure, our pots and pans, and in these days, our suits of clothes, last about as long. But apart from that, I suggest that the difference between forty years and seven is quite as significant as the difference between seven years' life and immediate consumption. Considerations of a more practical order are also pertinent. The State is not the chief buyer of machinery, as it is of longer-term capital goods. Moreover, these two classes of capital goods absorb largely different materials and are produced by different industries, which differ markedly today in their capacity to undertake additional work.

For these reasons, I contend that the national investment budget should be a really long-term investment budget, relating only to the most durable types of capital goods; and I attach considerable importance to this matter. It may be desirable in the interests of economic balance to restrain within moderate limits the amount of long-term investment work that is set on foot during the next few years. There are *not* equally good reasons for slowing down the work of renewing and modernizing industrial plant. Considerable confusion of thought has been caused, and policy may conceivably be distorted, by the lumping together in the White Paper calculations of these two different types of capital goods.

But that is somewhat of a digression and I return now to my main argument. Outside the important sector of investment work, the role of the State as the final purchaser of non-military goods is still a very minor one. It follows, I submit, that over the greater part of the economic system, quantitative programmes cannot play the part of 'directives to action' for purposes of increasing prosperity.

I pass to my second proposition. During the war it was permissible and necessary to disregard, for the time being, certain objects of policy which are of cardinal importance in peace. I refer in particular to three: first, the balancing of the budget; second, equilibrium between savings and investment, if I may be indulged in putting it that way; and third, equilibrium in the balance of international payments. Upon all those matters, the exigencies of war entitled and compelled us to take what was in one sense a short-sighted view. The paramount necessity was to win the war; and it would clearly have been wrong to have refrained from doing anything helpful to that end, because of post-war disadvantages, however serious. Therefore, among other things, we ran through our accumulated dollar assets and incurred heavy external indebtedness in the form of sterling balances owned abroad.

That is not a process which can possibly continue indefinitely; and indeed, there can be no two opinions as to the crucial importance in time of peace of living within our international income and of adjusting accordingly the balance between our imports and our exports. This relates to the third objective. If the other two are disregarded in time of peace, inflationary conditions may be perpetuated, carrying with them many dangers, including the one which recent events have brought home to us—that stocks of industrial materials and components may become insufficient to sustain continuous production.

Now each of these cardinal objectives of economic policy is concerned with a relation: not with one thing but with the balance between two. The kind of help which quantitative programmes can give is greatly affected by that fact. Consider first the task of balancing the budget. There the Government is in effective control of both sides of the account; and both can be and are expressed in precise quantitative terms. It rests with the Chancellor of the Exchequer and his colleagues to determine how much expenditure shall be allowed; and within the limits of the national taxable capacity, it is within their power to impose taxation sufficient to yield a corresponding revenue. The essential objective, however, is not to raise so much revenue or to keep expenditure down to a certain sum, but to keep the two in balance. True, it makes a great difference whether this balance is struck at a high level of revenue and expenditure or at a low level of both. Accordingly, past Chancellors have frequently declared it to be their aim to reduce expenditure and taxation to a lower level, and have occasionally been rash enough to specify the magnitude of the reductions which they hope to achieve over a period of years. When they have done that, they may be said to have set up targets defined in quantitative terms; and such targets may be of some use as guides or spurs to action, though history does not record that they have usually been reached. But they are essentially different from the quantitative programmes of war-time planning with their quality of directives to action. The parallel to the latter is supplied by the yearly Estimates and Finance Act. Thus, even in this financial sphere, where the Government is, as I have said, in effective control of both sides of the account, we see that quantitative programmes which represent acts of will are short-term and that any long-term programmes have the more dubious character of targets.

Let us turn now to the task of securing equilibrium in the balance of international payments. Here the immediate problem is that of closing a large gap between the two sides of the account. There are two ways of doing this, to cut down our overseas expenditure and to increase our overseas income; and so long as the costs of occupation forces and similar quasi-war-time Governmental disbursements play an important part in the total of our overseas expenditure, it is clear that we must attack the problem from both ends. As compared, however, with the pre-war position, it is undoubtedly preferable to close the gap so far as we can by restoring our income rather than by reducing our expenditure, which means by increasing exports rather than by curtailing imports. It is of value, therefore, to have the calculation with which we are all familiar, that we must increase our exports by 75 per cent. in volume above the level of 1938 if we are to import as much as we did before the war. That supplies us with a target which may be useful as a guide to policy.

But again this cannot be a directive to action. Nor is it possible for a short-term export programme, relating only to a single year, to have this quality. Here the point is important that for the balance of payments problem, the Government is not in effective control of both sides of the account. It can encourage and stimulate exports by various means; but since it is not the purchaser of the exports, it cannot determine their volume. It cannot do so even in a sellers' market when the limiting factor is production. Still less will it be able to do so when the limiting factor becomes the difficulty of finding purchasers abroad. Then the determining influences will be in part the prosperity and policies of countries overseas which are our customers, and in part the relation of costs and prices in Great Britain to those in countries which are our chief competitors.

The size of the export trade which we shall be able to maintain in these circumstances must be uncertain and unstable, liable to large fluctuations from year to year. Indeed, in the years that lie ahead, this uncertainty and this instability may be exceptionally great, in consequence of the dislocating impact of a total war upon the world economy. If international obligations do not prevent, it might be possible to do a great deal to limit the scope of the probable fluctuations and to introduce an element of reliability and steadiness into the flow of foreign trade by planned arrangements; for example, bilateral trade agreements between particular countries providing for the interchange of prescribed minimum quantities of each other's goods. Bilateral trade agreements of this sort belong to the category of quantitative programmes that can be carried out. But a main object of the conference upon commercial policy which is now in session at Geneva is to forbid such bilateral trade agreements altogether, and to work towards the elimination of other practices which qualify the power of international price competition to swing trade from one channel to another. Among these practices is the system of preferential import duties within the

H. D. H. 1947

British Commonwealth, which has contributed towards reliability and steadiness. The principle of non-discrimination, to which the conference on trade policy is dedicated, is indeed fundamentally incompatible with the principle of planning in the sphere of external trade. Planning implies that you choose; non-discrimination that you must not choose.

A curious paradox is worth noting here. The ideology which seeks to put the flow of international trade more completely than before the war at the mercy of the chances and vagaries of international price competition is accepted by many, though certainly not by all, of the strongest advocates of planning in our internal affairs. The inconsistency is to be explained by the spell still cast by the great Free Trade tradition. That tradition comprised two elements: first, a belief in the value of international trade, and second, the belief that international trade will be best conducted if governments do not interfere with it. For Great Britain, the first of these elements, the judgement as to the value of international trade, remains true and vitally important. But the second proposition becomes much more doubtful in conditions of extreme disequilibrium in the international economic world, and in these days when we are trying to regulate so much else. I do not believe that it will be possible to regulate our internal economy effectively, much less to plan it, if our external economy is left unregulated. Indeed, as I shall suggest in a moment, the continued regulation of our external economy seems to be inevitable on the import side of the account.

On the export side, however, our freedom of action is already seriously circumscribed by the conditions of the Anglo-American Loan Agreement and may perhaps be circumscribed still more in future. Even if it were otherwise, the extent to which the volume of exports could be determined by planned arrangements would be limited; and questions of costs and prices would still be vital. As matters are, the Government will best serve the purpose of an adequate export trade if the general policy which it pursues is such as to promote industrial efficiency and to help to maintain costs and prices at a competitive level. In the effort to overcome our export difficulties there will be need, I am sure, for many contacts and much co-operation between Government and industry; but it is an illusion, I fear, to suppose that any good can be done by formulating annual global export programmes and calling on industry to fulfil

Z

them. There may even be a danger that such programmes, which can only have the significance of wishes, may be treated as a substitute for the necessity for disagreeable action, that they may serve as a smoke-screen under cover of which the crucial questions of costs and prices and competitive efficiency are evaded.

Our essential objective, in the field of international payments, is to effect a large change in our import-export balance. In so far as we cannot do this by increasing exports, we must do it by curtailing imports; and here the Government is in a position to control events more effectively. Here, therefore, may be scope and need for quantitative programmes bearing the character of instruments of policy. In my judgement, we must expect that such programmes will be necessary for an indefinite future. I form that judgement, not only because of my sense of the difficulties of increasing our exports very greatly, but also because the link which used to connect the supply of internal purchasing power with the volume of our monetary reserves has been severed, almost certainly for good. Our internal purchasing power will probably be maintained at a level which would cause us to import much more than in 1938 if imports were entirely unchecked. Hence an indefinitely continuing need for quantitative programmes of import restriction. But there is no place for a long-term target on this matter. The restrictions, however necessary, will be restrictions of the irksome type, which we should all wish to diminish as much as possible. For completeness I should add, under this heading, that a more positive and expansionist purpose might possibly be served by medium-term contracts for the purchase of some of the staple foodstuffs and raw materials which we import. But this is a large and controversial question into which I cannot enter now.

It will be apparent from what I have said so far that the term 'quantitative planning' is often used loosely to include two very different things: first, quantitative programmes which are what Sir Oliver Franks calls 'directives to action', and second, rough and ready statistical targets. My general contention is that in peace, the scope for the former is very limited, except for the unwelcome though often necessary purpose of adapting ourselves to scarcity, and that the latter can only help by indicating the kind of policy which may be needed.

But there is a third type of statistical calculation which is also mixed up with the idea of quantitative planning entertained by some—namely the so-called 'model' type of comprehensive forecast. The distinguishing feature of this type of calculation is that it is hypothetical in the extreme. It first builds an elaborate algebraical apparatus to indicate the various factors which will combine to determine the matters which are being forecast, and then attempts to evaluate these factors in the light of such data as may be available. The intellectual ingenuity which goes to this work is often impressive; but for any practical purpose in the sphere of central economic policy, the method has the serious defect that the factors which are of dominating importance are often quite unpredictable, though the consequent unreliability of the final result is hidden from spectators by the massive bulk of the apparatus employed. Moreover, in the process of guessing the key factors, a sort of Gresham's Law is apt to operate, under which wishful thinking drives out common sense.

These defects are well illustrated by the 'model' calculation made by Mr. Nicholas Kaldor three years ago, which was published as an Appendix in Lord Beveridge's book, *Full Employment in a Free Society*, and was acclaimed at the time as a brilliant example of this method. Mr. Kaldor forecast that assuming that the war would end as it did in the summer of 1945, our productive capacity in Great Britain would be sufficient in 1948 to achieve the following objects:

1. To enable us to consume 19 per cent. more consumers' goods and services than we did in 1938—19 per cent. more; not, it may be noted, a rough 20 per cent.
2. To raise real investment activity to 25 per cent. above the pre-war level.
3. To eliminate completely the deficit in our international balance of payments.
4. To balance the budget with rates of taxation only 6 per cent. on the average above those of 1938.

This was an agreeable vision.[1] In times of strain and difficulty it

---

[1] Of the various over-optimistic assumptions that contributed to its creation, the most important was that in 1948 average output per person employed in Great Britain would be 13 per cent. *higher* than it was in 1938. In fairness to Mr. Kaldor, it should be said that his cheerfulness in 1944 upon this matter was in no way peculiar to him, but appeared at the time to predominate among economists and statisticians. This makes it the more pertinent, however, as an example of the psychological Gresham's Law to which reference has been made.

is always agreeable to escape from actualities into the realms of fancy; and Mr. Kaldor's fairyland picture of a notional 1948 may perhaps be regarded as an analogue to Sir Thomas More's *Utopia* or William Morris's *News from Nowhere*, in a medium appropriate to an 'age of sophisters, economists and calculators'. But if used as instruments of central economic policy, calculations of the 'model' type are unlikely in my view to do more than provide model dwellings for a Fool's Paradise.

More generally, I suggest that current notions about planning exaggerate greatly the aid which economic policy can receive from quantitative calculations relating to the future. It is all very well to say that the objects of policy should be precisely defined; or else action will be confused and ineffective. In peace-time, as I have tried to show, the central objectives of policy must be those of equilibrium or balance, not absolute magnitudes. Indeed, if I were asked to state in a single word the goal to which economic policy should be directed in Great Britain at the present time, I should answer, Balance; balance in the matters I have already mentioned, the budget, international payments, between savings and investment; but balance also in other matters, between primary and secondary production, in the labour market, and above all between aggregate demand and aggregate supply in the economic system as a whole. Balance in all departments of economic life is an essential condition of attaining a high level of productivity and material well-being.

The practical implications of the importance of balance are, however, not always palatable; and dislike of these implications seems to form in some minds the psychological basis of an exaggerated estimate of the virtues of planning. I have already referred to the danger that reliance on quantitative export programmes may distract attention from the price and cost conditions essential to the maintenance of an adequate export trade. This danger is not limited to the export field. A striking feature of the *Economic Survey for 1947* was its disregard, virtually complete, of forces of supply, and demand, and of the influence which they may exert on the attainment of the objectives stated. You might almost suppose that the time-honoured forces have ceased to operate in the modern world. The view that we should not allow impersonal economic forces to exert the absolute sway over our economic life that they once did, nay, that we should treat them as our servant instead of our master, is one to which I wholeheartedly subscribe. But to ignore them is stupid. They are actively at work today and our present economic troubles are partly due to the fact that they are working in directions which are ill-suited to our needs. In the labour market, for example, by drawing work-people away from more essential to less essential occupations, they are largely responsible for what we call the maldistribution of our manpower. To create conditions under which these forces will work more to our advantage should be a main preoccupation of economic statesmanship.

Nothing that I have said is intended to combat the view that we must have more State intervention and direction in our economic life than we had before the war. If the phrase 'economic planning' is given only what I described at the outset as its minimum content, I believe in economic planning. Nor have I any dislike of quantitative programmes, wherever they are appropriate, as for certain purposes, notably the regulation of imports, they undoubtedly are. We are faced in this country with the need to effect large-scale readjustments in several branches of our economic affairs; and I do not believe in the light of experience that large-scale readjustments will be made smoothly or satisfactorily if they are left to the forces of supply and demand, unaided and uncontrolled. Indeed, I have been partly moved to explore this particular subject on this occasion by the apprehension that disillusionment, following attempts to apply muddled notions about planning, may cause a reaction towards *laissez-faire* doctrine and practice which might prove unfortunate in the extreme. In overcoming our many difficulties, we may derive real help from planned arrangements of various sorts. The danger against which this lecture is designed as a warning is that, on the strength of the misleading analogy of our war-time experience, planning may be regarded as a magic talisman by which those difficulties can be charmed away.

2

THE PRICE SYSTEM[1]

A YEAR ago, my predecessor in my present role, Professor Dennis Robertson, devoted most of his address to a review of the controversy which was then active about the potentialities of economic planning. I had made my own contribution to that controversy, the Rede lecture which I gave in Cambridge and which I was moved to write, partly by what seemed to me the incoherence of the planning ideology which was prevalent, and partly by the suspicion that planning appealed to many as having the properties of a magic charm which would enable us, not to solve, but to shirk our problems. Since then the ideologues of planning have remained mostly on the defensive, while their opponents, marching under the banner of a return to the price system, have launched a general assault. I had better confess at once that this revivalist ideology seems to me marked by the same defects which repelled me in planning ideology, that is to say, incoherence and wishful thinking. The phrase 'the price system' is bandied about as though its meaning were self-evident, and as though it too had the properties of a magic charm. I propose in this address to examine it closely; and in order to minimize the risk of misunderstanding, I begin with a recital of first principles.

In its most general sense the price system is an inevitable outcome of the use of money. Wherever goods and services are bought and sold for money, there must be prices; and these prices must always exert a powerful and pervasive influence. Price provides the principal criterion for resolving every problem of economic choice, both the problems of an individual arranging the distribution of his personal expenditure, and those of a manufacturer in organizing his processes of production. Rationing and allocation schemes may narrow the area of choice, both for the consumer and for the producer; but where choice exists it is exercised by constant, if often tacit reference to the price criterion. In fact, the problems of choice which arise in ordinary private and business life, even in a highly

[1] Presidential Address to Section F of the British Association, 1948. Published in the *Economic Journal*.

controlled society, are very numerous; though they are nothing like as numerous as the problems which *might* arise, if they were not settled decisively, by a subconscious appeal to the price criterion, without, so to speak, coming into court. We do not actually have to worry our heads about replacing our china dinner service by more durable gold plate. Nor does a publisher have to spend a moment in considering whether to print his books on paper or on parchment. But, if there were no such things as prices, there would be an infinitude of such questions which someone would have to settle somehow.

The influence of the price system in this sense is far more pervasive than that of the profit motive. A private trader or manufacturer, operating in a highly competitive market, may be more vividly conscious of price considerations and more quickly responsive to them than the conductors of a publicly owned industry, but the latter do not and cannot leave them out of account. Their actions may diverge from those suggested by the price criterion, either from inattention or inertia, or because of decisions made deliberately for good reasons or bad. But in all their decisions, the price criterion is an essential factor. It is the needle which points out the course to follow where there is no reason to deviate from it. And here, too, the questions which call for deliberation are only a small fraction of those which escape attention because the answer given by the price criterion is categorical and obvious.

This then is the first proposition which I wish to emphasize: that even when our economic activities are subject to a multitude of physical controls, and even if most of our major industries were to be nationalized, the influence of the configuration of prices which exists at any time remains strong, far-reaching, and fundamental. It is important, therefore, that this influence should be a healthy one, that the configuration of prices should be such as to pull in directions which accord with the public interest. The price criterion may work very badly, as we have plentiful present reasons to know, if the relations between different prices are, to use a common phrase, distorted. We want price relations that are right, so far as that object is attainable. Unquestionably, this desideratum was unduly neglected in our governmental policy a year or two ago, and, by some planning enthusiasts, it seemed to be perversely denied. But here we must be careful not to beg a major question. In the matter of price relations, as in many others, it is easier to be sure that certain things are wrong than to know at all precisely what is right. In times of large-scale economic maladjustment, is there really such a thing as a right price for any commodity or service or factor of production; or are there merely widely separated limits within which the price should lie? If there is such a thing as a right price, how is it to be determined and established?

At this stage, I think I can most conveniently develop my argument by considering the answer that would be given to these questions by those whom I call for convenience, the ideologues of the price mechanism. In broad outline, their answer would be as follows: trust to the forces of a free market, operating under conditions of effective competition, and with the minimum of interference by the State. The right price will then be secured by the interplay of demand and supply on price, and of price on demand and supply. This will be for any particular commodity the price at which demand and supply will be in equilibrium; and the establishment of equilibrium prices throughout the economic system will carry with it the corollary that the relative prices of different things will be right, in the sense that their pull will be in the directions that are needed for the most efficient use of the productive resources of society. Something of this sort is what is usually meant by those who call today for the restoration of the price system.

I have stated this view, of course, in a crude and summary form. Perhaps nobody would associate himself with it without adding various qualifications or reservations. All would concede that due allowance must be made for the so-called 'wastes of competition'. Some regard these wastes as comparatively unimportant, others as extremely important; and differences of judgement upon this matter form one element in controversies about nationalization versus private enterprise. Again most economists would admit or affirm that large inequalities of income or wealth impair the claims that can be made for the results of a freely working economy; though those whom I call price-system ideologues tend to repudiate the inference that this may justify such expedients as controls or rationing schemes, and to insist that the appropriate remedy is to do more than is done already to abate the inequalities of wealth by redistributive fiscal measures. I say no more about these qualifications or the issues which they raise, but pass to a large reservation which brings us much nearer to the questions which I wish to examine.

The strongest advocates of a free economy are nowadays increasingly inclined to concede that, before it can be expected to work well, a prior condition must first be satisfied. A rough adjustment must be established between aggregate supply and aggregate demand; otherwise a freely working economy may result in inflation, if demand is overstrong, or in a prolonged *malaise* of depression and unemployment if it is too weak. Now this is a considerable admission. First it implies that if aggregate demand and aggregate supply are out of balance, or at any rate, if aggregate demand is greatly in excess of aggregate supply, controls and allocation schemes may be needed after all. Second, it implies that one of the reasons why they may be needed is that otherwise the prices brought about by a freely working economy may be far from right. Third, it implies that the necessary equilibrium between aggregate demand and aggregate supply cannot itself be ensured by trusting to the automatic responses of a free economy. This task, it is recognized, can only be discharged by deliberate policy, perhaps taking the form of a budget surplus in some conditions and a budget deficit in others, perhaps extending to such matters as the rate interest and the stimulation or restraint of capital investment; in any case deliberate State policy, which is thus assigned a positive role of key importance in the economic system. This takes us far from *laissez-faire*, a fact which most exponents of the views I am examining are eager to proclaim and to stress; for although eulogies of the price system and a free economy are again in fashion, the *laissez-faire* philosophy is not.

Without forgetting the qualifications mentioned earlier, we may therefore restate as follows the central prescription of price-system ideology: let the State attend to the balance between aggregate demand and aggregate supply. Let it concentrate on that one all-important equation, and leave to the free play of impersonal economic forces all the detailed adjustments of the economic system. Let the State see to it that global equilibrium is established, and it need not worry about particular disequilibria. It can then leave the producer free to produce what he chooses as he chooses, in response to the inducements and deterrents of the price system; and it can restore a similar freedom of choice to the consumer, including the choice between home-produced and imported goods.

I have cast this restatement in a topical form in which it makes a wide and growing appeal, and, to judge from recent publications, is especially attractive to economists. From different angles and with important individual variations Professor Jewkes, Mr. Harrod, Mr. Hicks, and Professor Meade, and many others in this country and abroad, can be observed converging on the formula: 'Equate aggregate demand to aggregate supply and set the price system free.' Nor is this formula propounded on purely practical grounds. It is suggested that it represents the fruits of the latest developments in abstract economic thought, the distillation of the genius of Lord Keynes, a profoundly thought-out synthesis of new facts and the wisdom of the ages, appropriate to the conditions of our time. We badly need such a synthesis, I agree; but for my part I cannot find it in this formula.

Up to a point, undoubtedly, it seems well adapted to our present practical requirements in Great Britain. In my opinion at any rate, it is vitally important to eliminate the excess of overall demand in our internal economy. Such an excess, if long-continued, depletes the stocks of finished commodities, raw materials, components and spare parts, which represent the indispensable lubricant of a smoothly working economic system. It increases the difficulty of making an adequate volume of goods available for export. It entails an inflationary trend of prices and wage rates, and a constant danger that the momentum of this trend may at any time become uncontrollable. I have no doubt, therefore, as to the paramount practical importance of eliminating the excess of aggregate demand as speedily as possible. It would be most rash, I would add, to relax our efforts towards this end, until we are quite sure that it has been achieved. All this, however, leaves unanswered the pertinent questions why this excess of aggregate demand should have arisen and why it should be so very hard to get rid of it.

To continue the main argument, I hope and believe that the elimination of the general inflationary trend in our economy would carry with it the substantial elimination of many particular maladjustments, and would thus enable us to dispense with many of the controls that irk us today, and to simplify others. But would it enable us to remove them all? I do not believe it. On the contrary, I am convinced that controls, that is to say, direct, physical controls, working otherwise than through the price system, will remain indispensable in some important sections of our economy. I have in mind, in particular, the regulation of long-term capital expenditure, which I expect will be desirable for a fairly considerable time, and the regulation of imports which I am certain will be necessary for a much longer time.

My dissent from the ideology I am examining goes much deeper than a distaste for what I am sure all sensible well-informed persons would agree with me in regarding as its over-sweeping claims in matters of practical policy. Its logical foundations seem to me unsound. The main idea on which it rests is the concept of an equilibrium price to be brought about by the forces of supply and demand. In times of large-scale economic maladjustment, this concept of an equilibrium price is, I submit, ambiguous. The theory of value comprises two parts, a short-term part and a long-term part, though as Alfred Marshall was careful to warn us 'of course, there is no hard and sharp line of division between long and short periods'. In the short run, the supply in any market may be taken as a more or less fixed quantity; and the equilibrium price is that which will so curtail an excessive demand, or so stimulate a deficient one, as to match the immediately available supply. In the long run, the supply of most things can be radically altered; and the equilibrium price is that which will evoke a rate of supply sufficient to meet the demand which will be forthcoming at that price. For a particular commodity, accordingly, the long-run equilibrium price corresponds to the cost of producing it, including in that term a fair profit margin.

Now in ordinary times, when the economic system has not been subjected to any recent large disturbance, the short-term and long-term equilibrium prices of most things are seldom far apart; and any small difference between them resulting from some small maladjustment between supply and demand serves as an effective and comparatively unobjectionable means of correcting that maladjustment. If, for example, the demand for some particular commodity or material expands so as to outrun the current rate of production, the price tends to rise, production becomes more than usually profitable, and the rate of production is increased until it becomes sufficient to meet the enlarged demand. For this purpose, a very moderate rise of price will usually suffice; and a very moderate rise is all that usually occurs when times are what I have called ordinary, though there may be important exceptions even then. These are the conditions in which the price mechanism in a free economy works efficiently.

The story is apt to be very different when the maladjustments to be corrected are very large. If it is a case of a large excess of demand over supply, the short-term equilibrium price may be very high indeed, much higher than is useful in stimulating additional production. For an exorbitant price does not stimulate production appreciably more than a good price; it frequently stimulates it less. Indeed it is a well-established paradox that an excessive price sometimes leads to a decline in output, because many classes of producers are disposed to work less hard when an accustomed income can be earned with less exertion. On the other hand, the disadvantages of an exorbitant price, or in more popular language, a profiteering price, may be very great.

Not that I wish to suggest that in the absence of controls a large excess of demand over supply will always lead to a price that is grossly in excess of costs of production. The actual price in such conditions will depend largely on the type of market in which the commodity is bought and sold. It will come near to the short-term equilibrium price for those things which are sold on organized exchanges, as are normally most staple agricultural commodities. But for goods which are produced to fulfil orders, as are most industrial products, the prices at which the orders are placed usually represent some sort of compromise between those which might result from a free auction on the one hand and the costs of production on the other; a compromise in other words between the short-term and the long-term equilibrium prices. The character of the compromise varies from one type of commodity to another. It is useful to note in passing that the deviation of price from the norm set by costs of production is usually least when the price is fixed by the unilateral decision of the producer, as it is for branded goods, that is to say where competition is most imperfect. It is not monopoly but competition which forces up prices most in conditions of shortage.

It is a mistake, therefore, to suppose that in such conditions the theoretical short-term equilibrium price is either what we want, or what we normally get in a free economy; or that relative prices would be 'right' if the State did not interfere with them by controls and subsidies. The paradox that the prices of second-hand motor-cars are often a good deal higher than the prices of new cars of the same makes can be observed today in the United States, no less than in Great Britain. This matters little, but it illustrates the anomalies that are apt to occur in price relations when shortages are widespread. Some of these anomalies do matter; and it is important to limit their growth. Unless we are to go out of our way to force up the less volatile prices to profiteering heights, this means that we must keep down the more volatile by appropriate restraints. Prices fail, in these circumstances, to discharge the function of lopping-off excess demand; and problems of allocation must be dealt with by other means or left unsolved.

It is true that shortages or surpluses are apt to be most wide-spread, and the consequential anomalies most serious, when there is a large maladjustment between aggregate demand and aggregate supply. But it is not true that the former disequilibria are always a mere by-product of the latter. They may sometimes have a common origin, as in the great economic disturbance caused by a major war; they may sometimes arise independently; or the relation between cause and effect may be the other way round, for sometimes particular maladjustments may play a big part, as I believe they do now, in causing or maintaining a maladjustment between aggregate supply and aggregate demand. However this may be, particular maladjustments of large magnitude and crucial importance may remain, after global equilibrium has been restored. Wherever such maladjustments exist, the short-term equilibrium price may diverge widely from the long-term equilibrium price; and real difficulties and problems may arise, for which the ordinary price mechanism affords no adequate solution.

These are the generalities which seem to be relevant. I am conscious that they come very near to being platitudes which it should not be necessary to labour at such length. I have felt impelled to stress them by the fact that they are so completely, and sometimes it seems so perversely, ignored in current price-system ideology. I pass now to consider their bearing on the most formidable of all our national economic problems—the large and persistent deficit in our balance of international payments.

Is there really any reasonable prospect that the restoration of balance between aggregate demand and aggregate supply in our internal economy would enable us to entrust our external economy to the price mechanism, that is to say, to remove restrictions upon imports, including imports from dollar or other hard currency sources? Is this even conceivable, so long as the prices of the food-stuffs and raw materials which we have to import are as high as they are today? The question is one which we are in a fair position to judge; for though we have not yet eliminated the excess of aggregate demand in our internal economy, we are not, I hope, very far now from doing so. The progress we have made in this matter has not, however, brought us within sight of closing the deficit in our balance of external payments. Even the target laid down in the *Economic Survey for 1948* went no further than a reduction of this deficit to £250 millions in the present year; and in the light of what has happened since, there is little chance that that target will be hit.

We are running a formidable deficit in this vital sector of our economy despite the fact that our total volume of imports is held down by means of an austere programme of import restrictions to about 80 per cent. of the pre-war level, and despite the fact that our commodity exports are considerably larger in volume than before the war, let us say by about one-quarter. Additional exports normally require additional imports of raw materials. Accordingly, the volume of imports available to satisfy the needs of our resident population is probably appreciably less than 80 per cent. of the pre-war volume, although this population is more numerous than it was. On the other hand, our consumption of goods and services as a whole, though its exact rate is a matter of some abstruse controversy, cannot reasonably be put much lower than before the war, at any rate when capital goods are included, as it is right to include them for the present argument. So we have the contrast: consumption of imported goods less than 80 per cent. of pre-war, total consumption about 100 per cent. of pre-war.

If the consuming public, together with manufacturers and traders, were free to choose between home-produced and imported goods, there is no reason to suppose that imported goods would represent a smaller fraction of their total purchases than formerly. It is true that in the absence of subsidies, imported goods would have risen more in price. Against this, however, must be set the redistribution of net income in favour of the lower income-groups, who spend a smaller part of their income than others on services, and a larger part on commodities from overseas. If, therefore, import restrictions were removed, it would seem only reasonable to expect that the volume of relevant imports would return from less than 80 per cent. to about 100 per cent. of the pre-war level, an increase of more than a quarter. At present prices, which might of course be increased by additional purchases, this would add over £400 millions to our national import-bill.

How would this result be affected by the definite removal of every vestige of inflation? This might serve to reduce our aggregate consumption somewhat, and the demand for imports correspondingly. Conceivably, our aggregate consumption may have to be reduced, failing a sufficient further increase in output. But no one, I imagine, would suggest, least of all the critics of austerity, that our aggregate consumption of goods and services may have to be reduced by 20 per cent. or more. This is the magnitude of the reduction that would be needed, if the removal of import restrictions were not to result in increased expenditure on imported goods.

It may be hoped that the elimination of excess demand will also help to increase our exports. That is one of the many reasons why it is so important to eliminate this excess. But we need a large increase in our export receipts in order to close the existing deficit in our balance of payments, which Marshall Aid is not enough to cover; and when Marshall Aid runs out we shall need in addition all the reduction in import prices for which we can fairly hope. In the meantime, we are in no position to contemplate a largely increased expenditure on imports. We have to keep our imports down and get our exports up as well. I cannot gainsay anyone who complains that once again I am labouring the obvious. I observe only that this disposes of the doctrine that if we re-establish global equilibrium we can leave the balance of payments to take care of itself.

The locker of price-system ideology contains, it is true, another shot. This is the idea that disequilibria in the balance of payments can always be corrected by variations in foreign exchange rates, though opinions differ widely as to how this idea should be applied. Professor Jewkes, in his *Ordeal by Planning*, argues that the level of exchange rates should be left to the free play of supply and demand in foreign exchange markets. Indeed, he seems to regard the fixing of even tentative exchange parities as constituting in itself an illegitimate interference with the price mechanism.[1]

[1] 'What would have happened in the free economy? The State would have confined itself to its legitimate role of restricting the volume of money sufficiently to prevent domestic inflation. Exports would have been stimulated because that would have been the only outlet for goods. The cramping effect upon industry of physical controls would have been avoided. No export targets would have been fixed, exports would have been left to find their own level. The long-period exchange rate would have been left to determine itself. A deficit in the balance of payments would have been met by a fall in the exchange rate, thus increasing exports and reducing imports. If the nation was living at a level beyond its means, the fact would have been immediately

In this, however, I think he is exceptional; and a more prevalent view is that exchange parities should be altered from time to time as a means of correcting balance of payments disequilibria. Those who hold this view are not all of one mind as to whether the pound sterling should be devalued in Great Britain at the present time. Some appear to advocate this course, or at any rate did so about a year ago; for on this matter minds not only differ but are apt to change. Professor Meade, in his inaugural lecture at the London School of Economics, expressly disclaims this proposition, and declares himself uncertain whether devaluation will eventually be needed. But he joins with the others in insisting that devaluation, in contradistinction to import restrictions, is the right remedy for our balance of payments difficulties, if they should prove obstinate. On the other hand, Professor Hawtrey, whom I think it is fair to class as a price-system ideologue, though of a highly individual type, urges the opposite course, the raising of our exchange rate with the dollar, on the ground that the pound is at present under-valued by reference to relative price levels, and that this gives us bad terms of trade and acts as an inflationary force.

I cannot attempt in this address a full examination of these diverse views. But I point to their diversity to illustrate my central theme. The ardent advocacy of exchange depreciation in the abstract, in which most price-system ideologues indulge, is attributable to the pivotal role which they assign to the concept of equilibrium price. There *must* be, they believe, some equilibrium rate of exchange which would equate the supply of and the demand for dollars. I reply that when our import-export balance is so far from adjustment, there is a huge divergence between the theoretical short-term equilibrium rate and the theoretical long-term rate. The former is that at which the demand for foreign exchange would be in balance with the supply accruing from business transactions. The relevant long-term norm for the exchange rate between two currencies, corresponding to the cost of production as the long-term norm for the price of a commodity, is, to use the phrase coined in the last post-war period by Professor Cassel, their purchasing power parity; not, of course, that that is likely to remain constant in unstable times any more than the cost of producing a commodity remains constant.

It is to this norm that Professor Hawtrey appeals in maintaining

signalled to all and the increase in domestic prices would have pressed down the standard of living to what was possible.' Jewkes, *Ordeal by Planning*, p. 234.

that sterling is too low relatively to the dollar. I am not quite sure that he is right in maintaining this; subsidized prices and changes in relative productivity make the relevant price level calculations a treacherous bog. But he may be right, or the trend of relative costs may soon make him right. If so, I infer that our exchange rate is about where it ought to be. For the price prescription which I offer for conditions of serious maladjustment is that the price should deviate from the long-term norm in the direction of the short-term equilibrium price, but only by a narrow angle.

It is important that the angle should be small. Just as an exorbitant price is seldom more effective than a good price in stimulating the output of a commodity, and may sometimes even lower it, so an exchange rate which is far below purchasing power parity is seldom more effective than one which is only slightly below this norm in improving the balance of payments of a country in deficit, and may even worsen it. It would be foolish, therefore, and possibly disastrous, to try to make actual rates of exchange correspond to the short-term equilibrium rates, when these would be far below current purchasing power parities. This is not a matter of *a priori* dogmatism. It is the principal lesson which was taught, even if we have failed to learn it, by the runaway currency inflations on the Continent of Europe in the 1920's. A marked and almost invariable feature of these inflations was that exchange depreciation in the country concerned moved far ahead of the rise in internal prices, so that the deterrent to imports and the stimulus to exports were as strong as any price-system ideologue could possibly desire. Yet the balance of payments was normally worsened, because the effect on the terms of trade outweighed the effect on the relative volumes of imports and exports.

The inflationary process was therefore cumulative. The rise in internal prices, though never catching up with the external depreciation, at least until the final stages, was always hurrying after it. It proved difficult to balance budgets in such conditions; and the process continued until eventually it was ended, whether before or after it had culminated in a complete *dégringolade*, by applying what came to be recognized as the indispensable remedy. This was to hold the foreign exchange rates firmly for a period, by means of foreign credits or the free use of the country's own gold reserves at a level in the neighbourhood of the purchasing power parity. So only could the breathing-space be secured in which any other

A a

measures that might be needed for stabilization could take effect.

These things happened in the days of unrestricted foreign exchange markets, when individuals were free to put their money abroad. This freedom, by the way, was regarded then, and indeed right up to 1939, as an essential feature of a free economy. Now that capital movements are tightly controlled in most countries, it is unlikely that an inflationary movement would conform to the model of the 1920's in all respects. On the essential point, however, of the capacity of exchange depreciation to improve a country's balance of payments, this experience is extremely pertinent. If contemporary experience is preferred, the large and rapid increase in French prices which followed the devaluation of the franc in January 1948 is equally apposite. British economists, I suggest, would do better to heed these lessons than to bandy calculations in terms of elasticities conceived as quasi-constant ratios, capable of measurement. In effect, all such calculations beg the crucial questions at issue, taking for granted first that a country can push exchange depreciation to any degree desired without affecting its internal price level, and second that the effect on the balance of payments, assuming this to be favourable, will increase without limit with the degree of the depreciation.

I submit, then, that for correcting a huge maladjustment in the balance of payments, such as still confronts Great Britain, counter-inflationary financial measures, though helpful, cannot suffice; and that exchange rate variations might be harmful. It is essential to keep down the volume of our import purchases as effectively as we now do by means of import restrictions. And not only to keep down their total volume, but more particularly that part of them that comes from what we call hard-currency sources. The principle of non-discrimination does not fit a world in which the whole international balance of payments has been upset.

There remains another aspect of the problem to which I should refer. Might not the necessary limitation of our import expenditure be secured by means more conformable, as the phrase goes, to the price mechanism than quantitative import regulation; for example, by high tariffs or by the auctioning of import licences, as Professor Meade persistently suggests? My answer is, where we are free to choose, that that method should be chosen which will secure its object most simply and most effectively. For some commodities, duties are unquestionably the most appropriate form of import limitation, notably for tobacco where the objects are mixed, and the indirect saving of dollars through the raising of revenue may well predominate over the direct saving accruing from a cut in purchases. But many of our import restrictions are prohibitions, complete or nearly so, at least on imports from particular countries. Nothing would be gained, not even a saving of administrative costs, by replacing these prohibitions by duties designed to be prohibitive. Here the quantitative method is simpler, more straightforward, and more certainly effective. For other commodities it may be important to avoid raising prices to the home consumer. Again, a large part of our imports is purchased at present directly by the State, and here manifestly it is impossible to evade the quantitative question, how much the State should buy.

The principle that I have suggested applies, of course, more widely. Wherever the need for effective regulation is made out, the question of the best method to employ should be settled on merits, in the light of the relevant circumstances, and not by ideological prepossessions, either for the price system or against it. Quantitative controls, allocation schemes, and the like are crude and clumsy instruments, which it is absurd to idealize. My own experience confirms the lively account which Professor Jewkes gives of the lengthy administrative process of quite unscientific haggling by which allocation schemes are apt to be constructed. But it must not be supposed that there are no defects in the so-called financial controls which some prefer. When, for example, it is suggested that the need to ration scarce essential commodities might be averted by redistributing purchasing power by really drastic fiscal measures, it is well to remember that taxes have their disadvantages and sometimes arouse criticism, that their incidence is not always just or scientific, and that officials have to be employed to assess and to collect them.

The same scheme of analysis which I have applied to foreign exchange rates and the balance of payments can be applied with appropriate modifications to the rate of interest and the balance between savings and investment. During the war, the production of capital goods for peace-time purposes was virtually suspended; consequently, the current demand for such goods is abnormally high. On the other hand, for various reasons the current rate of private saving is abnormally low. In these circumstances, an extremely high rate of interest might be needed to equate the rate of real investment to the rate of saving, if the demand for capital goods were uncontrolled. There is, therefore, a strong case for regulating this demand. The interrelations of the capital market and the monetary system introduce many complications; and I cannot pursue this subject further in this address. It is worth noting, however, that modern economic thought, over-impressed as I think by these complications, is inclined on this matter to abandon the notion of an equilibrium price altogether. It has been suggested that there are no limits, set by an underlying economic force, to the power of governments and monetary authorities to manipulate interest rates. This palpable exaggeration, as I have always thought it, served to encourage Mr. Dalton in the mistake which he undoubtedly made in carrying the cheap money policy to excessive lengths. The mistake lay in trying to force interest rates down below the long-term norm.

I have concentrated in this address on what I may call the mechanics of the economic problem. My main theme can be summed up in two short propositions; first that, in conditions of large-scale maladjustment, the optimum price is to be found, as a rule, between the long-term norm and the short-term equilibrium price, but lies much nearer to the former; second, that in such conditions, regulation and deliberate direction may be useful and sometimes indispensable. To anyone concerned in a responsible capacity with the actual problems that arise, the latter proposition at least is obvious common sense. I deplore the fact that it is necessary to argue it among professional economists. A century ago economists were laughed at as the practitioners of the dismal science. They scarcely deserve that taunt, or should I say that compliment, today. I fear it must be recorded that during a period in which the British people have been faced with most formidable economic difficulties, to surmount which it is important above all else to appreciate the magnitude of the effort required, the most extravagant propagandists of go-easy illusions, the most pushing salesmen of enervating Fools' Paradises, have been found among economists of diverse schools of thought. We have now, I hope, done with the illusion that a much better time could be had quite easily by all if only industry were mobilized for national purposes, as it was to produce Fido, and Pluto, and Mulberry. It would be no improvement to replace this by the illusion that our present austerities are unnecessary, and would vanish like the snow if the sun of the price system were allowed to shine.

3

THE FUNCTION OF EXCHANGE RATES[1]

I

THE idea that variations in foreign exchange rates can serve as an efficient regulator of a freely working international economic system has gained an astonishing vogue among British academic economists. It seems, indeed, to have become a main article of faith with those who still regard a return to a freely working international economic system as a righteous cause and a practicable goal. This, it is worth noting at the outset, implies a remarkable change of view. It is not very long since the extremists of economic liberalism were disposed to stress, and even to exaggerate, the advantages of fixed exchange rates. In the era of international economic expansion before 1914 a rigid fixity of exchange rates was, of course, secured by the nearly world-wide operation of the gold standard. After the First World War, when exchange rates were in confusion and runaway inflation widespread in Europe, international economic statesmanship concentrated on the restoration of exchange stability through the medium of a general return to the gold standard, as a central aim of reconstruction. This policy commended itself to public opinion at large, and to the economic liberalism of the day in particular, for many reasons. Among them was the consideration, emphasized in the resolutions of international conferences, that the restoration of exchange stability was an essential pre-condition of the removal of import prohibitions and quota restrictions and other new varieties of trade impediments. During the 1930's, after the collapse of the reconstituted gold-standard system, the persistent refusal of the British authorities to re-establish a definite gold parity for sterling was criticized and censured in ultra-liberal circles as a regrettable piece of self-regarding economic nationalism. To economists like Professor Robbins and Sir Theodore Gregory, to bodies like the International Chamber of Commerce, fixed exchange rates were still a condition of international economic health.[2]

---

[1] *Oxford Economic Papers*, January 1949.
[2] 'The bitter experience of the World Economic Conference has shown that, unless the future of exchange rates is tolerably certain, it is quite hopeless to

A Rip van Winkle familiar with the controversies of the last decade might, therefore, be startled if he were to wake up today to find that exchange-rate variations have been assigned a high constructive role in the ultra-liberal philosophy as the regulating spring of the future international mechanism, and the true alternative to the hated quantitative regulation. It may be instructive to consider how this change has come about. In the 1930's advocacy of fixed exchange parities implied acceptance of the whole gold-standard technique; and an essential part of that technique was that the amount of money and credit and purchasing power within a country was related to, and governed by, the volume of its gold reserve. This relation provided the regulator needed for a self-adjusting mechanism. A large or persistent deficit in the balance of payments of a country would lead to an outflow of gold; this would enforce a curtailment of the volume of credit and purchasing power, reduce incomes, prices, and costs, check imports and stimulate exports, and thus restore external equilibrium.

Such at least was the picture of the chain of remedial reactions which time-honoured theoretical analysis had imprinted firmly. Early in the inter-war period heretics had begun to mutter that in practice the process was less simple and less satisfactory. An outflow or inflow of gold might arise not only from disequilibria in the balance of payments on current account but from capital movements; and capital movements might represent not the long-term international investment which had won a good name in the nineteenth century, but a scurry of individuals or businesses in other countries to put their money abroad for greater safety or to bring it back again when their confidence recovered. Such erratic movements of 'hot' money were not a good reason for making credit in Great Britain abnormally easy at one moment and tight at another. Yet this was the natural outcome of the automatism of the gold standard.

After the fall of the pound in 1931 this consideration told strongly

expect any substantial abolition of the obstacles to trade. You cannot negotiate about tariff rates effectively unless you have some idea of the future course of values. And you can have no idea of the future course of values unless you can rely upon a more or less steady rate of exchange. After all, many of the obstacles which it would be most desirable to remove, actually came into being because of the difficulties caused by fluctuating exchanges. Until the exchanges have ceased to fluctuate, it is surely futile to hope that they will be removed.' Professor Lionel Robbins, *Lloyds Bank Monthly Review*, April 1935.

against returning to gold. By this time, moreover, 'hot' money movements had attained such large dimensions as to convince our authorities that a reserve of international purchasing power much larger than the traditional gold reserve of the Bank of England had become indispensable. The Exchange Equalization Fund was accordingly created in 1932; and as an incident of this, the link was severed which had hitherto connected the amount of our internal purchasing power with the monetary reserves available for external payment. It thus became possible to insulate our money market and credit system from the disturbing effects of quite large movements of funds whether in or out. Our monetary authorities came increasingly to appreciate how convenient this was for various purposes, notably for the uninterrupted pursuit of the policy of cheap money designed for the promotion of trade recovery. In this way a sense of the increasing disadvantages of the automatism of the gold standard under inter-war conditions gradually merged into a cautious sense of the positive advantages of a more insulated system in opening out new possibilities of deliberate and constructive policy.

The extremists of international economic liberalism, however, viewed these developments with disapproving eyes. They maintained that the firm re-establishment of definite exchange parities was the true corrective for 'hot' money movements, and that, for this, a readiness to stabilize sterling was indispensable. They were not attracted by the greater scope for deliberate policy under an autonomous monetary system, for they were predominantly *laissez-faire* in outlook. The more reflective of them expressly urged that the link between internal purchasing power and reserves of gold and foreign exchange should be restored.[1] Thus the free international economic mechanism which they wished to reconstitute would have contained its traditional regulator.

This is no longer true. Apparently there is no one left today who

---

[1] 'Fluctuations in the resources of the Exchange Equalisation Fund should be treated in the same way as fluctuations in the gold reserve in a centre finally stabilised on gold. If the reserve shows signs of serious depletion, then the rate of discount should be raised and steps should be taken to make it effective. No doubt this sounds disagreeable. We have become so accustomed to the drug of ultra-cheap money, that the thought that, to enjoy the benefits of international revival, we may be compelled to forgo the benefits of ignoring international conditions is very irksome. We like to think that international revival will be super-added to the delights of irresponsibility. We do not see that the failure of international revival to arrive is in part at least the price for the policy we have hitherto pursued.' Professor Robbins, ibid.

desires to make the volume of our internal purchasing power vary with the size of our monetary reserves. For the future, it is to be determined, according to the now fashionable prescription, solely with a view to maintaining full employment. Subject to some cautionary words about this phrase, Professor Robbins has declared his adherence to the policy. 'I favour something', he wrote in 1947,[1] 'which, if you like, you can call overall financial planning' designed 'to maintain overall stability of aggregate demand, while leaving the maximum flexibility between the various constituent items.' This, it should be observed, is recommended not for a temporary emergency but for the period 'when the problems of the transition are over'. Professor Robbins recognizes that it implies a certain change of view ('I confess that I have not always held this conviction as strongly as I do today'); but the change is far more radical than these words suggest. It means shifting the criterion by which the effective volume of our purchasing power is to be determined from one related to our international position to one related exclusively to our internal conditions. This would certainly have aroused Professor Robbins's strong disapproval before the war.

To all appearances this change of view is widespread. A purely internal criterion for regulating the volume of purchasing power is accepted today by those who still hope for a return to a free international economy no less readily than it is by others. Faith in the old regulator of the gold standard seems to have faded quietly away during the war years. Perhaps the appearances are deceptive; it may be that there are some who have not altered their views, but are merely silent and perplexed. Certainly it is somewhat curious that the war should have effected this revolution of opinion. For it would be possible to argue, not unreasonably, that the gold standard might work more satisfactorily in future, now that exchange control over capital movements has been introduced in Great Britain and many other countries. Not that this control is ever likely to be so effective as to prevent a slow, steady, capital leakage, if the underlying economic forces are set strongly in that direction. But it should suffice to avert large, sudden, fortuitous movements of 'hot' money. Accordingly changes in a country's monetary reserves may be expected to reflect more accurately than in the past the state of its balance of payments on current account, and are only likely to be modified or aggravated by a strong persistent tendency towards an

[1] *The Economic Problem in Peace and War.*

outflow or inflow of capital, to which it can be argued that internal credit conditions *ought* to be responsive. On these grounds, the line might well have been taken that the gold standard would be sufficiently modernized by retaining exchange control over capital movements, and that it should be an aim of policy to restore its essential elements, namely the fixity of exchange rates and a definite relation between internal purchasing power and monetary reserves.

In fact, however, the line taken has been quite different. During the war-time phase of post-war economic planning it became customary to do obeisance to a somewhat arbitrary potentate, known as 'the climate of opinion'; and on nothing, it was understood, was this potentate so insistent as on ensuring full employment and avoiding deflation in any circumstances. In this atmosphere the extremists of economic liberalism were chiefly concerned to argue that the object could be attained quite simply and without any serious interference with a free economy, by the expedient which Professor Robbins calls 'overall financial planning'. This contention was rendered more plausible by a new, ingenious, argumentative technique, invented, I think, by Lord Beveridge and widely adopted since. Awkward difficulties, such as the repercussions of a strong demand on wage rates and prices, which would previously have been recognized as belonging to the essence of the problem, were disposed of by recognizing them, with apparent candour, 'assuming' that they would be overcome somehow, and then ignoring them. With the aid of this device many economists have been able to hypnotize both themselves and the more sophisticated sections of public opinion into the remarkable belief that the problem of averting serious unemployment in future has been solved triumphantly by modern abstract economic analysis, unsupported though this is by experience, and resting though it does on the manifestly unreal hypothesis of a 'closed economy'.

They have been unable, however, to blind themselves to the fact that the new 'overall financial planning' must involve scrapping the old regulator by which maladjustments in the balance of international payments were corrected. The idea of deliberate regulation by such means as import restrictions and quantitative programmes is peculiarly repellent to all price-system ideologues, except as a strictly temporary expedient. For normal conditions they feel it essential to find a new automatic regulator; yet none appears to be available, other than exchange-rate variations. An optimistic view of their efficacy has become accordingly for many a necessity of the logic of their position. This goes far, no doubt, to explain the incomplete thinking and lack of critical sense and common sense with which exchange-rate variations are commended.

II

Let us consider what has to be assumed to justify the belief that exchange-rate variations might serve as an efficient regulator. First, it is clearly necessary to assume that a depreciation of a country's exchange rates will normally improve its balance of payments, and that this effect will be a lasting one. For this to be true an indispensable condition is that the level of internal prices and incomes should not rise proportionately to the depreciation even in the long run. On this hypothesis it is common ground that the effect of the depreciation on the balance of payments will be the resultant of opposing tendencies: on the one hand a worsening of the country's terms of trade, on the other hand an increase in exports and a decrease in imports in terms of volume. Therefore the further assumption is required that the latter tendency will preponderate over the former.

The reasonableness of this last assumption has been the subject of much discussion and controversy, necessarily inconclusive. The essential truth about it can be summed up, in my opinion, in the following propositions:

1. It is normally helpful in the long run to a country's balance of payments that its currency should be 'undervalued' rather than 'overvalued'; that is to say, that its internal value, representing its power to purchase labour and home-produced goods, should be somewhat higher than its external value, representing its power to purchase imported goods, and depending partly on exchange rates and partly on the price level in the outside world. The presumption that there will be a net advantage arises partly from the fact that an undervaluation involves a fall in the aggregate of national income and purchasing power, when reckoned in terms of other currencies. The effect on the volume of imports and exports tends, therefore, to be greater than that which would be produced by price influences alone.

2. Nevertheless, this net advantage will not increase indefinitely with the extent of the undervaluation. After a certain point

the unfavourable effects of a further undervaluation on the terms of trade will outweigh the favourable effects on the volume of imports and exports. This certainly is the conclusion suggested by the experience of runaway inflations, during which the extent of the undervaluation existing at any moment was usually extreme.

3. For correcting an adverse balance of payments there is, therefore, in principle, an optimum degree of undervaluation; and this, though it may vary from one country to another and from time to time, is usually, in my judgement, slight. I use the words 'in principle' because I do not wish to suggest that either the actual degree of a currency's undervaluation, or the degree that would be most desirable, can be precisely calculated.

I have dealt somewhat cursorily with this question because I do not regard it as the really crucial one. It seems to me more important to examine closely the questions that arise directly out of it. How is the optimum degree of undervaluation, whatever it may be, to be established and maintained? Is it likely, or even conceivable, that the expedient of exchange-rate adjustments could serve this purpose effectively? In considering these questions we must never lose sight of the fact that the undervaluation which has to be established is not a simple entity but a tripartite relation, in which rates of exchange are only one factor, the other two being the level of costs and prices in the country concerned and the level of prices in the outside world.

The effect of a depreciation of exchange rates on the above relation is likely to depend in practice on what is happening to the last factor, which, of course, lies outside the control of national policy. It can reasonably be expected to be a beneficial one, from the standpoint of the balance of payments, as from others, during a severe world depression, when prices in terms of gold and other currencies are falling sharply. In these conditions an exchange depreciation, within due limits, will not serve to raise internal costs and prices, except possibly by way of recovery from a very recent fall. The broad effect will be to avert or mitigate the need for a fall in wage rates and internal prices in order to maintain the country's competitive position in world markets. Now the process of adjustment to the need for a lower price level is notoriously slow and painful, and is apt to be incomplete. Wage reductions are never easy to bring about. Some prices and money incomes are more or less 'rigid' for long periods, or are at least 'sheltered' from the pressure of international competition. Thus the real incomes of many individuals tend, under deflationary conditions, to increase. This throws an additional strain on others; and the less sheltered producers must suffer a reduction of real income, as well as money income, if the country's competitive position is not to be impaired. To be relieved from the need to effect a readjustment of this sort, and from the pressure towards it, is a real service and may be a crowning mercy.

It was in conditions of severe world depression and deflation that the fall of the pound in 1931 proved of great advantage to the British economy, and helped for a time to improve the competitive position of British industries in world markets and the British balance of payments. The idea that exchange depreciation, previously regarded as a calamity, might rather be a blessing came into fashion as the result of this experience, and received an early and startling expression in the deliberate forcing down of the gold value of the dollar in 1933. The events that followed showed that this idea had serious limitations and drawbacks even in a deflationary setting. The depreciation of the pound and the dollar had disastrous repercussions on the economies of the gold bloc countries, notably France, which eventually were forced to devalue too; and there seemed at one time a real danger of a chaotic process of competitive exchange depreciation, which was averted by a 'gentlemen's agreement' between the United States, Great Britain, and France to avoid deliberate exchange depreciation for the future, known as the Tripartite Agreement of 1936. This experience does nothing to encourage the view that exchange-rate adjustments by particular countries would form a good basis for an orderly international economy. It remains true, however, that if serious world depression and deflation should recur, exchange depreciation would be useful and perhaps indispensable to countries in balance-of-payments difficulties.

It cannot be inferred that it would be equally helpful when world prices are rising, or even when they are more or less steady. In such conditions a lowering of exchange rates would cause internal prices to rise absolutely, and not merely relatively to prices in the outside world. The rise would not be confined to the prices of imported goods, but would spread gradually throughout the country's economy. In Great Britain more especially, an exchange depreciation would contribute either to a wage inflation, by raising the cost of living, or to a financial inflation, if the attempt were made to counteract this by additional food subsidies. In any other environment than that of world deflation, a substantial exchange depreciation must be a strong price-raising influence.

If it were not for the dynamic quality of inflationary movements, it would no doubt be arguable that the rise in internal prices and costs ought to be less than proportionate to the exchange depreciation; and attempts were, I think, made at one time to calculate the degree of inflation that would represent an appropriate adjustment on the basis of an assumed rigidity of certain prices and incomes. In practice, however, the extent of an inflationary movement, once it has been set going, cannot be forecast. The process is apt to be self-perpetuating, and indeed to gather momentum, unless and until it is checked by some obstacle or counter-force, for which there is no provision in the technique of exchange depreciation. There can be no assurance therefore that the rise of internal prices would stop at any theoretically appropriate points. It would be a happy accident if it did.

This raises an awkward question, to which it is important to know the answer. What is supposed to happen, under a system of exchange-rate variations, if the rise of internal costs and prices following a lowering of exchange rates should overshoot the mark, and instead of leaving some degree of undervaluation, helpful to the balance of payments, should result in an overvaluation? So far as I know the advocates of variable exchange rates are silent on this point. But clearly there are only two courses open. One is to lower the exchange rates again in the hope that there would be better luck next time. If this course were followed there would be no safeguard against the danger of a vicious spiral of exchange depreciation and internal inflation, gathering speed and continuing indefinitely. The other course is to call in aid whatever instruments may be most effective for forcing prices down, including perhaps the restriction of credit. These are the instruments which were brought into play more or less automatically under the gold standard, when gold was flowing out. If they have also to be used after an exchange depreciation, a further question arises. What would have been gained by the preliminary depreciation? If it may be necessary, after exchange rates have been lowered, to use the traditional deflationary instruments to establish a certain degree of under-valuation, why not use them in the first instance to establish the undervaluation at the original parities?

Reasons can be urged, it is true, for preferring an initial devalua-tion, which sometimes possess great cogency. For example, the real value of the interest payable on the national debt would be reduced by an inflation; and when the proportions of the debt charge to the national income and the public revenue are extremely high, it may be important that the public finances should obtain some such relief. Upon this issue much, of course, can be said on the other side; and I do not personally believe that the case for devaluation as a debt-relieving measure is nearly made out in Great Britain. But the point to note is that arguments of this sort for a once-for-all devaluation provide no support for the idea of using variations in exchange rates as a balance-of-payments regulator. If this idea were really to be applied, and if an exchange depreciation were followed by a fully proportionate inflation, there would be no escape from the other horn of the dilemma, namely a further lowering of exchange rates and the risk of a vicious spiral, in which the internal value and the external value of the currency would chase each other downwards.

The fundamental impracticability of the idea now begins to emerge; and, in order to bring it out clearly, it may be helpful and appropriate to use language of quasi-mathematical formalism. Price-system forces can only serve to regulate or improve the balance of payments by establishing and maintaining a favourable relation between three factors: exchange rates, internal prices, and world prices. One of these, world prices, is outside the control of national policy. Therefore, it must be possible to cause one of the other two factors to move in whichever direction is required, while the third is held firmly at a fixed point, or at least is effectively pre-vented from changing in equal proportion. It is possible to cause internal prices to fall, if that is the movement required, by the use of deflationary monetary and financial instruments, while the ex-change rates are held firmly at fixed parities; though there are limits to the extent to which this process can be carried in practice. This was the *modus operandi* of the gold standard. It is *not* possible to reverse the roles; i.e. to lower the exchange rates, and to keep internal prices stable or to ensure that they will not rise beyond a certain point. For the deflationary, or counter-inflationary, instruments are not precision instruments. If applied with sufficient force and for a sufficient length of time, they are capable of reversing an inflationary trend; they are incapable of the delicate work of allowing prices to rise so far and no farther. Still less could they hold prices and money incomes at a constant level, if exchange rates vary.

This would be a fatal weakness of the method of exchange depreciation, even if the regulation of internal prices were made the governing purpose of monetary and financial policy. In fact, however, this is not recommended, at least not ostensibly, by the advocates of exchange-rate variations. As I have indicated above, they subscribe, with whatever qualifying hesitations, to the doctrine that these instruments should be used to maintain aggregate demand at a level conducive to full employment. It is important to explore somewhat further the way in which this doctrine complicates the problem.

III

Nothing has done more in my opinion to lead modern economists astray than the practice which Lord Keynes brought into fashion in the 1930's of reasoning on the hypothesis of a 'closed economy'. Elaborate structures of theoretical analysis, purporting to supply light and guidance for the central economic problems of the actual world, have been built on what is in effect the assumption that there is no such thing as international trade, that all economic transactions take place within the boundaries of a single country and are therefore within the scope of its government's control. This assumption is, of course, supposed to be merely a provisional simplifying hypothesis, introduced to facilitate the orderly development of thought; and in principle it is recognized that all conclusions reached upon this basis must be subjected to subsequent revision in the light of the fact that our actual economies are far from being 'closed'. Unfortunately this final task is apt to be very perfunctorily performed and sometimes neglected altogether.

It is paradoxical that British economists should have led this intellectual fashion, at which Adam Smith, Ricardo, John Stuart Mill, Bagehot, and Alfred Marshall would certainly have knit their brows. International trade has been for centuries a factor of fundamental importance in the British economy. Even before 1914 our most serious economic troubles had their origins abroad; fluctuations in the overseas demand for British exports, both of consumers' goods and of capital goods, did far more to influence the level of our industrial activity than fluctuations in, say, the home demand for house-building, which frequently moved in the opposite direction to the general trend of trade. At any time, therefore, within the modern era, it would have been inappropriate and misleading to treat British economic problems as though international developments were a mere complication which could be ignored in a provisional analysis. That this fashion should have sprung up after the 1914–18 war is still more paradoxical. Today our main economic problems and difficulties are clearly those of international trade and international payment. So they were, in a somewhat different form, throughout the inter-war period. In such conditions, generalizations and prescriptions of policy, suggested by theoretical analysis proceeding on the hypothesis of a 'closed economy', are apt to be dangerously out of focus.

Yet it is on this basis, and with a complete disregard of this danger, that fashionable economic analysis has pursued its examination of the problem of unemployment, and claims to have 'discovered' its secret. This claim was readily accepted at its face value by a wishful-thinking public during the war years, and received some measure of official endorsement in the White Paper on Employment Policy issued by the National Government towards the end of the war. The key to the problem, according to this creed, is to maintain aggregate demand at an adequate level. Therefore, if a substantial contraction of demand should occur in some sectors of the economy, it is proposed that a compensating expansion of demand should be elicited in other sectors, by whatever means may be most efficacious for the purpose.

As a general proposition this seems attractive; but it includes the important special case that if our export sales were to diminish, so that the demand for labour in the exporting industries were to be reduced, a compensating increase of demand must be stimulated in the home market. Clearly this implies a passive acceptance of the worsening of the balance of payments resulting from the loss of export trade; and the policy contemplated would worsen it still further. The expansion of home demand would lead directly to an increased demand for imported goods. If it were to be large enough to overcome the serious 'structural' obstacles to a 'transfer' of labour, it would involve an increase in wage rates and costs of production detrimental to our competitive position in world markets. Furthermore, in so far as work-people displaced from the exporting industries were successfully absorbed in other industries, it would become more difficult for the former to reacquire a sufficient labour force if the demand for their products were later to revive.

As the doctrine of maintaining full employment through the instrumentality of a sufficient aggregate demand was evolved in a 'closed economy' setting, these difficulties were kept well in the background. Moreover, when attention was called to them, it could be argued in the 1930's, without evident absurdity, that they constituted no more than a minor drawback, and that the maintenance of full employment was greatly preferable to a better balance of payments. Today, however, it should be manifest that the complacent indifference to repercussions on the balance of payments which the policy presupposes is out of place. In the years that lie before us we shall be in no position to adapt our economy to a loss of export trade by measures which would make the balance of payments worse.

The policy in question would serve directly, in the circumstances in which it would be most likely to have to operate, to enlarge a balance-of-payments deficit. But this is not all. It would rule out the possibility of correcting the deficit by restricting the volume of internal purchasing power. It would therefore deprive us, if the instruments of quantitative regulation and direct control were also to be laid aside, of any effective means of maintaining exchange stability, if that were the desideratum. This again is not all. The policy would be fatal to any hope of correcting the deficit by the method of exchange depreciation, slender as this hope would be in any case, if my argument in the preceding section is correct. For it would be impossible to apply the instrument of a limitation of internal purchasing power to the difficult task of preventing the rise in internal prices and costs from outstripping the exchange depreciation. For any country in a weak balance-of-payments position the deadlock seems complete. Those who have concluded so hastily that the secret of maintaining full employment has been discovered in the formula of a sufficient aggregate demand must think again.

It is fair to say that the more recent statements of this formula reveal misgivings as to some of its implications. But these misgivings seem at present to be limited to the implications that are relevant to issues of internal policy. Professor Meade's recent book, *Planning and the Price Mechanism*, provides a curious example of this limitation. He is perturbed at the possibility that a high aggregate demand may lead to excessive wage rates, and he has a particular dislike for the practice of raising wages to meet increases in the cost of living. He refers to the danger that this practice may lead to a loss of export trade; and to this warning he attaches a footnote (p. 74) which is worth reproducing in full:

> Unless, of course, we offset the rise in our internal costs by a depreciation of the exchange rate, in which case the price of imported foodstuffs and so the cost of living would rise still further. If this in turn were followed by a rise in wage-rates, we should again either lose export markets or have to depreciate sterling still further, which would again raise the cost of living. And so on *ad infinitum*.

It seems reasonable to infer that exchange depreciation would be a most dangerous remedy for a balance-of-payments deficit. Yet, in his final chapter, Professor Meade advocates this expedient for long-run use with ardour, untroubled by doubt. He argues at length its superiority, as a price-system remedy, over import restrictions, ignoring altogether the possibility that incomes and prices might rise. Indeed he goes so far as to assert (p. 96) that 'the case for exchange rate adjustment is conclusive' if 'a relatively small reduction in the price of our exports in foreign markets [would] cause a relatively large increase in the volume of goods which we could sell'. This is a palpable *non sequitur*, if it is admitted that, owing to wage increases, there might be no lasting reduction in the export prices we were able to quote.

Professor Meade may perhaps suppose that, having urged that wages should not rise because the cost of living rises, he is entitled to assume that they will not do so. He does not, however, assume the difficulty away so wishfully in discussing questions of internal policy. He lays stress (p. 71) on the 'most bitter dilemma' with which society may be faced, if trade unions insist on exploiting their bargaining strength under high employment, in having to choose between continuous inflation and substantial unemployment. Professor Robbins in *The Economic Problem in Peace and War* discusses the same dilemma along very similar lines, and offers the formula that the aim should be 'to maintain aggregate demand at a level which, *at current or slightly rising rates of wages*, would secure a reasonably high level of employment and utilization of resources' (p. 71). (The italics are his own.) But he gives no hint that the dilemma has any bearing on our external economic problem.

Two crucial questions lie concealed within the folds of Professor Robbins's formula. Does he, too, mean that money wage rates should remain unchanged, or rise only slightly, whatever may be happening to the cost of living? And does he mean that the volume of purchasing power should be so regulated as to prevent wage rates from rising too much? If the answers to these questions are in the affirmative, it is evident that Professor Robbins is expecting a great deal from the financial and monetary instruments available. To prevent substantial wage increases following a sharp increase in the cost of living, it is probable that a drastic restriction of credit, involving heavy unemployment, would be required. A policy of this sort would differ radically from anything that has hitherto been thought of as a policy of full employment, however qualified. Under it, the criterion for regulating credit and purchasing power would have been shifted in effect from the state of employment to the movement of wage rates.

This suggests a further question. If the criterion for regulating purchasing power must be shifted in practice from the fair-seeming but deceptive one of the state of employment, with no further questions asked, might not the most satisfactory alternative in some conditions be the time-honoured criterion of the size of the monetary reserves, suitably adapted to modern conditions? No country, after all, can afford to permit its monetary reserves to disappear. If they are dwindling fast, action has got to be taken to arrest the decline; and it is important that this action should be timely and effective. Whatever general principles may be proclaimed, an undue loss of monetary reserves must, therefore, be a cogent and compelling reason for restricting the volume of purchasing power. It seems to me of real importance that the proclaimed principles should be revised so as to recognize this fact expressly. A subordinate issue also arises. Governments might take appropriate action to limit purchasing power from their own sense of the need for it, without being required to take it by statute. Indeed our main hope must be that they would do so. But there is always the danger that wishful thinking, indecision, obscurantist prejudice, political timidity or faction might cause them to do too little and too late. I agree with Professor Robbins in thinking it unwise on these vital matters to trust entirely to governmental wisdom and initiative, and in desiring to supplement them by formal regulations prescribing the action to be taken in defined circumstances, so long as these 'automatic' arrangements are well designed.

I suggest that it would be wise in Great Britain to provide that, if and when our monetary reserves fall below a defined figure, chosen as the minimum compatible with safety, a substantial reduction of the note issue must follow automatically, and that this arrangement should only be alterable by a new Act of Parliament. A reduction of the note issue would, of course, carry with it higher short-term interest rates and a restricted volume of bank credit. There are reasons, which in ordinary circumstances are probably good, for thinking this a clumsy method of curtailing aggregate demand, and for preferring others such as an over-balanced budget and the limitation of long-term investment work. Therefore, so long as the reserves are above the specified minimum, the discretion of the Government to use whatever means they think best for regulating aggregate demand should not, in my view, be fettered by automatic currency arrangements. Also governments should not be hampered by misconceived international obligations, or by ideological prejudices, in using the more direct methods of import regulation and trade policy to keep the reserves from falling to the danger point. But when this point is reached, other methods must be used as well. The method of credit restriction, clumsy though it may be, is one of proved, if limited, effectiveness; it would be essential to fall back on it as a weapon of last resort, and prudent to provide in advance that this should be done in time.[1]

This, then, is the basic principle which I suggest for the future regulation of the volume of purchasing power: above a specified minimum of gold and hard currency reserves, unfettered discretion for the authorities, who should, however, look to the movement of

---

[1] Since the arrangement would be designed to operate only if the situation had become serious enough to require really drastic action, the minimum figure might well be considerably less than the £500 millions, the maintenance of which has been declared to be an object of 'unalterable policy'. It might perhaps be put as low as £350 millions. On the other hand, it would be important to ensure that a fall of the reserves below this minimum would entail a contraction of currency and credit severe enough to produce results. The regulations should therefore be so contrived as to enforce a reduction of the note issue by some appropriate multiple of any short-fall of the reserves below the minimum, say three times.

the reserves as a main criterion of policy; below this minimum, an automatic and substantial curtailment of currency and credit. In putting forward this principle for consideration, I am not thinking only of Great Britain, though I have stated it for the sake of clarity in British terms. It might be of greater immediate importance to secure its effective application in other countries, e.g. France.

IV

The two essential principles of the gold standard were fixity of exchange rates, and a definite relation between internal purchasing power and monetary reserves. I have just suggested that we should do wisely to reincorporate the latter principle in our monetary arrangements, though in a greatly modified form. It will be evident from the general tenor of my argument that I also think it would be wise to reintroduce the former principle, though again with modifications.

The idea that exchange-rate variations might be used systematically to correct maladjustments in the balance of payments is not only, as I have argued above, fundamentally impracticable. It misconceives the attributes of exchange rates; it overlooks their special fitness for a function of real importance. They are one of the few things in the economy which can be definitely fixed; and it is well that something should be fixed. The true function of exchange rates is to provide a constant factor round which the more variable elements may move, and by reference to which they can be adjusted; in other words, to provide a focus of stability in an orderly price system. The confidence which was felt in the fixity of exchange rates under the gold standard contributed much to the remarkable development of international economic life during the nineteenth century. It also contributed more generally to the comparative efficiency with which an unregulated price system then worked. Something valuable is lost when this confidence has disappeared. The value may have been overrated formerly; today it is certainly underrated. In Great Britain the force of this general consideration is greatly increased by the special considerations relevant to her position as the centre of the sterling area.

The modifications which are desirable under modern conditions can best be judged by reviewing the interrelated defects and mistakes that were responsible for the breakdown of the attempt to restore the gold standard as an international system after the 1914–18 war. Prominent among these was the instability in the purchasing power of gold, expressed in the heavy fall in commodity prices during the world crisis of 1929–33. If in the future severe world depression and deflation should recur, any arrangement designed to ensure stable exchange rates would again break down. In such conditions, as I have tried to show above, individual countries can derive a much-needed relief from exchange depreciation, and the use of this expedient might become imperative in countries with balance of payments difficulties. For different and more complex reasons, a continuing inflation of world prices would also prove incompatible with fixed exchange rates. Therefore, a reasonable stability in the purchasing power of gold, if that is to remain the standard in terms of which exchange parities are defined, is an essential condition of international exchange-rate stability.

In practice the purchasing power of gold will depend mainly on the policies pursued by those countries which are untroubled by balance-of-payments anxieties and equipped with abundant gold reserves. Therefore, a special responsibility for creating the conditions in which exchange-rate stability can be maintained rests upon these countries, outstanding among which is, of course, the United States. In the meantime, uncertainty upon this matter would suffice to forbid the idea of attaching to modern exchange parities the sacro-sanctity which they possessed in the hey-day of the gold standard. The possibility of modifying these parities, as a *pis aller*, must be left open, though it must not be supposed that a new and more orderly international system can be built upon this basis.

Another main cause of the breakdown of the gold standard in 1929–33 was the excessive strain which was thrown upon its mechanism by large maladjustments in the balance of international payments. Since the maladjustments that have now to be corrected are far larger, it is important to interpret rightly the lessons of this experience. No blame can fairly be attached to the principle of exchange-rate fixity. Some responsibility is attributable to the fact that the exchange rates for sterling were over-high as the result of the decision of the British authorities to return to gold at the traditional parity. But from the international standpoint the chief mistake that was made, in my opinion, was to entrust the task of restoring equilibrium far too exclusively to the forces of the price system. Half-hearted attempts to assist these forces by deliberate policy and measures of direct control were deprecated and discouraged as contrary to sound principle and obstructive to international trade. Countries in balance-of-payments difficulties were persuaded to rely instead on the aid of foreign loans, floated in the centres of the more strongly placed countries, and organized and developed on a large scale with the help of the goodwill and public-spirited exertions of the dominating figures in the banking world and the officers of the League of Nations. The tradition of economic liberalism was then too strong and self-confident for any other type of policy to have been feasible. The event proved, however, that the aid given by private international lending was unreliable and fitful, and that the more automatic forces of the price system were too weak to do the work expected of them.

For the much larger task of readjustment which faces us today, deliberate policy, using such instruments as systematic import programmes and trade arrangements, is not only indispensable for the time being, but will remain indispensable in my judgement for many years to come. To suggest, as is sometimes done, that, though import restrictions are necessary now, they may become superfluous comparatively soon if an improved price system is given freer play, is to nurse illusions. As I have argued elsewhere,[1] the British balance-of-payments deficit could only be corrected by price-system forces at the cost of a huge, unnecessary, and impracticable lowering of the standard of life.

A further cause, and superficially the most important, of the 1929–33 breakdown was the overwhelming magnitude of the short-term capital movements which developed. Despite their imperfections, the systems of exchange control which have been introduced in many countries should provide, it may be hoped, a fairly effective safeguard against a recurrence of this particular disorder. So far as can be foreseen, the need to retain exchange control for the purpose of limiting capital transfers will continue indefinitely. This represents, therefore, an essential change in the arrangements by which fixed exchange parities used to be maintained.

In ways like these it is important to adapt our monetary arrangements to the altered conditions of the difficult modern age. It is a profound mistake, however, to suppose that it would be wise or helpful to invert the principles which underlay the traditional monetary scheme, by making variable that which was formerly

[1] Address delivered at the British Association. *Economic Journal*, December 1948.

fixed, and by trying vainly to fix that which was formerly variable. The economic failure of the inter-war period was due less to the imperfections of the monetary system than to the policy which left it, insufficiently supported, to perform a task of readjustment which was beyond its powers, and would have been equally beyond the powers of any other arrangements of a price-system type. Exchange-rate fixity, like other desirable things, may prove unviable in times of extreme disorder; but it is a most desirable thing, and it should be an important aim of policy to establish and maintain it.

4

THE INTERNATIONAL ECONOMIC PROBLEM[1]

In the handling of our internal economic and social affairs, we congratulate ourselves that we have made much progress since the days of Queen Victoria. We have no cause for similar self-praise in the international economic sphere. International trade and international investment were the chief dynamic elements in the remarkable economic expansion of the Victorian age. It was mainly owing to the growth in the volume and in the range of overseas trade that this small but then prolific island was enabled to sustain a rapidly increasing population at a steadily improving standard of life. As part of the same process, the vast but hitherto untapped resources lying in the hinterlands of new continents were opened up, and the peoples of the New World were able to make amazing progress by drawing on the industrial heritage of Europe. This grand international division of labour proceeded in the setting of a freely working economic system, assisted by the facilities for international payment supplied by the common adoption of the gold standard, but otherwise unplanned by governments. The initiative was left to private enterprise, working under the incentive of profit, spurred by competition, and regulated only by impersonal economic laws, by the quasi-automatic correctives of the price system. The forward march was not, of course, unmolested by trouble and disturbance. Trade set-backs and slumps, financial crises and defaults, occurred from time to time. But no one who compares the economic condition of the world at the time of the battle of Waterloo with its condition just before the outbreak of the First World War can doubt the reality or the magnitude of what was achieved in the interval, or the leading part in this achievement that was played by the expansion of international trade.

This is in sharp contrast to what happened in the period between the two world wars. Whereas international trade had previously led the way in the process of expansion, and helped everything else forward, it now lagged behind and held everything else back. The economic troubles of the inter-war years were centred in the

[1] Stamp Memorial Lecture, 1946.

international sector. It was there that disorders were most grave and problems most intractable. It was there that a freely working economic system seemed to work worst, and that the remedial efforts of economic statesmanship seemed most futile or most misconceived. For the future it is clear that the most difficult economic problems for the world, and by far the gravest for this country, will be the international problems. In order to understand them aright, we must first ask how the inter-war failure is to be explained.

The answer to this question must be considered under two broad headings: causes of trouble independent of the war, and causes attributable to the war. First, it seems probable that from early in the present century the conditions which underlay the successful working of the free international economic system were being slowly transformed by new fundamental tendencies, and that serious difficulties might have arisen sooner or later in consequence, even if the First World War had not been fought. The motive force of the constant expansion of international trade and international investment during the nineteenth century was the need of the swiftly growing populations of industrial Europe, and especially of Great Britain, for ever-increasing supplies of food and raw materials. This need could only be met, so long as the rate of technical progress in agriculture was comparatively slow, by opening up new areas for agricultural production; hence the large scope for international investment. Under these conditions there could be no prolonged fall of agricultural prices to levels that were disastrous for the agricultural producers overseas. Moreover, the fact that Great Britain, which was the chief international lender and the chief supplier of the capital goods on which the loans were spent, was also the chief market for the additional primary products which the loans brought into being, helped greatly to keep the balance of international payments in reasonable equilibrium.

In the past generation there has been a marked speeding-up of the rate of technical progress in agriculture, which has had the effect of increasing greatly the quantities which the existing agricultural areas can supply. On the other hand, there has been a marked decline in the rate of increase of the populations of Great Britain and Western Europe. Here we have tendencies, independent of the war, which, reinforced as they were by certain other influences that may perhaps be partly attributable to the war, gave rise to one of the most difficult problems of the inter-war years—the problem of

a persistent excess of supply over effective demand for many staple
agricultural commodities, with ruinously low prices as a consequence. This phenomenon only gradually became apparent after
the shortages of the early post-war years had been made good, and it
was countered at first by various schemes for holding supplies off the
market, which aggravated the subsequent trouble. Eventually, the
heavy and sustained fall of agricultural prices served to derange
the balance of payments of the many countries whose exports consisted mainly or largely of agricultural commodities; and this cast
a new strain on the self-adjusting mechanism of the international
economic system. This played a part in the troubles of the inter-war
years which should not be underrated. Incidentally it removed, for
the time being at any rate, the conditions which had previously
made a constantly expanding volume of international trade to the
manifest advantage of all parties to it.

But even more serious were the disturbances and maladjustments
left behind by the war. Some of them were palpable. When the dust
of conflict cleared, it was found that the international gold-standard
system had broken down. Many currencies were undergoing serious
inflation, some of them runaway inflation, with a fall in the foreign
exchange rates, representing a currency's external value, leading
the way and keeping far ahead of the decline in its internal value,
represented by the rise of internal prices. Throughout the world
exchange rates were unstable and liable to fluctuate. These conditions were necessarily prejudicial to international trade, the difficulties of which were further increased by the oscillations of
industrial activity in the early post-war years; a short but intense
reconstruction boom marked by a sharp rise of prices, followed by
a severe though not prolonged set-back. Behind these palpable
phenomena lay more fundamental maladjustments, including especially disequilibria in the balance of payments of many countries,
resulting from large changes left behind by the war in their import-
export balance and in the relation between the debts they owed and
the debts that were owed to them.

Faced with this situation, the economic statesmanship of the
period concentrated its energies first upon the palpable troubles,
and set itself to the task of restoring what we should call today an
effective system of multilateral payment, by stabilizing currencies
and exchange rates. This was a sufficiently difficult and complex
task; and many prior conditions had to be satisfied before it could

be done. The effective balancing of budgets and the provision of external loans and credits to countries that were in difficulties were essential items in the general prescription; and for the problem of Germany it was recognized that something more was needed, that her Reparation obligations, which had led to so many crises and so much friction, must be put upon a basis which left no doubt as to her capacity to discharge them. It was no easy task to carry out this programme; many formidable obstacles stood in the way. But eventually, after a lengthy series of efforts, which were marked by the close and cordial co-operation of the Governors of the Bank of England and of the Federal Reserve Bank of New York with one another, and with the economic and financial organization of the League of Nations, the obstacles were surmounted one by one. The problem of German Reparations was provisionally settled by the adoption of the Dawes Plan. In addition to the Dawes Loan, which formed part of that plan, special Reconstruction Loans were raised for Austria, Hungary, Bulgaria, Greece, and other embarrassed countries; budgets were balanced nearly everywhere, and exchange rates were stabilized by a general return to the gold standard. A freely working multilateral economic system was at length restored.

To this work much public-spirited and idealistic endeavour, much expert skill and practical resource, were devoted. Englishmen were prominent in every phase of the work, and in the most difficult task of all, the settlement of German Reparations, a leading part was played by the man in whose honour these lectures have been instituted. When I recall the qualities which Josiah Stamp, then at the height of his powers, brought to the wrangles of the Dawes and Young Committees, the quick intelligence, the resourceful ingenuity, the indefatigable energy, the good sense and the radiant good humour, and when I reflect that he was one of a band of gifted men working in related fields, and all inspired by faith in their mission, I should be glad if I could feel assured that qualities half as effective will be at the service of the international economic conferences and organizations which are being projected for the future in such exuberant profusion.

The sustained and temporarily successful efforts to reconstruct the international monetary mechanism were made in the hope that conditions would thereby be restored under which a self-adjusting economic system could once more work efficiently. For a brief period it seemed as though this hope might be realized; and that the nineteenth-century paradise would be regained. Between 1924 and 1929 international trade made a remarkable recovery, increasing in volume by about 20 per cent.; and in most countries internal production went rapidly forward also. This was made possible by the highly 'expansionist' conditions which prevailed in international finance. The Central Banking authorities and League of Nations experts had always hoped that if they could succeed in stabilizing European currencies, this would pave the way for a revival of international lending on a large scale, and they had also hoped that the American public could be induced to play a much larger part in this lending than heretofore. The nursery tales warn us that when the fairy grants our wishes, disconcerting results may sometimes follow. So it was on this occasion. The Dawes Loan and the League Reconstruction Loans served their purpose of 'priming the pump'; financial institutions both in the United States and in Great Britain lent substantial sums on short-term to central Europe; and the American investor was induced to buy foreign bonds by the use of the most modern methods of commercial salesmanship. By these means dollars were made available for central Europe and Latin America on a larger scale than is contemplated for the future under Bretton Woods. So long as this continued, it undoubtedly supplied a stimulus or a lubricant to international trade. Impoverished countries were freed for the time being from any necessity to take steps to reduce their imports, and were enabled to go on buying from abroad much more than they could pay for from their current earnings.

But this phase was short-lived. After a few years the flow of American lending slackened and ceased, and many of those who had lent money on short-term to central Europe attempted to recall it. Then followed the world financial crisis of 1930 and 1931. Runs were made upon the currency of one country after another, rather like the runs on banks that used to cause an internal banking crisis. The pound sterling became the victim of a 'bear' attack, and the international gold-standard system which had been reconstituted despite so much difficulty by so much devoted labour was destroyed once more. The foreign exchanges were again thrown into confusion and disorder, though in many countries the disorders took a form significantly different from that of the first post-war phase. Those countries which had experienced runaway inflations during the early post-war years were determined to do all they could to avoid a repetition of that experience. They elaborated, therefore, increasingly effective systems of exchange control; they prohibited free dealings in foreign exchange markets, and supplied gold or foreign exchange for their currencies, at the parities which they chose to maintain, for 'approved' transactions only.

This second breakdown of the international monetary mechanism in 1930 and 1931 is the key event in the economic story of the inter-war years. Many factors played some part in bringing it about. But beyond doubt a major influence was the persistent disequilibrium in the balance of international payments on current account. During the First World War some countries had been largely cut off from their accustomed markets; other countries, less absorbed in the war, had gained a hold upon these, and local production had also been stimulated. Thus war conditions had left enduring effects on the flow of international trade; and the balance of creditor-debtor relations had also been radically altered. There was, therefore, a large-scale maladjustment in the balance of payments of many countries which had to be corrected. Some progress in the direction of equilibrium was made during the brief phase of 'paradise regained' in the later 1920's; but not nearly enough, and the world financial crisis of 1930 and 1931 caught many countries in a danger-ously unbalanced position.

In the strict sense of the term, the United Kingdom was not one of those countries. The enduring effect of the First World War on our position was not to give us an adverse balance of payments on current account, but merely to deprive us of the huge favourable margin which we had enjoyed before 1914, and which we had used year by year for fresh productive overseas investment. None the less, the loss of that favourable margin proved a source of weakness when the world financial crisis came; for the issuing of overseas loans had been in the pre-1914 world the main business of some of our leading financial houses, and a disposition to continue to issue such loans naturally persisted despite the change in our balance of payments. This led us as a people unconsciously into the always dangerous course of borrowing short and lending long. While that was the position of the United Kingdom, many countries in central Europe had adverse balances, which were covered over for the time being by external borrowing; and, as I have already indicated, the heavy and prolonged fall in the prices of agricultural commodities deranged the balance of payments of agricultural exporting countries in Latin America, in the British Dominions, and in eastern Europe. At the other end of the scale, the United States had in most years a large favourable balance on current account, and no satisfactory answer was found to the problem of how the rest of the world could pay the United States for what it bought from her under conditions of 'non-discrimination'.

Several lessons, as it seems to me, are taught by the story, as far as I have carried it. First, the quasi-automatic correctives of a freely working economic system may be strong enough to effect small readjustments, and may be adequate accordingly in the absence of any major disturbance to preserve a condition of equilibrium once it has been established, by correcting departures from this equilibrium before they have gone far. But it is rash to infer that they will be strong enough to effect the large readjustments that are needed after the huge disturbance of a total war.

The second lesson is the fundamental importance to any orderly international economic life of the objective of equilibrium in the balance of international payments. It is shallow and short-sighted to suppose that the maximum expansion of international trade is all that matters. Undoubtedly expansion, rather than contraction, should be the aim; but unless expansion can be reconciled with a reasonable measure of equilibrium in the balance of payments, it will not be long maintained; it will give place to a severe contraction. In the long run, a large uncorrected disequilibrium in the balance of international payments is a contractionist influence of the first importance.

The third lesson relates to the uses and abuses of financial aid. It may be of great help to a country which is short of international purchasing power and faced with a large deficit on its balance of payments to obtain credits or some form of financial accommodation either from a strongly placed country or from an international institution. The assistance will relieve the intensity of the immediate pressure on the country in difficulties, and supply it with a breathing period in which it can adjust its import-export balance gradually, and thus cause less hardship to its own population, and less damage to the trade interests of other countries, than must result if it has to make the adjustment suddenly. But, whatever form the assistance takes, it will lead to mischief in the long run if it is used to evade the task of adjustment; and if it is given on conditions which are likely to hamper the task of adjustment it becomes a doubtful blessing.

I have said that the international monetary breakdown of 1930–1 is the key event in the inter-war story. It constitutes a watershed dividing the 1920's sharply from the 1930's. Some erroneous views which are in vogue on both sides of the Atlantic spring from a failure to distinguish between these two very different decades. To suppose, for example, that the 1920's witnessed an orgy of economic nationalism is to distort the sequence of events. Tariffs, it is true, were higher in the 1920's than they had been before 1914. For the most part this was due to considerations that are entitled to respect, and are certain to exert a powerful influence in future; for example, the desire on the part of agricultural countries, greatly stimulated by war conditions, to develop industries, and thus diversify their economic life, and the desire which was felt here to maintain branches of industry, the absence of which had been found to be a source of weakness in time of war.

But the tariff increases of the 1920's were not so great as sometimes seems to be implied. They did not prevent the increase in the volume of international trade of 20 per cent. between 1924 and 1929 to which I have already referred. Moreover, tariffs were in the later 1920's the only important trade obstacle. Exchange control, exchange clearing agreements, payments agreements, and 'barter' trade agreements were still virtually unknown; and there were very few import restrictions. The tariffs, moreover, were upon lines which gave practically complete effect to the principle of non-discrimination. The Ottawa Conference was still to come. The most-favoured-nation clause was accepted as sacrosanct. Whether this was to the advantage of international trade is another question; it involved the consequences that the dissolution of the Austrian-Hungarian Empire into a number of independent states was accompanied by the erection of new tariff barriers between areas which had previously traded freely with one another. But, however this may be, it was a non-discriminatory and multilateral economic system which plunged into the disasters of 1930–1.

After the monetary breakdown it was inevitable that international trade should be drastically reduced, and that to defend currencies new measures which were incidentally deleterious to international trade should be introduced. But, apart from that, the breakdown was accompanied by a trade depression severe beyond all parallel; unemployment and agricultural distress became the main preoccupations of public opinion throughout the world, and they carried an obvious threat, which in some countries proved fatal, to the stability of political régimes and social structures. Governments felt constrained accordingly to experiment with new policies, without paying much regard to the repercussions of their actions upon other countries. These new policies were of various types; there was an experiment with a new technique of deliberate exchange depreciation in the United States; there was the system of exchange clearing agreements evolved in central and eastern Europe; there were bilateral trade agreements; there was the development of Imperial Preference in the British Commonwealth from rudimentary beginnings into a comprehensive system; there was a widespread use in many different fields and for many different purposes of the method of quantitative regulation. Since these new policies were evolved for the most part, under the pressure of events, as emergency remedies for immediate evils, it is not surprising that they should all have been defective in various ways, and that many of them should have been open to grave objections. None the less, it seems to me stupid to sweep away everything that was done during this decade with schoolmasterly disapproval as something which should not have occurred, and must not occur again. Even from those experiments which were most distasteful to us, there may be something to be learnt, especially upon the question how a number of countries with complementary needs, and each of them poorly equipped with gold or general international purchasing power, may be enabled to live within their international means and to safeguard their currencies against disaster, without a senseless curtailment of their trade with one another.

That is a question to which it may be important for us in future to find an answer. A second world war has been fought and leaves behind it an international economic problem similar in many respects to that which followed the first. There is once again the prospect of a large disequilibrium in the international balance of payments; but on this occasion the United Kingdom must be reckoned among the countries with a large adverse balance to correct. We shall not, of course, be the only country in this position; yet our task may well prove more formidable than that of any other. We are far more dependent on imports than any other important country; a large-scale flow of imports is indeed essential to our existence. The total burden of external indebtedness which rests on us as a direct consequence of our war effort is commensurate

C C

with that imposed on Germany as Reparations under the Dawes Plan or the Young Plan. We are still incurring military expenditure overseas on a substantial scale; which adds, so long as it continues, to our adverse balance of payments. Meanwhile our export trade has been reduced under war conditions to comparatively trifling dimensions; and it is never easy to recapture export markets which have once been lost. We have, therefore, a large and most difficult readjustment to effect in order to bring our balance of payments back to equilibrium.

It is disconcerting in these circumstances to find that the plans which are being evolved for the reconstruction of the world's economy resemble so closely the plans which failed after the First World War, when the problem was far less difficult, and when we had not the lessons of that failure to instruct us. The main idea seems to be once again to re-create the essentials of a freely working economic system in which the flow of trade will be determined by the chances of international competition. The emphasis is laid on non-discrimination. Convertible currencies and stable exchange rates are prescribed. Bilateral trade arrangements are proscribed. The aid of large-scale international lending is again to be invoked as the main solvent of every difficulty. There are, of course, points of difference between the remedies recommended now and those which failed before. International lending is not to be left so much to the enterprise of the investment market; but is to be arranged in large measure through new international institutions. Rates of exchange are not to be fixed so rigidly as before. Some limited recourse is to be allowed rather grudgingly to methods of quantitative regulation. Exchange control is to be permitted and encouraged for the purpose of regulating capital transfers. This last is a really important difference. It should be of great value in checking speculative bear attacks on weak currencies. This, we may trust, should enable us at the worst to avoid the danger of a runaway inflation such as overtook the currencies of every continental ex-belligerent during the 1920's.

On the other hand, the disequilibrium which the war has left behind in the international balance of payments is larger and more serious than it was twenty-five years ago; and it seems optimistic in the extreme to suppose that it can be corrected by the free play of competitive prices under the conditions which are now being laid down. Indeed, the question arises whether the insistence, which is so prominent in current plans, on the principle of non-discrimination is not fundamentally irreconcilable with the solution of this vital problem. For in practice this insistence comes very near to a demand that the flow of trade must not be influenced in any way by the requirements of the balance of payments position.

I at least find it impossible to believe that plans which are so inspired can work even moderately well in the difficult years that lie ahead. Yet no international plans which are differently inspired are practicable for the time being; and we have therefore to expect, as it seems to me, a prolonged period of friction, trouble, and re-crimination, before a genuinely constructive approach to the international economic problem can be attempted. Undoubtedly there is need to devise a code of good international behaviour to restrain the purely self-regarding policies of individual states, and to make them conform to the general welfare. But this code should be one which will fit the conditions, the needs, and the aspirations of the modern world; not a code of Queensberry rules for an old-fashioned competitive prize-fight. It must leave countries free to regulate their economic life effectively, both in order to adjust their balance of international payments, and for such purposes as steadiness in the flow of trade and stability of employment. The trend towards an increasing degree of collective organization and State intervention in internal economic affairs must necessarily exert a far-reaching influence on external economic policies; and a wise code of good international behaviour must be based upon an acceptance of that fact. Consistently with this, it should be directed to ensuring that countries show due consideration for each other's interests, and that they refrain therefore from acts calculated to cause serious disturbances to another country's economy, such as might result, for example, from a sudden and violent switching of their purchases from one source to another.

Sooner or later, I believe, we must address ourselves to the task of evolving a code along these lines. But it cannot be attempted now. Ideas first must change; and in all countries men must become more ready than they have been in these matters to learn the lessons of experience.

5

THE HAVANA CHARTER[1]

In their bulk and mass, the International Trade Charter and the organization which is to administer it resemble a mountain rather than a mouse. Yet the significance and value of what has been achieved with such prolonged and expensive toil are far from clear. The basic principles which the Charter was originally intended to express and to enforce are wrapped up and swaddled in thick layers of exceptions and saving clauses, through which it may be hard for them to penetrate. Nor, speaking generally, is it possible to blame those who have insisted on the exceptions and saving clauses. The basic principles, it is increasingly manifest, could not possibly be applied immediately. Accordingly, the prevailing disposition among supporters of the Charter is apparently to stress its negative value as a restraint. Progress towards the goal of a non-discriminatory, freely working international economy cannot, it is reluctantly conceded, be made just now; it may even be necessary to acquiesce in various movements in the opposite direction. But such retrograde movements must be carefully controlled and kept within the limits which circumstances really justify. This, it is claimed, is a function of great importance; and for it the International Trade Charter and the Organization are supposed to be well contrived.

This is so modest a claim that it may seem ungracious to question it. Yet I feel obliged to record my fear that the Charter may do more harm than good and may prove more of a hindrance than a help to the creation of a healthy international economy. The harm, it is true, may not be very great, and will mostly be of a less immediately tangible sort than there was once reason to apprehend. Countries to which import restrictions are indispensable in order to correct a large deficit in their balance of payments will not be debarred from effective action by their Charter undertakings. For these and many other contingencies, the exceptions and saving clauses make what should be adequate, though by no means wholly satisfactory, provision.

[1] *American Economic Review*, June 1949.

The Havana Charter 389

None the less, the question is pertinent whether the basic principles of the Charter are really sound and wise. Is the present difficulty of applying them only a transient one? Or does it spring from the fact that these principles are fundamentally ill suited to the conditions and problems of the modern world? If the latter is true, the consequences of proclaiming them as the goal of policy are bound to be unfortunate. At the least, we must expect disillusionment, cynicism, a sense of frustration, and considerable prejudice to the idea of international co-operation. On unfavourable hypotheses, there are more serious dangers to be feared in the years that lie ahead—friction and recrimination, charges of bad faith on the one hand, and undue interference on the other, bedevilling the relations between friendly countries and Anglo-American relations in particular.

THE PRINCIPLES OF THE CHARTER

Certainly, if such risks are to be avoided, it seems to me important that what I have called the basic principles of the Charter should be discussed far more freely, critically, and objectively than has been customary hitherto. In the lengthy process of semi-official exchanges and fully official conferences which preceded the signing of the Final Act at Havana, discussion of these principles upon their merits played no part. They were a *chose jugée*. The principal governments concerned were already committed to them by the terms of the various Mutual Aid Agreements. It was only the manner in which they should be applied that was still open to argument.

The course of public discussion has been much affected by the same inhibition. British opinion especially has been influenced by a desire to avoid the impropriety of seeming to challenge principles to which we are committed. This reluctance is increased by considerable uncertainty and confusion upon the merits of the case. On the one hand, the principles in question do not seem to square with the policies which it is necessary to pursue. On the other hand, they are in full accord with a long-established national tradition which still makes a wide appeal.

Confusion is indeed the chief characteristic of such discussion of the principles as has taken place. It is remarkable how seldom the arguments of the disputants seem to meet. This reflects, in my opinion, a deep confusion of thought in the principles themselves.

Desirable aims are mixed up in them with false inferences and unwise behests; and I think it of real importance to try to disentangle them. The desirable aims may be formulated as follows: (*a*) a large and expanding volume of international trade, which will permit the fullest possible realization of the advantages of an international division of labour; (*b*) as a condition of the foregoing, the utmost practicable scope for the processes of triangular or multi-angular trade and payment; (*c*) commercial policies which satisfy the desire for equity and fair-dealing between nations.

To these aims all sections of British opinion subscribe wholeheartedly and without reserve. It is a commonplace that Britain is far more vitally dependent on imports than any other country of comparable size. The ampler the dimensions of world trade as a whole the easier are we likely to find it to maintain the large external trade that is essential to us. We certainly desire conditions under which we can use exports to one market to defray imports from another, and thus avoid the need for a precise balancing of accounts with each country with which we trade. No country has better reason than Great Britain to fear the spread of 'autarkic' ideas throughout the world, or to welcome the establishment of a code of international good behaviour which would restrain arbitrary self-regarding acts of national policy injurious to the interests of others.

It may seem only a short step from these propositions to the principles of the Havana Charter, which may be summarized thus:

1. non-discrimination;
2. reduction of tariffs on the basis of reciprocal concessions;
3. subject to a long series of reservations, the outlawry of import restrictions; to which should be added, though it appertains strictly to Bretton Woods, rather than Havana;
4. free convertibility of currencies.

At first sight, admittedly, these seem appropriate means for achieving the accepted ends. How can international trade be enlarged unless trade barriers are reduced? Are not import prohibitions and restrictions usually the most drastic type of trade impediment, and the one which lends itself most readily to abuse by high-handed application? How can triangular trade be developed without facilities for exchanging one currency for another? What causes more ill feeling or conflicts more obviously with the instinct of fair play than discriminatory treatment? Surely, then, the Havana principles are proper ones to proclaim and press, provided that the detailed obligations make due allowance for the difficulties of applying them. All this is plausible, undoubtedly, but in my view it is seriously misleading.

It is misleading because the list of desiderata given above is incomplete. This list omits equilibrium in the balance of payments. The unhappy international economic story of the inter-war period, the scarcely more promising experience of the last few years, both show that this is a requirement of paramount importance. Nor is it one which is adequately met by the technique of escape clauses and exceptional provisions. Disequilibrium in the balance of payments is the central problem of modern international economics. No expansion of international trade can be soundly based, nor, therefore, can it prove enduring, unless this far-reaching disequilibrium has been overcome. This is indeed the chief task that confronts international economic statesmanship today, as also European statesmanship and the national statesmanship of many countries. It is a task, moreover, which calls pre-eminently for constructive action.

NON-DISCRIMINATION

There could be no more impressive recognition of this truth than that contained in the Marshall Plan. The central features of this plan are, first, the generous provision of dollar aid over a limited period of years, and second, the promotion of greater economic co-operation between the countries of Europe. The latter objective comprises in its turn two elements: appropriate financial arrangements, including aid from the relatively strong to the relatively weak, and the development of intra-European trade. Now this last policy embodies a principle which is very different from that of non-discrimination. In effect, the Marshall Plan says to the embarrassed countries of Europe: 'You are finding it difficult to buy all the things you need from the United States. Well, we are prepared to help you for a time, in so far as you really need our help. But you must reduce your calls on us to a minimum. In particular, you must not look to the United States for supplies which you might obtain from one another without much difficulty.' On the other hand, the principle of non-discrimination says in effect: 'You must not buy from one another (unless indeed you go so far as to form a Customs

Union) goods that you might obtain from the United States or elsewhere at a slightly cheaper price.'

There is a contradiction here which seems to me more fundamental and more significant than is commonly admitted. It is true, of course, that the Havana Charter virtually exempts countries which are in serious balance of payments difficulties from the restraints of the non-discriminatory obligation, so long as these difficulties remain. And it can be argued without any logical incoherence that this obligation will become appropriate and desirable under 'normal' conditions, when these difficulties are supposed to have disappeared. But it is precisely this sharp distinction between the exceptional and the normal which is fundamentally unreal. The restoration of basic equilibrium in the international balance of payments is no mere passing problem of the transition from war to peace. It is a long-term, large-scale task. Actual balance of payments deficits must, it is true, be eliminated, willy-nilly, fairly soon; and disagreeable measures, including drastic import programmes and discriminatory trade arrangements may be needed in many countries for this purpose. But it may be no less necessary to retain such measures, however modified, for many succeeding years, to prevent these deficits from reappearing.

Again, it is true that by forming a Customs Union or Free Trade area, or by making an 'interim agreement' designed to lead to either of these things, European countries can obtain leave to discriminate permanently in favour of each other. In thus distinguishing between Customs Unions and preferences, the Havana Charter is, of course, in full accord with tradition; the same distinction used to be recognized in the application of the old-fashioned most-favoured-nation clause. The justice of this distinction has, however, long been doubtful. The members of a Customs Union discriminate much more decidedly in favour of each other, as against the outside world, than do the parties to a preferential trade arrangement. It is far from clear why it should be equitable and praiseworthy to practise discrimination in an extreme degree, but inequitable and reprehensible to practise it in a moderate degree. The distinction may be defended by various arguments resting on the plane of practical convenience, but its ethical basis is not easy to discern.

It is a distinction, moreover, which does not fit modern problems and modern facts. Benelux notwithstanding, a genuine Customs Union, in the sense in which the term has been understood in the

past, is quite impracticable in the Europe of today. In many countries, import policy has now become, and is likely to remain, one of
the main and most vital functions of government. In Great Britain,
for example, the standard of living that can be enjoyed immediately,
and on the other hand, the prospect of overcoming our balance of
payments difficulties and maintaining our monetary reserves depend
very largely on the rate of expenditure on imports of different commodities from different sources; and this is regulated by our governmental import programmes. This is not a function which the British
Government could allow to pass outside its effective control. Nor,
I suggest, could the government of any other country which is faced
with similar difficulties, and which intends to keep any substantial
measure of independence. The idea of forming an effective Free
Trade area, with a uniform treatment of imports from countries
outside it, is only really feasible between countries that are prepared to unite politically, and to unite, not in a loose federation,
but under a highly centralized form of government.

This truth, however, is not yet as manifest as I believe it will
become. Although any full Customs Union is clearly impracticable
in Europe for the time being, it is easy to cherish illusions that the
obstacles may eventually be surmounted. It might even be possible,
though in practice it would not be easy, to make early progress in
adjusting tariff rates towards the requirements of a Customs Union,
and to lean more heavily for the essential work of regulating imports
on quantitative restrictions, assumed to be an emergency expedient.
It may well be, therefore, that the Charter will serve to stimulate
arrangements claiming to be 'interim agreements' within the meaning of Article 44. In considering whether such claims are justified,
the Organization will presumably adopt extremely tolerant standards, under the influence of the prevalent idea that any arrangements of this type represent a desirable development conducive to
the general cause of European unity.

For my part, I doubt whether this idea is justified. It is certainly
of the utmost importance to develop intra-European trade and to
secure a 'closer integration' between the economies of different
European countries. But it is premature to suppose that we know
today at all precisely how these ends can best be served. Arrangements that are really helpful must be highly flexible. To try to force
them within the framework of a project for a Customs Union may
well prove profoundly unwise. It may lead to subsequent deadlock

and breakdown, injurious to the larger cause, which might have been forwarded by less ambitious arrangements. It is almost certain to involve an immense amount of make-believe and casuistry, corrupting to those who take part in it, and exasperating to others. Indeed, if any 'interim arrangements' are approved, and a serious attempt is made to enforce the non-discrimination rule elsewhere, countries which find themselves hampered by it will have good reason to complain that the dice are loaded against them.

Here I may observe that in British eyes the dice of the non-discrimination rule seem already to be loaded against the preferential system of the British Commonwealth. A Customs Union between Great Britain and the Dominions is clearly impracticable; and no 'interim agreement' could be made between them purporting to lead to this. But that is not all. Article 15 permits, subject to certain conditions, the establishment of new tariff preferences between countries which 'are contiguous one with another' or which 'belong to the same economic region'. No such possibility is open to the countries of the Commonwealth which are separated by the oceans. Here the Havana Charter departs from tradition; for preferences between countries belonging to the same political system (and after all the British Commonwealth, despite the looseness of its formal structure, is an association which has stood the test of two world wars) were not regarded as violating the most-favoured-nation clause.

It is scarcely an exaggeration to say that the reduction of tariff preferences within the British Commonwealth is the only consequence of the Charter which is definite and certain. I appreciate the strength of the objections of American opinion to the arrangements of the Ottawa Conference of 1933. None the less I find it difficult to understand what useful purpose can be served by a reduction of Imperial Preference in the altered circumstances of the present day. Its maintenance, and where desirable its extension, could do no real injury to American export trade; for the Commonwealth will always be ready and anxious to import from the United States to the full extent of the dollars it can earn both directly and indirectly by export to other markets. On the other hand, the reduction and restriction of these preferential arrangements must tend in some degree to make it more difficult to restore and maintain equilibrium in the balance of payments between the sterling and the dollar areas.

THE REDUCTION OF TARIFFS

I have already indicated my opinion that one of the main weaknesses in the philosophy which underlies the Charter is the distorted perspective in which it views the problem of balance of payments equilibrium. This should be recognized as a key objective; it should be a primary purpose of economic policy, both national and international, to establish and maintain it; and the provisions of the Charter should have been largely directed to this end. In fact, the Charter treats this vital matter in an essentially passive way. It takes it for granted that the balance of payments will normally be in equilibrium, and thinks it sufficient to concede, almost by way of afterthought, that when countries are threatened by serious deficits they may be allowed to indulge in practices which would otherwise be forbidden to them.

This misconception vitiates the approach to the problem of reducing tariffs. The Charter contemplates that tariffs should be reduced by negotiations between particular countries, based on the principle of reciprocal concessions. This, of course, is the fundamental principle of the American Trade Agreements Act; and it is easy to understand, in the light of the history of the measure, supported as it has been by the low-tariff and criticized by the high-tariff school of thought, that substantial tariff reductions could not be effected at present in the United States on any other basis. This, however, does not alter the fact that the principle in question ignores the possibility of a serious balance of payments problem, and is therefore ill fitted to serve as the basis of international economic policy in the world of today.

Here again, indeed, there is a fundamental contradiction which is insufficiently appreciated. The principle of reciprocal concessions comes very near to saying that tariff reductions, calculated to increase American imports, can only be made in return for tariff concessions by other countries, calculated to increase American exports by an equivalent amount. This, in turn, comes very near to making it a *sine qua non* of tariff reductions that they should do nothing to solve the dollar problem or to readjust the balance of payments of the world. In practice, doubtless, the principle will be interpreted and applied more reasonably. None the less, it must serve as an obstacle to the rearrangements that are urgently desirable.

The true logic of the problem can be stated in a simple syllogism. To secure a balanced international economy, it is essential that the United States should increase her import purchases by much more than she increases her export sales. Therefore she should be ready to reduce her import duties, although other countries may find it necessary to maintain and even to increase theirs. More generally, it should be for countries to reduce their tariffs and encourage imports, not in proportion to the reciprocal concessions they are able to secure, but in proportion to the strength of their balance of payments position.

This, I submit, is one of the main principles on which a wise code of international good behaviour should be based. Doubtless it is still far removed from the region of acceptability to American opinion. Yet the logic behind it is so strong, and is likely to be driven home so insistently by the lessons of events, that I am not without hopes that it will gradually win an increasing measure of recognition and acceptance in the years that lie ahead. To this process, unfortunately, the embodiment of the opposite principle in the Havana Charter must be an obstacle.

In the meantime, it is important to note one influence which the treatment of tariff reductions in the Charter must be expected to exert. It is likely to stimulate and to prolong the use of quantitative import restrictions. If countries that find it necessary to curtail their expenditure on imports are unable to raise import duties for this purpose, they will rely increasingly on the alternative technique of quotas. This will be a paradoxical, and it may be a somewhat unfortunate, consequence. As will soon become clear, I do not personally share the extreme dislike of the quantitative method which forms a main element in the philosophy of the protagonists of the Charter. On the contrary, I believe that concrete or quantitative regulation is likely to play an important part in international economic life for a more or less indefinite future. For many commodities, however, imports are better regulated by duties than by quotas; and it is possible that for some commodities a combination of the two methods would be the most satisfactory arrangement. It is undesirable from every point of view to force the use of the quantitative method. Yet this may well be an unintended result of the provisions of the Charter. If so, it will be attributable to the false assumption that import restrictions can be abolished altogether at an early date.

QUANTITATIVE REGULATION, EXCHANGE RATES, AND THE
PRICE SYSTEM

As it emerged finally from the Havana Conference, the Charter allows quantitative regulation in so many different forms and for so many different purposes as to obscure the fact that the original intention was to prohibit the use of this method, save in the most exceptional circumstances. It is under this heading more than any other that exceptions and escape clauses were multiplied during the long-drawn negotiations that preceded the Final Act; and in practice, as I have just suggested, the Charter may well do more to stimulate than to check the spread of quota restrictions. It remains true, none the less, that in the minds of those who have done most to initiate and to push forward the project of the Charter, a strong dislike of quantitative regulation, as something inconsistent with, and inimical to, a self-adjusting price system, has played throughout a prominent part. It is, I think, more useful to consider the broad issue of economic policy which arises than the detailed provisions of the Charter relating to quantitative regulation.

The position from which I approach this question may be stated summarily as follows. When there are no large maladjustments that must be corrected, or no large readjustments that must be made, the economic system can be entrusted to the forces of the price system with the prospect of reasonably satisfactory results. But in any situation which calls for large-scale readjustment, it is necessary to supplement and sometimes to supersede these forces by more direct measures, consciously directed to the object which has to be attained. The forces of the price system are strong enough to effect small adjustments smoothly; but when the work they have to do is large, they are apt to prove clumsy, wasteful, and ineffective.

As a special case of this general rule, countries in balance of payments difficulties must use the direct method of quantitative regulation to limit their expenditure on imports, and also apply appropriate measures of control to promote their export sales. That this may be necessary, as a strictly temporary expedient, is not now seriously disputed, even by those whom I call for convenience the ideologues of the price system. But many of them take the line that no difficulties can justify the continuance of such expedients for a prolonged period. If the maladjustment continues for several years, in the sense at least that it would reappear if the direct controls were removed, this proves, they would argue, that there is something radically wrong in the underlying price relations of the country concerned; and they believe that if this error were corrected, the maladjustment would disappear fairly soon. In other words, they concede that direct controls may be useful as a stop-gap; but insist that the work of readjustment must be taken over as soon as possible by price-system correctives. The particular corrective which appears to be most fashionable at the moment among adherents of this school of thought is the depreciation of exchange rates.

This is a point of view which appeals especially to academic economists, who are tempted by a semi-aesthetic appreciation of the harmonious interrelations of the price system, as pictured by theoretical analysis, to exaggerate its actual virtues. It represents the essence of the answer which some would give to many of the arguments I have used in the course of this article. They would readily agree, for instance, that equilibrium in the balance of payments is no less important than the expansion of international trade. But they would argue that the former object can only be secured by establishing proper price relations through such means as the adjustment of exchange rates, and that tariffs, import restrictions, or other trade impediments, though they may be of some temporary help as a stop-gap, can be no substitute in the long run for correct price relations. Therefore, they would conclude, it is right to concentrate on lowering trade barriers, and in particular on eliminating quantitative restrictions as soon as possible.

Such arguments have an appearance of profundity, which in my view is misleading. It is always important, I agree, to secure price relations which will help rather than hinder any readjustment which has to be made. It does not follow that price relations can be relied upon as the main active force for effecting the readjustment. In particular, there could be no more dangerous idea than that a depreciation of exchange rates is the sovereign remedy for a balance of payments deficit. It is doubtless true that it is helpful to a country's balance of payments that its currency should be 'undervalued' rather than 'overvalued', though a high degree of 'undervaluation' may be harmful. It is most rash to assume that the right degree of 'undervaluation' can be brought about by lowering exchange rates. This must tend to raise internal costs, prices, and incomes; and since an inflationary movement is never easy to control, the ultimate result may be to raise internal prices to the full extent of the exchange depreciation. If the idea is that exchange rates should then be lowered again, in the hope that next time the luck will be better, there is an obvious danger of a vicious spiral of internal inflation and devaluation. The recent experience of Italy and France shows that these are not fantastic possibilities. Nor should these object lessons have been necessary. The pertinent story of the nineteen-twenties should have been enough.

Of course, if internal inflation has led to a serious overvaluation of a country's currency, exchange devaluation may be essential. Indeed, the recent fall of prices in the United States makes it probable in my opinion that it will prove necessary in the end to devalue sterling (together perhaps with other European currencies) relatively to the dollar; though it would be much better, if conditions permit, to defer this until *after* the inflationary trend in our own economy has been brought unmistakably to an end. It is vital, moreover, that any exchange-rate adjustments that are made should be once-for-all adjustments. The idea that frequently occurring exchange-rate variations might provide the regulating spring of an automatic international economy will not, I believe, stand up to critical examination; and the prominent part which it has come to play in modern price-system ideology is a most curious phenomenon. Before 1914, when an otherwise unregulated price system worked tolerably well, exchange-rate stability was regarded as an essential feature of it; and it is still, in my opinion, an important desideratum.

Behind the practical dangers which would arise if an attempt were made to apply the new doctrine of exchange-rate variations, lies a more fundamental consideration. A country which has to adapt itself to straightened international means must readjust the structure of its economic life. It must alter its habits of consumption and production. Any necessary reduction of imports will be less injurious to its standard of life, if it is *selective*, falling heavily on some items and sparing others, than if it is indiscriminate. Therefore, a radical change in the composition of the country's imports may be needed. It is an illusion to suppose that such changes can be quickly brought about by price-system forces of any type, unaided by direct controls. In a sense, it may still be true that the need for such controls may prove to be only temporary. It may not continue after the new production and consumption habits have become established, and the country's economy has been recast securely in a new and appropriate mould. But the time required for this is certainly far longer than any that the conception of a transitional post-war period is apt to suggest.

Moreover, it is not only for the work of readjustment that quantitative regulation may be needed. It may also be useful for the purpose of maintaining stability, of minimizing the vicissitudes and disturbances which are apt to occur in an unregulated economy. The experience of the inter-war years shows how serious such disturbances may be, and how unsafe it is to rely on the price mechanism to prevent them. This truth is indeed recognized in the Charter in a few applications. It concedes the legitimacy of import restriction, for the protection and development of certain types of infant industry; and it must be expected that extensive use will be made of this concession.

The chapter on Inter-Governmental Commodity Agreements is based on the proposition that for primary commodities there may be a 'tendency towards persistent disequilibrium between production and consumption, the accumulation of burdensome stocks, and pronounced fluctuations in prices'. Here, accordingly, the Charter gives some positive support to the idea of quantitative regulation in the form of 'commodity control agreements' on an international basis, though it seems unlikely that many such agreements would succeed in practice in running the gauntlet of the elaborate procedure and the rules and principles of Chapter VI. Similarly, Bretton Woods makes provision for the permanent retention of exchange control for the purpose of regulating capital movements; and no one who recalls the mischief that was done in the inter-war period by the large erratic scurries of 'hot' money can seriously dispute the necessity of this control in a world which has lost its faith in the stability of exchange rates.

Economic instability, however, may arise from many different causes and may take many different forms; and there is a correspondingly large variety of circumstances in which it may be wise to apply direct controls to the external sector of a country's economy in the interests of steady and orderly development. It is foolish to suppose that these circumstances can be adequately provided for by any list of exceptions which is drawn up now. Such exceptions will be apt to emphasize the arbitrariness of banning direct controls in other circumstances in which it may come to seem more justifiable and important to employ them. I can see no escape from the dilemma that those provisions of the Charter which are directed against quantitative restrictions must either be treated as a dead letter, or will arouse a resentment so strong as gravely to prejudice the idea of international arrangements.

These are the reasons why I think it probable that the Havana Charter will do more harm than good. It is ill related to the very difficult problems which exist and which loom ahead. The true aims of international economic statesmanship are in my view, first, to facilitate the large readjustments in the flow of international trade that are needed to restore equilibrium, and second, to ensure that readjustments are made in such a manner as to cause the minimum of avoidable injury and disturbance to the economic life of the world as a whole, and in particular to that of the United States.

At present the United States is generously providing large-scale financial aid to cover the deficits of Europe. It is very reasonable that Americans should insist that this arrangement cannot continue for very long. But the cessation of Marshall Aid implies an economic readjustment which must take the form, either of a greatly diminished demand for American exports, or a greatly increased importation of European or other goods into the American market, or possibly both; in any event, a large change in the import-export balance of the United States. If at the same time the sellers' markets of recent years are replaced by buyers' markets, the dangers of serious dislocation in the American economy are obviously great. It is urgently desirable that constructive thought should be directed to the problem of how these dangers can best be minimized, without obstructing the task of readjustment. This can only be done along very different lines from those of the Havana Charter.

6

THE PROBLEM OF RETRENCHMENT[1]

EMBARRASSED public finances are a normal sequel to a major war. The balancing of the British budget by the instruments of taxation then available remained a difficult problem for several decades after Waterloo. Indeed, the national debt charge probably represented then a higher proportion of the national income than it does today; and, as Sydney Smith's famous diatribe indicates, complaints were no less widespread that the taxation imposed was oppressive and injurious to trade. But hitherto after wars, even that of 1914–18, time gradually brought relief. Defence expenditure quickly returned to peace-time levels; the debt charge was reduced by sinking funds or by conversion operations; and, what was more important, its effective burden was greatly eased by the agreeable tendency which our ancestors termed the buoyancy of the revenue. The national income increased rapidly, reflecting partly the growth in the numbers of the income-earning population, and partly the growth in their average earnings per head. The yield of taxes increased correspondingly and it was thus possible both to reduce taxation rates, and to embark on new policies involving additional expenditure.

Such has been our experience in the past, and most of us are apt to assume subconsciously that it will eventually be repeated. Unfortunately, there is little in the basic facts of the present day to justify this cheerful supposition. The phase of falling aggregate expenditure which followed the war has already come to an end; and for the future it seems not unlikely that expenditure on the basis of existing policies will increase a good deal faster than taxation yields. Various elements, some raising difficult issues for practical politicians, others more fundamental and intractable, enter into this prospect; and it may be well to review them briefly.

The main headings of our budgetary expenditure are defence, the service of the national debt, the social services, and administration. Expenditure on defence has come down from its war-time heights to a figure which is still well above £700 millions. The com-

[1] *Lloyds Bank Review*, January 1950.

parable figure for the 1920's was about £120 millions; and, if we assume that the value of money has fallen by one-half, the real cost now is about three times as great. Clearly, however, in the present uneasy condition of world politics, it would be rash to assume that further large reductions could be made. It may well be that our present arrangements might be improved so as to obtain a greater degree of effective military strength from a given expenditure. But nothing could be more short-sighted or dangerous than to plead economic or financial difficulties as an excuse for failing to play our full part in the defensive system contemplated by the Brussels Treaty and the North Atlantic Treaty.

Still less is there any reasonable prospect of relieving the budgetary charge for the service of the national debt. During the war, we were amazingly successful, by past standards, in keeping down the interest rates at which the huge war-time borrowings were made; but this success rules out the possibility of obtaining further relief now by conversion operations. It is fairly arguable, indeed, that relatively to the huge capital burden of the debt, the present interest charge is artificially low. It would certainly undergo a material increase if Bank Rate or short-term money rates were to be raised at any time. The desire to keep the debt charge down is thus a major element in the problem of money rates, and constitutes a powerful obstacle to the use of the chief traditional instrument for countering inflation.

It is true that our present financial policy is based on the principle of seeking to maintain for the time being, and for as long as conditions remain prevailingly inflationary, a budget surplus, as reckoned by the accounting standards of the past. For various reasons, however, this seems unlikely to do much, if anything, to relieve the burden of debt. First, the surplus is precarious. It might quickly disappear in the event of a reduction of profit margins; it may be abandoned because of the difficulty of maintaining it in face of the rising tide of expenditure; and it is part of the current economic philosophy that it should be replaced by a budget deficit, as a matter of deliberate policy, if unemployment or trade depression were to develop. Second, even under existing conditions, it does not now do more than cover additional Governmental borrowings for new capital purposes, many of which are financially unremunerative. Much credit is undoubtedly due to the present Chancellor of the Exchequer for presenting the national accounts in a more realistic manner. But it would be optimistic to suppose that our modernized financial technique will do as much to repay debt over a period of years as would have been achieved by a moderate sinking fund of the old-fashioned type.

Thus the factors which have contributed most to lower expenditure after previous wars contain little promise of relief today. It is, however, when we turn to the other side of the picture that the prospect becomes alarming. In the last few years, there has been a large and rapid increase in expenditure upon the social services; and this expenditure must be expected to continue to grow rapidly as a more or less automatic consequence of policies which are already operative. On some of the purposes falling under the category of the social services increased expenditure was, of course, inevitable in order to repair the ravages of war. This is notably true of housing; a big house-building effort was clearly necessary; and it was no less clear that large Exchequer subsidies would be needed to finance it. In fact, the eventual cost of the housing programme will necessarily be increased by the much higher standards of space and equipment laid down for the new houses. For the most part, however, the increase in social service expenditure arises from the adoption of three new, ambitious schemes: comprehensive National Insurance, the Education Act, and the Health Service. The existing cost of the insurance scheme is mainly defrayed by the contributions of employers and employed; but the Exchequer is to bear the burden of future increases in this expenditure, and for old-age pensions a very large increase is expected mainly because of the large inevitable growth in the numbers of the elderly and aged. The Government Actuary has estimated the probable cost of retirement pensions as follows:

				£ millions
1948	.	.	.	238
1958	.	.	.	301
1968	.	.	.	421
1978	.	.	.	501

The Royal Commission on Population, in citing these figures, adds the observation that they are based 'on assumptions which make no allowance for any future fall in mortality, and therefore probably understate the cost for future years'.

Expenditure on education and the health service may perhaps increase even more rapidly. This is kept down for the time being by physical limitations—by lack partly of schools and hospitals; partly of teachers, doctors, nurses, and dentists; partly of certain drugs and medicines. It is obviously important to overcome these limitations, but, in proportion as we succeed in doing so, the expenditure will necessarily increase. This applies more especially to the health service. The cost of this is already far larger than was estimated; yet it is clear that the demand for its facilities has not been nearly satisfied. This demand, moreover, is certain to increase steadily in future as another consequence of the growth in the numbers of the elderly. Men and women over 65 have a much more frequent need for medical attention than have those in the prime of life.

According to the calculations of the Royal Commission on Population the number of those over 65, which was about 5,000,000 in 1947, is likely to increase to about 7,300,000 in 1977, even if there is no further fall in mortality rates, and to about 8,200,000 if they continue to fall further at the rate at which they have fallen hitherto. If the health service fulfils its purpose it would be natural to hope for a speeding-up in the process of reducing mortality, so that, catastrophes apart, the latter assumption seems very moderate. This would mean an increase over the next generation of about 64 per cent. in the number of those over 65 years of age, who will then represent about one-sixth of the total population. There is no means of computing the additional demands which this charge will throw upon the health service, but it is obvious that they will be heavy. This prospect has to be considered in conjunction with the fact already mentioned that the demands which the health service is designed to meet are at present only partially satisfied because of the physical limitations which we are striving to overcome. It is not easy in these circumstances to set limits to the probable growth of the health service expenditure, now some £300 millions.

The budgetary outlook is affected by the prospective change in the age distribution of the population in yet another way. While the numbers over 65 will grow rapidly in the next thirty years, the numbers of those of working age will probably remain fairly stationary. We shall thus be deprived in future of the aid of one of the main factors which have contributed to the buoyancy of the revenue in the past; namely the growth in the numbers of the income-earners. It is only in so far as we earn more per head that we can expect the yield of taxes to increase during the next generation. No doubt we may fairly hope for a considerable increase from this source as the result of continued technical progress. But this provides a somewhat precarious basis for an expanding revenue. It is exposed to the vicissitudes of trade fluctuations, and of our national economic fortunes in a highly uncertain world. It is easy to make optimistic calculations, it is less easy to feel confident that the expansion of revenue resulting from increased productivity will suffice to keep pace over a period of years with the semi-automatic increase in expenditure on our existing social schemes.

The grim financial outlook to which these considerations point is relieved to some extent by other possibilities. Not that it would be wise to hope for large net savings in the costs of administration. It should be possible to reduce gradually the size of the staffs now engaged in administering controls; but against this some further increase will most likely be needed in the staffs which administer the expanding social services; and sooner or later the claims of civil servants for higher salaries will have to be met. A much more promising field for future economies is to be found in the £450 millions or so which are at present spent on the food subsidies. As a short-term matter, the problem of effecting substantial savings in this expenditure is peculiarly difficult, bound up as it is with the endeavour to stop wage increases in a sellers' labour market. On a long view, however, the maintenance of the greater part of this expenditure, i.e. that part which is directed merely to keeping down the cost of living, cannot possibly be justified. Eventually, it should undoubtedly be possible to effect a considerable saving under this heading, even though expenditure on children's allowances may be increased in partial compensation, and though the consequences may be a further fall in the purchasing power of money accompanied by somewhat higher money incomes.

This leads to another consideration. The revenue yield is increased by anything that raises the level of money incomes; that is to say, subject to time-lags, it is increased as much by inflation as by greater productivity. Unfortunately, the former tendency serves, as the latter does not, to increase public expenditure correspondingly, subject again to time-lags, under almost every heading. But there is one category to which this does not necessarily apply, namely the service of the national debt. If, therefore, as the devaluation of sterling and the recovery of trade and prices in the United States combine to make probable, we move gradually towards a further moderate reduction in the purchasing power of money, the budgetary position may derive therefrom some appreciable relief. Our need for such relief may indeed be regarded as one of the many reasons why the 1949 devaluation was essential.

This, however, is a treacherous line of argument. To resist inflation, to keep the rise of prices and costs consequential upon devaluation down to the minimum is a main objective of official policy. And rightly so. The problem of the balance of payments and the dollar gap has still to be solved. It can only be solved if British export prices remain relatively cheap over a wide trading range. The margin which this condition leaves available for future increases in costs of production in Great Britain is certainly a narrow one. As international competition becomes keener with the return of Germany and Italy to world markets, it may well prove narrower than now appears. Nor does any hope lie in the possibility that an excessive level of British selling prices might again be corrected by a further devaluation. Along that road, the danger of a vicious spiral of inflation and exchange depreciation would be very real. In the process, moreover, the possibility, relevant to the present argument, that the budgetary stringency might be eased by a reduction in the real burden of the debt charge, would almost certainly be destroyed by the need for a much higher level of short-term interest rates.

Thus the favourable elements in the financial outlook are neither big nor sure; and the broad impression emerges that it may not be easy, in practice, to keep the total of public expenditure from growing as fast as the revenue from existing taxes. Then comes the most formidable fact of all. Our existing taxes are extremely high—far higher, there is only too good reason to fear, than is reconcilable in the long run with full efficiency in the working of the economic mechanism, and far higher, it may be suspected, than would be regarded as permanently tolerable by any section of public opinion. There are some, no doubt, whose first impulse would be to dispute this proposition, because the idea of high taxation is still associated in their minds with taxation concentrated on the wealthy in the interests of egalitarian redistribution. But this process has long ago been carried as far as is practicable, or at any rate helpful to the revenue. The present rates of many of the most prolific of our indirect taxes, as well as of our direct taxes, are essentially emergency rates, and were in fact justified by emergency arguments when they were first imposed. This applies notably to the tobacco duties and to the purchase-tax, which were raised to the present heights on dollar-saving or counter-inflationary grounds. Any suggestion that these taxes should be maintained permanently at their present rates would be especially repugnant to most of those who acclaim high income-tax, surtax, and death duties. Nearly everyone still cherishes the hope that the day will come when some tax or other which he finds particularly onerous will be drastically reduced.

The slenderness of the chance of a material improvement in the budgetary position implies, of course, that there is a correspondingly small margin available for new types of expenditure, including any that might be necessitated by unforeseen contingencies. Before 1914, when the income-tax was in the neighbourhood of a shilling in the pound, proposals to increase the income-tax were frequently criticized on the ground that a high income-tax was an instrument which should be kept in reserve for the possibility of war. Such precepts may arouse a nostalgic smile today; but it is a serious defect of our present arrangements in the sphere of public finance, as indeed in that of our balance of payments and of the efforts to eliminate inflation, that they all assume the continuance of fair weather, and contain no safety margin.

The picture is not yet complete. There is no real public awareness of the seriousness of the financial problem that has been described. The prevailing mood on questions of Government expenditure remains astonishingly complacent. On other matters, notably, for example, dollar purchases, the need to economize and to put up accordingly with irksome deprivations is widely recognized throughout the community. The response of the trade-union movement to the appeal for a wages standstill indicates a growing readiness to subordinate sectional interests to the national needs in a sphere in which the pursuit of a self-regarding policy was previously regarded as mandatory. But on matters of Government expenditure there is a deep psychological resistance to the very idea of economy, as something which is supposed to be both socially reactionary and intellectually outmoded.

This state of mind, which accords so ill with the underlying facts, is due partly to the persistence of illusions which war-time conditions always generate and partly to new currents of economic thought issuing from the depression of the 1930's. These include a repudiation of the old orthodox belief that budgets should be balanced year by year. The modern prescription is that budget deficits are appropriate in times of depression and budget surpluses in times of inflation or boom. In principle, this is a very reasonable idea, though it is permissible to doubt whether its application will prove consistent in practice with long-term budgetary solvency. But the point to note is that the prevalence of this idea, and its application in the past two years in the form of an ostensible budget surplus designed to check inflation, greatly weaken the association in the public mind of increased expenditure with increased taxation. The consideration that a proposal, estimated to cost a given sum of money, would necessarily mean so much on the income-tax or so much on beer used to act as a much stronger restraining influence than is ever likely to be exerted by calculations that it would cut down a budget surplus below the figure needed to absorb inflationary pressure.

This represents a serious flaw in the idea of trying to check inflation by a budget surplus. So long as a surplus is believed to exist, the power of a Chancellor of the Exchequer to resist increases of expenditure, still more to enforce economies, is greatly weakened *vis-à-vis* the members of his Party, and *vis-à-vis* his colleagues; and perhaps his own determination may be weakened too. Now increasing expenditure is inherently inflationary. It is an illusion to suppose that its inflationary influence is cancelled if it is matched by a commensurate increase in taxation, for the taxation may be largely or even mainly defrayed by reduced savings or by capital consumption. Such forms of increased taxation as the capital levy of 1948 or the higher death duties of 1949 must be met almost wholly in this way. If, therefore, a budget surplus, raised largely by such means, weakens the restraints upon Government expenditure, its ultimate effect may well be to strengthen the inflationary pressure it was designed to relieve.

The strongest of the influences which make the idea of public economy unpalatable is, however, the hold which the concept of the Welfare State has gained over the public mind, and more especially the popularity of the health service. It is upon the social services in general, and the health service in particular, that expenditure has increased most rapidly in recent years and is most likely to continue to increase. This is the field in which revisions of policy are most needed, if the growth of public expenditure is to be kept within tolerable limits. But it is precisely in this field that the idea of economy is most repugnant, for reasons which it is easy to understand.

The leading part in the development of the social services in the present century has been taken by Great Britain, together with New Zealand and Australia. But they no longer represent a peculiarly British institution. Though there are important differences of method, degree, and pace, measures of a welfare-state type are being introduced today throughout a large part of the world. Indeed, the common pursuit of policies of this type by countries with very different economic philosophies, and including notably the United States, constitutes one of the outstanding economic and social phenomena of the present time. Nor can there be any reasonable doubt that this is, in the main, a desirable tendency. The establishment of the social services in Great Britain has been justified by their results. They have done much to improve health and vigour, and to abolish the destitution which was so widespread forty years ago. This achievement is the more remarkable in view of the exceptional economic troubles by which the British economy was afflicted in the inter-war period, resulting from the large-scale loss of export trade by major industries of a highly localized type. These troubles served to obscure the important part which our social expenditure almost certainly played in sustaining demand in a period of depression and thus acting as a steadying element in the national economy. Nor was the fact that social expenditure formed one of many factors involving rates of taxation as high as those of the inter-war years a really cogent objection. Up to a point, and indeed to quite an advanced point, there is truth in the claim that the advantages of a less unequal distribution of net income outweigh the disadvantages of the deterrent effects of high taxation.

It is my view, at any rate, that for these reasons the good name which the idea of the social services has acquired is well deserved. Hence the manifest widespread reluctance, almost universal in Parliament at present, to adopt any line of argument or to make any suggestion which could plausibly be represented as an attack on the social services. Public controversy insists on sharp contrasts and clear-cut issues, and rejects like high Heaven 'the lore of nicely calculated less or more'. Yet, in this matter, the 'less or more' is the crux of the problem. Before the recent war the expansion of the social services was undertaken gradually and cautiously, and due regard was paid at every stage to financial consequences and resources. But during the war, in the planning of the new welfare world, caution and moderation were in effect abandoned. A hazy notion prevailed that internal financial considerations did not matter, and that objections on grounds of finance to any expenditure which could be represented as a mere redistribution of purchasing power were in some way fundamentally fallacious. Thus the way was cleared for the introduction, with the support of all Parties, of the three new large measures named above, and for their development, in face of only intermittent and half-hearted criticisms, along peculiarly lavish lines.

In the health service, in particular, it is clear that the principle of free collective provision, as distinct from subsidized provision, has been carried much too far—further than would be justified even if our national financial position were a fairly comfortable one. It is an illusion to suppose that the need for medical attention or treatment or medicinal supplies is always a simple clear-cut objective matter, in which it is fundamentally wrong that the ability of the individual to pay should exert any restraining influence. That is true of some complaints, and of some types of treatment; it is by no means true of all. The responsibility which our present arrangements throw on the decision of the doctor, subject to general exhortations to avoid extravagance, is dangerously great, and is likely to lead increasingly to anomalous and indefensible differences in the treatment of different individuals. The introduction of a shilling charge on prescriptions marks the recognition of the need to make some retreat from the principle of free provisions. But the retreat will have to go much further, and extend over a much wider front, if health-service policy is to be brought into accord with economic realities.

It is not, however, the purpose of this article to adumbrate a programme of retrenchment, but to plead for a wider and clearer understanding of the need for one. Since the end of the war attention has been concentrated mainly on our external difficulties: the balance of payments and the dollar gap. Undoubtedly, these difficulties call for concrete remedial measures, such as import restrictions, which operate directly in the external sphere. It may often be justifiable to adopt measures which are calculated to save dollars at the cost of some addition to the budgetary burden, though this is a principle which should be only cautiously applied. But our internal and external economic affairs cannot be treated as though they belong to separate watertight compartments. Our internal financial policy is linked with our balance of external payments by the influence which it exerts in maintaining an excessive aggregate demand in our economy, and thereby serving both to raise the prices of our exports and to reduce the volume of goods that can be made available for export. The importance of this connexion has been officially recognized by the economies of last October, though whether these economies will prove adequate for their purpose remains doubtful in the extreme.

The complete removal of the inflationary pressure from our economy is vital to the solution of our external problem; and retrenchment in public expenditure is an essential condition of the removal of inflationary pressure. Devaluation, and the recovery in the United States from what was never more than a mild recession, have given us further time in which to achieve this task. But the events of 1949 contain a warning which we should do well to heed. They show how serious are the dangers we shall run if sellers' markets disappear in the outside world before inflation has been arrested at home. That is a conjuncture of circumstances which a country in a weak balance-of-payments position must do its utmost to avoid. Yet, if the argument of this article is correct, this is a danger which is almost certain to recur unless we make haste to introduce into the sphere of our public finance something of the austerity which is applied in so many other branches of our economic life.

7

CONTROLS AND THE PRICE SYSTEM[1]

DURING the past generation the economy of Great Britain has been
subjected to strains the severity of which is not I think sufficiently
appreciated. There have been two major world wars. The first of
these accelerated and intensified certain inevitable changes which
would in any case have given rise sooner or later to problems of
adjustment of some difficulty. With the advantage of after-know-
ledge we can see that it was inevitable that industrialization would
spread gradually throughout the world, and that this would prejudice the position of some of our older-established exporting
industries, of which the Lancashire cotton industry is the most
obvious example, which had done an immense and rapidly growing
trade in the days when Great Britain had a virtual monopoly of
industrial exports. The disturbance of normal trade relations during
the First World War speeded up this change, which might otherwise have come about more gradually. The industries which suffered
from inability to regain their pre-1914 export markets happened to
be highly localized industries, concentrated in areas in the economic
life of which they played so prominent a part that most trades in
their neighbourhood suffered from their depression. Thus there
arose the problems of depressed areas and depressed industries,
which were quite foreign to our previous experience, and which
called for measures of readjustment to which the ideas that then
prevailed were not attuned. Moreover, our attempts to solve those
problems were embarrassed by the onset during 1929 of a world
depression of unparalleled severity and obstinacy which dislocated
the established mechanism of international exchange, and left behind it increased difficulties for most types of international trade.

The Second World War has left us with a problem of readjustment of another sort, the problem of restoring equilibrium in our
balance of external payments. Many other countries were faced
with a similar problem after the First World War; and the difficulties of those countries played a major part in the collapse of the free

[1] The Herbert Lecture, 14 March 1950.

international economic mechanism to which I have referred. But in Great Britain, though we emerged from the First World War with a greatly weakened balance of payments position, and with a much smaller margin available for fresh overseas investments, we had still a margin on the right side of the international account, at any rate until the very end of the inter-war period. We could thus accept the decline of British export trade, and seek a remedy for the unemployment it caused in increased production for the home market.

Such policies are not open to us today. We have now to establish a balance between our export earnings and our expenditure on imports radically different from that with which we made shift before the war. We have not only to establish this radically different balance; we have to maintain it during the years that lie ahead, in times of bad trade as well as in times of good trade, or at least as an average over bad times and good; and we have to do this under world conditions which remain far less friendly to the expansion of international trade than were those of the Victorian age.

This has been our central problem in economic policy since the end of the war, and it is likely to remain our central problem for a long period to come. The task is not one which we can take up or lay down as we please. It represents an inexorable need, as all profess to recognize. None the less, our approach to this problem has not been, perhaps it could hardly be, single-minded. It is complicated by controversies about the structure of society in which public opinion is in fact more keenly interested, and by which policy is largely influenced. It is with the bearing of these controversies on our formidable task of readjustment that this lecture is concerned.

In these basic social and economic controversies, it is possible to distinguish three main issues. The first is the issue of public ownership versus private enterprise. The second issue is about the use of the instrument of taxation to redistribute wealth and income, to promote the development of what is called the Welfare State and also to maintain full employment. The third is the issue which I have taken as the title of my lecture, namely Controls and the Price System.

In a sense, the first of these issues, that of private enterprise versus public ownership, is the most far-reaching and fundamental. This is the issue raised by the old Socialist slogan of the nationalization of the means of production and exchange; a slogan which has never been disclaimed. None the less, there seems to be a growing recognition that the extension of the area of nationalized industry is not really the most appropriate or effective way of satisfying the two basic desires from which that slogan sprang. The first of these was the desire for a more equal distribution of income and wealth. It was believed that the nationalization of industry would promote this object by transferring the profits of industry from private individuals to society as a whole. As soon, however, as the principle is accepted that fair compensation must be paid to the owners or shareholders of the industries that are nationalized, it becomes apparent that this belief is essentially fallacious. Those who before nationalization drew large sums in dividends will continue after nationalization to receive large sums as interest on Government securities. True they will be deprived of the chance of gain if profits should increase by more than had been expected; but, against this, they will be safeguarded against the chance of loss, if profits should decline, or increase by less than had been expected. On balance there is no clear presumption that nationalization, based on fair compensation, will reduce the sums to be paid out as investment income. Of course, that investment income can be taxed, but so it can when more of it takes the form of dividends; and the moral to which this possibility points is that the key to redistribution of income and wealth, in so far as this can be brought about by public policy, may be found in the sphere of finance rather than in that of the organization or ownership of industry. That is a moral which in its positive aspect Left-wing thought is perfectly ready to accept and to apply. There are signs I think of a growing readiness to accept its negative implications also, and to recognize that the cause of egalitarian redistribution is not really advanced by extending the area of publicly owned industry.

There is, however, a second main motif in the advocacy of nationalization, on which increasing emphasis has been laid in the past generation. This is the desire for a more efficient economic system, which will make a fuller use of the productive powers of modern society. The waste of productive power throughout the world during the long-drawn depression of the 1930's was preposterously large; and this undoubtedly constitutes a formidable criticism of the economic arrangements which then prevailed. Moreover, since those arrangements were essentially what may be called *laissez-faire* arrangements, in which the main reliance was placed on the free play of economic forces, this experience provides a cogent argument for trying to secure better results by deliberate organization—an argument, in other words, for some relevant type of economic planning. The idea of nationalization has derived some support hitherto from a hazy belief that it in itself represents economic planning of this sort, or at any rate that it forms an essential part of it.

This belief rests, as it seems to me, on a confusion of thought. The case for planning, as I have just stated it, is that it may be desirable to organize deliberately matters that have hitherto been left to chance. But in what parts of the economic system are these matters to be found? Not in the internal affairs of particular businesses, where a high degree of organization already exists, or even in the affairs of particular industries; but rather in the relation between different industries and in the global sphere of the relations between total demand and productive capacity as a whole. This then is the field for policies of economic planning, intended to introduce purpose and organization where they have been lacking hitherto. To nationalize industries, which means to take over what is organized already, is to follow a false scent.

This moral, too, is I think beginning to be more widely appreciated. There remains, of course, other arguments which can be urged in favour of nationalization, the force of which varies greatly from one industry to another; there are, also, of course, many arguments which can be urged against it. It is clear that for some time to come proposals to nationalize particular industries will be the subject of keen dispute. None the less, I believe that this issue will exhaust itself comparatively soon; and that we shall settle down in Great Britain, and indeed throughout the Western world, to a working compromise as to the area within which the technique of public ownership is appropriate. After all, the chief arguments urged in favour of particular nationalization projects cannot reasonably be given a wide application. The argument, for example, that seems most in fashion at the moment is that nationalization means a transference of power; and power, it is implied, in the hands of private individuals is an obnoxious thing. But surely there are limits, and limits not far away, to the extent to which any sensible person would wish to concentrate power over the details of our economic life in the organs of the State. Surely it is an essential part of the values of a free society that power and the things that go with it, initiative and responsibility, and the right to take decisions and to try new courses, should be widely diffused.

If controversies about public ownership may be expected to fade gradually during the next generation, the opposite is likely to hold true of the second of the broad issues which I distinguished, namely the uses which should be made of the instrument of public finance. Here it seemed, on a superficial view at least, as though a substantial measure of agreement had been reached during the war years between the different parties and the schools of thought they represent. In the first place, there was apparent agreement, embodied in the Coalition Government's White Paper on Employment Policy, about using financial policy, that is to say, adjusting the balance of the budget and regulating the volume of capital expenditure with the object of maintaining full employment. This is a principle which it is easy enough to state; its application raises various difficulties concerned with inflationary possibilities and repercussions on the balance of payments to which I shall revert.

There has also been a remarkable measure of agreement in recent years about the development of social services at the expense of the Exchequer. The National Insurance Scheme, the Education Act, and the Health Service have all been passed without any opposition, and indeed without criticism except on comparatively minor details. The absence of fundamental controversy upon these matters has led to results which are decidedly disconcerting. The expenditure upon the social services is growing very rapidly, far more rapidly than had been expected. Moreover, on the most costly of these services, namely the health service, the growth of expenditure seems for the time being to have escaped from effective control. The time-honoured system of Treasury control by which public expenditure used to be kept within reasonable bounds has in effect been abandoned or by-passed under our present arrangements. It is the decisions of the doctor, the consultant, the dentist, the optician, and the hospital board which mainly determine how much money shall be spent upon the health service; and it seems inevitable that these decisions will be such as to cause expenditure to mount steadily and rapidly from year to year. The demand for the facilities which the health service provides is not yet nearly satisfied. Moreover, this demand will be greatly increased in future by the steady growth in the number of old people, who have a much more frequent need for medical attention than persons in the prime of life.

The growth of public expenditure on the health service, on other social services, and on defence is in my judgement a most menacing factor in our economic outlook. It is not merely that it seems likely to require us to maintain our present high rates of taxation, both direct and indirect, without any material reduction, for an indefinite future. It constitutes a powerful and persistent inflationary influence in our economy, which obstructs in more than one way the attempts to bring our export receipts and our import expenditure into balance. I do not believe that we can allow this drift—for that is what it is—towards ever higher public expenditure to continue uncontrolled much longer. But the problem cannot be solved without major revisions of policy, which will inevitably be unpopular and will almost certainly give rise to bitter controversy.

This, however, still lies ahead. In recent years, economic controversy has been concentrated rather on the third issue; that of controls versus the price system. On this subject, a vehement dispute has raged, in the course of which controversialists on both sides have tended as it seems to me to adopt increasingly extreme and increasingly indefensible positions. On the one side are those who urge that we should rid our economy as soon as possible of any type of concrete, physical control, including the regulation of imports and of capital investment, and who seem to suggest that given a genuine desire to do so, this could be done to the general advantage at an early date. On the other side are those who seem to wish to extend the area of controls indefinitely, and who oppose measures to eliminate the inflationary pressure which at present exists in our economy, or to restore better price relations, on the ground that the disadvantages of inflationary pressure or distorted price relations can easily be countered by appropriate controls.

I have called these extreme positions. But it is not a mere matter of finding a reasonable middle course between extremes. The essence of the argument which I wish to submit upon this issue is that in conditions such as those which confront us in the post-war world, conditions in which there is an inexorable need for difficult large-scale readjustments, the issue between controls and the price system is a false issue. We must continue to use the instrument of direct controls, wherever this is appropriate and helpful. We must also strive to ensure that the forces of the price system are working in the right direction. We can dispense with neither instrument, because each is needed to supplement the deficiencies of the other.

The forces of the price system are too indirect, too erratic, too slow, and too weak to accomplish large readjustments by themselves. Controls are much more immediately effective. But their effectiveness is apt to diminish steadily, if the forces of the price system are working strongly and persistently the other way. It is not a question, therefore, of choosing between them in accordance with our preferences or our sociological prepossessions; but of using them both in harmonious combination.

Those who press for the early removal of all controls seem to me singularly forgetful of what happened between the wars, or singularly obtuse to the lessons which that experience should have taught. The decisive fact in the troubles of those years was the international breakdown in 1930 and 1931—the collapse of the gold standard and the chaos in foreign exchange markets, the widespread defaults on international loans, and the sharp contraction in the volume of international trade which ensued. It was this international breakdown which made the depression so extensive, so severe, and so prolonged. At the root of this breakdown lay the fact that there was then as now a large maladjustment in the balance of international payments, though not as large a one then as there is today, and though we were not then one of the countries in a deficit position. The work of correcting this maladjustment proved beyond the powers of the semi-automatic forces of the free international economic system which had been re-established with much toil and trouble during the course of the 1920's.

The moral to which this experience points is that an unregulated price system is a fair-weather system. The corrective forces which it brings into play can make small adjustments quite effectively, but when large readjustments are needed, they are liable to fail, or even to work perversely. Consider, for example, the influence exerted by speculation in foreign exchange markets, commodity markets, and the like. When equilibrium exists and when there is general confidence that it will be maintained, speculative activity, taking such forms as dealings in futures, often plays a useful and even a stabilizing role, widening the effective market over both space and time. Accordingly in books written before 1914, organized speculation received on the whole a good name. But when there is serious disequilibrium, and a prevailing lack of confidence, speculation serves to intensify instability, and to accentuate price movements, sometimes to the point of chaos. Speculation in foreign exchange markets played a prominent part in the runaway currency inflations on the European continent in the early 1920's. It was for this reason that countries which had undergone such inflations and which saw their gold reserves disappearing rapidly in the crisis of 1930 and 1931 took the step which has had such far-reaching consequences, the abolition of free markets in foreign exchange and the introduction of exchange control.

In Great Britain we were spared any such experience in those days; and it is easier to entertain illusions as to the feasibility in the circumstances in which we now find ourselves of removing controls in the external sector of our economy. It is most improbable, however, that either exchange control or import regulation could be abandoned for a long time to come without disastrous consequences. The crux of our balance of payments problem, as I said earlier, is the need to alter radically our pre-war balance between imports and exports. So far as we can, it is better to do this by increasing exports than by reducing imports; and we have, of course, succeeded in increasing our exports by a large percentage. Yet even under the conditions of the last few years, when sellers' markets have prevailed generally and it has been especially easy to sell goods in the sterling area, we have not come within sight of closing the gap in our balance of payments by increased exports alone. We have also kept our imports down by drastic import controls to somewhere about 85 per cent. of the pre-war level. And even so there remains the dollar gap, which we have got to close before Marshall Aid runs out. It is only precariously and from time to time that we have attained what is called equilibrium in our overall balance.

For the future, much uncertainty necessarily attaches to our export prospects. At the moment our export trade seems to be going well, but the set-back last year showed how vulnerable it is to even a mild American recession. In these circumstances it would be very rash to allow a large increase in our expenditure on imports. On the contrary it is only prudent to assume that it may be necessary to keep a tight control over imports for a long time to come, and what is perhaps even more vital, to shift our import purchases as far as possible from countries such as those on the North American continent who we find it difficult to pay to other countries where there is no real difficulty. Now it is idle to suppose that readjustments like these might happen of themselves if we get rid of restrictions and controls. Why should they? Why should the consuming public, for example, if given its pre-war freedom of choice between imported and home-produced goods continue, as is necessary, to spend a much smaller portion of its income upon imports, particularly from the dollar area? It is not true that the forces of demand and supply, if unaided and unrestricted, would bring about the desired results. What they would bring about would be a rapid exhaustion of our monetary resources, carrying the threat of a vicious spiral of exchange depreciation and inflation.

Whenever large readjustments have to be made, we cannot leave them to the vagaries of the price system. We must use means that are more direct, more certain, and more immediately efficacious; in other words, such expedients as import controls and export pressure. It is true that controls have many disadvantages. Their administration absorbs much time and labour, both in the machine of government, and also in business and private life. They involve uncertainty and delay. They are crude and clumsy instruments; and they can never be anything else. There could be no more dangerous illusion than to suppose that the defects of controls might be overcome by extending them and making them more elaborate. In practice, this could only make them more costly, more arbitrary, and more frustrating. Controls, those at least of the type which rely on the technique of licensing, can only be justified as a *pis aller*, that is to say, on the ground that the alternative of no control would be worse. That, as I have argued, is often true; and it is pre-eminently true of the external sector of our economy in the post-war world. But it is certainly desirable to avoid unnecessary controls; and for this purpose it is important that policy in other fields should be such as will keep the area within which controls are needed as small as possible.

This brings me to the other aspect of my theme. Though we cannot afford, when large adjustments have to be made, to throw the reins to an unregulated price system, it is important to ensure that the forces of the price system are helping to promote these adjustments. The influence exerted by these forces is continual and pervasive, and if this influence is working in the wrong direction the result may be to throw an excessive strain on the mechanism of control.

On this point too the set-back of last year supplies a warning. It became apparent then that British export prices were too high over a large and increasing range of trade. This served to reduce our export sales to countries which could afford to buy from alternative sources of supply, and it caused much discontent from which serious consequences might have followed in sterling area countries whose purchases had to be directed to us under the mechanism of exchange control. It thus became essential for us to establish more favourable relations between the prices of British goods and those of other countries if we were to avoid a steady erosion of our export trade. This was the essential justification of the large devaluation of sterling which was undertaken last September; and for the time being this measure has put our prices on a reasonable competitive basis.

This, however, will not remain true if costs and money incomes in Great Britain continue to increase, nor can we have recourse a second time to the expedient of devaluation if our selling prices again become too high. It is therefore vital to the solution of our balance of payments problem that we should arrest the inflationary trend in our economy before the level of costs and money incomes has risen much further.

So much is fairly generally admitted. But a large issue on which a fundamental discord appears to be developing lies behind. Can we hope to arrest the upward movement of costs and prices so long as its main underlying cause, namely the persistent though comparatively slight excess of aggregate demand over aggregate supply in our economy, is allowed to continue? It is here that controversialists at the other extreme on the issue of controls versus the price system are toying with an idea which seems to me both unrealistic and dangerous. The idea is that an excess of demand over supply ought to be retained in the interest of full employment but that any consequential increase of prices and costs should be prevented by multiplying restrictive controls and granting additional subsidies. In my judgement the propagandists of this idea underrate the ultimate strength of the forces of demand and supply as seriously as the propagandists of *laissez-faire* exaggerate their immediate efficacy. It is possible by all sorts of expedients to slow down the upward movement of prices in a fundamentally inflationary situation. But it is not possible to do more than slow it down, or indeed to slow it down for very long, if that fundamentally inflationary situation is allowed to continue. We cannot, I believe, evade the need to eliminate the excess of aggregate demand. Nor can we prudently afford to delay much longer in doing so, though the American recovery and the upturn of prices there has given us a further breathing-space.

Now to eliminate the excess of aggregate demand in face of the rapid growth of public expenditure to which I have referred is not an easy task. The measures adopted with this end in view, such as the disinflationary budgets of the last few years and cuts in capital programmes, are apt to prove inadequate in practice. They are also apt to be unpopular, and it is for this reason that the vogue of the idea which I have just been criticizing may prove dangerous. The need to continue a broadly disinflationary policy is not likely to be disavowed; but it is very likely indeed that this policy will continue to be half-heartedly applied.

Let me try to restate the problem so as to bring out its intrinsic difficulties more clearly. There are two social or economic objectives which have won such favour in recent years that few practical politicians in any party would dare to challenge them. These are the development of the social services, and the maintenance of full employment. Reasonably interpreted and judiciously pursued, these are both eminently desirable objectives. But they can be so interpreted and pursued as to constitute a most formidable complex of obstacles in the path of a balanced economy. The rapid increase of expenditure on the social services in general, and on the health service in particular, supplies a strong direct and inflationary influence. This cannot easily be corrected by increasing taxation to correspond, for as we have seen in the last few years, the result is apt to be a decline in the rate of personal saving, which indeed has gone so far in Great Britain as to give grounds for most serious misgivings. For this and other reasons it is an important and urgent requirement of sound policy to bring the expenditure on these services back under effective control, with a view not to reducing this expenditure below the present level, but to limiting the rate at which it increases in future to a reasonable proportion of the growth in the real income of the community. This is in one sense a modest aim; but it raises obvious difficulties for practical politicians operating under conditions of the keenest competition. And to these difficulties must be added the inhibition exerted by the preoccupation with the danger of unemployment. 'Disinflate to some extent, perhaps; but be very careful not to overdo it.' Many voices can be heard insinuating so from time to time, and their numbers seem lately to have increased under the influence of the notion that controls and subsidies can perhaps keep costs from rising in an environment of excess demand. The trouble with this prescription is that as these matters never lend themselves to exact calculation, if we pursue the objective of disinflation in this mood, we shall almost certainly fail to disinflate enough.

It is a serious question whether in view of the overriding importance of the balance of payments problem, we can afford to give full employment, as it is currently interpreted, this priority among our aims. A country in a weak balance of payments position will, I fear, find itself in Queer Street if the disappearance of sellers' markets in the world generally overtakes it before it has rid its own internal economy of inflation. It seemed for a time last year as though that phase might have come. It is almost certain that it does not lie far off.

8

THE ECONOMICS OF INTERNATIONAL TENSION[1]

I. THE ECONOMIC TASK

THE reaction of Western opinion to the warning from Korea has been rapid and far-reaching. The demonstration of the military efficiency of the Communist invaders, the perception that the same technique of aggression masquerading as civil war might be applied elsewhere and that the analogy between Germany and Korea is particularly menacing, the revelation of the unpreparedness of the Western Powers to resist any such attempt, the appreciation of the need for prompt and vigorous rearmament, the Strasbourg call for a European Army, have followed one another closely. In this process, the United States Administration have played a leading and impressive part. By his quickness in announcing a large programme of American rearmament, and in offering aid to others if they will rearm also, President Truman has gone far to avoid the twin dangers of an exclusive concentration of American opinion on the immediate imbroglio in Korea, and of isolationist or defeatist inaction in Western Europe. As the outcome of this strong and timely initiative rearmament has become the order of the day throughout the Western world; and Great Britain and France in particular have declared their intention of increasing their defence expenditure over the next three years to a level equivalent to about 10 per cent. of their national incomes. It is true that the execution of these programmes is made dependent, not only on the provision of American aid on certain defined lines, but in the case of France on other conditions which may give rise to lengthy international debate. None the less, that so much should have happened within fifty days of the outbreak of fighting in Korea is remarkable.

From the economic standpoint these developments are perhaps less reassuring. It is clear that large-scale defence expenditure will be a dominating influence in economic life, both internal and international, for many years to come. The broad nature of some of the

---

[1] *District Bank Review*, September 1950.

economic consequences to be expected is obvious enough; e.g. that inflationary pressure will be intensified, this indeed has been realized only too quickly by the consuming public of the United States. But all the problems with which economic statesmanship has been preoccupied in recent years assume now a new perspective—those of the balance of international payments, of financial and monetary policy, of the degree to which the price system should be given free play or supplemented by physical controls, together with those of more concrete projects such as the European Payments Union and the Schuman plan.

In the first place, it is important to appreciate one crucial feature of the defence problem itself. It calls both for urgent action and for sustained effort. It is important to lose no time in developing an immediately available fighting strength in Western Europe, which may serve to deter aggression; but when this fighting strength has been developed it may have to be maintained for a very long period. Negotiation from strength has become the accepted formula: and indeed it represents the only policy which seems to offer a reasonable hope of avoiding a third world war. But the process of reaching a comprehensive and convincing settlement with the Communist world will not be short or easy. This end can only be attained, apart from the interposition of war, through a *modus vivendi* which must remain for many years uneasy and precarious, and in which confidence can only develop slowly. Meanwhile strong defensive forces will have to be maintained. The Western world has therefore to evolve arrangements which will enable it to maintain sufficient fighting strength as part of its normal way of life. This is a hard doctrine, and a distasteful prospect; but the realities of the iron-curtain era are bound to be disagreeable. To allow rearmament to rest on a makeshift economic basis might, among other disadvantages, give a dangerous cogency later on to arguments for preventive war.

This feature of indefinite duration differentiates the economic problem of the period which lies before us from that of war. War-time economic policy is based on the assumption that wars come to an end, and that while they last capital assets can be expended and capital renewals left unmade. Resources are accordingly made available for war purposes by cutting out almost altogether, or cutting down severely, certain types of activity which in the long run are among the most essential. Prominent among these is the production of capital goods and other durable goods for civilian use, including house-building and the manufacture of plant and machinery for the industries which make consumers' goods. Production for export can also be curtailed to the extent permitted by a country's holdings of gold and marketable foreign securities together with its capacity to borrow abroad or enlist external aid. The production of capital goods and production for export account for a considerable proportion of normal peace-time output in most countries, and the proportion is especially high in Great Britain. Britain's war effort was effected in large part by restricting these forms of production, though at the expense of the post-war balance of payments problem, and of a shortage of housing and other forms of capital equipment.

It will certainly be necessary to make some use of the same expedients during the next year or two, if the scale and *tempo* of rearmament are to match the need. The demands of the defence programme, including both military and civil defence, will be concentrated largely on engineering, iron and steel, shipbuilding, and building; that is to say, on the industries which produce capital goods. Of these, moreover, engineering, including the manufacture of motor-cars and other vehicles, has played a leading part in the export drive of recent years. Some decrease in the volume of capital investment and of exports is thus an inevitable corollary of rapid rearmament, and must be accepted unhesitatingly as part of the price of safety. None the less, it will be important to keep this decrease within narrow limits. The balance of payments problem cannot be disregarded in peace as it was disregarded in the war. It may be eased by the American aid which has been foreshadowed, or complicated perhaps by more systematic arrangements for an international pooling of the burden of defence. The special problem of the dollar shortage may be eased by America's own large-scale expenditure on rearmament, and on military operations in Korea. Such developments may help us to live within our international means while rearming; but they cannot absolve us or other European countries from the need to live within our means. We must be ready to sustain a heavy burden of defence expenditure for a long time, and if need be indefinitely; and we cannot do this on the basis of dwindling monetary reserves or growing international indebtedness.

Nor can we afford to suspend or to slacken seriously the process of industrial re-equipment and modernization. It is to this process that the gratifying increase in national production since 1947 is mainly attributable; and our new defensive requirements make it the more important that our production should continue to increase, if possible at an accelerated pace. It would be equally out of the question to suspend for an indefinite period the building of houses, schools, or hospitals. In short, adequate provision for capital maintenance, extension, and improvement, and equilibrium in the balance of payments, are essential elements in the economics of preparedness, as distinct from those of war.

This elementary truth must be kept clearly in mind, if the magnitude and nature of the new economic problem are to be rightly judged. Stated in ordinary financial terms, the defence programmes that have been announced seem very big. Certainly the British figure of £3,400 millions to be spent on defence over the next three years would have seemed appallingly large to Mr. Gladstone. Expressed, on the other hand, as has now become the fashion, as percentages of the national income, and compared with the corresponding war-time percentages, they are apt to seem almost trifling. For Great Britain, the percentage works out at little more than 10 per cent., as compared with over 50 per cent. at the peak of the war effort; and the American percentage is no higher. These, moreover, are the equivalents of the total defence expenditures that are contemplated. The increases to be made over the current (or pre-Korean) rates of expenditure are equivalent to only about 3 per cent. of the national income for Great Britain, and about 4 per cent. in the United States. The increments in the national income which should come from three years of technical progress in either country should be at least twice as great on a very moderate computation. In other words, in the United States, in Great Britain, and probably in other countries too, rearmament on the scale at present contemplated should not absorb more than about half the increase in production which can reasonably be expected in the course of the next three years.

This way of measuring the problem brings out its fundamental realities accurately enough. Unquestionably the rearmament programmes announced so far, and indeed materially larger programmes, if these should prove necessary, should be well within the capacity of the economies of Great Britain and the Western world. The execution of such programmes should not even entail hardships or sacrifices in the sense of any lowering below present standards of either the average consumption of individuals or the amenities of the welfare state. All that is needed is to dedicate for a few years to the purposes of defence most, and perhaps nearly all, of the increment in the real national income to be expected from increased production. Obviously, this can be done, given the will to do it; and we can count ourselves fortunate, if we can secure peace and safety at no higher cost than this.

II. THE DANGER OF INFLATION

None the less, the practical difficulties of the task are considerable, and it would be unwise to minimize them. It is not a simple matter to make available for defence, or any other collective purpose, the greater part of the annual economic increment. An increase in the volume of production is normally associated with an increase in the incomes of many individuals, and consequently with an increase in personal consumption. Indeed, the automatic correlation between variations in production and variations in effective purchasing power is of fundamental importance, and is the secret of the comparative efficiency with which a mainly *laissez-faire* economy used once to work. In the aggregate, it is true, an increase in production can be prevented from generating an increase in the net incomes of individuals by raising taxation; and if the increase in incomes were evenly spread throughout the community, this expedient might be enough to put the increment of productivity wholly at the disposal of the Government. In practice, however, the increase in incomes is apt to be distributed most unevenly; so that an increase in taxation commensurate with the increase in production must leave some individuals better off, while making others worse off. The former will increase their personal consumption; the latter will resist any reduction of theirs, so far as they can, by cutting down fresh saving or drawing on accumulated savings; and aggregate personal consumption will be increased.

Stated in these general terms, the difficulty may not perhaps seem very great, but our experience in Great Britain during the last two or three years shows that it may be formidable. During this period we have not succeeded in eliminating the inflationary tendency in our national economy, despite a high rate of increase in our national production and despite repeated doses of the medicine of an overbalanced budget. By various devices, including the official appeal for a wages standstill and the substantial response thereto of the trade union movement, the pace of the increase in prices and money incomes has been kept reasonably slow so far; but an excess of aggregate demand over aggregate supply has persisted throughout in the labour market and in our general economy. This is because only a small part of the increment in output has been available for personal consumption, most of it having been absorbed by two competing claimants:

(i) the increased exports required to put our balance of payments in order, and

(ii) increased Government expenditure, largely upon goods and services for the health service and the social services generally.

Before rearmament, that is to say, the share of personal consumption in the national economic increment was already about as small as it seemed feasible, or at any rate at all easy, to contrive. Clearly, the present position is very different from that of 1937, when rearmament against the German menace was first begun. Then there was a large margin of unemployed manpower and resources, and a large amount of industrial slack which could be taken up. In that setting, rearmament, though it gave rise to some bottle-neck difficulties, involved no general inflationary danger. Today, the demands made by the defence programme on manpower and resources fall on an economy which is already fully extended.

In these circumstances, the danger of a marked speeding-up of the *tempo* of inflation is very real. Trade union acquiescence in the wage-restraint policy has been slowly breaking down in recent months; and though a new situation has now developed, it is most unlikely that any appeal for its re-acceptance would succeed. Indeed the Government is no longer in a position to promote such an appeal by its own example as employer; for increases of pay in the regular forces have clearly become essential, and the higher Civil Servants are now to receive the salary increases which were deferred last autumn. The cost of living is almost certain to go on rising, owing to higher import prices. Wage-earners will, therefore, be disposed to press for substantial wage advances, and the general condition of excess demand, accentuated as it will be by rearmament and by any lengthening of the period of national service, will put them in a strong position to enforce their demands.

For a time, it is true, and up to a point, the effects of a more rapid increase of costs and prices in Great Britain should not be as harmful in the new situation as they might have been a few months ago. The chief danger that had then to be feared, namely that our exports might become too dear for effective international competition, is now lessened by the probability that the tendency towards inflation may become world-wide, and the possibility that sellers' markets may be given a new lease of life in some lines of trade. From the balance of payments standpoint, this is an important reassurance. It will, however, only be efficacious provided that inflation does not proceed faster and further in Great Britain than it does elsewhere. Moreover, it is a reassurance of a two-edged sort; for higher prices in the outside world will stimulate inflation here—and the reaction upon the balance of payments is only one of many disadvantages of an inflationary trend. A substantial rise in the price level over the next two years, amounting to a further fall in the value of money has unfortunately become overwhelmingly probable, if we are to play our full part in Western defence; provided it is held within definite limits it need not be taken tragically. But it will be of the first importance to keep this inflationary tendency from acquiring a gathering momentum, and to bring it to an end as soon as practicable.

III. RETRENCHMENT OR TAXATION?

How can this best be done? What sort of policy offers the best chance of avoiding undue inflation while releasing adequate resources for defence? The present disposition in official quarters is to reply by stressing the importance of increasing production as much as possible. Undoubtedly the problem will be eased if the current rate of increase can be improved upon; and it seems reasonable to hope that this may be done in some degree. The manufacture of most types of armament lends itself fairly readily to mass-production methods; and the length of the ordinary working week being what it is, systematic overtime in the industries on which the pressure of defence requirement falls most heavily would be an appropriate arrangement. On the other hand, emergency expedients for increasing production in general, such as a lengthening of the standard working week throughout industry, or the large-scale re-employment of married women in factories, cannot prudently be used in a phase of preparation, but should be held in reserve for the contingency of actual war. Subject to this, a speeding up of the increase in production would help greatly; none the less it would be a mistake to regard the problem solely or mainly in these terms. It is highly probable, as has been said above, that production will increase in the aggregate by more than the additional expenditure upon defence. The problem is to keep down sufficiently the competing claims upon this increase. As has been indicated, exports and capital investment will probably have to be denied any share at all of this increase for a considerable time to come, if only for technical reasons. There remain the claims of Government expenditure and personal consumption.

If only it were feasible to cut Government expenditure for purposes other than defence by quite a moderate percentage, how simple the problem would be! After all, the additional expenditure upon defence is to average no more than £250 millions per annum over the next three years, say about 7 per cent. of the total budget figure; and it will presumably be much less than this for the next year or eighteen months. Nor can it be disputed that our current Government expenditure contains many lavish items. It is obvious, for example, that the Festival of Britain is not strictly necessary, and it will soon become obvious that a mood of festivity will not be appropriate in 1951, or at all in keeping with renewed appeals for austerity in personal consumption. The reports of the Public Accounts Committee contain many instances of manifestly extravagant expenditure.

The greater part of the expenditure that must be deemed unduly lavish is, however, of a kind which could not be cut down so easily. Mr. Bevan has told us more than once that he would feel anxious about the health of the British people if he thought that the 'cataract' of medicine which has sprung from the prescriptions of the health service had all gone down human throats, instead of much of it, as he suggests, down scullery sinks. Despite this air of amused tolerance for an amiable idiosyncrasy, Mr. Bevan is doubtless doing his best to restrict this and similar abuses, so far as this can be done by administrative action. But such action can only be of limited efficacy under the present arrangements which put so much of the health service expenditure outside effective Treasury or departmental control. At present the demand for the facilities which the service offers, including that of hospital accommodation, is so greatly in excess of the supply, as to necessitate the use of a rough and ready system of priorities; and this demand will continue to grow rapidly, especially in view of the steady growth in the numbers of the elderly, so long as the principle is retained of providing free of cost to the individual any treatment which a doctor deems desirable or prudentially expedient. The radical revision of this basic principle has indeed become urgently necessary if the expenditure on the health service is to be stopped from growing indefinitely; but any attempt to revise it will raise many difficulties, some real and some political, as the abortive attempt to introduce a small charge for prescriptions sufficiently shows.

In other fields too, notably education, the application of existing policies, if these are left unrevised, will absorb both public money and real resources on a steadily increasing scale; and a similar complex of administrative, idealistic, and political obstacles obstructs the path of revision. To overcome these difficulties, which are formidable, a new impulse will be required. Is it too much to hope that this may now be forthcoming in response to the gravity of the times? This question may well supply a crucial test of British statesmanship. For if this task is shirked, a lowering of the present average standards of personal consumption will then become inevitable; and this can hardly be effected without much friction prejudicial to production and deep internal dissensions which may paralyse the national will.

Consider the dangers which lie along this road. In face of the rise in personal incomes which is inevitable, there are only two means by which personal consumption can be forced down or kept from growing; increased saving or higher taxation. The outlook for personal saving is anything but good, and it becomes still worse if taxation is further increased. Taxation, both direct and indirect, is already very high, so high as to involve long-run injurious consequences which are now beginning to appear. It is true that since the end of the war there have been various remissions of income-tax, affecting more particularly the lower ranges of income, and amounting in all to a substantial sum; and that in an extremity, as Sir Stafford Cripps has pointed out for our reassurance, the remitted taxes might be reimposed. But this is another instance of the sort of expedient which should be held in reserve for the contingency of war, and not used up for the purpose of peace-time preparation. Furthermore, a simple reimposition of these taxes would necessarily fall most heavily on those who have benefited most from their remission; that is to say, on the lower income groups. The larger surtax payers who have been carefully excluded from any share in the concessions would not be hit at all. Such a financial policy would not commend itself to mass opinion. Yet the rich are at present so heavily 'soaked' that it would be anything but easy to devise a scheme for substantially increased taxation which would not be open to egalitarian attack and yet be defensible on merits. Mr. Strachey's recent speech is enough to show how easily class antagonism might be exacerbated over the issue of the distribution of the burden of increased taxation, if a burden big enough to hurt should have to be imposed.

It is doubtless arguable that the exploitation of class antagonism cannot be excluded from our party politics in ordinary times. But no one with a sense of responsibility can suppose that we could afford to indulge in it today. National unity has always been an essential condition of effective military strength. It is today an essential condition also of greater solidarity in Europe and the Western world. Progress towards European unity and the development of a sense of partnership in, and obligation towards, a common cause cannot be reconciled with the pursuit of bitter social controversies in Great Britain, in France, or in any other of the member countries of the commonalty of Western civilization. For this reason there is sense in the caution conveyed in the British Government's reply to the United States that it would be unwise at this juncture to push rearmament so fast as to endanger economic recovery. Certainly it is important to avoid drawing the bow too tight. But the opposite danger is at least equally great, that a desire to evade awkward economic problems may cause individual countries to hang back, to do less than they should, to wait upon each other in a manner reminiscent of Lord Chatham and Sir Richard Strachan. The common cause will not prosper unless, as Mr. Churchill has well said, the rivalry is as to who can give most. Much will turn on the example which Great Britain sets; and the effort which we succeed in making, and in sustaining over the next few years, will depend largely on the discernment we display in economic policy.

Published Work of Sir Hubert Henderson

[Papers, &c., reproduced in this volume are marked with an asterisk]

I. *Books*

(*a*) The two following books were published under his own name:

(i) *Supply and Demand*: published in London by the Cambridge University Press in 1922 as one of the Cambridge Economic Handbooks.

(ii) *The Cotton Control Board*: published in Oxford at the Clarendon Press in 1922 for the Carnegie Endowment for International Peace, in the British series on the Economic and Social History of the Great War.

(*b*) In addition he was largely responsible for:

(iii) *The Agricultural Dilemma*: published in London by P. S. King and Son, Ltd., in 1935, being 'A report of an enquiry organised by Viscount Astor and Mr. B. Seebohm Rowntree'.

[Lord Astor, in his preface, stated that he and his colleagues were indebted to Henderson for 'drafting the present report'];

made a substantial contribution to:

(iv) *Britain's Industrial Future*: published by Ernest Benn, Ltd., in 1928, being the report of the Liberal Industrial Inquiry (the Liberal Yellow Book);

and contributed a chapter to:

(v) *Harold Wright; a Memoir*: published in London by George Allen & Unwin in 1934, and edited by C. Ernest Fayle.

II. *Pamphlets, &c.*

(i) 1926. The New Way Series, No. 15, published by the Daily News, Ltd., *Inheritance and Inequality. A practical proposal*.

(ii) 1939. Oxford pamphlets on World Affairs, no. 7. *Colonies and Raw Materials*.

*(iii) 1946. The University of London; the Stamp Memorial Lecture, published by the Oxford University Press. *The International Economic Problem*.

*(iv) 1947. The Rede Lecture; published by the Cambridge University Press. *The Uses and Abuses of Economic Planning*.

Also, in conjunction with J. M. Keynes:

(v) 1929. *Can Lloyd George Do It?*, published by the Nation and the Athenæum.

III. *Other publications*

(i) 1935, in *International Affairs*, the journal of the Royal Institute of International Affairs, vol. xiv, no. 1, pp. 108–16 (Jan. 1935): 'American Economists and the Slump'.

(ii) 1935, in *Lloyds Bank Monthly Review*, new series, vol. 6, no. 64, pp. 338–45 (June 1935), 'The Case Against Returning to Gold'.

(iii) 1936, in *The Banker*, vol. xl, no. 130, pp. 92–97 (Nov. 1936), 'Devaluation—the future of sterling'.

°(iv) 1937, in *The Journal of the Royal Society of Arts*, vol. lxxxv, no. 408, pp. 603–16 (May 1937); 'The Displacement of Labour by Machinery'.

    Also published, in part, in *The Human Factor*, vol. xi, nos. 7–8, pp. 241–53 (July/Aug. 1937).

(v) 1937, in *Lloyds Bank Monthly Review*, new series, vol. viii, no. 88, pp. 290–8 (June 1937), 'The Trade Cycle and the Budget Outlook'.

(vi) 1937, in the *Sociological Review*, vol. xxix, no. 3, pp. 258–71 (July 1937), 'Economic Consequences and Problems'

    [of the altered trend of population in the Western world.]

°(vii) 1938, in *Oxford Economic Papers*, old series, vol. i, no. 1, pp. 1–13, 'The Significance of the Rate of Interest'.

(viii) 1941, in the *Economic Journal*, vol. li, nos. 202–3, pp. 338–47 (June–Sept. 1941), 'Josiah Charles Stamp, Baron Stamp of Shortlands'.

    [An obituary notice.]

(ix) 1946, in the *Bulletin of the Institute of Statistics, Oxford*, vol. viii, no. 1, pp. 1–13, (Jan. 1946), 'The Anglo-American Financial Agreement'.

(x) 1946, *The Royal Commission on Equal Pay*, Appendices to minutes of evidence, Appendix IX, memoranda of evidence submitted by a number of economists, no. 3, pp. 93–99 (published by H.M.S.O.).

(xi) 1947, in *The Review of Economic Studies*, vol. xiv (2), no. 36, pp. 76–81, 'The International Economy'.

    [A comment on 'National Central Banking', by R. Tiffin, in the same issue.]

(xii) 1947, in the *Bulletin of the Oxford University Institute of Statistics,* vol. ix, no. 8, pp. 274–82 (Aug. 1947), 'The Implications of the Marshall Speech'.

(xiii) 1947, in the *Economic Journal*, vol. lvii, no. 227, pp. 265–71 (Sept. 1947), 'Cheap Money and the Budget'.

(xiv) 1948, in *International Affairs*, the Journal of the Royal Institute for International Affairs, London, pp. 19–29 (Jan. 1948), 'The European Economic Report'.

°(xv) 1948, in the *Economic Journal*, vol. lviii, no. 232, pp. 467–82 (Dec. 1948), 'The Price System'.

    [Presidential address to Section F of the British Association, delivered at Brighton on 10 Sept. 1948.]

°(xvi) 1949, in *Oxford Economic Papers*, new series, vol. i, no. 1, pp. 1–17 (Jan. 1949), 'The Function of Exchange Rates'.

(xvii) 1949, in the same, no. 2, pp. 157–8 (June 1949), 'A Comment'.

[On a criticism of xvi by Professor Hawtrey.]

*(xviii) 1949, in the *American Economic Review*, vol. xxxix, no. 3, pp. 605–17 (June 1949), 'A Criticism of the Havana Charter'.

(xix) 1950, in the *Journal of the Institute of Bankers*, 'The Emerging Pattern of International Trade'.

[An inaugural lecture read at Oxford on 5 Sept. 1949 to the summer school of the Institute.]

*(xx) 1950, in *Lloyds Bank Review*, new series, no. 15, pp. 1–12 (Jan. 1950), 'The Problem of Retrenchment'.

*(xxi) 1950, in the *Journal of the Coventry Engineering Society*, vol. xxxi, no. 3, pp. 39–48 (May–June 1950), 'Controls and the Price System'.

[The first Herbert Lecture.]

*(xxii) 1950, in the *District Bank Review*, no. 95, pp. 3–13 (Sept. 1950), 'The Economics of International Tension'.

(xxiii) 1950, in *Economia Internazionale*, vol. iii, no. 4, pp. 3–15, (Genoa, Nov. 1950), 'Internal Financial Policy and the Problem of External Disequilibrium'.

[A paper read at an informal meeting of European Economists at Geneva, 9 Sept. 1949.]

(xxiv) 1951, in the *Journal of the Royal Statistical Society*, vol. cxiv, part 1, pp. 40–42, 'A discussion of the Report of the Royal Commission on Population'.

[N.B. Nos. xv, xvi, and xix were translated into Italian and published in *Moneta e Credito*, the quarterly journal of the 'Banca nazionale de Lavoro' under the title 'Realta economica e illusioni di neo Liberisti'.]

IV. *Three broadcasts published in the 'Listener'*

28 Aug. 1947: 'Is Britain in danger of inflation?'
7. July 1949: 'Fair play for parents—a comment on the report of the Royal Commission on Population.'
11 May 1950: 'The Budget and Economic Policy.'

V. *The two Royal Commissions on which Henderson served were:*

1. The Royal Commission on the West Indies.
   Report published by H.M.S.O., Feb. 1940, Cmd. 6174.
2. The Royal Commission on Population.
   Report published by H.M.S.O., 1949, Cmd. 7695.

Among the published papers of that Commission is included in vol. iii, the Report of the Economics Committee published by H.M.S.O., 1950. Henderson was chairman of that Committee.

INDEX

Agriculture: and the Beveridge Insurance Scheme, 205; effect of falling prices in, 138, 251, 379; exchange crisis in, 253; expansion of, 139; mechanization of, 126, 137–9, 254, 257, 378; organized marketing by quantitative regulation in, 280, 281; protection of, 139, 251; surplus capacity of, 253, 256; unemployment insurance in, 163; wheat production revolution, 134.

All Souls College, 152.

American Economic Review, article on the Havana Charter, in (June 1949), 388.

Anglo-American Loan Agreement, 337.

Argentina, imports into, from the U.K., 61.

Artificial silk, duties on, 19.

Australia: gold discoveries in, 52; trade with Great Britain, 87, 88.

Austrian-Hungarian Empire, dissolution of, 384.

'Autarky', 241, 244.

Baldwin, Stanley, 2, 12, 14, 29.

Balkans, the, and Exchange Clearing Agreements with Germany, 266–71.

Bank of England: raises Bank Rate, 5; bank rate and business enterprise, 180; credit policy of (1932), 104; drain of gold from (1931), 84; suspends gold payments, 81.

Bank for International Settlements, and International Certificates (1932), 103, 104.

Bank Rate: and business enterprise, 180; and suspension of gold payments, 81.

Beaverbrook, Lord, 43; and Imperial Preference, 53.

Benelux, 392.

Bevan, Aneurin, M.P., and the Health Service, 432.

Beveridge, Sir William (later Lord Beveridge), *Full Employment in a Free Society* by, 339; *see also* Beveridge Report.

Beveridge Report, the: comprehensive

unemployment insurance in, 200–5; flat rate of contribution in, 206; pensions and the Means Test in, 192–200; principles of social insurance in, 192; retirement pensions in, 198–200; subsistence benefit in, 206.

Birkenhead, Lord, 2.

Birth control, 3.

Birth-rate in Great Britain, 144, 145.

Blum, M., takes office, 261.

Bonar Law, Andrew, 2.

Bradbury, Lord, article in *The Times* by (1933), 111, 112, 113, 118.

Brand, R. H. (later Lord Brand), and international monetary problems (1933), 112, 118, 119.

Brazil, trade with Great Britain (1932), 88.

Bretton Woods: and exchange control for movements of capital, 400; comparison of, with Dawes Plan, 381.

British Association, presidential address to section F of (1948), 342–56.

British Commonwealth: Havana Charter and reduction of tariffs within, 394; preference within, 336, 337, 385, 394; and trade with U.S.A., 394; *see also* Havana Charter; Imperial Preference.

Brüning, Herr, 264.

Brussels Treaty, 403.

Buckmaster, Lord, 2.

Budgets: belief in balancing, 408; deficits in, 59; expenditure on defence, national debt, and social services in, 402, 403; and falling prices, 54, 55; financial orthodoxy in, 317, 318, 319, 321, 322; and quantitative programmes, 335; use of to increase purchasing power, 286, 287, 319, 403, 409.

California, gold discovery in, 52.

Canada, 11; wheat pools in, 141.

Capital: development, 15, 16; demand for capital goods and cyclical unemployment, 281, 282; expenditure of and rate of interest, 182; risks of, 6.

Carson, Lord, 2.

Cassel, Professor, and purchasing power parity, 352.

Catholic emancipation, 2.

Centre Party, 2.

Chamberlain, Austen, 2.

Chamberlain, Joseph, 38; and Imperial Preference, 53.

Chatham, Earl of, 434.

Cheeryble brothers, 20.

Children's allowances, 191, 406.

Church Establishment, 3.

Churchill, Sir Winston: and budget of 1925, 18–22; and budget of 1926, 23; improvidence of, 37; and re-armament, 434.

'Circular 8213', 13.

Civil Service, increase in pay in higher ranks of, 430.

Clynes, J. R., 2.

Coalition Government, White Paper on Employment policy, produced by, 417.

Coal industry: Act of 1938, 303; and German Reparations, 93, 94, 95; and international problem, 38; in-dustry losing ground, 25; coal mines, 15, 23, 29; growth of Communism in coal mines, 30; owners' attitude to, 27; stoppage in, 23, 28.

Cobden, and Commercial Treaty of 1846, 52.

Commons, House of, 12, 13, 17.

Controls: *Controls and the Price Sys-tem*, 413–24; disadvantages of, 421; a false issue, 418.

Corn Laws, Repeal of, 52.

Cost of living index, 7; rise in, owing to higher price of imports, 430.

Cotton industry: and budget of 1925, 19; loss of export markets in, 252, 414; short time in, 31.

Credit: cheap, 8; expansion of, 6; internal and external credit policy, 81–86; restriction of, 5, 6.

Cripps, Sir Stafford, and remissions of income-tax, 433.

Cromwell, 20.

Currency: inconvertible paper, 8; les-son of currency inflations of 1920's, 353; possibility of a managed cur-rency system, 123.

Curzon, Lord, 2.

Customs Union: impracticable for the British Commonwealth, and for Europe, 393, 394; and the Havana Charter, 392; *see also* International Trade.

Dawes Plan, solves problem of Ger-man reparations, 380.

D'Albernon, Lord, and Economic Mission to South America, 1930, 61, 62.

Dalton, Rt. Hon. Hugh, his cheap money policy, 356.

Defence: and danger of inflationary pressure, 426; expenditure on, in face of Korea, 425; scale of defence programmes, 428.

Denmark, organized marketing of bacon in, 280, 281.

Derby, Lord, 2.

Disarmament, 3.

Distribution charges, high level of, 52.

District Bank Review, article in (Sept. 1950), 425–34.

Divorce reform, 3.

Dockers' strike, 7.

Dominions, British, and tariffs, 52.

Economics: *The Economics of Inter-national Tension*, 425–34; *Interna-tional History of Economics in Inter-war period*, 236–95; Keynes's Theory of, 79; economic liberalism versus economic nationalism, 245, 357, 359, 384; economic liberalism after World War I, 360, 361; eco-nomic planning, 327–41; quantita-tive economic programmes, 328, 329, 330, 334, 335; *Economic Sur-vey of 1947*, 340; *Economic Survey of 1948*, 350; place of principle in, 41, 42.

Economists Committee (1930), memo-randum circulated to, 66–70.

Education: religious, 3; necessity for revision of existing policy in, 433.

Empire Marketing Board, 140.

Employment: conditions necessary for maintaining full employment, 152, 220–35, 264, 294; *see also* Unem-ployment; Trade cycle.

European Payments Union, 426.

Exchange Equalization Fund (1932), 108, 111, 119, 359.

Federal Reserve Board, 8, 380.

Financial News, 69.

Fiscal issue, theological atmosphere of, 43, 44.

Fiscal system, changes in, 9.

Fixed debt charge, and trade depression, 55.

Food, Ministry of: as bulk purchaser, 284; food subsidies, 406.

Foreign competition, and the home market, 52.

Foreign exchange: British policy in 1933, 107–9; clearing agreements in Europe, 385; control of, 241, 242, 246, 247, 248, 273, 420; deliberate depreciation of, 291, 292, 385, 398; depreciation of the dollar (1933), 258, 292, 385, 398; exchange control for regulating capital transfers, 386; Exchange Equalization Fund, 259, 260, 262, 264; 'Function of Exchange Rates', *Oxford Economic Papers* (1949), 357–76; Havana Charter, policy regarding, 390; new doctrine of exchange-rate variations, 399; speculation in, 419–20; *see also* International Trade.

Foreign policy, British, 3.

France: and monetary conditions (1930), 51; and budget equilibrium (1931), 73.

Franco-German War, 52.

Franks, Sir Oliver, lecture by, on 'Central Planning and Control in War and Peace' (1947), 328.

Free trade in England, 9; and antagonism to exchange control, 242, 251; and McKenna Duties, 43–47; formation of free-trade area, 392, 393; movement away from, before 1914, 378; our traditional commercial policy, 272, 337; *see also* Foreign exchange; International trade.

Garvin, J. L., 18.

Geddes, Sir Eric, 5; Geddes Axe (1921–2), 318.

Geneva, conference on commercial policy at (1947), 336.

Germany: and reparations, 67; elections (1930) in, 67; import restrictions in, 271–4; rearmament in,

271, 272; reparations and British industry (1932), 91–102; reparations and the Dawes Plan for, 239, 380; return of, to world markets, 407; Young Plan for, 67, 95; *see also* Reparations.

Gibbon's theological barometer, 2.

Gladstone, W. E., and cost of present-day defence programme, 428.

Gold exports, embargo on, 16.

Gold prices, stability of, 8.

Gold standard, 8; and foreign exchange stability, 120–2; breakdown of, 245, 379; Britain's departure from, 247, 251; conditions of remaining on (1931), 75; essential principles of, 373; fixity of exchange rates under, 373; return to, 16, 17, 19–21, 24, 25; in the Victorian age, 377.

Government expenditure: inflationary effect of increase in, 409; resistance to idea of economy in, 408; need for retrenchment in, 412, 413; *see also* Budgets.

Graham, William, and tariff truce, 42, 47.

Great Britain, 3, 24; industrial problems of, 68, 69.

Gregory, Sir Theodore, and fixed exchange rates, 357.

Gresham's Law, 339.

Grey, Lord, 2.

Haldane, Lord, 2.

Harrod, Mr. Roy, and price system ideology, 346.

Havana Charter, the: and non-discrimination, 392; and quantitative regulations, 396, 397; article in *American Economic Review* (June 1949), on, 388–401; basic principles of, 389, 390, 391; harmful effect of, 401; *see also* British Commonwealth; Tariffs.

Hawtrey, Professor, and price system ideology, 352, 353.

Health Services, the: extravagance of free provisions under, 411; increase in cost of after World War II, 404, 405; need for revision of basic principles of, 433; popularity of, 409; *see also* Social Services.

Index

'Herbert Lecture', the (March 1950), 413–24.
Hicks, Professor John, and price system ideology, 346.
Hitler, Adolf, and world economic crisis, 264, 289, 290.
Horne, Sir Robert, 2.
Hotel industry, neglect of, 64.
Housing: and rate of interest, 183; estate development in, 298, 300, 320; post-war problems in, 285, 286, 297; state subsidies for, 158.

Imperial Preference, development of, in British Commonwealth after 1931, 385; see also Foreign exchange; Tariffs.
Income-tax: evasion of, 35, 36; reduction in standard rate of, 19, 22.
India: imports from Great Britain, 87.
Industrial Institute, 79.
Industry: demand for labour in, 126–50; development of, 25; new industrial revolution, 28–32, 61–64; metallurgical group, 14, 15; north of England losing ground in, 25–32; obsolescence in mechanized industry, 135, 146, 181, 182, 333; re-equipment, need for, 427.
Inflation: danger of speed up in, 430, 431; not eliminated after World War I, 429; policy for holding, 431.
Interest, the rate of: Keynes's theory of, 167, 168, 169, 170, 171, 172–6; orthodox theory of, 167, 172, 173, 174, 176; significance of (Oxford Economic Papers, Jan. 1938), 178–90.
Inter-governmental Commodity Agreements, chapter on, in Havana Charter, 400.
International Chamber of Commerce, 243; and fixed exchange rates, 357.
International trade: balance of payments problem, 210–12, 336, 379, 382, 383, 391; bilateral trade agreements, 330; cessation of American loans for, 256, 257; customs union and discrimination, 215; the economic problem of today, 368; exports, 15, 24, 60; future problems of, 378; import restrictions, 271–6, 338, 399; industrial cartels, 283; in the inter-

war period, 377, 378; loans for, in the 20's, 255, 256; low-tariff clubs, 285, 286; post-war commercial policy, 210–19; quantitative regulation of, 214, 294, 338, 355, 385, 386; types of restriction in, 275–7; in the Victorian Age, 377; see also Foreign exchange; Tariffs.
Italy, return to world markets, 407.

Japan, the yen and pound sterling (1933), 113; and Ottawa Conference (1932), 249; and Lancashire cotton industry, 252.
Jewkes, Professor J.: and price system ideology, 345; Ordeal by Planning by, 351; and quantitative controls, 355.

Kaldor, Nicholas, his model calculation of productive capacity, 339, 340.
Keynes, J. M. (later Lord Keynes), 17; and a 'closed economy', 367; and employment policy, 315–25; and international note issue, 123; and international stabilization (1933), 116; and price system ideology, 346; his 'General Theory', 161–77; his 'Tract on Monetary Reform', 123.
Korea: American operations in, 427; analogy with Germany, 425; warning from, 425.

Labour: mobility of, 15, 16; surplus of, in coal and cotton industries, 60.
Labour Party, 1, 14, 34; and McKenna Duties, 40; policy of, 3, 4.
Laissez-faire, 278, 291, 294; and lesson of the 30's, 415, 416; danger of reaction to, 344; disclaimed by price mechanism ideologues, 345; exaggerates efficiency of forces of supply and demand, 422; former efficiency of, 429; return to after World War I, 317, 318, 359.
Land values: Notes on Problem of (1944), 296–315; 'Planning Authority' and land developer, 305, 306; Uthwatt doctrine of 'floating value', 311, 312, 314, 315; Uthwatt proposals on, 296, 298, 300, 301, 302, 304; Uthwatt proposals on State acquisition of development rights, 305, 309, 310, 314.

Lansbury, George, 2.
League of Nations: and foreign loans, 375, 380, 381; and reparations, 239, 242; booklet on *Quantitative Trade Controls* (1943), 234, 236; 'survey of commercial policy' (1919–39), 243.
Liberalism, definition of, 1.
Liberal Party, 1, 14; definition of, 2; and *The Nation*, 43.
Licensing, 3.
Lloyds Bank Review, article in (Jan. 1950), on 'Problem of Retrenchment', 402.
Lloyd George, David (later Earl Lloyd-George), 2, 15, 16, 17, 43, 238.
Locarno, Treaty of, 24, 244.
London: a free gold market, 24; expanding industry in, 58; and other financial centres, 69, 88, 247.
Lords, House of, 2, 3.

MacDonald, J. Ramsay, 2.
McKenna, R., 9.
McKenna Duties, 9–12; repeal of, 9, 10, 39–47.
McKinley Tariff, 52.
Malthus, 255.
Manchester Guardian, 43.
Marks and Spencer, 230.
Marshall Aid: and deficit in balance of payments, 351; central features of, 391; implications of cessation of, 401, 420; *see also* United States.
Marshall, Professor Alfred: his theory of value, 347; and a 'closed economy', 367.
Marshall Society, 161.
Massingham, H. W., 1.
Meade, Professor James: and exchange parities, 352; and price system ideology, 346; and tariffs, 354; *Planning and the Price Mechanism* by, 370.
Mill, John Stuart, Professor, 367.
Miners' Federation, militant policy of, 30.
Ministry of Labour Gazette: tables of employment in, 26; of insured persons in, 30; of uninsured persons in, 31.
Mond, Sir Alfred (later Lord Melchett), 2, 13.
Money market, 5; and cheap money, 81; and dear money, 5, 82.

Monetary policy, 5–8, 16; and fall in monetary reserves, 372; international (1933), 110–25; and suspension of gold payments, 81.
Montevideo, conference of American States at (1933), 286.
Motor industry, the British, 9; export trade in, 63; and McKenna Duties, 41; employment in, 10–12; mass production in, 136, 137; protection of, 10; taxation of, 63.

Nationalization, 6; an old Socialist slogan, 414; not an aid to more equal distribution of wealth, 415; planning motif in, 415, 416.
National debt, and 1949 devaluation, 406.
National expenditure, Report of committee on (1931), 69–75.
National income, increase in after World War I, 402.
National Insurance, 28; numbers of insured persons, 30, 31; principles of, in Beveridge Report, 192; *see also* Beveridge Report.
National production, increase in, since 1947, 428.
Newbold, W. H., 2.
New Deal, 262.
Newspapers: city columns in, 5; city editors of, 5.
New York: Exchange, 5; Federal Reserve Bank of, 239.
New Zealand, trade with Great Britain (1932), 87, 88.
North Atlantic Treaty, 403.

Observer, 18.
Ottawa Conference (1932), 249; effect of, on Dominions, 286, 287; effect of, on the U.S.A., 274, 394.
Ouchy Convention, 285, 286.
Oxford: Economists Research Group in, 186, 187; *Oxford Economic Papers* (Jan. 1949), 357; Oxford Political Economy Club, paper read to (May 1935), 151.

Petrol, duty on, 63.
Pigou, Professor A. C., 169.
Poor Law Commission, 155.
Popular Front (1936), 261.

Index

Population: and land values, 299, 303; changes in age distribution of, 405, 417, 432; effect of growth of, in the nineteenth century, 143, 145, 146, 165, 257, 378; effect of decline of, in the twentieth century, 144, 145, 150, 158, 165, 184, 188, 197, 198, 299, 378; Royal Commission on, 404, 405.

Pound sterling, the: and the balance of trade (1932), 87–90; danger of flight from, 36, 37; devaluation of (1949), 422.

Prices: implications and reactions of falling prices, 49–55; probability of rise in, 431.

Price system, the: ideology of, 344, 349, 361, 397, 399; presidential address to section F, British Association (1948), on, 342–56; versus controls, 413–24.

Private enterprise: in the Victorian age, 377; versus Public ownership, 414; versus Socialism, 294.

Productivity, increase of and the demand for labour, 126–50; see also Industry, mechanization of.

Profits, Labour's hostility to, 7.

Profiteers, 7.

Prohibition, 3.

Proportional representation, 3.

Protection: and falling prices, 52, 53; and industry, 45; and repeal of the McKenna Duties, 42; and world slump, 69; and world trade, 59; see also International trade.

Public authorities, as owners of capital goods, 183, 184.

Public expenditure, 3; growth of, on social services, 418; an inflationary influence, 418.

Public works: arguments for and against, 151–60; as aid to transfer of labour, 152, 159; as permanent policy to absorb savings, 153, 156, 157, 188, 225; as trade cycle tap, 152, 156, 221, 321.

Railways, development of, 134, 135.

Rearmament: and economic recovery, 434; for defence, 426, 427; in 1937, 430.

Reconstruction, Ministry of, 9.

'Rede Lecture', the, Cambridge (1947), 327–41.

Reichsbank, and drain of gold (1931), 84.

Reparations: and foreign loans, 245; and inter-Allied debts (1930), 67; see also Germany.

Retrenchment, the problem of, 402–12.

Rhineland: evacuation of, 244, 247; occupation of, 242.

Rhondda Valley, 164.

Ricardo, David, 367.

Ricardo, Joseph, articles in *The Times* by (Sept. 1933), 116.

Road Fund, 72, 76.

Road Transport, 151.

Robertson, Professor Sir Dennis, address to the British Association (1947) by, 342.

Robbins, Professor Lionel: and economic liberalism, 360, 361; and fixed exchange rates, 357; *Economic Problems in Peace and War* by, 370, 371.

Roosevelt, Franklin D., President of the U.S.A.: and American price level, 116; and World Economic Conference (1933), 110; devalues the dollar, 260.

Rothermere, Lord, 43.

Rowntree, Mr. Seebohm, survey of York (1936) by, 191, 195.

Rubber: schemes for limiting production of, in the 1920's, 282; Stevenson scheme for, in the 1920's, 282.

Ruhr, the, 5, 8; occupation of, 93.

Salisbury, Marquis of, 2.

Savings, effect of increased taxation on, 433.

Scandinavia, trade with Great Britain (1932), 88.

Schacht, Dr., President of the Reichsbank: and exchange-clearing agreements, 264–71.

Schuman Plan, the, 426.

Shipbuilding industry, transference problem in, 228, 229.

Simon, Sir John (later Lord Simon), 2, 14.

Sinking Fund: a deflationary influence, 322; raiding of, in 1930, 69.

444

Smith, Adam, 367.

Smith, Sydney, his famous diatribe, 402.

Snowden, Philip, Chancellor of the Exchequer, 2, 9, 12, 17; and budget of 1924, 18; and budget of 1930, 33–38; and budget of 1931, 319; and the McKenna Duties, 39–42.

Social Services: development of, 3; increase in expenditure on, after World War II, 404, 417, 423; justification of, 410.

Socialism, 3; as remedy for unemployment, 13; 'Limits of Insular Socialism', article in *The Nation*, 33–38.

South Africa: trade with Great Britain (1932), 88.

South American Republics, and exchange-clearing agreements with Germany, 267.

Stamp, Sir Josiah (later Lord Stamp): memorial lecture to (1946), 377; personal qualities of, 380.

State, the: as 'Entrepreneur-in-Chief', 233–5, 331, 332; as wholesale dealer in utility goods, 229–32.

Steel-Maitland, Sir Arthur, 17.

Stock Exchange, 5; effects of slump or boom on, 185; speculation on (1920's), 245.

Strachan, Sir Richard, 434.

Strachey, John, and distribution of taxation, 434.

Strakosch, Sir Henry, memorandum in *The Economist* (1932), 98.

Stresa Conference (1932), 285.

Strikes, 7.

Sugar industry, in West Indies and Porto Rico, 215, 216.

Supertax: yield in 1928–9, 33; evasion of, 34.

Supply, Ministry of, as bulk purchaser, 284.

Tariffs: and falling prices, 52; Anglo-American trade agreement on (1938), 216, 218; as alternatives to quantitative control, 214, 217–19; Hawley–Smoot Act (1930), 249, 285; Imperial Preference, 214–16, 236, 244, 249, 255, 286, 336; international tariff truce, 49, 50; introduction of general tariffs in Britain

(1932), 249; the Havana Charter, 390; Non-discrimination, principle of, 337, 386–91; *see also* Havana Charter; Ottawa Conference; Protection.

Taxation: as means to develop the Welfare State, to maintain full employment, and to redistribute wealth, 414; income-tax, 408; tobacco duties and purchase-tax, 407.

Town and Country Planning, Ministry of: and compensation of land values, 301, 304; Planning Acts, 310; Report by, on Preservation of the Countryside, 312.

Trade: depression of, 6, 14, 23, 51, 52, 59, 67; fluctuations in volume of, 6, 7, 14.

Trade cycle, the: description of, 6, 8; explanation of, 6; Keynes's theory of, 174; mastery over, 6, 8; and public works, 156, 160; and rate of interest, 189; and time lag, 3, 4; *see also* Employment; Unemployment.

Trade Unions, and wages standstill, 408, 429, 430.

Transvaal, gold production in, 53.

Tripartite Agreement, the (1936), 261–3, 364.

Truman, Harry S., President of U.S.A., and American rearmament, 425.

Unemployment: crux of problem, 6; 'cyclical', 165, 166; different types of, 56–60; 'export' of, 250; and export markets, 53, 320, 324; increase of (1925), 13–16; and increased productivity, 126–50; insurance funds for, 13, 69, 72, 73, 155; in interwar years, 318; and repeal of McKenna Duties, 46; live register of, 56, 58, 59; and return to the gold standard, 17; 'transfer', 165, 166; solution of, 15; unemployment pay, system of, 70; *see also* Employment.

United States, 8, 15, 16; claim to German reparations, 252; a creditor country, 251; departure from the gold standard, 110; depreciation of the dollar, 258; European travel from, 64; exchange stability in, 374;

experiment in economic recovery in, 118; Federal Farm Board, 141; Federal Reserve policy (1932), 107; great slump in, 73; international speculation in (1933), 107; and Korea, 425, 427; labour turnover in, 58; Marshall Aid, 401; new industrial development in, 62; responsibility for maintaining exchange stability, 374; standardization of wages in, 58.

U.S.S.R., and inter-war import restrictions, 274.

Van Zeeland Plan (1938), 286.

Victorian Age, economic expansion in, 377, 414.

Wages: disputes, 7; standardization of in U.S.A., 58.

Wall Street: slump (1929) on, 41, 46, 185, 323; boom on, 240.

War debt, weight of, 3.

Waterloo, battle of: economic condition of world at time of, 377; budgetary difficulties after, 402.

Webb, Sydney (later Lord Passmore), 2.

Welfare State, the, concept of and public economy, 409.

West Indies, and preference on sugar, 215, 216, 287.

White Paper: *Economic Survey for 1947*, 328; on unemployment policy towards the end of World War II, 368.

Woolworth's, 230.

World depression: and balance of payments, 419; and foreign investment, 210; a cause of import restrictions, 274; immediate causes of, 245; and increasing productivity, 142; a cause of new techniques in international trade, 385; nadir of (1932), 258; and price system, 278; and speculation, 147–9; a cause of general unemployment, 318, 384.

World Economic Conference (1930), 42, 47, 110, 140; and currency stabilization (1933), 258; and tariffs, 243.

World financial crisis (1930–1): key event in inter-war years, 384; sweeps away the international gold standard, 381, 382, 414.

World War I: economic condition of the world at outbreak of, 377, 378; effect of, on international trade and balance of payments, 382, 386, 413.

World War II: comparison of problems set by, with those of World War I, 386, 413, 414.

PRINTED IN
GREAT BRITAIN
AT THE
UNIVERSITY PRESS
OXFORD
BY
CHARLES BATEY
PRINTER
TO THE
UNIVERSITY